SELLING THE STORY

SELLING
THE
STORY

Transaction and Narrative Value

in Balzac, Dostoevsky, and Zola

JONATHAN PAINE

Harvard University Press

Cambridge, Massachusetts

London, England

2019

Library of Congress Cataloging-in-Publication Data

Names: Paine, Jonathan, author.
Title: Selling the story : transaction and narrative value in Balzac,
Dostoevsky, and Zola / Jonathan Paine.
Description: Cambridge, Massachusetts : Harvard University Press, 2019. |
Includes bibliographical references and index.
Identifiers: LCCN 2019008949 | ISBN 9780674988439 (alk. paper)
Subjects: LCSH: Authorship—Marketing—History—19th century. |
Balzac, Honoré de, 1799–1850—Criticism and interpretation. |
Dostoyevsky, Fyodor, 1821–1881—Criticism and interpretation. | Zola,
Émile, 1840–1902—Criticism and interpretation. | Economics and
literature—History—19th century. | Serialized fiction—History and
criticism. | Publishers and publishing—History—19th century.
Classification: LCC PN161 .P26 2019 | DDC 809.3/034—dc23 LC record
available at https://lccn.loc.gov/2019008949

For Julie, Claire, Alex, and Olivia

Contents

Notes on Citation

REFERENCES TO PRIMARY WORKS by Honoré de Balzac are, unless otherwise indicated, to the twelve-volume Pléiade edition of *La Comédie humaine* of 1975, edited by Pierre-Georges Castex, and are identified in my text by volume and page number in arabic numerals, with the text of *Splendeurs et misères des courtisanes,* edited by Pierre Citron, at 6:425–935. Similarly, references to Balzac's correspondence, unless otherwise identified and other than with Eveline Hanska, are to the five-volume Pléiade edition of 1960–1969 (*Correspondance,* edited by Roger Pierrot) and are identified by the label *Corr.* followed by volume and page number. References to Balzac's correspondence with Madame Hanska are to the two-volume Editions Laffont edition of 1990 (*Lettres à Madame Hanska,* edited by Roger Pierrot) and are identified by the label *EH* followed by volume and page number in the text.

References to Fedor Dostoevsky's works are to the Voskresen'e 2003–2005 edition, *Polnoe sobranie sochinenii F. M. Dostoevskogo v XVIII tomakh,* edited by G. N. Seleznev and others, eighteen volumes with three supplemental volumes, hereafter referred to in the text and notes by volume and page number in arabic numerals. References to editorial text in this edition are identified by the label *PSS 2003–2005* preceding volume and page numbers. Supplementary volumes are identified as *PSS 2003–2005,* suppl. 1–3.

References to primary works by Emile Zola are, unless otherwise indicated, to the five-volume Pléiade edition of *Les Rougon-Macquart: Histoire naturelle et sociale d'une famille sous le Second Empire,* edited by Henri Mitterand (1960–1967), and are identified in my text by volume and page number in arabic numerals.

All translations are my own unless otherwise indicated.

J'ai l'espoir de devenir riche à coups de romans.

HONORÉ DE BALZAC to Laure Surville, August 1820,
Correspondance, ed. Roger Pierrot and Hervé Yon,
2 vols. (Paris: Gallimard, 2006), 1:70

[Lady Carbury] had taken to the writing of a novel because [her publisher] had told her that upon the whole novels did better than anything else. She would have written a volume of sermons on the same encouragement, and have gone about the work exactly after the same fashion. The length of the novel had been her first question. It must be in three volumes, and each volume must have three hundred pages. But what fewest number of words might be supposed sufficient to fill a page? The money offered was too trifling to allow of very liberal measure on her part. She had to live, and if possible to write another novel,—and, as she hoped, on better terms, when this should be finished. . . .

Whether the work might have been better done she never asked herself. I do not think she prided herself much on the literary merit of the tale. But if she could bring the papers to praise it, if she could induce Mudie to circulate it, if she could manage that the air for a month should be so loaded with 'The Wheel of Fortune' as to make it necessary for the reading world to have read or to have said that it had read the book,—then she would pride herself very much upon her work.

ANTHONY TROLLOPE, *The Way We Live Now* (1875), ed. John
Sutherland (Oxford: Oxford University Press, 1982,
reissued 2008), 2:364–366

SELLING THE STORY

Introduction:
The Economics of Narrative

"WHAT'S THE STORY 'WORTH'?" asks Roland Barthes in *S/Z*. He continues, "Narrative is, by a vertiginous trick, the representation of the very contract on which it is based: in the example of these stories, narration becomes the (economic) theory of narration: . . . stories are told as a means of exchange, and this transaction becomes the subject of the story itself: narrative is at once product and the means of production, merchandise and commerce."[1]

Narrative, Barthes suggests, is an economic commodity in an exchange which contains a record of its own transactional agency. Stories nowadays have indeed become big business, in a financial as well as a metaphorical sense. We describe narrative in terms of business deals: we buy a story just as easily as we buy milk from the corner store. We sell a line, swap an anecdote, trade jokes. Publishers may set prices, but readers buy the stories; the process requires an exchange that implies at least temporary agreement on a value for literary output. Readers invest time in a text in the expectation of a return and call the process "taking an interest." The act of buying the story turns the credibility of the narrative into the creditworthiness of the author. And authors respond, by following fashions or by challenging them, in order to create markets for their own works, and in doing so they leave an imprint of the process in what they have written. Narrative is just as much an economic commodity as a creative act, and the issues Barthes raises are fundamental to any consideration of narrative as an economic activity.[2]

Barthes is, however, better at asking questions than answering them. How do we judge the "value" of texts? How can we relate economic to aesthetic value? What role does the reader, or the author's perception of the reader, play in establishing value? And how can the text itself provide clues to its own economic activity? That is the subject of this book. I explore narrative as a self-reflexive commentary on the conditions of its own production. I ask whether a detailed examination of the story *(récit)* itself can provide evidence of how an author conceived of its value, constructed its value, and manipulated its value. By focussing on the text itself as an economic instrument, I want to develop a pragmatic, rather than theoretical, approach to an underrecognised area of literary analysis, that of economic criticism.

The Role of Economic Criticism

Discussing the economic context of artistic production has never been easy. The very notion of commercial influence on art has been repeatedly denied, treated as relevant only to populist output, pigeonholed as belonging to a particular political viewpoint, or regarded simply as an offshoot of biography. Even today, our growing appreciation of the value of historical context still hesitates to include the economic dimension fully. Attempts over the past thirty years to develop "economic criticism" as a distinct point of view have largely foundered through attempts to impose a theoretical framework or through perceived political bias. More recently, and more in some literatures than in others, there has been a revival of interest in the role of economics in literary criticism, not from any theoretical standpoint but as a practical reflection of the need to understand how the commercialisation of artistic production affects the process of aesthetic creation itself.

Economic criticism has been far more extensively developed as a critical tool in some disciplines than in others.[3] In the field of English literature, analysis of the underlying economics of the publishing industry, the growth of literacy, and the evolving tastes of the reading public began early with, for example, Richard Altick's investigation of mass readership in nineteenth-century England in *The English Common Reader*, first published in 1957.[4] This established the groundwork for a discussion of the role of economics in literature that focussed, in part, on how novels represented external economic developments and systems of political economy and, in part, although to lesser extent, on how the representation of economics affected the act of writing itself. An early and influential contribution to the latter debate was made by John Vernon's 1984 *Money and Fiction,* which drew parallels between the failure of traditional stores of economic value, such as money, to deliver predictable value, and the failure of fiction to mimic reality.[5] These twin tracks have begun to converge, and there now exists a flourishing array of critical literature, produced largely by scholars in the United Kingdom and the United States, on the representation of external economic conditions in prose fiction, on the relationship between literature and political economic theory, and, increasingly but from a very narrow base, on my particular area of focus, narrative as a commentary on the conditions of its own production. I return to all of these later.

Studies in French literature and economics have taken a rather different turn. The development of the publishing industry was documented at an early stage, in particular by Claude Bellanger's 1969 *Histoire générale de la presse française*[6] and Roger Chartier and Henri-Jean Martin's four-volume *Histoire de l'édition française,* published from 1982 to 1986.[7] This early work revealed a rich seam of investigation on the economic, social, and cultural history of publishing which has almost developed into its own discipline. René Guise's 1975 thesis established the importance of the *roman-feuilleton* as an economic driver of the periodical in the 1830s;[8] Jean-Yves Mollier documented the histories of the key publishers of the nineteenth century;[9] Françoise Parent-Lardeur the role of the *cabinets de lecture.*[10] Current work on journalism and its relationship to popular culture is being led by Dominique Kalifa, Philippe Régnier, Marie-Eve Thérenty, and Alain Vaillant, most recently in a wide-ranging and much-needed survey entitled *La Civilisation du journal.*[11] Guillaume Pinson has explored the growing interaction between the worlds of journalism and the novel throughout the nineteenth century.[12] Judith Lyon-Caen has investigated contemporary reader reception as evidenced by readers' letters.[13] Christophe Charle has supplied complementary research into economic history and culture,[14] while others, in particular Martin Lyons[15] and Vaillant, have successfully compiled statistical databases and applied techniques of economic analysis to aspects of literary consumption.[16] Most recently, Edmund Birch's work on the two-way interaction between the press and the novel has done much to dispel earlier hierarchical assumptions that "literature" could remain unaffected by its increasing proximity to the commercial press.[17]

But in the area of literature as a reflection of theories of political economy, French criticism has historically been heavily influenced by a long tradition of Marxist analysis in French literature, dating back at least to the influence of György Lukács, whose 1916 *Die Theorie des Romans* and series of articles on Honoré de Balzac in 1934–1935, translated into French as *Balzac et le réalisme français* in 1951, had proposed a method of showing how Balzac's exuberant, totalising, and commercial perspective could be taken as a realistic portrayal of a society in the throes of capitalist disintegration, despite the author's opposite personal convictions.[18] This seems to have resonated with French aesthetic hierarchies, already established in literary criticism from the time of Charles Augustin Sainte-Beuve and his excoriation of "industrial literature" (*la littérature industrielle*), which rejected popular art and literature as an appropriate subject for academic study unless otherwise redeemed by a political justification.[19] The Marxist focus is visible in a wide range of sociological, critical, and economic perspectives, from Pierre Bourdieu's concepts of cultural capital,[20] to Pierre Barbéris's notion of the text as the home of the proletariat,[21] to Jean-Joseph Goux's proposition of counterfeit coin as the founding metaphor for a debased society.[22] Even more recent works, such as Alexandre Péraud's 2012 *Le Crédit dans la poétique balzacienne*, which explores the relationship between financial debt and moral bankruptcy, acknowledge a debt to a long Marxist tradition.[23] Although the influence of this viewpoint now seems to be on the wane, over time it has, I think, rather restricted the scope of French critical thinking and perhaps hindered the development of new approaches to economic criticism.

In Russian scholarship, even the basic tools for economic analysis are underdeveloped. It was not always thus: in fact, the ur-texts appeared much earlier than in many other European countries. Mikhail Kufaev's 1927 *History of the Book in Russia in the 19th Century (Istoriya russkoi knigi v XIX veke)*[24] and Mikhail Muratov's 1931 *Publishing Trade in Russia in the 19th and 20th Centuries (Knizhnoe delo v Rossii v XIX i XX vekakh)*[25] provide the foundation for analysis of the evolution of the readership and the role of changes in printing technology, distribution mechanisms, and economic inputs, but neither is as comprehensive as its equivalents in the English or French market. For almost half a century, little more was added until William Mills Todd III's 1978 *Literature and Society in Imperial Russia, 1800–1914,* which began the process of filling some of the "serious lacunæ in the study of Russian literature as a social institution" identified by his analysis in its very first sentence.[26] In part this is due to real evidential voids—for example, in literacy statistics until the first census of 1897, or in central bibliographical records of publications (despite Russia's having more continuous censorship laws than anywhere else in Europe). In part it reflects a genuine absence of original basic research into what is, or might be, available in terms of the publishing history, the readership, and the social culture of the nineteenth century.

The relative absence of basic research has complicated efforts to develop a more sophisticated debate on economic and literary interactions. Nonetheless, advances have been made in understanding the readership and the culture of reading, most notably by Abram Reitblat[27] and Jeffrey Brooks.[28] Todd has done the same for the role of serialisation in Russian periodicals;[29] Louise McReynolds for the development of the mass-circulation press;[30] Deborah Martinsen for that of literary journals;[31] Boris Mironov in the field of social history and sociological change;[32] and Susanne Fusso for the role of that most influential of all Russian publishers in the nineteenth century, Mikhail Katkov.[33] But economic criticism as a separate branch of study has yet to become established. A seminal 1999 text, which I shall discuss later, entitled *The New Economic Criticism: Studies at the Intersection of Literature and Economics,* edited by Martha Woodmansee and Mark Osteen,[34] was indeed published in the Russian journal *Novoe literaturnoe obozrenie* in 2002, along with contributions to the economic debate by Todd, Mikhail Makeev, Séamas O'Driscoll, Kirill Postoutenko, and Lev Usykin.[35] Postoutenko also published other articles on the topic around the same time.[36] But I can find little more.

Economic criticism is hardly a new phenomenon, even though it has only recently begun to be recognised as a separate branch of interdisciplinary study. It has always been difficult to define. When Woodmansee and Osteen launched their attempt to establish it as a distinct discipline, their introduction suggested a redefinition by reference to four separate "approaches to the economics of literary texts." "Production" meant a focus on the "social, cultural and economic contexts in which . . . works have been produced": a branch of New Historicism focussing mostly on the external conditions of production, though oddly they barely mention the publishing industry itself. "Internal circulation" argued that the representation of money, finance, and transaction within a work can not only provide clues as to the author's own hierarchy of value but can also mirror and critique external economic conditions both through content and through stylistic device. "External circulation and consumption" considered the economics of reception, the process of canonisation, and the impact of changing tastes, as well as the author's "debt" to precursors from all possible intertextualities. Lastly, "metatheoretical" provided a heading under which the methodology and theory of economic criticism could itself be discussed.[37]

In the intervening years, the increasing volume of works on and around the subject of economic criticism (particularly in English literature), and parallel evolution in other aesthetic disciplines such as the fine arts and music, has allowed revised definitions to emerge from actual practice. Mary Poovey, writing in 2008, presages a reformulation when she suggests three broad categories: "one that treats economic matters as ideas (or 'thought'), logics, metaphors or structural paradigms; one that focuses on the economic problems of Literary production, and one that deals with the formal, generic, and commodity features that have allowed Literary writing to attain a degree of relative autonomy since the late eighteenth century."[38]

In practical terms, what has actually happened is the emergence of a far greater degree of economic awareness across three largely preexisting approaches. The oldest of these is the "literature as commerce" approach. In its earliest incarnations, this almost always takes a pejorative line, representing the threat posed to aesthetics by populism—Paul Delany provides a good summary of the origins of this approach in *Literature, Money and the Market,* from Plato's preferment of ascetic Sparta over consumerist Athens to recent Marxist criticism.[39] The influence of economics on narrative was implicitly admitted by its very rejection, as witness Rémy de Gourmont's 1907 argument that serious art was essentially incomprehensible to the populace at large.[40] More recently, Theodor Adorno's reading of aestheticism and art-for-art's-sake discourses, in his posthumous *Ästhetische Theorie,* argues that, despite their claims to despise the commercial market, these remain wholly dependent on it.[41] The original approach has long since given way to serious analysis of the business of publishing, and, at least in France and England, a solid database of information about the growth of publishing as an industry and about the evolution of the readership now exists. The one area in which all these analyses are still lacking is that of the availability and sources of capital to finance growth. We know from other industries, particularly transport, how vital an enabling tool this is; publishing is little different save in scale, and more information on this point would give us another measure of value for literary production.

The second strand of current economic analysis is the "literature as economic critique" approach. This divided historically into two closely related subfields: "literature as socioeconomic commentary," which saw literature, and in particular realist and naturalist literature, as a critique of the social and economic conditions of contemporary society, and "literature as political economics," which saw literature either through the prism of a political or economic interpretation imposed by the critic, as in much of Marxist criticism, or as a representation of a contemporary theory of political economy. The early foundations of both were laid by studies of the way in which realist writers depicted the society they lived in through the prism of fiction. Thus modern criticism of Balzac, for example, begins with extensive analyses showing how Balzac's fictional representation of the emergence of a commercialised and consumerist bourgeoisie corresponded to the historical and sociological evidence. Jean-Hervé Donnard's 1961 *Balzac, les réalités économiques et sociales dans "La Comédie humaine"* is, as its title suggests, a good example of this approach,[42] but many of the earlier critical works, such as Bernard Guyon's analysis of Balzac's political and social thinking,[43] André Maurois's biography,[44] or Harry Levin's survey of how realist writers write realism,[45] tend towards this perspective. At around the same time, economists and sociologists were examining literary representations of society as evidence of public attitudes, as, for example, in Louis Chevalier's *Classes laborieuses et classes dangereuses à Paris pendant la première moitié du XIXe siècle* (1958),[46] which compares the available evidence about the lower classes from economic, sociological, and scientific observations against their representation in contemporary works of literature, in particular by Balzac, Eugène Sue, and Victor Hugo, as well as against contemporary theorists of political economy such as Henri de Saint-Simon, Charles Fourier, and Pierre-Joseph Proudhon.

The same evidence was also repurposed by other critics to impose a reading from a political economic perspective. For decades the link between political economics and literature had been close. Political economics had explained, and was explained by, literary creation: Lukács[47] and Walter Benjamin[48] reinterpreted Balzac and Charles Baudelaire in the light of urban commodity capitalism, while Karl Marx used Johann Wolfgang von Goethe's *Faust* to articulate his theories on the power of money.[49] The dangers of this approach were amply demonstrated by the wholesale imposition of Marxist theory in the Soviet Union between the early 1930s and the early 1980s, a move that severely limited the value of much Soviet criticism during this period. But new attitudes were also evolving. Regenia Gagnier's *Insatiability of Human Wants: Economics and Aesthetics in Market Society*, published in 2000, traced the shift in nineteenth-century political economic thinking from "notions of Economic Man as producer (Smith, Ricardo, Mill, and Marx) or reproducer (Malthus) to a view of Economic Man as consumer [(Jevons, Menger)]." She illustrated this with examples from contemporary literature to show how artistic products both were subject to and could represent this transition, and in doing so she provided an intellectual basis for considering reception theory as an economic force.[50] It was now thinkable to enquire in more detail about how demand for aesthetic products could be produced and, more importantly, manipulated by their creator to be made even more desirable.

At the same time, the field of literature as economic critique was also undergoing radical change towards a final category of economic criticism that I call "literature as economic self-commentary." To an extent, this dates back to the very emergence of the extended debate about realism as simultaneously representation and critique of the conditions of its own conception: the very form of realism is seen as a necessary condition of its ability both to represent the realities of nineteenth-century industrial society and to attract readers to read that representation. The inflection point at which economic critique becomes economic self-commentary is clearly shown in Christopher Prendergast's *Order of Mimesis*, which treats narrative as an item in an economic exchange with readers in which readers have an expectation of a profitable return on both their time and their investment of trust in the narrative credentials. In his chapter on Balzac, Prendergast uses Balzac's representation of transaction and commerce as a way of asking what we can infer from this about the transaction between narrator and reader.[51]

At the same time, the scope of literary criticism and its ability to access economic tools also underwent a significant change. Terry Eagleton's

1983 *Literary Theory: An Introduction* called into question all received attitudes to literary criticism and to literature itself.[52] Vernon's comparison between prose fiction and categories of texts that were then only beginning to be considered as part of the literary system, such as banknotes,[53] highlighted the benefits of a broader horizon, particularly when combined with the then recent reception theories of Wolfgang Iser[54] and Hans Robert Jauss.[55] Albeit slowly, this led to Poovey's proposition that virtually all forms of writing, from banknotes to treatises on political economy, should be treated as genres within a broad definition of narrative.[56] In turn this has legitimised the application of literary criteria to financial narratives and that of economic criteria to aesthetic representation.

But this new form of interdisciplinary criticism needed more input from the economics side. Pioneers such as Marc Shell and Goux had become overfascinated by the correspondence between linguistic and economic systems, as Delany argues, and had failed to develop a broader model for bringing the literary and economics together.[57] Catherine Gallagher, in *The Body Economic: Life, Death, and Sensation in Political Economy and the Victorian Novel* (2006), proposes a model which brings together an understanding of how the literary representation of a political economy can influence the composition and style of the narrative itself. She uses the example of Charles Dickens's *Hard Times,* which she argues is an attempt to represent and critique Benthamite political economy. The attempt, she contends, is reflected in the style of the work itself. "The prose doesn't just mime the monotony of the environment but announces that the novel is both product and produce of the severe workfulness it seems to criticize. *Hard Times* relentlessly belabors its effortful prose and its unhappy (in both senses of the word) allegories. Workfulness is not just an attribute of people of this novel, it is a mode of representation and an angle of vision on the world in general."[58] This is perhaps the closest example I have found to an illustration of my perspective, in that it shows clearly how the act of composition could be influenced by an economic objective. In this case, as she argues it, it is the representation, in fiction, of an economic theory rather than the variation of the perceived value of the text by the reader that is being achieved, but the principle is the same.

Literary historians have also started to make similar use of stylistic analysis. Franco Moretti's *The Bourgeois: Between History and Literature*

(2013) argues that the rise of the bourgeois in nineteenth-century Europe is reflected in the evolution of literary devices. Changing patterns of adjective use, for example, reflect a shift from the descriptive purposes of eighteenth-century prose to the "incrustation of value judgements over matters of fact" that, Moretti argues, characterise Victorian fiction. The new technique of "filler" narratives around the main plot offers *"the kind of narrative pleasure compatible with the new regularity of bourgeois life"* (Moretti's emphasis). The implication is that the act of composition itself is influenced, whether consciously or not, by external economic and social factors.[59]

Even so, both Gallagher and Moretti miss a point. As the tone of Gallagher's analysis makes clear, she evidently thinks that the resulting stylistic changes have not improved the book's readability—in other words, its value to the reader. Many subsequent critics have agreed with her. Yet at the time of its publication in 1854, *Hard Times* succeeded in doubling the circulation of *Household Words*. John Ruskin thought it one of Dickens's finest.[60] What does this tell us about the literary and stylistic devices that made it attractive or valuable to the contemporary reader? Is there evidence to suggest Dickens was aware of what some now see as the novel's shortcomings and, if so, are countermeasures visible in subsequent works? Gallagher's approach concentrates on the political economy angle and successfully demonstrates the interrelationship between theory and narrative structure, just as Moretti's links social to stylistic evolution, but both omit the additional angle that an appreciation of literature as commerce might have brought.

My own approach, and the one I want to explore in this book, is to treat the text as something that its author is, typically, trying to "sell" to the reader, in both a strictly economic and a metaphorical sense—the title of the book, *Selling the Story*, encapsulates this very duality. The text itself will show the evidence of this activity both in the author's choice of subject and in his or her choice of style, genre, or literary device. This is what I mean when I say that every narrative is, in some part, a self-reflexive commentary on the conditions of its own production. I suspect this may be true of all narratives, whenever produced, but my focus here is on the nineteenth-century "professional turn," the point at which the writing of prose fiction became a commerce and writers were able to make a living, of sorts, from the business of selling narratives. An author's output encountered a commercial market where consumers, often through powerful publishing intermediaries, defined the parameters of value and influenced, at times even dictated, the terms of trade. It is only to be expected that what is produced will reflect an awareness of what sells. Even the asserted absence of a commercial objective is itself a form of commentary.

Understanding the market into which an artistic product is launched thus becomes part of understanding the work itself. How creators define the value of their products—and there are many yardsticks of value, from economic, to critical, to posterity-driven—is related to the reception of those products in target markets. Understanding market context, in terms of both contemporary conditions and emerging trends, can alert a modern critic to authorial strategies used to modify the value of an artistic production. Such strategies, particularly if commercial and related to canonical works, are rarely recognised in current critical discourse. Exposing them can reveal a hitherto underevaluated and underappreciated awareness of, and responsiveness to, economic influences.

This, then, is the starting point for my investigation. The process relies on three rather basic analytical steps, which I will discuss in more detail later. These can be summarised as follows.

Understanding the context—economic and cultural, but most specifically the *publishing context*—of a given work provides the tools to detect the pressures of artistic production at work on the author. An awareness of these pressures helps to recognise possible authorial responses in the text.

Unbundling the role of *transaction* in narrative is the next step. At an obvious level, nineteenth-century novels frequently use transactions—monetary, legal, psychological—as essential elements of plot. Behind this, though, the narrative itself can be viewed as the object of a real transaction between author and reader in which the reader trades time against the anticipation of textual gratification. An awareness of both roles for transaction allows the reader to ask all sorts of rather down-to-earth questions more normally associated with commerce than with creativity: "What am I being sold? Why should I buy it? How much? How do the in-story characters value the very same narrative? If they buy the story, should I?" Analysing narrative as transaction helps to isolate the economic effects of literary devices more normally approached in aesthetic terms.

Finally, the two prior steps lead directly to a discussion of the constituents of *literary value*. Here I am less interested in the subjective reader response than in gathering evidence from the text itself of how the author tried to mediate or manipulate the value of the narrative to the reader, and thence attempting to deduce how the author might have conceptualised literary value. The result is a rather practical approach to literary value that I call the *point of sale* perspective, which focusses on mining the text for what it reveals about the author's understanding of transaction and anticipated reader response at the point of composition. It prompts a series of questions about what tools authors have to mediate value, where the tools came from, whether there is textual evidence of their use, how effective they have been, and how effectiveness is itself to be judged.

In isolation, none of these steps is particularly original. Woodmansee and Osteen's suggested approach in *The New Economic Criticism* contains all of these elements.[61] What is different is my focus on the synchronic viewpoint of the author at the point of sale, to the extent demonstrable from contemporary evidence including the text itself, as a way of examining how economic considerations might have influenced the composition of the same text. The role of the economic critic is to identify these economic drivers (or, indeed, their absence) and to link them to textual structures such as genre, subject, or literary device, which can be shown on the basis of contemporary evidence to influence reception. It is not, in my view, necessary to demonstrate authorial intention or awareness in this process, although in many cases evidence of an all too acute consciousness of the author's economic standing is clear. Fedor Dostoevsky and Balzac, for example, are famously and vocally indigent, while Gustave Flaubert and the later Dickens are just as demonstrably aware of their financial independence. The implication, though, is that because no writer exists independently of his or her economic context, their works will also be in some measure a self-reflexive response to that context. Texts can reveal conscious authorial strategies to address economic issues of reach and reception, while reception, both immediate and through posterity, can reveal economic effects that may have been far from conscious at the point of sale. More, the act of writing itself compels every author to become, in effect, a character in his or her own novels responsible for mediating reader reception. Economic criticism is an effective way of identifying and analysing this phenomenon.

To an extent, this different viewpoint affects everything else: the focus of my perspective on transaction, for example, is on the various negotiating strategies an author can adopt depending on his or her per-

ception of how readers assess literary value. It is important to emphasise, though, that this is not a work of critical theory and it makes no
claims to stand as such. My economic perspective is just that, a different
point of view informed by experience of another discipline that can, I
think, provide a new approach even to major canonical texts that have
been exhaustively analysed within existing critical frameworks. It is,
emphatically, not exclusive: economic criticism complements aesthetic
approaches and seeks to add rather than to supplant. Since it is essentially a pragmatic approach, it is best illustrated by demonstration of its
application. For reasons discussed more fully later, I have chosen three
authors from across the nineteenth century and from across widely separated geographies and cultures, each represented by canonical works
already familiar to critical attention: Balzac's *Splendeurs et misères des
courtisanes*, Dostoevsky's *Brothers Karamazov*, and Emile Zola's *L'Argent*.
But first, a better understanding of my three analytical steps is perhaps required.

The Importance of the Publishing Context

Changes in the wider economic and cultural contexts can have far-
reaching effects once translated to the publishing environment. One of
the themes I shall follow is the divergent evolution of the book as a publishing format in different countries. My chapters on Balzac, Dostoevsky, and Zola will examine this in greater detail, but a general overview will provide a summary of the overall publishing context.

In England the early phases of the Industrial Revolution had created
a literate middle class with enough spare time and money to buy and
read the works of Samuel Richardson, Jane Austen, and Walter Scott,
as well as an economy with enough access to capital to invest in printing
technology and distribution. Demand for all forms of printed matter
grew as literacy, education, and new publishing technologies expanded
the market. Railways arrived to reach new readerships at ever-growing
speed. This thriving market could support multiple publishing formats,
from newspapers to periodicals to stand-alone books, most notably the
nine-hundred-page, forty-five-chapter, three-volume "triple-deckers"
required by Mudie's and bemoaned by Lady Carbury in my introductory quotation from Anthony Trollope's *Way We Live Now*. Indeed, triple-
deckers remained an important publishing format throughout the

century until the mid-1890s despite competition from serialised novels, cheap "yellowback" reprints, and eventually cut-price book-format editions of original works. Other formats were able to coexist and grow alongside the book, including periodical miscellanies such as *Blackwood's Magazine,* more literary weeklies such as Dickens's *Household Words,* and the mass-market newspapers such as the *Daily Mail* introduced by the Harmsworth family in the 1890s. Authors had access to, or at least direct experience of, multiple and evolving formats, and the most successful, like Dickens, could even dictate their own choice of format.[62]

By contrast, authors in nineteenth-century France were confronted by a rather different publishing environment. In comparison to England's economy, that of France started the century in a less developed state and continued to grow more slowly. Both population and productivity growth were weak; industrialisation and urbanisation took longer to happen; education and literacy followed suit. The publishing industry found itself in a vicious circle of high costs, low productivity, intrusive censorship, piracy, and slow growth in the readership, which led to widespread failures and a government bail-out of Parisian printer-publishers in 1830. When, in 1836, the first lower-priced periodicals appeared on the market, the industry found itself in no state to support competing formats. For the next half century, the book format would remain subservient to the dominance of the periodicals and the newspapers. Not that the book disappeared as a format; rather, the readership penetration achieved by the roman-feuilleton at the foot of the first page of a popular periodical or newspaper was so much higher than that of a stand-alone book, unsupported by the shop window of the periodical, that it became far less profitable for authors and publishers to choose the book format unless independently wealthy.

Not until the late 1870s would technological advances and the development of a mass readership change the equation and allow the book format to return as the leading marketplace for new, original prose fiction. The virtual requirement, during the entire middle of the century, to publish in a journalistic medium, in serialised format, in physical proximity to the news and scandal of the day that sold newspapers, in return for payment by the line or column, is of inescapable importance in understanding French authors of the period, even those who, like Flaubert, could afford to buy their way free of the system.[63]

The Russian market was, as usual, idiosyncratic. Its size, geography, and economic backwardness created vast barriers to the development of a mass readership. It had developed its own hybrid publishing format, the "thick journal," a monthly periodical often of several hundred pages in bound hardback-book format, containing entire chapters of novels alongside essays on subjects from science to farming, which reached readerships of rarely more than a few thousand. Since the days of Peter the Great, much of its aristocracy, thus a substantial proportion of the potential book market, had looked to the West for imported taste, manners, and technology. The link with France was particularly close, though it remained very much a one-way street from France into Russia until late in the century. Publishers appropriated the latest developments in the French publishing market and applied them to a Russian market which lagged far behind in the development of its readership. Authors throughout the century found themselves addressing a readership a fraction the size of that in France which their publishers were attempting to develop using tools designed for a wholly different market. Nonetheless, the French market had demonstrated the potential of a mass market yet to come. So which market should an author address? I think it is difficult to understand an important aspect of nineteenth-century Russian literature without an appreciation of this point.[64]

Writers themselves document the translation of general economic trends into specific publishing strategies or pressures. Wilkie Collins, writing in *Household Words* in 1858, records his surprise at discovering "a reading public of three millions which lies right out of the pale of literary civilisation," evidenced by the proliferation of penny journals as urban population growth and literacy begin to explode.[65] The relentless domination of the French press by the periodical and newspaper sector is chronicled and satirised by, among many others, Balzac in *Illusions perdues* (1837–1843), the Goncourt brothers in *Charles Demailly* (1868), and Guy de Maupassant in *Bel-Ami* (1885). Zola finally, and virtually singlehandedly, overcomes the power of the periodical, reestablishes the book as a profitable economic entity in its own right, and documents the process, as I shall argue, in *L'Argent*. The publishing context acts as filter and focus, bringing the implications of wider economic and cultural changes for the business of producing literature into sharper relief.

Literature as Transaction

The notion of transaction implies a process, an act, and an account of both.[66] The process involves a negotiation through time to discover value and the levers that affect value, to compare the values of different commodities in an iterative process which may involve modifications and repeated reassessments, and finally to reach a point of compromise at which the parties to the transaction agree on an equivalence of value between two different commodities. The act involves the completion of an exchange between two or more parties or, alternatively, the completion of a performative process that results in a transfer of value even without a counterparty, as, for example, through a legal process, as in a will or a dowry, or through coercion, as in theft or extortion. Both cause a discontinuity, a sudden and radical change of state occasioned by, for example, a signature on a contract. Finally, transaction can be seen as an account, a narrative of itself, as in the transactions of a learned society; not merely the act but the story of the act as well.

Since Barthes we have become used to thinking of narrative as a commodity and of the *récit* as a contract between author and reader that can credibly be described as an actual transaction. The author offers a narrative in exchange for the reader's attention, often mediated by a publisher who establishes a monetary equivalent for the initial value of the narrative. The author's perception of value may extend beyond the reception of an immediate readership towards possible future readers and a concept of future value. The text becomes a commodity capable of establishing a form of exchange rate between the Marxist value of the author's labour, Samuel Taylor Coleridge's concept of the absolute or perpetual value of art, and the Jevonian marginal utility value of the work's reception over time. Georg Simmel discusses whether relationships based on a transfer of intellectual property can qualify as genuine exchanges in *The Philosophy of Money*. He establishes two criteria for defining what is, and what is not, exchange. Each party, he says, must offer to the other more than he or she possessed before; and each party must sacrifice a good in order to obtain the commodity he or she wants. The author-reader exchange satisfies both conditions: each reader, present and future, offers "reach"—a larger audience and the possibility of eventual canonisation—and, indirectly via the publisher, a financial return to the author, who has sacrificed time to create the narrative as the commodity of exchange. The author offers to the reader the prospect of enjoyment or education to be derived from the narrative: the reader sacrifices time and attention to achieve these objectives. In Simmel's terms, it seems clear that the author-reader exchange would qualify as a genuine transaction.[67]

It seems justifiable, therefore, to think of literature as a form of transaction. In part this simply reflects reality; in part the discipline of allocating an economic category to a creative process provides a useful tool for unbundling the economic agency of individual parts of that process. It also provides an alternative lexicon for describing narration and narrative types that is sufficiently unfamiliar as to force us to reappraise previous commonplaces. It also allows us to apply some of the same techniques to a literary text as would be applied to the analysis of a transaction, by seeking to establish how the reader assigns value to the text, what methods the author uses to mediate that value, and whether the value of the story as perceived by its characters is the same as that adjudged by its readers.

It seems particularly appropriate to apply these techniques to the prose fiction of the nineteenth century in the light of the commercial revolution, which tracked its industrial counterpart across Europe at varying speeds over the course of the century. In France the sale of state-owned assets *(biens nationaux)* in 1789 and 1792 was probably the single largest series of connected transactions of that or the following century. Robert Gildea argues that the opportunity this created may have been the catalyst for the rise of the commercial bourgeoisie in France.[68] In Russia the process of commercialisation began far later: arguably, the negotiation of land reform that followed the 1861 emancipation of the serfs fulfilled a similar function to that of the sale of the French *biens nationaux* in making transaction an issue of national rather than merely individual significance. The development of literature from an aristocratic hobby into a profession required authors to transact with publishers. The "industrialisation" of literature through its assimilation for extended periods of time by the newspaper or periodical industry required many authors to become part-time journalists, aware quite literally of the value of their product per column inch. An author's personal experience of transaction was likely to become more frequent, more intensive, and more intrusive as the century progressed. It seems plausible that this should be reflected in literature, particularly in the prose narratives of novelists claiming in many different ways to offer a realistic portrayal of the money-obsessed, speculative, and deal-driven world in which they found themselves.

Considering narrative as a form of transaction also has the advantage of recognising the importance of the recipient of the narrative as an equal and necessary partner in the exchange. Lee Erickson, in *The Economy of Literary Form,* describes the process in terms that many economists would find familiar: "Since readers read within a framework of desire, the economy of literary forms can be described from the perspective of reception as well as that of production. In this way, literary forms can be viewed as historical, aesthetic products of market forces reaching a momentary equilibrium between the aspirations of writers and the desires of their audiences."[69] Erickson's perspective is essentially diachronic, and he sees reception as a process that follows on from the publication of a literary text by means of criticism, appraisal, or approval: a transaction only revealed as such by the distance of history. My more synchronic approach looks at the "point of sale" itself (a definition to which I shall return) and asks three questions:

How does the author represent transaction within the story? How do the in-story characters construct the narratives they tell to others? What techniques do they use to modify its value and what effect do they have on the credibility of the narrative in the eyes of the recipient? How are the processes of negotiation and completion represented? Understanding how the author conceives of and portrays the process of transaction gives us a yardstick with which to judge how he or she might approach the broader transaction of selling the narrative to the reader.

What clues does the story afford about how the author approaches the transaction with the reader? What techniques does the author use to make the narrative more attractive or valuable to the recipient? Has the author introduced dissonances or gaps between the way the characters perceive the value of a narrative and the way the reader perceives it, and what can this tell us about how narrative value is created and manipulated? Is there evidence within the text of the inclusion of devices that demonstrably created narrative value in related publishing formats (most obviously the periodical or newspapers within which the texts were usually published and where the link between narrative value and increased subscription or copy sales could be demonstrated with some accuracy)? How has the author reacted to external factors—censorship, editing, the process of serialisation? Building a comprehensive picture of the tools used by an author to mediate narrative value is the practical aim of this part of the analytical process.

How does narrative value change with time? Within the author's creative lifetime, what evidence can be deduced from the alterations in the tools used by a novelist to create value? In particular, is there evidence of a cycle of feedback from readers, publishers, critics, or other market forces within the publishing market? Many writers, including all three in this study, leave evidence of such exchanges in correspondence or diaries. Serialised works or works written over an extended period provide particularly compelling evidence of shifts within an established value hierarchy. Anticipated changes in the composition of the readership can also cause shifts or conflicts within systems of narrative value: what pleases one generation will not necessarily please the next. Over longer periods, changing tastes alter perceptions of literary value, allowing the formation of a literary canon and creating a notion, to which I shall return, of "posterity" or "perpetuity" value. At this point the synchronic and diachronic axes fuse temporarily, in that authors can and do "write for posterity"—allowing their views about the eventual reception of their works by posterity to act as a direct influence on current output.

Of course, not all authors, or even critics, would agree with the proposition that literary value is created through a process of transaction. William Wordsworth, for example, evidently thought that the artist could prescribe his or her own literary worth and said so emphatically in the extended preface to his *Lyrical Ballads* of 1815: "Every author, as far as he is great and at the same time original, has had the task of creating the taste by which he is to be enjoyed."[70] But there are different types of transaction which can take account of differing perceptions of value creation, and this is perhaps the moment to introduce three categories that I will later use extensively in my examination of all three of the authors I shall discuss.

The approach I explore categorises texts according to their mode of economic agency. Most nineteenth-century prose fiction can, I believe, be usefully considered within a framework that describes its economic functions in relation to three fundamental methods of "value discovery": *prospectus*, *auction*, and *speculation*. The categories are intended only to serve as a *grille de lecture*, one further perspective among many others that may usefully clarify one particular aspect of the text. They are not proposed as a theoretical approach to either novelistic construction or reception.

Prospectus

The prospectus approach reveals value through assertion by author, narrator, or character, just as a prospectus typically advertises goods in relation to a value fixed by the offeror. The recipient or buyer's task is simply to decide whether to buy the offered commodity at the price stated; the opportunity to bargain or to assert a revised view of price is either absent or limited within a range defined by the seller.

All didactic and most sacred texts would typically belong to this category, as would any form of rhetoric that seeks to persuade, from legal argument to business opportunity. The category thus incorporates extremes, from credo to credit, and provides a useful tool for testing the economic agency of concepts not generally considered in an economic framework. At one end of the scale, for example, it would include Mikhail Bakhtin's definition of "authoritative discourse" as assertion outside the dialogic process. Bakhtin neither relates this to economic function nor perceives it as part of a continuum with other forms of utterance, but the ability to classify religious texts as a form of prospectus will lead to a new perspective when we come to Dostoevsky.[71] At the other extreme, prospectus, because of its ability—indeed, propensity—to lie, is far closer to fiction that is generally assumed, as Poovey points out in *Genres of the Credit Economy,* which, in a sense, licensed an expansion of the notion of genre to include "financial writings" such as prospectus.[72]

The prospectus of the nineteenth century differed radically from our modern notion of a formal legal document. Its antecedents would have linked it to fraud and speculation in the shape of eighteenth-century stock exchange crashes such as the South Sea Bubble of 1711 or John Law's 1720 Mississippi Company failure, which had led to a general financial crash in the French market. The demand for huge volumes of capital to finance the investments of the Industrial Revolution across Europe in the nineteenth century led to a proliferation of share and debt issues, all sold by prospectus. Even new literary works were advertised by prospectus, as we shall see in the case of Balzac's *La Comédie humaine.* Many literary journals were themselves sold by prospectus and subscription. In essence, the prospectus was a story about a story, a narrative asserting value that its readers were expected to evaluate and decide whether they bought the story. It was associated with hyperbole and sensation, genres that also characterised the popular press for much of the century. Contemporary readers, I think, must have been well aware of the prospectus's ability to project false as well as genuine value and of their own role as arbiters.

Auction

The auction approach is, in many ways, the opposite. It recognises that in many circumstances authors have no way of knowing the value of their work other than through reader reception. The author thus offers his or her narrative via a process of value discovery, akin to an auction, which allows readers to establish the value of the narrative in competition amongst themselves. Goux argues in *Frivolité de la valeur* that the shift from fixed values to market-driven prices determined by those who had previously been the price-takers is an intrinsic factor in the emergence of the realist novel in nineteenth-century France, represented both in its pages and by its existence. "Every activity, every thought, every product of the intelligence or the imagination is dragged into a market, a stock exchange, where in [Marie-Esprit-Léon] Walras's model its value, which has no other basis than its exchange rate from moment to moment, is determined by 'open outcry.'"[73]

In France, at least, auctions would have been a thoroughly familiar method of sale, since the sale of the *biens nationaux* following the revolution had been conducted using this technique, with reduced lot sizes to ensure maximum reach amongst the population. Even in a literary context, value is established as much by financial results as by critical response, in the shape of increased copy or subscription sales, translated into cash by the intermediation of the publisher. Much of nineteenth-century prose fiction is affected, not least because narratives published in a journalistic context—most serialised novels of the century, for example—become auction texts by default through their participation in the sales strategy of the publication.

Speculation

Finally, the speculative approach recognises that neither author nor reader may be able to assign value to a given narrative on anything but a transient basis and that values may fluctuate significantly at each repetition as the narrative travels through time. It relies on iteration, either in the hope that multiple valuations are, over time, more representative than any methodology relying on a single point or simply in recognition of the inevitability of value change over time. Again, it is a motif drawn from actual experience: contemporary accounts reveal, rather surprisingly, that by the 1870s Paris had become the most speculative bourse in Europe, its longer settlement periods, more favourable options terms, and high liquidity giving it a decisive edge over the more staid London market.[74] The gaming resorts of Europe, from Bad Hombach to Monte Carlo, where the first casino opened in 1856 (after, of course, raising money by prospectus), were well known to travellers from as far afield as Russia and feature in correspondence from Dostoevsky and Ivan Turgenev among others.

Speculation has close links to narrative value. Thomas M. Kavanagh, tracing the history of speculation in France, quotes evidence that roulette players invent systems to beat the wheel despite knowing that none exists and that, by definition, their solutions are pure fictions that have value only to their authors.[75] The narrator of the *Arabian Nights* is clearly aware that narrative has variable value and that iteration of similar narratives can change the cumulative perception of their worth, but has no real guide as to the impact of each individual narrative iteration on overall value. Over the century, the figure of the gambler, epitomised in tales such as Dostoevsky's *Gambler* (*Igrok,* 1867) and Paul Bourget's *Autre joueur* (1884), shows how narrative outcomes, just as much as the player's wallet, can fluctuate with each roll of the dice.

The distinction between prospectus, auction, and speculative narrative seeks to identify, from the evidence of the text itself, how authors perceive their own ability to value their output. The framework proposed is comprehensive, in that all transactions other than gifts must fit at least one of the three types.[76] It differs from approaches that rely on subsequent reader reactions to texts, in that it focusses on evidence about the author's behaviour and state of knowledge at the point of composition. It is behaviourally credible, in that it corresponds with most people's personal experience of transaction and with established distinctions between transaction formats. Finally, it is particularly relevant to the nineteenth century, in that there is ample contemporary evidence of the existence of each transaction type in both commercial and literary sources, from prospectuses for railway shares to Dostoevsky's Roulettenburg.

The Notion of Literary Value

If literature is to be seen as a form of transaction, then we will need a practical method for understanding what we mean when we talk about literary "value." For all the difficulty of definition, a closer understanding of the concept is essential to bridge the difficult gap between economic value and aesthetic worth.

The idea of text as a repository for the transmission of value is one that takes root in the growth of literacy which characterised the nineteenth century across much of Europe, represented axiomatically by paper money, which exchanges value into the narrative of value. The French Revolution brought with it a revolutionary currency in the shape of *assignats*, a paper currency issued by the Assemblée nationale from 1789 to 1796 backed by the security of the property expropriated from the Catholic Church. Doubts over both legality and liquidity soon led to the *assignats* trading at substantial and growing discounts to their face value. The prospectus, or assertion of value, on the face of the notes was routinely reassessed and translated into a fluctuating valuation that formed the basis for exchange transactions. A similar experience occurred in Russia, where the paper rouble, the *assignatsiya*, had collapsed in 1817. Jillian Cooper, in *Economies of Feeling*, argues persuasively that the continuing changeability of the value and form of paper money in Russia during Dostoevsky's lifetime finds aesthetic expression in his representation of the fantastic.[77] In England the gold standard had temporarily been abandoned during the Napoleonic Wars for almost twenty-five years, from 1797 to 1819. The previously gold-backed currency had been replaced by competing paper "fiat" currencies issued by both the Bank of England and a variety of local banks.[78] Users had to act, in effect, as literary critics, comparing the value of one story of solidity and respectability with another to establish methods of differentiating value. Banks, meanwhile, discovered that by enhancing the credibility of the paper they circulated, they could also boost their creditworthiness. The motto of the London Stock Exchange, "My word is my bond" (Dictum meum pactum), perhaps the ultimate assertion of the equivalence of credibility and credit, dates from 1801.

It did not take long for the association of text and economic value to become established in more formally literary texts. Thomas Bridges, writing in 1770–1771, casts a twenty-pound note as the hero of his *Adventures of a Bank-Note,* implying that this symbol of value could also function as a focus of narrative interest and cannily taking advantage of a popular fad for "object narratives" to enhance the value of his own.[79] Goethe, perhaps with tongue rather in cheek, represents the economic agency of inscription as Mephistophelean alchemy in the second part of *Faust* (published 1832):

> To whom it may concern,
> this note is worth a thousand crowns.
> It is secured by a specific pledge
> over untallied buried treasure in the Emperor's lands.
> Now let it be provided that this rich treasure,
> once lifted from the ground, shall serve as quittance.[80]

The devilry may lie rather in the implied equation between narrative as financial value, as offered to and accepted by the in-story characters, and the same narrative as literary treasure offered to Goethe's readers.

By the time of Trollope's Melmotte in *The Way We Live Now* (1875), devilry had become sleaze, and the story's ability to carry economic value had sloughed off any last reliance on Goethe's underlying security, *vergrabnes Gut,* as his narrator acerbically observes: "As for many years past we have exchanged paper instead of actual money for our commodities, so now it seemed that, under the new Melmotte regime, an exchange of words was to suffice."[81] The role of narrative as a carrier of value had been so well established that it could even be parodied: an article by Dickens's subeditor, W. H. Wills, in *Household Words* entitled disingenuously "Review of a Popular Publication: In the Searching Style" turns out to be a critique of a Bank of England banknote as a work of literature: "Few can rise from a critical examination of the literary contents of this narrow sheet, without being forcibly struck with the power, combined with the exquisiteness of the writing. It strikes conviction at once. It dispels all doubts, and relieves all objections. There is a pithy terseness in the construction of the sentences; a downright, direct, straight-forward, coming to the point, which would be widely imitated in much of the contemporaneous literature that constantly obtains currency (though not as much)."[82]

The professionalisation of the business of writing and the rise of journalism throughout the middle of the century and more or less across

Europe offer another way of attaching financial value to literary production. Balzac, writing to Eveline Hanska in 1836, is so explicit about the equivalence as to be worth an extended quotation:

> Over a 15-day period I sold 50 columns to the *Chronique* for a thousand francs, one hundred and twenty columns to *La Presse* for eight thousand francs, 20 columns to a *Revue musicale* for a thousand francs, an article to the *Dictionnaire de la conversation* for a thousand francs, which makes eleven thousand francs in a fortnight. I worked 30 nights without going to bed, and I completed *La Perle brisée* (for the *Chronique*, out already), and *La Vieille Fille* (for *La Presse*, out tomorrow). I did *Le Secret des Ruggieri* for Werdet. In a couple of weeks the last two volumes of *Etudes de Moeurs* will be published, then I'm quits. I sold my third dizain for *two thousand francs* (so that makes 13,000fr.) Then I'm going to do *La Torpille* and *La Femme supérieure* for *La Presse*, and *Les Souffrances de l'Inventeur* for the *Chronique*. At the same time I'm in the process of selling, for *18,000 francs*, the reprint rights to *La Torpille* and *La Femme supérieure*, together with *Un grand homme de province [à Paris]* and *Les Héritiers Boirouge*, both begun, which makes a total of *thirty-one thousand francs*. Then, since I don't have to rely on that rotten plank of a Werdet any more, I'm going to do a deal with a rich, solid publishing house for the 14 remaining volumes of *Etudes de mœurs*, volumes 12 to 26, which should be worth up to 56 thousand francs for the author's rights, out of which I'd want 30,000 up front. If that all comes off, I'd have raised 63 thousand francs through the last two deals, which I'm going to put my back into, and that would save me from everything. Not only would I be free of debt but I'd even have some money over. But I'll need to work day and night for six months and then at least 10 hours a day for two years.[83]

As a love letter this may lack finesse, but it shows convincingly how conversant Balzac was with the details of literature as a business, from the value of journalistic writing compared to prose fiction to the structure of contracts with publishers. Dostoevsky, who habitually ends his letters with a request for money or a complaint about its absence, was variously publisher, editor, and contributor to his own and others' periodicals, as well as novelist. Dickens established his own weekly publications, *Household Words* followed by *All the Year Round*, partly in order better to control the commercialisation of his own literary production, a move that was evidently successful, to judge by a comment from the *Economist* in 1852: "The works of Dickens are [as] sure to be sold as the bread which is baked is sure to be sold and eaten."[84] Trollope's autobiography contains a list of all his works to that date and the money he had made from each, totalling £68,939 17s. 5d: a later biographer refers to it as the "profit-and-loss account of his life and work."[85] Even independently wealthy writers like Flaubert and Tolstoy seem to have been acutely aware of the financial value of their output—Flaubert broke with his publisher, Michel Lévy, in a bitter disagreement over Lévy's interpretation of the terms for the publication of *Salammbô*.[86] Tolstoy gifted the copyright to some of his works, in tacit acknowledgement of their financial value, to support the migration of the Dukhobor sect to Canada. Writing had become a business, literature had become a traded commodity, and its value was regularly and pragmatically established by publishers.

Many contested that financial reward could ever be a proxy for aesthetic worth and advanced other criteria for defining literary value.[87] In England the Lakeland poets asserted their right to prescribe the nature of reader reception, and thus to control the mode of valuation for their output, according to an abstract notion of absolute aesthetic value, but fell foul of their own need for income, the declining popularity of poetry in the 1820s after Lord Byron's death, and the vagueness and subjectivity of their surrogate value yardsticks. But their insistence on the incommensurability of aesthetic and economic value announces a common theme across other European cultures that will eventually lead to various permutations of the argument for a separate dimension of aesthetic activity capable of being valued only on its own, self-referential terms. In England the public debate between Walter Besant, Henry James, and Robert Louis Stevenson in the pages of *Longman's Magazine* in 1884 attempted to define the laws of fiction as they related to the representation of reality—and thus, presumably, to a value hierarchy based on compliance with those laws.[88] In France, contested rules that promoted artistic values over accurate representation would pit Théophile Gautier, the Goncourt brothers, and eventually Joris-Karl Huysmans and Stéphane Mallarmé against the realist and naturalist schools.

The enthusiastic and influential participation of literary critics in these debates—Sainte-Beuve in France,[89] Ruskin in England,[90] and Stepan Shevyrev in Russia,[91] to name but a few—suggests yet another definition of value in the shape of the critical appreciation of "literature" as selected by a self-appointed elite. Ruskin adds further to the list with claims for pedagogical value, through the transmission of information and the power to excite noble emotions or intellectual visions, as he puts it in *Munera Pulveris* (1872)—a combination of informative and moral value.[92] He also, importantly, recognises the importance of posterity value, distinguishing in his 1864 *Sesame and Lilies* between "books of the hour" and "books of all time."[93] Other critics extend the list still further, as, for example, Pierre Bourdieu does with his claim for literature's ability to confer social or cultural capital on its recipients.[94]

This hardly helps in arriving at a workable definition of literary value. The list of the different approaches to value is too long—financial, artistic, critical, pedagogical, moral, social, or cultural—and the criteria are too woolly and subjective. Nor do more purely economic models help in practice. A commercial definition of literary value would, I think, be based on a calculation of "reach over time," or the cumulative number of readers of any given work, in all media, since its first publication. Our current definition of the literary canon can probably be seen as a non-scientific way of evaluating the relative penetration of the overall (and evolving) readership over an extended time between different works. In theory some kind of proxy framework for relating readers to copy sales (in whatever format) might then give us a financial approximation of literary value. But there are too many holes in this approach for it to be genuinely useful. The time period required for assessment is too long to deal accurately with any but the older works in the canon. Reach is difficult to define—does reading, for example, an anthologised extract from a longer work count? Do we need to make adjustments, for example to reflect smaller possible readerships for earlier works? And how should we now deal with free distribution, made possible by the internet, as works fall out of copyright?

So all formulations of literary value, whether aesthetic, ethical, philosophical, or economic, have their problems. The definition that I have found most helpful, and that I shall by and large retain here, is based on what I call the point of sale. It asks how an author might have assessed the "value" of a manuscript as he or she creates it. It is pragmatic and empirical. It admits different forms of value, from the aesthetic, through the reputational, to the commercial. It is synchronic and thus sufficiently restricted in time to be more capable of delimitation and definition than diachronic approaches that seek to address value in the *longue durée*. It can be supported by contemporary evidence of market, culture, and readership. Perhaps most importantly, it attempts to re-create the actual tensions between economic and literary value that confront every author and to deduce from the evidence of the text how the author dealt with the issue.

Part of the authorial assessment would, for any author dependent on publishing as a main source of income, be based on the financial value of the work in progress, as expressed in terms of reasonably visible and predictable income streams—for example, from serialisation, from publication in book format, from the sale of foreign rights, from theatrical royalties if the work could be turned into a play, and even from merchandise sales for the most popular works. As we have seen in Balzac's letter quoted earlier, this exercise certainly produced a definition of literary value of practical use, in that it not only paid the bills but gave authors a fairly clear guide as to how to vary their output to increase their income, if they were so inclined.

Another part, closely connected to the first, might be based on perceived initial reach. It relates specifically to the expectations of the author or publisher (who might have different views) around the initial publication of a work of prose fiction as to the size of readership it could reach over a limited period of time—typically the duration of its serialisation plus the initial publication in book format. We know that publishers were prepared to pay for texts that expanded circulation and attracted new readers, so to an extent "reach value" overlaps with financial value. But it is not just a financial or economic measure of literary value. Authors self-evidently had their own reasons for seeking increased reach, perhaps as a way of broadcasting text that they wished to be recognised for its aesthetic, intellectual, or, indeed, purely entertainment qualities, perhaps as a measure of influence or prestige. Zola's spirited defence of the commercialisation of publishing in an article entitled "L'Argent dans la littérature" for both Russian and French periodicals in 1880 included a clear recognition of the important part that increased reach had played in the development of the market: "As a first step, the spread of education creates thousands of new readers. Newspapers get everywhere; even in the countryside people buy books. Inside half a century the book, which used to be a luxury item, becomes an everyday consumable."[95] And Zola's own nineteen attempts to be elected to the Académie française seem to indicate that he thought the reach he had achieved had created a right to have its value publicly recognised.

Finally, an author might be aware of precedents which indicated that substantial changes to the readership were likely in the foreseeable future, even though they could not affect conditions at the time of publication. Stendhal's dedication of four of his works—*Promenades dans*

Rome, *Le Rouge et le noir, La Chartreuse de Parme,* and *Lucien Leuwen*—to the "Happy Few" is usually taken to be a reference to a future readership able to comprehend his works. Dostoevsky's ability to compare the French publishing market, where the development of a mass readership was under way, with that in Russia, where the process had yet to begin, is crucial to understanding his relationship with his Russian readers. The initial panning that *L'Assommoir* received led Zola to look to posterity for redress, as he writes to the critic of *Le Gaulois:* "Perhaps it is necessary for the vast ensemble of novels to which I have dedicated myself to be completely finished for it to be understood and judged. And I'll happily wait another ten years."[96] This creates a third component of value: posterity or perpetuity value, itself a measure of future reach based on the anticipation of a mass, or simply a more receptive, readership to come.

The concept of reach, whether immediate or over time, is far more than a purely financial or economic yardstick. Authors write for many reasons: to achieve artistic expression, to illustrate moral or philosophical concepts, to describe the human condition—the list is long and the grubby business of making enough money to live on may be well down the hierarchy even for journalists. But every author needs reach, for without it the writer is a voice crying in the wilderness. Broad reach suggests a work's ability to travel across geography, across social boundaries, across intellectual barriers, and through time. Reach is a measure of reception, a process of evaluation and classification that builds forms of temporary or more durable consensus out of multiple subjective experiences. The different manifestations of reach, from the canonical novel to the viral blog, are far beyond the scope of this book to investigate, save to observe that each manifestation will commonly imply, though it does not presuppose, a financial return, even if this takes time or rewards others apart from the author, as many recipients of the work will be prepared to pay for the benefit they expect from reading it.

Reach, as I have suggested, is best determined in terms of the cumulative volume of readers over time, insofar as this can be measured or, more likely, approximately deduced. Several alternative definitions of literary value would insist on a further component, a measure of the quality of reach. Critical value, for instance, relates to reception within a small (but influential) subset of the possible readership; pedagogical value to another subset. When we distinguish between "literary" and "nonliterary" texts, we implicitly create a value-based hierarchy between different subsets of readers. I have chosen not to incorporate these distinctions into my definition of literary value, partly because their subjectivity undermines their usefulness, but mostly because in the long run it seems to me that many of the differences they seek to highlight are, in fact, captured by a rolling concept of reach. Critical value merges over time with posterity value as assimilation into the literary canon proceeds or fails. *Harry Potter* may be as widely read as Shakespeare for a period, but reach over time is the only effective means of establishing a long-term yardstick of value.

So when I refer to the "literary" or "narrative" value of a text for publication, as will frequently be the case in these pages, I mean a measure of value based on reach over time. In nineteenth-century France and Russia, it is implicitly (though still only partially) an economic concept, in that novels published by serialisation in newspapers or journals relied on the economic success of their vector to achieve initial, short-term reach. Subsequent medium-term extensions of reach could be achieved if the initial platform had provided enough penetration, through different formats, markets, or media. It also includes the longer-term potential reach that could be anticipated given contemporary trends in demographics, the evolution of the readership, and publishing strategies. Authors, I think, write by and large for the readership they can see at the point of sale plus the new readers they think they might acquire as a result of reasonably foreseeable developments in the readership over a relatively short time horizon—a few decades, a century at most. "I'm writing this, I hope without lying or pulling the wool over my eyes, just like a pleasurable letter to a friend. I wonder what that friend will think of it in 1880?" asks Stendhal in *Vie de Henri Brulard*.[97]

All three metrics are proxies for reader reception that allow the author to form a view of the value of his or her enterprise. The first asks how early reader reception translates into short-term economic gain and provides an immediate exchange rate between reception and monetary value. The second allows market analysis by subsegmenting reception between different demographics or reader communities. The third allows forward projection—business planning—by rationalising assumptions about market evolution, or changes in reception.

Importantly, my definition recognises the transactional nature of the exchange in that it explicitly allows for both the vendor's and the buyer's perspectives of value. Serialisation provides an unparalleled opportunity for reader response, and there are copious examples across the nineteenth century of letters to authors, from complete strangers as well as from friends, offering advice, criticism, requests, and even their own personal stories as plot. Prendergast estimates that the four hundred surviving letters from readers to Sue in response to his enormous and hugely successful *Les Mystères de Paris* represent only about a third of the likely total volume.[98]

The measure is, of course, crude: none of the three components of value can be estimated with precision, nor do they share a common unit of measurement, nor can they be satisfactorily summed. But they do, on the other hand, accurately reflect the practical issues facing an author or a publisher who intends to create or distribute a text and who must find a way to add apples and oranges. Life is, perhaps, simpler for a publisher prepared to reduce additional reach to a direct proxy for further financial returns, and more complex for an author or contemporary critic worrying about the quality of that reach—will the work reach the "right" readers?—but the essential need to make important judgements based on a combination of anticipated return and reach does not vary.

If my definition seems to insist overly on the economic aspects of reception and reach, it is because this perspective has been largely ignored in critical debate. My intention in foregrounding it is to rectify the balance rather than to suggest that novelists write only for money. The artistic, philosophical, metaphysical, religious, and biographical influences and objectives of each of my chosen authors have all been extensively analysed. All have demonstrably played important roles in artistic creation. But in analysing an era when writing prose fiction was becoming a profession, a modern critic ignores the impact of economics on the very text itself at his or her peril. The economic approach complements, rather than excludes, aesthetic and intellectual assessment. It is, in fact, essentially interlinked with artistic evaluation. In many instances economic drivers have direct aesthetic effect, as, for example, when financial considerations influence a choice of genre or literary device, and all three chapters on the chosen authors will discuss this interrelationship at length.

My definition may also seem rather subjective and prone to "intentional fallacy" objections, but in fact each of my three components of value can, I think, be adequately supported by external evidence. An author's perception of financial value can be deduced from many different sources—from correspondence, as we have seen in the case of Balzac; from the terms of contracts with publishers; from contemporary comparisons of payments per page, column, or line, which we know obsessed some authors. Strategies to increase reach can be evidenced by a comparison between those works and contemporary literature in its broadest sense, comprising both journalism and fiction, to identify trends in reporting and representation that can then be compared with the author's output to detect whether and how the author has imported, for example, devices of proven popularity in other media. Awareness of posterity value can be implied from the speed of change in the readership, as evidenced by growth in literacy; improvements in reader access to printed materials (most notably, in the nineteenth century, by the extension of the railway and road networks); the growing affordability of publications through efficiencies, technological advances, or rises in disposable income and leisure time; and the invention of new publication formats, such as the boulevard newspapers of the mid-1860s in both France and Russia, specifically designed to address a growing mass readership.

A crucial advantage of my point of sale approach is that, by postulating a measure of literary value at a point in time that coincides with the creation of the text in question, it allows us to see narrative device as a direct means of modifying that value and to identify and analyse these mechanisms in terms of economic value creation. Further, it allows us to recognise how frequently authors discuss and represent concepts of narrative value within their texts. On occasion they write directly about the value of literary or artistic production, as Balzac does in *Illusions perdues,* or Zola in *L'Œuvre.* More often they describe in-story characters telling and receiving stories and show the mechanisms that determine credibility from the points of view of a story's narrator and of its recipient. Entire genres—detective stories, crime novels, courtroom dramas—depend on this device. The external reader is required to become involved as critic of these mimetic narratives, attributing more value, for example, to the narrative of one character than another, modifying the perception of value as new narratives are presented, and understanding, even if intuitively rather than explicitly, what it is that has caused value to shift. Assessing the value of a literary narrative, even if we do not express it in those terms, is something that we all do routinely.

So when I talk of value in this intratextual context, I am essentially describing another layer of textual reception. Just as the value of an entire text depends on its reception over time, so authors use the building blocks of that text as tools to manipulate value and provide their own representations of the functioning of this process within the text. An author's choice of literary device can affect the economic value of the overall text. We see examples of this every day in, for example, the different treatments of the same subject between broadsheet and tabloid newspapers: stylistic variation is used to maximise demand within different target readerships. In this way the traditional tools of critical analysis can be repurposed to show how an author uses literary device to manipulate value. Plot, for example, has an evident economic function in acting as "the motor forces that drive the text forward," as Peter Brooks describes it in *Reading for the Plot*.[99] A more accurate description might be "the motor forces that drive the reader through the text" and thereby create demand for the product. Brooks barely admits an economic dimension in his entire discussion, but some of his examples show economic agency at work. Balzac's ambitious heroes, from Rastignac to Rubempré, impel readers to read on to the very end to find out what happens. The rambling plots of Sue's *Les Mystères de Paris,* serialised daily over almost eighteen months, suggest that equivalent value could be created simply by persuading readers to read to the end of a single episode rather than requiring the conclusion of the entire work. Detective stories increase demand by deliberately frustrating their readers' desire to know the end. Authors whose works subvert plot, as Brooks argues of Flaubert's *L'Education sentimentale,* describing it as a novel of "tenuous readability," may pay an economic price if their readers get bored.[100]

Genre is also a powerful driver of economic value. At the very core of the shift from romanticism to realism, and thence to naturalism, lies an economic motive force. Reaction against the remoteness of romanticism to a broadening readership, the attraction of the taboo-breaking novelty of realism, the increasing influence of periodicals and newspapers as the carriers of prose fiction, and the influence of developing journalistic techniques of sensation seem to have coalesced into a product that attracted readers from an ever-widening demographic. Similar stories unfurled across Europe: Scott gave way to Dickens, François-René de Chateaubriand to Balzac, Nikolai Karamzin to Nikolai Gogol and Aleksandr Pushkin. There is no mistaking the intimate connection during the nineteenth century between the evolution of literary genre and the expansion of the readership as literacy and demand grew. The circularity of the relationship confers real economic agency on genre: improvements in literacy and education produce more readers, who in turn fuel demand for new or evolving genres of reading material, which in turn attract more readers. Critical opinion, though, has taken some time to come around to this point of view. Tzvetan Todorov typifies the more traditional point of view when he describes the link between genre and society as principally constative rather than performative, more a simple reflection of society than an agent for change: "Genres bring to light the constitutive features of the society to which they belong."[101] In *Qu'est-ce qu'un genre littéraire?* Jean-Marie Schaeffer admits no economic dimension to his entire discussion.[102] Poovey, on the other hand, argues that we can extend generic classification much further to encompass not just imaginative genres but ways of creating money (monetary genres, including the role of bank notes and bills of exchange as narrative in their own right) and ways of talking about money and economics (financial writing, including journalism about finance).[103] In an era when the boundaries between fact and fiction were not easy to define, when the real value of bank notes belied the stories on their face, when prospectus became puffery, when reporting blended with invention, the use of genre as a tool to mediate economic value was widespread.

Much the same can be said of other aspects of literary construction. Format is, to a large degree, a response to economic pressures. Robert Darnton's history of the publication of Denis Diderot's *Encyclopédie* shows just how important a part the competing quarto and octavo formats played in ensuring the penetration of this key tool of the Enlightenment. "[The documentary evidence] show[s] how the book changed in shape as the publishers adapted it to an ever-widening audience and how publishing consortia succeeded one another as the speculators scrambled to exploit the biggest best seller of the century."[104] Serial publication enabled newspapers and periodicals to exploit the evident commercial attractions of prose fiction in a journalistic format to drive subscriptions and copy sales. It also functions, as Todd has pointed out, as a means of shifting economic and ethical risk between publisher, censor, and author.[105] Boulevard newspapers catered to a mass readership in a similar way to modern tabloids, though, as Tim Farrant has pointed out, their contribution to the fragmentation of literature through serialisation and mass distribution may eventually have had the opposite effect by reinforcing the aesthetic and moral standing of the novel when it reemerged as a separate format.[106] The Russian "thick journal" grew out of one publisher's attempt to devise a monthly compendium with content broad enough to attract urban and provincial readers in a format that could be distributed in the provinces without falling apart before it reached its readers: such are the practicalities of publishing.

Finally, many everyday literary devices can also be shown to have economic influence. My discussion of Dostoevsky relies in part on the economic power of iteration—the repetition of a single story over and over again in different narrative modes in order to maximise the chances of attracting readers, the literary equivalent of a reinsurance contract. In the case of Zola, I argue that his appropriation of journalistic devices, in particular hyperbole and compression, plays a crucial role in the development of a literary style that enabled the book to reemerge as an economically viable format.

Balzac, Dostoevsky, and Zola

If my thesis of the novel as an implicit commentary on the conditions of its own production is to hold water, then it must be flexible and broadly applicable. In choosing works by Balzac, Dostoevsky, and Zola as my test beds, I hope to be able to show that the concept is relevant across time, geography, and culture. To avoid spreading the butter too thinly, I have concentrated on the French and Russian literary markets of the nineteenth century. The core of this book consists of three extended and interlinked chapters, one on each of the three writers, in which I have approached three major works from the economic perspective I have set out here. All three authors have been extensively covered in critical analysis, and each chapter will discuss the critical context of each. The combined volume of works about them would dwarf their own output, which is perhaps another comment on literary value.

In Chapter 1, "Balzac: Narrative as Business," I show how Balzac's own commercial experience is reflected in his narratives. The large majority of his writing occurs at the precise moment of the migration of prose fiction from book format to that of the serialised roman-feuilleton in the periodical, from the mid-1830s to the mid-1840s. The interaction between fiction and format is traceable throughout his works. The fact that his works also depict an unmistakeably Balzacian plethora of transactions affords a particular opportunity to study the relationship between the representation of transaction as a subject for fiction and the rapidly changing external realities of transacting with publishers and readers to sell his output. His own constant financial difficulties, until the final years of his life, lead to a well-evidenced concern for his own financial solvency throughout his writing career, which translates, as we have seen, into an acute awareness of the economic value of narrative. His head-to-head rivalry in the early 1840s with Sue, possibly the most financially successful writer of his generation, allows a side-by-side contrast of very different approaches to creating literary value.

Given this perspective, *Splendeurs et misères des courtisanes (Splendeurs)* suggests itself as the text of choice. The span of its composition, over twelve years from 1835 to 1847, covers seminal changes in the French publishing market and in the demographics of the readership, Balzac's own move into fiction as a serialised format in a journalistic context, and his painful evolution from serial debtor to established and, once married to Eveline Hanska, solvent chevalier of the Légion d'honneur. Of Balzac's major works, it is the only one to have been written over such an extended period. Its nine-year publishing history comprises two parts in book format from different publishers, three as serialised romans-feuilletons in different journals, and one appearance in a compilation volume of collected works. The commercial history of *Splendeurs* is in itself a mirror of the rapidly evolving world of publishing during the 1830s and 1840s. I present it as an extended discussion of the constituents of narrative value, which tracks Balzac's own growing disenchantment with the need to write for money and acts as an increasingly savage parody of the hierarchy of literary value emerging from the newly commercialised press. Balzac's initial confidence in his ability to create narrative value on his own terms, as the new era of the roman-feuilleton begins, degenerates into an introspective disassembly of the constituents of value to find out why the printing press seems to have broken as he competes with Sue in the early 1840s, and from there to a cynical misassembly to find out whether the reader has noticed that the prospectus was false as his creative career draws to a spectacular close in 1847.

Dostoevsky, by contrast, represents a different culture, a different literary market, and an opportunity to test whether my approach applies to this new environment. In Chapter 2, "Dostoevsky: Who Buys the Story?," I argue that his major works all reflect real uncertainty about the nature of the readership for which he wrote. His novels mirror the volatile economic and publishing context in which he lived. The economic ramifications of the Great Reforms represented the greatest experiment with the structure of the Russian economy in the entire nineteenth century. The outcome of that experiment was far from clear at the time of Dostoevsky's death. Over the last two decades of his life, Dostoevsky had witnessed a switchback series of policy initiatives, partial successes, defeats, and relaunches. The literary economy had followed suit as it copied developments in western Europe. But whether either would prove capable of developing solutions suitable for the Russian context, with its different history and culture, remained unclear. Writing in the Russia of the 1860s and 1870s, Dostoevsky perforce addressed a relatively small and demographically narrow readership, since at the time the conditions for the development of a mass reading public did not exist in Russia. But an awareness of the possibility of a mass readership did exist, as for decades the Russian press had been following and copying French printing strategies designed for a far wider French readership. So Dostoevsky's literary technique blends Russian and French formats, content, and genres in an attempt to create a literature that might have value both in the contemporary literary market and to a much larger readership in posterity. But since writing for this future audience could be based on nothing much more than speculation as to its tastes and culture, Dostoevsky, I argue, adopted strategies to hedge his bets.

The Brothers Karamazov (published in serial format in 1879–1880, in book format in 1881) is Dostoevsky's final work and to an extent draws together themes from across the entire body of his work. The struggle to find a mode of writing that had sufficient immediate commercial attraction to pay the bills, but that also dealt with serious philosophical issues in the hope that eternal truths would attract a perpetual readership, is played out in its text. So this chapter argues that *The Brothers Karamazov* is a novel about how to write a novel. It explicitly and repeatedly questions how recipients of narratives value what they receive and forces the reader of the novel to participate in experiments designed to contrast the reader's experience with that of the in-story characters. It shows how the uncertainty over the identity of his target readership is visible in Dostoevsky's narrative technique, which mixes stylistic devices from contemporary journalism developed for the mass market with religious and philosophical text addressed to a narrow, educated audience. It suggests that Dostoevsky develops the device of iteration, which allows the same story to be retold many times in different genres to experiment with reader reception, into a key economic tool ensuring that his narrative appealed to as broad as possible a contemporary audience, as well as to an emerging but still future mass readership.

Chapter 3, "Zola: The Business of Narrative," documents the rise of big business and its impact on narrative. Unlike Dostoevsky, Zola was able to address a mass audience, which he himself had helped to create. His novels, written contemporaneously with Dostoevsky's major works, describe a world in which mass culture and big business affect all aspects of life, from department stores to mines. But the process that the novels describe also affects their own composition, as Zola combines the techniques of the populist press with a highly commercial approach to the business of writing that he had learned at the feet of one of its leading entrepreneurs, Louis Hachette. Naturalism migrates from literary theory to promotional platform to stylistic template, sanctioning the wholesale importation of journalistic devices. The effect is to release the book, as an independent commercial format, from a half-century-long subordination to the newspaper serial, completing the cycle of which Balzac had recorded the beginning.

L'Argent (1891) is the eighteenth in the twenty-volume cycle of *Les Rougon-Macquart,* and also the third story about Aristide Saccard. *La Fortune des Rougon* (1870), the first of the series, describes his early beginnings as a journalist. *La Curée* (1871 / 1872) tells of his first fortune as a Parisian land developer and is the second novel in the series. *L'Argent* is the story of his reincarnation and eventual failure as a banker. The three novels are linked by more than a hero. The twenty-year gap between them charts Zola's own rise from obscurity to fame and wealth as a writer. By tracking the techniques Zola uses to construct his output from the early days of *La Curée* to the maturity of *L'Argent,* I illustrate how Zola's use of literary device is closely associated with external developments in the commercialisation of the novel in book format, as well as with the rise of big business itself in the French economy.

His role in the industrialisation of narrative mirrors the rise of the story itself as a key tool of commercialisation—through advertisements, prospectuses, corporate presentations, and public relations—and its ever-growing dissociation from underlying reality. *L'Argent* tells the story of how Saccard fashions a narrative of business that, like the schemes he proposes, depends for its value more on its credibility as narrative than on the economic viability of the projects it sells. Zola, too, is enamoured of his own virtuosity as a storyteller and begins to take liberties with his readers in just the same way that Saccard does with his shareholders, presaging the gradual attrition of his own value as a novelist as he moves beyond the cycle of *Les Rougon-Macquart*.

Selling the Story contends that economic criticism represents an underexploited resource that has yet to deliver its own full value, both in developing new tools and in extending its geographic reach. The ambiguity in its very title encapsulates the critical process it proposes. On one hand, "selling the story" is simply descriptive, shorthand for the commercialisation of literature during the nineteenth century. On the other, it is a literary device, a metaphor, representing an author- and publisher-driven process of positioning, presentation, and promotion and hinting at an equivalent, opposite, and reception-driven process of "buying the story." Economic criticism, too, has value as both descriptor and metaphor. It allows us to highlight the economic pressures on authors operating in a commercial environment with more focus than is usual. It suggests we should look for evidence of the external economic context within the text itself. It forces us to recognise the transactional nature of the relationship between reader and writer. And it makes us realise that the process of selling and buying the story is one in which we are all involved, each and every day. Modern life bombards us with narrative, through media, through politics, and through finance just as much as through literature and journalism. We have all learned to be wary of the false prospectus, to avoid being "sold a line." We have developed our own personalised tools to rank and classify narrative. We are all economic critics.

1

Balzac: Narrative as Business

"L *A COMÉDIE HUMAINE*. The complete works of Monsieur H. de Balzac. De luxe edition at a great price. First instalment 3 pages of in-8° plus a vignette. . . . The complete work in 12 volumes. Each volume comes with eight decorative engravings and will consist of 10 instalments. Subscribe here."[1] Thus runs an advertisement accompanying the April 1842 prospectus for *La Comédie humaine*.[2] The emergence of the novel as a commercial driver behind a new generation of periodicals and newspapers that revolutionised the French press coincided closely with the span of Honoré de Balzac's career as a writer. The extended composition of *Splendeurs et misères des courtisanes*, occupying a twelve-year period from 1835 to 1847, tracks both and provides a consistent thread by which to follow the impact of this process of commercialisation on Balzac's writing. Like most of Balzac's works, it represents, and comments on, a world in which transaction and commerce seemed to have replaced morality with masquerade, fraud, and dissemblance. The story begins with a Faustian pact and ends with the erstwhile devil doing a deal to join the establishment. What begins as a prospectus for a new and vibrant form of literature ends as a false prospectus, a travesty of the value promised. What is delivered is not what was advertised, whether to the in-story characters or, ultimately, to the reader.

A summary of the plot of *Splendeurs* perhaps overplays the melodrama but serves to remind us that this is a work in a different genre from its precursor, Balzac's rather better-known *Illusions perdues*. This had ended with the rescue of Lucien de Rubempré, aspiring author, journalist by necessity, and fallen social climber, by a mysterious Spanish priest. In *Splendeurs* we discover that this arch-manipulator, ex-convict, and hinted-at homosexual, variously known as the *abbé* Herrera, Trompe-la-Mort, Jacques Collin, and Vautrin, is on the verge of reestablishing his beloved Lucien in Parisian society. But the cost has been huge, so to defray expenses he exploits the attachment of the lovelorn banker Nucingen to Lucien's mistress, Esther, a ravishing and unconventional courtesan, to extort money in return for Esther's favours. Eventually the plot is discovered, but not before Esther has committed suicide rather than betray her love for Lucien just hours before she would have received a windfall legacy that would have wiped out the debt. Both Vautrin and Lucien are imprisoned and investigated: Lucien cracks, confesses, and hangs himself, while Vautrin trades on compromising letters from high-society ladies and his inside knowledge of the criminal world to end up as chief of police.

The novel was written in four widely separated episodes of composition. Since dates of composition are more relevant to this analysis than dates of publication, I shall refer to the four parts of *Splendeurs* by abbreviations relating to these four episodes of composition. *La Torpille* (6:425–481), written during July / August 1838 and first published in September 1838, covers the opening scene at the Opera ball where Esther is unmasked as Lucien's mistress, her rescue and subsequent reinvention by Vautrin, and her eventual reuniting with Lucien. In Balzac's final edition of the work, known as *Furne corrigé*, this section represents roughly the first third of the first part, *Comment aiment les filles*. My shorthand title for this section refers to the title under which the work was first published: *La Torpille* then connoted an electric eel and only subsequently acquired its modern meaning of torpedo.

The second, *Esther* (6:481–696), was written in the months up to May 1843, first published in May 1843, and deals with the seduction of Nucingen up to Esther's death and Lucien's arrest. In the final edition it covers the remainder of the first part and all of the second, *Les Amours d'un vieillard*. The third, *Lucien* (6:697–798), written between December 1845 and May 1846 and first published in July 1846, covers Lucien's imprisonment, confession, and suicide and corresponds to the third part of the final edition, *Où mènent les mauvais chemins*. The final part, *Vautrin* (6:799–935), written in December 1846 and January 1847 and first published in April 1847, describes Vautrin's investigation, negotiation with the authorities, and reincarnation as police chief, and maps to the fourth part of the final edition, *La Dernière Incarnation de Vautrin*.[3]

Unlike any other of Balzac's works, the novel's long gestation also provides a commentary on the emerging role of fiction and of the author as agents of the commercialisation of the press in the hands of a new generation of newspaper and journal publishers. In the hands of Emile de Girardin and his emulators, the novel had become a commercial tool that sold newspapers. *Splendeurs* is Balzac's investigation of the consequences of this process and a repudiation of the assumption that fiction reliably delivered predictable value to readers. The transactions he describes between its characters mock the notion that any represented value is deliverable. And, as the plot gradually goes off the rails (a process this chapter will uncover), the reader discovers that the text also fails to deliver on any conventional view of novelistic value. This novel of the false prospectus is itself a false prospectus, purporting to deliver value but in reality subverting its own claims. The analogy is more than mere metaphor and accurately describes the transaction between reader and author.

This chapter examines how Balzac establishes, develops, and experiments with this concept over the course of the evolution of the narrative as we now know it. As we shall see, the false prospectus is at once the emblem of the compromised morality of the rising bourgeoisie of the 1830s–1840s, a commentary on the breakneck commercialisation of the contemporary novel, and a literary device that exploits the willingness of the subscriber—both commercial and literary, of course—to accept fantasy as reality. Through the four main episodes of composition of the novel, Balzac moves from the prospectus as the subject of the novel, through a behind-the-scenes exposé of its construction and operation, to an experimental disassembly of its mechanism, and finally to a self-reflexive and self-destructive critique of its effects on the literary environment. Central to the novel's theme is the issue of how the reader-subscriber not only is able to interpret fantasy as a kind of enhanced reality but is even prepared to collude in the process of self-deception. The title itself has the ring of a playbill that attracts subscribers by the lure of excess, by *splendeurs* and *misères*, by intensity beyond everyday experience, by the transgressive attractions of the *courtisane*—and also by the implied reference to the speculative switchback of commerce. The plot rehearses the montage and exposure of a series of deceptions by Balzac's version of a novelistic superhero. But this fantastic avatar, by turns Herrera, Collin, Vautrin, and Trompe-la-Mort, runs riot, switching personalities as frequently as identities, disrupting narrative continuity just as he undermines the rules of characterisation, parodying the contemporary conventions of commercial fiction, and forcing readers to consider at what point they stop buying the story. .

However, as Balzac's own firsthand experience of inventing stories to fob off his creditors amply demonstrates, fantasy and deception regularly play a part in real life: credibility and credit are inseparable bedfellows. Where is the dividing line, Balzac seems to be asking, between buying and rejecting the story? If the fiction is successful, then it is because reality and fantasy have become so intermingled that the recipient can no longer tell them apart. If it fails, then a discontinuity occurs: fiction no longer commands credibility, and artistic device collapses into exposed manipulation. What causes this loss of credibility? Does not the process of commercialisation of the novel lead of itself to a Faustian pact with the reader in which satisfying the increasingly jaded customer eventually exposes the fraud? As *Splendeurs* gradually assumes its final shape, both author and reader are required to recalibrate their notions of narrative value: literally, from the point of view of the author, in terms of what sells in an increasingly commercial environment; and figuratively, from the point of view of the reader, in terms of when he or she loses faith in the story. The questions raised by the end of the novel about the nature of narrative credibility and the compromises that the contemporary novelist is required to endure lead to an exhausted withdrawal from the transaction, symbolized by a failure to complete the novel to its original plan and Balzac's almost total silence as a novelist after 1847.

Perhaps the very difficulty of pigeonholing *Splendeurs* has led to its virtual absence from modern critical discussion. Early critics tended to be dismissive—"a . . . mediocre work" *(un . . . livre médiocre)*—but were often working from incomplete texts.[4] The wave of interest in Balzac in the 1960s tended towards more general reviews that referenced *Splendeurs* in passing but typically spent more time on other texts, with the exception of Jean Pommier's exploration of the origins of *La Torpille*.[5] The most recent monograph, Agathe Novak-Chevalier's 2010 *Splendeurs et misères des courtisanes*, is a useful compilation of background and themes that essentially views *Splendeurs* as an attempt to represent the totality of reality, from the highest to the lowest social milieu, through the widest possible range of novelistic and stylistic devices.[6] In doing so, she follows one side of Lucien Dällenbach's argument, set out in two influential articles (1979 and 1980), that Balzac's ability to link each fragment to the whole gives him a genuine claim to a totalising, comprehensive viewpoint of contemporary society.[7] Dällenbach does not specifically focus on *Splendeurs,* but Christopher Prendergast, following a parallel track, uses it as an extended example in his own argument for Balzac's totalising realist vision, which leads him to conclude that even Vautrin's final incarnation as chief of police is plausible in a world where Balzac can perceive the moral uniformity of criminal and authority.[8] By the time of his 1986 *Order of Mimesis,* however, Prendergast seems to have swung around towards Dällenbach's subsequent argument regarding the failure of the integrating vision in the face of a disintegrating world. The more explicitly economic perspective that Prendergast adopts in the latter work, in treating the novel as an item of economic exchange and Balzac's representation of a commercialised world as a proxy for his attempt to sell his narrative to the reader, is a line that I shall develop in my own analysis.

"Phrase-Mongers" (Marchands de phrases)

To chart the episodic creation of *Splendeurs* is to follow the evolution of the relationship between the novel and the press in microcosm. To understand the gradual emergence of *Splendeurs* as a completed and integrated narrative requires an appreciation of how the writing, commercial sale, and mode of publication of each of the four principal parts interrelate to the swift evolution of the publishing market.

La Torpille was conceived as a serial but was eventually published in book format in 1838 following two rejections by *La Presse* as too racy for its readership. *Esther* did appear in the feuilleton of *Le Parisien* almost five years later in 1843, but without its final chapters, which were withdrawn, apparently due to the uncertain financial standing of the journal. The completed text finally appeared in book format the following year, under a contract that had been retraded through three different publishers since its origin two years earlier. *La Torpille* was almost immediately republished as part of the 1845 Furne edition of *La*

Comédie humaine, but this time without *Esther,* presumably to allow the earlier edition to sell out first. *Lucien* appeared in serial form in *L'Epoque* in 1846 and was almost immediately reprinted in book format, but under a different title, possibly to hoodwink at least some gullible readers into a double purchase. The final part, *Vautrin,* was intended for *L'Epoque,* but its financial problems forced an on-sale to *La Presse,* where it formed part of a spectacular climax to Balzac's career as he published three novels simultaneously in the feuilletons of three different journals. The commercial history of *Splendeurs* is in itself a mirror of the rapidly evolving world of publishing during the 1830s and 1840s.

From the early 1830s it had become economically inevitable that book production would decline relative to that of newspapers and periodicals. The overall market for literary products of any kind was limited: the French population overall had grown from 30 million in 1815 to 32.5 million in 1830, but that of Paris, the centre of literacy, had risen only from 713,000 to 785,000 over much the same period.[9] Parisian literacy rates, far higher than those in the provinces, were still no better than 60 per cent, giving an approximate Parisian total market across all social classes in 1830 of under half a million readers.[10] A provincial readership existed but was difficult and expensive to reach: the road network was only expanded in the 1830s, to be followed by the railways in the 1840s.[11] Provincial tastes were different from those of the capital, and the stock-in-trade of the colporteurs who served the provincial markets outside the main towns was works of piety, almanacs, and the *bibliothèque bleue.*[12] This was emphatically not a mass audience, which would only emerge in generations following the mass literacy campaigns initiated by François Guizot's education reform of 1833 and by the gradual inclusion of women in literacy initiatives following the *loi Falloux* of 1850. It was a readership of urban bourgeois, actual and aspirant, whose novelistic tastes still centred on the classics of the seventeenth and eighteenth centuries with only occasional excursions to current in-vogue writers, as Martin Lyons's examination of best sellers in France over the first half of the nineteenth century demonstrates.[13]

The book-publishing industry in the 1830s was in a mess. Average book prices were unaffordable for much of the prospective readership: as late as 1845, a generously typeset edition of Alexandre Dumas *père's Le Comte de Monte-Cristo* occupied ten volumes at an overall cost of 135 francs, or around a month's wages for a good worker.[14] Inefficiently small print runs of around one thousand copies and multiple editions were the order of the day.[15] There is a tendency to blame this on technical factors such as inefficient presses and poor distribution channels, but the evidence suggests that, when properly organised, volume production was possible: Louis Hachette's success in the educational publishing business following the 1833 *loi Guizot* seems to be confirmed by an order in 1835 for five hundred thousand copies of *Alphabet des écoles,* one hundred thousand of *Livret élémentaire de lecture,* and forty thousand each of *Arithmétique, Géographie,* and *Histoire de France*—all apparently successfully fulfilled.[16] Belgian piracy, much inveighed against by Balzac,[17] undoubtedly took part of the already small market, but French publishers seem to have encouraged the habit by selling directly to pirates, as demonstrated by François Buloz's sale of an unpublished proof of *Le Lys dans la Vallée* to a Russian publisher in 1835.[18] The public reading rooms *(cabinets de lecture),* in their heyday in the 1820s,[19] were effective at maximising readership but less so at converting readership into revenue, and Balzac certainly thought they did more economic harm than good.[20] But by and large these are symptoms of a more serious underlying malaise: a lack of capital and credit. The book-publishing industry was largely owned by self-made entrepreneurs, hence fragmented, and without inherited wealth, hence either risk averse or financially volatile, as evidenced by the spate of publisher bankruptcies, including those of Balzac himself and his sometime publishers Urbain Canel and Louis Mame, leading up to a government bail-out of the industry in 1830.[21] Both author and publisher bills of exchange were regularly circulating at large discounts. If capital was available, it was only to the *haute banque* who used it to fuel their own speculations, while elsewhere the Banque de France followed a highly restrictive credit policy throughout the first third of the century which, though it failed to stop a property bubble, effectively restricted the provision of credit in the remainder of the economy.[22]

By contrast, the platform offered by newspapers and periodicals must have looked increasingly attractive as the 1830s progressed. Girardin introduced three crucial innovations: the ability to attract new readers through variations in format, illustrated by the success of the 1830 *Journal des connaissances utiles* and the slightly later 1833 *Musée des familles* in developing female and family readerships; the ability to create new subscriber demand by reducing price, illustrated by the 1836 launch of

La Presse at an annual subscription of half that of the competition; and the ability to mobilise capital for investment in the periodical press, evidenced by the 800,000 francs raised to fund the start-up costs of *La Presse*. This becomes a virtuous circle: volume production allows unit costs to fall, permitting not only cover price reductions but also the absorption of distribution costs, thus opening up a new provincial audience that, in turn, creates more volume growth. Girardin offered free delivery across France for the *Journal des connaissances utiles* as early as 1831.[23]

René Guise illustrates at length that the attractiveness to readers of prose fiction, initially in the shape of the short story, had been proved from the beginning of the decade in what he calls the craze for the short story, the *folie du conte*, of 1832–1834, and that many of the extensions of literary genre—for example, into the fantastic of E. T. A. Hoffmann—into new subject areas such as the prisons and the courts, and into the exotic of Russian or Arab tales, were first introduced at this time.[24] The craze confirmed the importance of short fiction as a tool for selling newspapers, though it could not solve the other problems of scale of the newspaper market, which were not addressed until 1836 when Girardin successfully initiated a volume market that combined lower prices with the serialisation of longer works of fiction. By 1847 the total circulation of the Parisian press had risen, from 80,000 in 1836, to 180,000. "The novel-as-book has abdicated, the novel-as-feuilleton reigns and rules," writes an unknown correspondent in the *Gazette de France* of November 12, 1843.[25]

The speed and scale of change in the publishing world at this time, as publishers experimented with the impact of differing forms of extended fiction in the pages of the newspaper or periodical to drive and retain subscriptions, must have presented particular difficulties for contemporary authors.[26] Balzac's own awareness of the economic role of narrative had been evident for some time: "Eventually we have to get to the point where a volume is produced, distributed and sold just like a loaf of bread," he writes in 1830.[27] But what would readers value? Or publishers? Did the two notions of "value" coincide? And did either coincide with the author's own perception? Writing about how value is projected and established within the fictional universe is a logical strategy both for experimenting with different approaches and for testing whether an authorial assertion of how value is created, and what constitutes value, is shared by publishers and readers.

Many of Balzac's early stories had, indeed, dealt with precisely these issues. *Sarrasine* (first published in the *Revue de Paris* of November 21 and 28, 1830) not only describes Zambinella as a valuation conundrum, a literally seductive projection of apparent value camouflaging a quite different reality, but provides a frame audience to judge the literary quality of the fictional medium as well. In-story, Sarrasine records how Zambinella's value deflates: in the frame story, the unidentified marquise to whom the tale is told in expectation of sexual favours delivers her own verdict by refusing. Both *La Peau de chagrin* and *Le Chef-d'œuvre inconnu* (both 1831) externalise and reify an object of apparent value—asses' skin or artistic talent—as the central focus of the narrative and describe the process by which its value is shown to be illusory or transient. In *La Peau de Chagrin* the gradual discovery that Raphaël's fortune is a trick is metaphorically measured by the shrinkage of the asses' skin, while in *Le Chef-d'œuvre inconnu* the illusory nature of Frenhofer's talent is symbolised by the gradual overpainting of his masterpiece until only a foot remains.

In *L'Auberge rouge* (1831) and *Madame Firmiani* (1832), the role of the object to be valued is taken by the narrative itself, with the in-story audience and the reader cast separately in the role of valuers. Prosper Magnan's story of his role in the murder at the Auberge Rouge, described as "a German tale" (*une histoire allemande;* 11:90), and thereby associated with Hoffmanesque fantasy, is consequently disbelieved by the authorities who put Magnan on trial. But the story is nonetheless represented by its teller as "true" to the frame audience, who pass conflicting judgements on its value to the narrator, who is in the process of deciding whether to marry the rich daughter of the murderer. Simply telling the facts of a story is insufficient to create value: value is generated during the process of reception by the individual point of view of the receiver. Facts may, ultimately, have nothing to do with it: "Where would we all be if we had to delve into the origins of fortunes?"[28] asks a Balzacian lawyer. On the one hand, credible fiction is preferable to inconvenient facts. On the other, the spectre, true or false, of past turpitude may itself be an important constituent of current social narrative and interpretation. In either reading, narrative emerges as the defining location of value in the hands of the recipient. *Madame Firmiani* suggests that perhaps a concept of consensus value exists: the seventeen individual responses to Madame Firmiani's public persona are quite different

(2:142–145), yet the reader emerges with a distinct, if ill-defined, feeling that a credible fictional character has been created.

Le Colonel Chabert (1832 in its original incarnation as *La Transaction*, 1835 in its pre-Furne final form) is essentially a narrative about the value of narrative. Chabert as a person acquires or sheds value in direct correlation to the credibility of his narrative. Doubts over credibility lead directly to financial consequences: "You may have to compromise, said the lawyer"—the French uses the verb *transiger*, with overtones of transaction.[29] *Illusions perdues* (1837) even refers to the concept of asserted and punctured value in its title. The conflation of duplicity, narrative, and transaction as Lucien the poet writes "exquisite embroidered verbiage" (*délicieux verbiage brodé;* 5:176) to Mme de Bargeton, as Lucien the journalist sells out to Vernou (5:458–459), or as Lucien the debtor forges bills of exchange on his brother-in-law (5:545) shows Balzac's awareness of the link between text and value—both affective and economic.

Using narrative to assert value, then playing out models of acceptance or rejection within the fictional environment allows an author both to experiment with alternative representations of authenticity and to get actual feedback from contemporary readers. For Balzac this is far from a theoretical concern. René Bouvier and Edouard Maynial's analysis of Balzac's accounts shows an opening debt at the beginning of 1835, when *La Torpille* first makes Balzac's to-do list, of just over 61,000 francs, set against prospective income of around 20,000 francs. By the beginning of 1838, the year of its eventual composition, his debts had risen to just under 179,000 francs as a result of the 1836 failure of his own periodical, *La Chronique de Paris,* and sunk investment (quite literally, given its subsequent problems with subsidence) in his new property in Sèvres, Les Jardies. Bouvier and Maynial link literary output to financial pressures: "It seems beyond doubt that in many cases Balzac was by turns driven to write or discouraged from writing depending on the extent to which he was harried by his financial difficulties."[30] By default, the novel is an object of commerce whose value Balzac cannot reliably assess but equally cannot ignore.

In circumstances where value is difficult to assess, the prospectus is an important tool. Value itself can only be determined by the relationship between supply and demand, whether established by auction or by changes in demand in response to a fixed price. The prospectus is a means of asserting value by means of narrative. It is often the first public incarnation of its subject: most of the major infrastructure developments of the 1830s and 1840s, in particular the railways and canals, were first introduced to the public by means of a prospectus published in contemporary newspapers, just as *La Comédie humaine* was introduced to the readership through Balzac's own prospectus in 1842.[31] The prospectus in the hands of the speculator becomes a symbol of the age, described by the Vicomte d'Arlincourt in an eponymous article in the 1840 *Les Français peints par eux-mêmes:* "Oh, how fine is the speculator, limply draped over a Voltaire armchair, voluptuously reading the prospectus of an astonishing business to which he will bring all his skills and his friends all their money. How he studies its prospects! It appears to him all the more magnificent that it seems almost completely impracticable."[32]

Paper money is one of the simplest forms of prospectus, carrying a straightforward assertion of a fixed exchange value often supported through imagery, such as a historic monument or a ruler, that suggests solidity and continuity: prospectus as pure sign.[33] The very origins of paper money in France at the beginning of the preceding century had indissoluble links with John Law's Compagnie d'Occident (subsequently to become the Mississippi Company), set up to raise money for the Crown by, effectively, privatising its trading privileges. When the scheme ran into difficulties in 1718, Law was granted further privileges, including the right to issue paper money through his Banque Générale, which thereby became in practice the first French central bank. Law's scheme required repeated share issues to keep growing: ever-brighter visions of future prospects were published and, to finance share purchases by the public, Law offered loans in the paper money issued by his bank, collateralised by the shares they were to buy. Inevitably, the shares soared; inevitably, the dislocation between asserted and real values became apparent, though it took until 1720 for this to happen; inevitably, both shares and paper money, like the contemporaneous South Sea Bubble in England, then crashed.[34] Much later in the century, the population was again reminded of the volatility of paper money by the *assignats* issued during the French Revolution, which lost their entire face value in the space of seven years, from 1789 to 1796.

The prospectus itself would have been an entirely familiar, real, and everyday concept to the contemporary readership of the late 1830s and 1840s. The boom in road and railway construction that began in the late

1830s and accelerated in the 1840s necessitated such large amounts of capital that new markets to provide it had to be developed. The newly established banking dynasties, led by the Rothschilds, were increasingly able to source investment from public markets, leading to a wave of speculative new share issues.[35] Advertising was proliferating through billboards, posters, and the back pages of newspapers.[36] The press was full of prospectuses for new share issues and advertisements for proprietary medications. A search of *La Presse* around the time Balzac was writing *La Torpille* yields a prospectus for the Chemin de Fer de Paris à Tours par Chartres—"We must draw attention to the return on capital which, on the basis of the most reliable statistical research, will yield a dividend of 18fr 71c per cent"—and advertisements for both pectoral syrup and paste "made from ARABIAN HIBISCUS, . . . the ONLY pectoral medicines approved and recognised as SUPERIOR to all others by a REPORT of the Faculty of Medicine, a Patent and by 54 Certificates from the most celebrated doctors."[37] A modern reader will no doubt wonder whether either could deliver on its promises, and Balzac's *César Birotteau* (1837), with its exploration of the illusory claims of Birotteau's scalp oil, *huile céphalique*, suggests that contemporary reactions were perhaps not so different.[38]

La Comédie humaine itself contains fifty-two instances of the word *prospectus*, in twelve separate novels or stories (though not, incidentally, in *Splendeurs*).[39] Most are literal references to the promotional material that accompanied newly launched literary works or investment opportunities and that provided a financial lifeline for an army of journalists, from hacks to struggling authors, in the cutthroat world of the press. This exchange between Anselme Popinot, entrepreneur and future cabinet minister, and Andoche Finot, future press baron, in *César Birotteau* summarises nicely the equal relevance of the prospectus to the financial and literary markets:

> "Monsieur," said Popinot, "a prospectus is often an entire fortune."
> "And for ordinary people like me," said Andoche, "fortune is just a prospectus."[40]

But Balzac also uses the word figuratively. Gaudissart is called a living prospectus, a *prospectus vivant*, to illustrate his marketing skills (4:568). "The prospectus for a muse" *(le prospectus d'une muse)* is how Balzac describes a character in a sketch for *La Femme auteur* who is more show than real talent (12:611). And with the figurative comes the ironic: the description of the dandy Vauvinet in *Les Comédiens sans le savoir* as "a species of prospectus" *(une espece de prospectus)* shows Balzac's awareness of the illusory and superficial nature of the concept (7:1179).

The reading public was clearly quite well attuned to these distinctions. As Marie-Eve Thérenty argues, the rising importance of literature as an economic process gave rise directly to a market in fakes, from plagiarism, pastiche, and pseudonymous works to actual counterfeit, and to commoditisation in the shape of collected works, anthologies, or status editions designed to look impressive on the bookshelves of the *nouveaux riches*.[41] The demand for volume production led authors to pass off the works of associates as their own, as Dumas *père's* partnership with Auguste Macquet to develop a production line of romans-feuilletons illustrates. Publishers also created a "junk bond" market in the works of their own authors as the pressure to clear out slow-moving stocks led to discount sales.[42] Then as now, buying the story was an activity that was an increasingly explicit part of everyday life.

Balzac seems instinctively to understand how this works and parodies its effect in *César Birotteau:* "The Lotion of the Sultan's Wife and the Carminative Water products were introduced into the worlds of fashion and commerce by advertisements in colour, at the head of which stood these words: Approved by the Institute! This formula, rolled out for the first time, had a magical effect."[43] Both Birotteau and Balzac understand that the key to the success of the prospectus is the reader's own desire to be convinced. Given the promise of a coveted objective, the reader's own propensity to believe changes, allowing him or her to accept as credible that which he or she would otherwise have rejected as fantastical or defective. Birotteau behaves precisely in accordance with this rule: "[He] himself drafted a prospectus, the ridiculous phraseology of which became an element of its success: in France people only laugh at things and people they notice, and nobody notices what doesn't succeed."[44] Birotteau's prospectus plays on the reader's willingness to accept hyperbolic fantasy as the expected and appropriate genre of the sales pitch.

In doing so, recipients place their faith in the projected narrative of a commodity rather than in their own analysis. But how does this process work? Helpfully, Balzac would have found parallels in a literary genre with which he would have been intimately familiar, that of melodrama, with its direct links to the Parisian boulevard theatre and the theatrical origins of many of Balzac's own early works.[45] Melodrama depends for its effect on a complex interaction of several processes: the establishment of an initial antithesis through cultural stereotypes, the intensification of the antithesis through a process of iteration, and the exploitation of the audience's ability simultaneously to sustain two alternative interpretations of a text. Prendergast asks, in his examination of Balzacian melodrama, how Balzac persuades the reader to believe the exaggerated or fantastical elements of his plots, and argues that he is able to do this by reflecting a set of cultural values and conventions that his readership would recognise as part of the prevailing stock of social knowledge, in the same way that we can accept the concepts of reality of a Jean Racine or a Pierre Corneille as governed by the rules of tragedy or *bienséance*.[46]

The melodramatic convention is governed by a relationship between the real and the fantastic that depicts the universe in terms of antithesis, of polarisation between good and bad, of moral values that are assumed to be absolute, constant, shared by author and audience alike. The contrast between the real and the fantastic is often heightened by the narration of the fantastic in the medium of the factual (the opening of Eugène Sue's *Les Mystères de Paris,* which embeds a Gothic tale of princely derring-do in a gritty description of the Parisian underworld, *les classes dangereuses,* is a good example). The resulting combination gives the reader reason to accept the narrative and simultaneously accentuates the antitheses of which melodrama consists.

This reliance on shared values accepted by the recipients of these texts was also potentially attractive to the new breed of newspaper publishers whose need to drive subscriptions depended on the ability to deliver constant value to readers, the more predictable the better. The origins of melodrama in accepted convention create a problem for the author, though: How to create an original script out of received value? Melodrama answers this through a process of iteration, which typically finds novelty in fresh modes of representation of expected and conventional oppositions. Finding continuing ways to keep the model current, both between different works and particularly within a single text, tends to lead to a process of increasing hyperbole to maintain surprise or, simply, to engineer a climax. The fantastic from which melodrama starts thus tends to become more so, and Guise's analysis of the *folie du conte* of the early 1830s identifies just such a trend.[47] This intensification of the fantastic is frequently accompanied by an equivalent and counter-balancing emphasis on the factual, "the way [man] lives in the ordinary," as Peter Brooks puts it, to give the appearance of grounding the narrative.[48]

Buying the story depended on the recipient's willingness to accept the coexistence of two alternative methods of valuing text. Charles Maturin's preface to his *Melmoth the Wanderer* asserts a defence against accusations that he has concentrated too much on "the horrors of the Radcliffe-Romance" by a stout assertion of mundanity: "that I had made the misery of conventual life depend less on the startling adventures one meets with in romances, than on that irritating series of petty torments which constitutes the misery of life in general."[49] That his subsequent narrative bears this out only in its detail, never in its substance—for the ensuing tale is a Gothic compendium described in realistic detail—is a revealing reflection on the interplay of the real and the fantastic within the genre of melodrama. A simultaneous awareness and rejection of an alternative, more factual but less emotionally satisfying, variant of reality lies at the heart of successful melodrama. The recipient must be aware of two parallel interpretations and must find reasons to prefer the melodramatic or hyperbolised version to a more mundane alternative that serves to anchor fantasy to reality.[50] Creating the tension that allows the reader to collude willingly in creating this illusion provides a new toolkit with which to vary the perceived value of the narrative in the eyes of the recipient—but also creates major challenges for an author. If the hyperbole of a sales pitch is taken too far, buyers tend to back off: the balance is so delicate that a single misplaced phrase can turn the tables. In just the same way, if the melodramatic genre in narrative is pushed too far, there comes a point at which the reader will simply close the book, or turn the newspaper page.

But where does this point lie? And does it depend solely on content, on what is represented, or is it affected by the manner and medium of representation? Is this consistent with delivering a product that publishers will want to buy? Finally, does it allow the artist to produce a text that is not irretrievably compromised by the requirements of the market? There is, evidently, no straightforward correlation between realistic representation and credibility, since the evidence of the popular literary market, from the melodramatic theatre of the boulevards to the *folie du conte*, suggested public willingness not merely to suspend disbelief but actively to seek out the fantastic. The customers for Birotteau's *pâte des sultanes* and *eau carminative,* however, pass judgement not just on content but on delivery: they are explicitly willing to swallow an overblown prospectus in the context of a commodity they want, even though the commodity itself may be fraudulent. The parallels with Balzac's literary competitors are too obvious to be ignored. And just as it explains why the fraudulent can become credible, so it poses the question of why this process can also fail, why the commodity can suddenly appear ridiculous rather than enticing, why the recipient can suddenly switch focus from the embellishments to the implausibilities of the narrative; why narrative value, both literally and figuratively, can disappear. This question lies at the very heart of *Splendeurs,* which can be seen as a record of Balzac's evolving attempts to answer it, as the only text of his that travels throughout this central period in the emergence of the roman-feuilleton and the commercialisation of the novel.

La Torpille: *Experiments in Narrative Value*

La Torpille seems to have been conceived as a *conte,* first mentioned in a to-do list of stories about female criminals on the manuscript of *Le Père Goriot* of January 23, 1835 (6:1309). Its conception as a short story reflects the emergence, over the preceding few years, of the *conte* and, increasingly, of the longer-form *nouvelle* as drivers of subscriptions for the new breed of commercially driven periodicals. Although Balzac's prolific capacity as a writer attracted publishers, his choice of subject matter was to prove an immediate problem. Reader reaction to his *La Vieille Fille,* Girardin's first serialisation in 1836, was deemed serious enough to provoke a formal complaint from the editorial board that was to have an immediate effect on the marketability of *La Torpille:* "To the author of *La Vieille Fille.* We are in receipt of such a number of complaints about the choice of subject and the unrestrained nature of certain of the descriptive passages . . . that the management of *La Presse* requires the author of *La Vieille Fille* to choose a subject other than that of *La Torpille.*"[51]

Balzac no longer had the option of publishing the (so far unwritten) narrative in his own *Chronique de Paris,* which had gone bankrupt earlier in the year, at least partly because of competition from Girardin's new and cheaper rival. The story, comprising only the scene at the Opéra and Esther's subsequent rescue and reinvention at the hands of Herrera up to the point of her reunion with Lucien, seems finally to have been written during Balzac's 1838 stay in Italy and was complete by the end of July, when it was again offered to Girardin, this time in substitution for *La Maison Nucingen,* which Girardin had rejected as too politically sensitive. Yet again Girardin rejected it, this time after having it typeset, on grounds of unsuitability for the audience of *La Presse.* It finally appeared in book form, published by Edmond Werdet on September 24, 1838, sandwiched in between *La Femme supérieure* and *La Maison Nucingen,* in a quite possibly unfinished state since in this version it ends almost midsentence (6:481, note *d*). The preface to the first edition (6:424–428) indicates both an intention to write a sequel and a frustrated defence of the work's morality that reflects a growing tension between the commercial appeal of mild eroticism and the public face of bourgeois prudishness.[52]

La Torpille bears the hallmark of this hybrid creation: a *conte* that became a novel, a feuilleton that became a book, a failed attempt to write for the evolving market of newspaper subscribers. It starts as a celebration of the power of narrative and its author's virtuosity. It ends with a whimper, as Balzac's plot unravels and his narrative command evaporates. Its subject matter, appropriately, is the projection, manipulation, and reception of a series of false identities. Lucien pretends to nobility and fortune; la Torpille to a romantic dream. Herrera poses as a Spanish priest; Esther as a convent novice. The manner of its narration illustrates, self-reflexively, an inconclusive attempt to establish a credible proposition for publisher, reader, and author.

It is constructed from two almost separate narrative instalments written in quite distinct genres with equally distinct commercial qualities. The first of these, the Opéra narrative (6:429–446), is outwardly an exuberant projection of the power of narrative and of the existence of narrative values that will generate predictable responses from its readership. It was intended for the roman-feuilleton and starts by establishing a link, through a report of the Opéra ball, with the presumed readers of Girardin's *La Presse* as an "unbuttoned" version of its "Nouvelles Diverses" columns, which relayed the doings of the aristocracy— whom the king had dined with, who had newly arrived, who had attended the latest balls—mixed with the spicier freedoms allowed in the columns of the feuilleton. It plays to a voyeuristic desire still evident in today's tabloids to spy on the goings-on of the rich and famous, to know who was seen at the theatre, what they were wearing, what the latest scandal is. The masked ball adds an element of the exotic, a genre symbolised by the *Mille et une nuits* and of proven commercial value to the periodical, as had been shown during the period of the *folie du conte*, when libraries of short stories from Arabia to China had been ransacked for material.[53] The figure of the anonymous dandy, introduced in the fourth sentence (6:430), plays both to the power of fashion—Girardin, trendsetter as well as trend spotter, had founded *La Mode* in 1829—and to the voyeuristic demand to know who lies behind the anonymity. The narrative asserts, from the outset, the notion of projected value, a system that only works if it is based on a system of shared values between transmitter and recipient. The narrator, as transmitter, implies that he understands what the reader wants and is in a privileged position to access it: secrets are known only to a few select onlookers, "quelques flâneurs émérites," in whose number he clearly figures and, while the rest remain in the dark—"la foule observe peu la foule"—readers can rely on the unwavering attention of the narrator to bring them the latest goings-on at the Opéra ball (6:430). He understands how his readership responds, and reflects its own values back to it. The subject of his narrative is, indeed, his ability to detect and unmask fraud for the benefit of his readers: "Who there has not noticed that . . . there is a way of being which reveals what you really are"—he can see the prostitute behind the domino.[54]

But behind this confident facade is a constant concern about the ambivalent power of the word to create and to pervert in equal measure. The group of observers, journalists, and publishers who will later form the publishing world of *Illusions perdues*, Finot, Blondet, Vernou, and Bixiou, are described as examples of the compromises inherent in combining authorship and the commercial pressures of the press: "Whoever has dipped his toes into journalism, or still has a toe in the water, is under the cruel necessity of being polite to men he despises, of smiling at his worst enemy, of coming to terms with the most offensive behaviour, of dirtying his hands trying to pay back his attackers in the same coin."[55] Their narrative virtuosity is unimpaired—a group of journalists, suggests Blondet, would have transformed Esther into a grand courtesan: "Between us we could have made a queen of her. . . . Vernou would have done her publicity, Bixiou would have written her lines"—but it is somehow sullied by cliché—the standard "queen," a received value instantly recognisable by an audience—and by commercialism, "publicity," the projection of an asserted value.[56]

The narrator's own position is ambiguous. On the one hand, the very virtuosity of his description of the group of journalists, and of Blondet's dialogue, with its parody of the pedantic and showy style of the *Journal des débats*, in particular, asserts that his own text should not be seen as compromised (6:441). On the other, his characterisation of Lucien as the dandy, or of de Châtelet as the starched representative of the ancien régime, is itself a caricature that depends on similarly established commonplaces. Narrative certainly has the power to create value, true or false, but how that power is to be used is unclear. The disguise of Esther's mask at the ball is demolished by the unleashing of a single word: her name. Rebuilding it requires, literally and literarily, a change of genre, the introduction of the fantastic in the shape of the masked figure of Herrera, and a simultaneous demonstration that the reader will accept this because it plays to the established narrative conventions of melodrama: that readers will prefer the more positive outcome even if they know it is the less credible, and that they will favour an open-ended narrative to an apparent full stop.

The second part of the story, that of Esther's attempted suicide and redemption, starts to raise questions about how this process works. It is essentially a narrative about rewriting. Balzac starts by writing the alternative, tragic end to *La Torpille* in which Esther commits suicide. He then passes the pen to Herrera, who rescues her, deus ex machina fashion, and rewrites her as a reformed sinner. When this fails to work, she is again rewritten, this time in her final version as a courtesan.

The opening version offers us a logical conclusion to the *conte* of the first part, and one that responds to Balzac's expressed desire in the preface to the 1845 Furne edition to write a work "which depicts in total honesty the lives of the spies, the prostitutes and those at war with society who swarm in Paris."[57] But it situates it in a melodramatic cityscape in whose flickering pools of light alternative endings are possible (6:446). Balzac's description of the sinister rue de Langlade is a literary landscape with genre signposts to tell the reader what to expect: "The fantastical world of Hoffmann the Berliner is there."[58] The imagery of melting words—"some of those words which Rabelais thought had been frozen and which were melting"—suggests the malleability of reality through the medium of language.[59] This is a landscape of inversion: "Atmospheric conditions are different there: winter is hot, summer is cold."[60] Inversion can convert reality into the fantastic: Esther's suicide is underpinned by a series of details probably taken, as Antoine Adam records, from a wide variety of contemporary sources: Auguste Ricard, Paul de Kock, Alphonse Esquiros, Sue, Nestor Roqueplan, Maurice Alhoy, and, most important of all, Alexandre Parent-Duchâtelet, in his 1836 treatise on the commerce and social hierarchy of the prostitute world, *De la prostitution dans la ville de Paris*.[61] But in this melodramatic landscape, factual detail simply serves to make suspension of disbelief seem more plausible: the irruption of Herrera into this landscape seems not only desirable but inevitable. As the 1845 preface concludes, "You have to acknowledge the modern God, the *majority,* this colossus with feet of clay."[62] The commercial call for longer fiction compounds with the reader's desire for the story to be continued.

The stage is set for a melodramatic tale of demonic power, "pactes infernaux" (6:502), and moral redemption or compromise. At one level that is indeed what happens, and many critical appraisals have viewed it in this light. Kyoko Murata follows the evolution of Balzac's treatment of the Faustian pact through Balzac's work and presents it in terms of the way in which the eternal struggle of the demonic pact, the *pacte diabolique,* against the *pacte angélique* comes to grips with the modern world of commerce and contract.[63] But at another level there is a nagging undertone of questioning. Are the assumptions about stable values really right? In this new environment, in front of the growing feuilleton audience for which Balzac expected to be writing, are the conventions of melodrama, of fixed narrative values and predictable reader response, really tenable?

In earlier stories Balzac had experimented with challenges to the canon. *Melmoth réconcilié* (first published June 1835; 10:345–388) comprehensively debunks the Faustian pact which fails to survive its encounter with the modern world of financial transactions. The process relies not on any inherent implausibility of doing a deal with the devil but on the bathos of recasting the deal as a tradable security. Castanier, the bookkeeper led astray by Melmoth, commits fraud by narrative: he issues circulating notes *(des circulations)*—the link between fraud and the press is hardly accidental—that represent a fraudulent prospectus in which the value advertised does not exist: "notes which represented neither merchandise nor deposited monetary securities."[64] The scam works only for as long as the transacting parties believe them to be credible and creditworthy. The Faustian pact proposed by Melmoth is similar: a shared narrative that only retains value to the extent that the buyer shares the same valuation methodology as the seller. Castanier, by profession a cashier, understands the parallel, and so when the time comes to pass the pact to the next recipient, he does what comes naturally: he trades it on the stock exchange (10:383–384). But exposing its value to a wider audience calls into question the convention that upholds its value. Once the value of the pact has been called into doubt, it takes a mere six pages out of forty-three for its entire value to dissipate (10:383–388). As the fantastic is reduced to the humdrum, so meaning itself starts to disintegrate. "This man is pyramidal"—the translation follows the original, "Cet homme est pyramidal"—is how the startled German demonologist researching the story finds himself described, in terms more reminiscent (if anachronistically) of Ubu Roi than of Balzac (10:388).[65]

Balzac also seems to find it difficult to accept the melodramatic turn his narrative appears to have taken without simultaneously questioning it. The theme of inverted value continues. Herrera, it is hinted, is himself a pervert, an *inverti*, a man "insensible to the pretty curves of a breast."[66] Esther's narrative must be inverted: within a few pages, we discover that "she was no longer a courtesan, but an angel picking herself up after a fall."[67] Having offered us the possibility of a logical, if tragic, end to the story, Balzac seems to be asking why we prefer the false coin of this inverted, sentimental redemption. We are left in little doubt that this is a primarily literary makeover. It has already begun by a performative act of rewriting as Esther submits her formal declaration to the police to be removed from the register of prostitutes (6:452). Balzac makes it clear that Herrera is the author of this version of the proofs. As we gradually discover, Herrera is more the personification of false value than of Mephistopheles. He is described exclusively in terms of the facade of his appearance: what lies inside is compared to a mirage: "No gaze could have discerned what was then going on in this man, but for the bravest there would have been more to shudder at than to hope for from the aspect of his eyes, formerly sharp and yellow like those of tigers, and over which austerity and privation had now cast a veil similar to that which forms on the horizon in a heatwave: the ground is hot and luminous, but the mist renders it indistinct, vaporous, almost invisible."[68] Almost every detail we learn about him will later prove to be wrong. His real name is not Herrera. He is not a priest. His backstory is politically implausible in both the 1838 and 1843 editions (6:472–473, 1346–1347).[69] His own fictional creation is inverted: the composition of this narrative, which dates from July / August 1838 and which describes an established relationship between Herrera and Lucien, *precedes* that of the final part of *Illusions perdues,* where Herrera first meets Lucien (started April / May 1839, not finished until 1842).

And as an author, Herrera has clear shortcomings. He is pompous, full of classical allusions that Balzac even took the trouble to reinforce between the manuscript and the published edition, book-learned, exclamatory (6:458–460). Balzac seems to be sending up his literary pretensions—much of the "pompous" passage was shifted from the narrator's mouth to become the implied thoughts of Herrera in the published edition. Even his authorial omniscience is mocked: "So at this moment this man saw the depths of human nature"—and yet his analysis of Esther is immediately shown to be wrong.[70] His first attempt at constructing Esther's new narrative as a redeemed sinner fails the test even of the in-story audience, in the person of the convent superior, whose judgement of Esther's sincerity as "edifying" is tellingly reserved (6:466). Balzac himself seems to have found it difficult to make this narrative flow fluently: the numerous alterations in different drafts of the manuscript to the description of Esther in the convent, for example, testify to his compositional difficulties (6:463–464). The former deftness of authorial touch so much in evidence in the Opéra narrative seems to desert him: Esther's hands are described as "as white as the hands of a woman giving birth to her second child"; her eye at rest as "like a miraculous egg in a nest of silken strands."[71]

The conclusion of the story, in which Balzac seems to take back the narratorial *parole* from Herrera as the narrative shifts from dialogue to third-party reportage, is tentative, contradictory, and incomplete. His descriptions of Herrera are couched in the form of unanswered questions and declarations of ignorance: "None could answer these questions, nor measure the ambition of this Spaniard, just as none could predict what would be his end."[72] He shifts genre from the melodramatic to the sentimental: "And so the passion of a poet becomes a grand poem where human measure is oft surpassed."[73] The narrative reverts to cliché as Balzac reunites Lucien and Esther at the point of Esther's first communion. We feel that Balzac's own interest in the narrative may have narrowed to the purely economic: "Don't break the die that coins us money," says Herrera to Lucien—a "tart with a heart" is a more marketable literary commodity than a nun.[74] Unable to survive these contradictions, the narrative limps to a halt in a tacit acknowledgement that there are significant questions about how to maintain its value (6:481).

It is difficult to avoid the conclusion that *La Torpille* is an unsatisfying narrative, a tale that fails to live up to its original promise, a prospectus that has not delivered the value it promised. The momentum and vigour of its opening are not maintained. Faced with the need to expand what was essentially a short story into a longer narrative to address the changing requirements of the roman-feuilleton for which he expected to be writing, Balzac has created a narrative that seems to be full of false starts and changes of direction.[75] It is certainly a text that takes as its subject matter the projection of false value, from Esther at the ball, through Esther at the convent, to the multiple deceptions of Herrera. It gives the impression of being a text driven partly by commercial factors, in that at each narrative check, it seems to revert to a literary commonplace, a device that will sell well, the world of Hoffmann (6:447). It is therefore doubly ironic that the reason for its rejection by *La Presse* was the publisher's view that Balzac had misjudged the limits of acceptability to the journal's readership. Successful narrative requires a delicate balance between artistic imperatives and the evolving commercial needs of publishers and readers. *La Torpille*'s suspension in midflow is indicative of an unresolved problem.

Esther: *The Prospectus, Production Model*

Balzac was not to return to *Splendeurs* for almost five years. In the meantime, his debts had peaked in 1839 at over 230,000 francs and had hardly moderated by 1843 despite continuous publication and a reduced lifestyle. In the meantime, his level of financial sophistication, particularly in procedures for evading debts, had increased considerably, and his experience in concocting stories to deceive creditors, to divert the questions of Mme Hanska, and to delude himself about his financial position had grown exponentially. He regularly put assets in the names of straw men to avoid attachment. The apparent sale of Les Jardies was a legal charade intended to force creditors to agree to write down outstanding debts. His apartment in Passy, where he lived under a false name, had two exits on separate streets to facilitate evasion.[76] The need to project value that did not exist was constant.

By 1842 the power of the longer-format novel in serialised form to drive subscriptions to periodicals of all sorts was conclusively evidenced by Sue's *Les Mystères de Paris*, which helped propel its platform, the staid *Journal des débats*, from 3,600 to 25,000 subscribers in a month and thereafter to 40,000.[77] For some authors this offered, at last, a way to financial independence and the ability to live from the earnings of their pens, but Girardin himself, writing in his own *Musée des familles* in November 1834, estimated that only two dozen writers in France could hope to sell more than 600–900 copies of a work and be paid more than 500–800 francs per volume on a consistent basis.[78] Furthermore, this serialised platform could also monetise additional reach—for example, through the *cabinets de lecture*—in ways not open to the book, such as advertising and product extensions—almanacs and keepsakes were among the many variants tried. Finally, fiction offered a way around increasingly intrusive press legislation from the new law of 1835 onwards, as the government attempted to reconcile a commitment not to impose censorship with an urge to do exactly that.[79] Indeed, fiction based on the depiction of real life offered novelists an easy way of mixing social comment and literary invention in ways that both made a point and provided a defence, making the choice of a genre closer to journalism both popular and practical.

It is against this background of the novel as an increasingly integral part of the newspaper industry, and of the author as a hybrid extension of the journalist, that the next part of *Splendeurs* emerges. The narrative of *La Torpille*, now entitled *Esther, ou Les Amours d'un vieux banquier*, doubling its length to thirty-nine feuilletons and dealing with the entire story of Esther up to her suicide, finally reached the pages of the newspaper through serialisation in *Le Parisien* from May 21 to July 1, 1843. For the first time, it is possible to put an accurate monetary value on this narrative: Balzac's contract with the publisher of *Le Parisien*, J. Amyntas David, entitled him to a payment of 5,000 francs. But both narrative and payment remained incomplete: the final thirteen chapters were withdrawn by Balzac, probably because of his fears of nonpayment by *Le Parisien*, which he took to court on July 1, 1843 (according to a letter to Mme Hanska from the same day).[80] The text once again reverted to book format, finally complete to the point of Esther's death and now for the first time under the title *Splendeurs et misères des courtisanes,* appearing first in a separate three-volume edition published at 22.50 francs on August 28, 1844, by Louis de Potter under a contract that had been concluded with Louis-Fortuné Loquin, a banker, in 1842, immediately ceded to the publisher Louis Dumont, invalidated for nonperformance by the publisher, returned to the original banker, and finally acquired by Potter in August 1844. It reappeared in the eleventh volume of the Furne edition of *La Comédie humaine* one month later. The last of the seven instalments that composed the eleventh volume contained, however, only the 1838 *La Torpille* narrative, presumably to allow the Potter edition to be sold first. The missing instalments were subsequently published in 1845.[81]

The *Esther* narrative has often been seen as Balzac's attempt to emulate Sue's success with *Les Mystères de Paris,* published in the conservative columns of the *Journal des débats* from June 19, 1842, to October 15, 1843. "All the world devoured *Les Mystères de Paris,*" writes Théophile Gautier in 1844 in a review of a theatrical adaptation of the novel, "even people who cannot read: they got some educated and willing porter to read it aloud to them."[82] "I'm doing Sue, pure and simple," writes Balzac to Mme Hanska on May 31, 1843, and the French phrase, "Je fais du Sue tout pur," has passed into the critical lexicon.[83]

But what did this really mean? Sue's narrative depends on a system of fixed exchange rates within which stock characters, plots, and narrative devices can deliver predictable reader reception. It relies on an understanding of how techniques of journalism and popular fiction were merging to respond to the tastes of a rapidly growing readership, as well as on an appreciation of fiction's commercial role as a driver of subscriptions. Anne O'Neil-Henry describes Sue as a market-savvy literary entrepreneur who exploited genres of proven commercial success—the maritime novel, the *roman de mœurs*—to advance his literary career and who consciously recycled his own material to improve productivity.[84] The very first words of the first three sentences of the narrative of *Les Mystères de Paris,* set out as separate paragraphs in the feuilleton of the *Journal des débats* of June 19, 1842, instantly create a quite specific and calculated effect: "a low pothouse," "a former jailbird, "a crime." If the reader has not got the message, Sue spells it out in the fourth sentence: "This opening alerts the reader that he must be witness to sinister scenes." And for good measure, the fifth sentence, referring to James Fenimore Cooper and Walter Scott, lays claim to a literary tradition and asserts a link to a genre with which the audience would have been familiar.[85]

The same objective is visible in the use of realistic detail to retain an apparent anchor in the observed world and to make the fantastic and the imaginary appear more plausible as the level of intensity in the plot grows. "We will conduct the reader into this miserable lodging," writes Sue as he introduces the Morel family: there follows five pages of detail of their attic apartment, which itself has been preceded by four chapters of preparation in a previous iteration.[86] As the reader responses to Sue's *Les Mystères de Paris* indicate, what we might now see as the fantastical element of the ensuing plotline, as Rodolphe interprets his standard role of saviour, was taken by at least some readers as an observed or at least psychologically "true" fact. It seems that the desire to believe uses the realistic detail to justify its right to believe: "I had read his book, I had drunk of his potion, I had become intoxicated by his magic," writes one of Sue's readers.[87] The essence of Sue's success lies in replaying to his audience their own preconceptions, prejudices, and tastes. Jules Janin, portraying the journalist in Léon Curmer's 1842 *Les Français peints par eux-mêmes*, confirms the importance of popular response: "At the same time, above even the editor in chief, to give a lead to the paper and to point it each morning in the direction it must follow, is the public the paper represents, for it is the public which inspires it, which imposes its outbursts of anger and vengeance."[88]

But what was the message coming from this new readership? Prendergast's study of reader response to *Les Mystères de Paris* illustrates a clear channel of communication between writer and reader made possible by the format of serial publication. But it also shows the diffuse nature of that exchange, the conflicting points of view expressed by readers, and the difficulty of drawing any specific conclusions about particular textual influence.[89] The feedback is neither homogeneous nor representative of any single point of view. I suggest that in this environment, the default editorial response was to go for readability—the *juste milieu* hybrid, in the shape of a format designed for piecemeal consumption, stylistically manipulated to draw the reader on to the following episode in the next instalment, *la suite au prochain numéro*—and for content that responded in predictable ways to contemporary fashions. Helping the reader to define who he or she is, and just as importantly who he or she is not, is an obvious place to start, as Judith Lyon-Caen argues, and one that goes a long way toward explaining the ubiquitous image of the mirror on society, reflecting a representation of the entire contemporary world, not just of the particular social stratum the reader happened to inhabit.[90] Christiane Mounod-Anglès, in her analysis of Balzac and his female readership, *Balzac et ses lectrices,* argues that Balzac took particular care to establish himself as a writer who understood the female demographic by delivering a potent mixture of what they demonstrably read—romance—carefully combined with sensation and scandal, which gave the impression of pushing at the bounds of what they could or should read. The result proved to be a real commercial success in this fast-growing part of the new literary market.[91]

Throughout French literary output of this period, whether literary or journalistic, there is evident a compulsion to name, describe, and classify, based in what seems almost a national obsession for attempting to understand and define what being French in the postrevolutionary, postempire era really meant. Janin describes *Les Français peints par eux-mêmes* as an attempt to record a slice of history for posterity, but the obsession extends from Stendhal's mirror to Honoré Daumier's cartoons and beyond.[92] Lexicographers and encyclopaedists attempt to classify language and record knowledge, from Denis Diderot's *Encyclopédie* to the 1835 *Dictionnaire de l'Académie française,* and by the middle of the century the task had been taken up and appropriated for profit by Emile Littré and Pierre Larousse. Balzac satirically categorises his colleagues in his *Monographie de la presse parisienne,*[93] classifies society into zoological species in the 1842 *avant-propos* to *La Comédie humaine,* and attempts to describe it in its entirety in the work itself. In the same vein, Sue's *Les Mystères de Paris* can be seen as a taxonomy of *mœurs,* from the aristocracy, through the bourgeoisie and the working classes, to the criminal. But its point of view is always that of the reader of the roman-feuilleton. This is a literature that may be *about* the people but is certainly not *of* the people: it is written for the subscribing public, for an elite, middle-class audience peering over the author's shoulder and shivering with carefully cossetted horror at the lower classes, at Le Chourineur and La Chouette, at the untamed Paris of the old Ile de la Cité.

It is no coincidence that this theme links so strongly with the journalistic point of view of the miscellany column, the *fait divers,* which shares a similar preoccupation with the sensational, the prurient, and the criminal and which will eventually form the basis for a new genre of proto-tabloid journalism in Moïse Millaud's 1863 *Le Petit Journal*. Even Sue's rather tepid treatment of the theme reflects the limits of public morality: he is well aware of its power to stimulate the reader's attention but tactfully self-censors at the critical moment, or deflects to make a social point, or intervenes with a sententious sermon, or conjures up another Rodolphus ex machina rescue. Reader response provided a useful way of checking on changes in reader concerns. The letters addressed to Sue throughout the course of the publication of *Les Mystères de Paris*, whether from admirers, victims, or political sympathisers, are remarkable for the way in which they talk more of the senders' problems or reactions than of their views on the text. The narrative itself has simply become the catalyst for often unrelated outpourings that act as silent testimony to the accuracy of the text in touching communal nerve points and that, in turn, provide the novelist with a means of sensing changing attitudes in order to play them back more accurately.

Even the critics respond in the same way: Alfred Nettement's castigation of the work as immoral reveals more of the contemporary royalist and Catholic prejudices of the *Gazette de France* than of the work's own shortcomings, which are barely addressed.[94] The very format of Sue's platform, the roman-feuilleton, is the emblem of its topical and transitory relevance, which can only be maintained by constant performance. It is driven by events and trends of the moment, and its continual process of self-renewal makes it an ideal mirror of the fashionable and the ephemeral.

Perhaps for this reason, the reader is implicitly prepared to trade literary aspiration for immediacy or, simply, for more product—Sue's blend of sententiousness and sentimentality, along with lapses in characterisation and continuity, are proof enough of that. It is precisely Sue's lack of the literary qualities we admire elsewhere that makes his success so intriguing, and I suggest that this very lack of literariness (despite apparent literary aspirations) is an essential part of the newly evolving bourgeois taste. It is probably no coincidence that Sue's style is closer to that of contemporary journalism, which also needed to self-censor the prurience of the faits divers, which holds and broadcasts both social and political views, and which is full of the sententious tub-thumping demonstrated even by its fiercest critics, led by Charles Augustin Sainte-Beuve's castigation of journalistic influence in *De la littérature industrielle*. The runaway success of *Les Mystères de Paris* is created by a kind of autosuggestion induced by the author's understanding of popular taste, rather than by the strength of his own views. The Goncourts will later describe exactly this process in *Charles Demailly*:

> So the man with three francs in his pocket has bought and paid for you and taken you away under the influence of this kneejerk reaction [the runaway success]. He goes home, he retreats into himself. You are a new name so he mistrusts you. He knows himself and mistrusts himself; he's scared of his own judgement, he isn't used to thinking on his own, an opinion always seems to him to be public property, something lent by all to each. . . . On top of that remember that this man is a member of the public: he envies you just like a reader envies a writer. You have to clamber over all of these preconceptions so that when he reaches the last page the three franc man is convinced that he believes you have talent.[95]

This ability to manipulate readers by playing back to them their own concerns and prejudices, the subsuming of the author's character within that of the reader, is at the heart of bourgeois literary culture and perhaps explains why Sue's work was only able to resonate with a particular audience in a particular era.

For Balzac, it must have created a dilemma. Aping its success would, indeed, be financial salvation. Fixed narrative exchange rates were evidently productive of more stable revenues for their authors. Sue's early extravagances had led to bankruptcy in 1836 and to the need to write for a living, as they did for Balzac: writing was as much about discovering the cash value of narrative as it was about realising its artistic worth. Sue's earlier success with *Arthur* in *La Presse* (1838) had allowed him to buy a house in Paris. Girardin had secured another success for Sue with *Mathilde* in 1840–1841 and was the underbidder for *Les Mystères de Paris* against *Le Journal des débats*. What was good for authors was also good for publishers, as *La Mode* sniffily observes in 1842: "*La Presse*'s business has done well from this long immolation of its virtue on the paper's cash register."[96] Sainte-Beuve estimates that *Les Mystères de Paris* had earned Sue 30,000 francs by the middle of 1843.[97] A *succès de scandale* was beneficial to author, publisher, and creditor alike.

It would hardly be surprising, therefore, if Balzac had wished to emulate Sue's success. But to do so involved a significant compromise of authorial identity. The novelist must, to a greater or lesser extent, become a novelist-journalist, *romancier-feuilletoniste*. Appropriately, we have evidence of the extent of the dilemma from both fictional and historic sources. Balzac's portrait of Lucien de Rubempré's descent from the romantic author of *L'Archer de Charles IX* to the mercurial journalist in the pay and at the bidding of Vernou—"we are phrase-mongers" *(des marchands de phrases)* (5:458)—implies a received attitude that this is a degeneration of his talent, but it is quite evident that Lucien is a far better journalist than he ever will be a novelist and that as a journalist his work has an immediacy and an ability to connect with an audience that may, Balzac seems to imply, be one of the hallmarks of a true writer "who revolutionised journalism by the revelation of a new and original style."[98] By contrast, this readership is incapable of any kind of sophisticated critical reaction: Lousteau's audience of provincial worthies in *La Muse du département* do not even notice that the manuscript of *Olympia, ou Les Vengeances romaines* that he reads to them has the page order scrambled (4:703–719).

Balzac's own contemporary journalism reveals a confused vacillation between a rejection of the apparent artistic standardisation required by this new literary culture and an enthusiastic embrace of the financial opportunities it represented. His 1834 "Lettre adressée aux écrivains français," published in the *Revue de Paris,* complains that piracy and unauthorised theatrical versions effectively robbed authors of part of their already compromised intellectual identity and their financial independence: "Let's talk about capital, let's talk about money! Let's commoditise and tally up intellectual output in a century which prides itself on being the century of positive thinking. No writer succeeds without a tremendous investment in study that is the equivalent of time or money: time is money, he deserves it."[99] His satirical sketch of the press in his 1842 *Monographie de la presse parisienne* levels a series of charges at the industry of which enforced authorial anonymity, lack of originality, political venality, and greed are only the beginning: "The *Premier-Paris* [the main editorial in contemporary newspapers], which exists only through its continuing ability to divine the thoughts of its subscribers, takes them quite by surprise the following morning by rolling their own thoughts out in front of them."[100] This notwithstanding, his solution to the novel's reliance on the press, in the shape of the proposed *Société d'abonnement générale,* is essentially that of a periodical in disguise. The fact that his plan to publish eighty to one hundred works a year, distributed by subscription largely to underdistracted provincial readers, never finds a commercial backer is probably an eloquent commentary on the inability of the novel to sell itself as a pure product unmixed with journalism—though it may also reflect a thwarted desire to preserve the purity of the novel as a genre still apart from journalism.

But the reality was that the move to a journalistic platform involved a considerable blurring of the notion of authorial identity. Who, indeed, is the author when publishers and readers, and indirectly politicians, regulators, and investors, all have influence over content? Even the selection of what to create becomes a subject of negotiation between publisher and author, with contracts based on synopses, volume, and delivery dates. Content that failed to resonate with readers could be summarily withdrawn, as Balzac found to his cost in 1844 when Girardin replaced *Les Paysans* with Dumas *père*'s *La Reine Margot* after only sixteen episodes: *Les Paysans,* previously puffed as a "phenomenon of the feuilleton novel in political and social vein," was apparently boring readers because Balzac's extensive character description in the opening chapters infringed public expectations of sensation and pace.[101]

Balzac was evidently capable of writing about subjects that attracted readers, as his success during the *folie du conte* of 1832–1833 had shown. But it must also have been clear that Sue's narrative style adapted more easily to the feuilleton format than did Balzac's. Lyon-Caen asks whether Sue's work is more extended piece of journalism than novel.[102] Thérenty points out the difficulties that Balzac experienced in aligning chapter and instalment and quotes Georges Sand's view that Balzac lacked Sue's talent for cliff-hanger endings to instalments.[103] Guise notes how this affected Balzac's writing career during the period between *La Torpille* and *Esther,* as Dumas *père,* Frédéric Soulié, and Sue all succeeded in publishing more in the roman-feuilleton than Balzac.[104] Even Balzac's method of writing and revision differed fundamentally: each narrative episode, usually consisting of multiple feuilletons, needed to be complete and painstakingly corrected at proof stage before the go-ahead for printing, the *bon à tirer,* could be given, while Sue wrote by instalment and appears to have been untroubled by the inconsistencies that this engendered.

Esther, therefore, had to be a narrative capable of sustaining multiple alternative readings. It needed to be a financially viable narrative, capable of finding a place in the feuilleton and of exploiting the tricks of Sue to entice publishers and subscribers. Balzac's correspondence with

Mme Hanska makes it quite clear that he thought of the competition with Sue in economic terms: in a letter dated September 17, 1844, he writes, "I can't, I shouldn't have to, I won't put up with the way Sue's dealings have devalued me and dragged me down and by the bally-hoo which his works create."[105] On the other hand, it needed at the same time to be a method of differentiation from Sue and of rejecting the notion of fixed narrative value. Its choice of subject—the creation of the prospectus for Esther's public offering to Nucingen—betrays its construction: a text intended, by the very act of emulation, to debunk Sue, to demonstrate that his system of narrative fixed exchange rates where stock characters, plots, and narratives devices can deliver predictable reader reception is bankrupt and credible only to those with no literary discernment. Its victims may even include Balzac himself, attempting to create a financially viable narrative out of his parody while simultaneously trying to demonstrate that he does not have to conform to the normative values of the roman-feuilleton to survive.

At one level, therefore, it is essential that the *Esther* narrative is capable of being taken as pure Sue, "du Sue tout pur." In two pages, Balzac sweeps away the baggage of *La Torpille:* the now unnecessary disguise of Herrera is cast aside; Esther is reinstated as a queen of the stage, "une reine . . . de théâtre"; and the diabolical powers of the "Spaniard" (l'Espagnol), with anonymity reinforcing mystery, are reinflated (6:481–482). The characters of Europe and Asie acknowledge public taste for both the exotic and the taxonomic (6:483–485). The figure of Esther as the spiritually reformed but physically practising prostitute allows Balzac to offer the promise of voyeuristic titillation while retaining a defence against immorality. The passage of time—"four years of happiness" in the original chapter title—allows a new scene to be set in which Esther's seclusion enables her to be repositioned as the maiden in distress (6:487). L'Espagnol can be revealed as Jacques Collin, *dit* Trompe-la-Mort, escaped convict (6:502–503), who can do battle on a level playing field with Sue's Chourineur.[106] Literary references are marshalled to guide the reader to established and familiar repositories of narrative value. Lucien and Esther's love affair is linked to a canon of romantic literature, *Paul et Virginie,* and to the classic of the exotic genre, the *Mille et une nuits* (6:486, 491). References linking Herrera to Faust, which had begun as soon as the masked figure appeared in *La Torpille* (6:434, 445–446), culminate at the beginning of *Esther* in an overt allusion to the

Faustian pact that Lucien has concluded with Herrera—"one of those infernal pacts you only see in novels."[107]

The allusion to the novelistic setting is no accident: these are all attempts to anchor narrative value in known categories that produce predictable responses from the contemporary audience. Readers of Maturin or Hoffmann would find reference points for the Mephistophelean presence and powers of Herrera in Melmoth or the Archivarius Lindhorst of Hoffmann's *Der goldne Topf.* Readers of romantic literature would have found parallels for Esther's redemption across social and cultural divides in François-René de Chateaubriand's *Atala.* These were literary commonplaces that could be relied on for stable value. Iteration combined with growing fictional intensity, the stocks-in-trade of melodrama and of Sue's narrative construction in particular, carry the story to its climax. Nucingen fails four times to win Esther: when he fails to find her after the first, accidental, midnight meeting (6:495–499); when he is tricked by Europe into a meeting with a false Esther (6:552–556); when he is refused by Esther in an exchange of letters that reveals the seriousness of intent on both sides (6:599–604); and when his final triumph is rendered hollow by Esther's suicide (6:690–693). Balzac seems to follow Sue in his blend of the fantastic and a social commentary based in recorded observation. The depiction of the Parisian underclass, as represented, for example, by Europe, a character described as "worn down by all the corruptions of Paris" *(fatiguée par les corruptions parisiennes)* (6:485), relies on the admixture of hyperbolised detail and the received prejudices of the bourgeois target readership about the generic menace of the lower classes, which Louis Chevalier analyses in his *Classes laborieuses et classes dangereuses à Paris.*[108] The romance of Lucien's relationship with Esther is balanced against the financial realism and social hypocrisy of his courtship of Clothilde, illustrated by the original titles of succeeding chapters: "A Girl of Good House" and "A Good Girly-House."[109] The candlelit drama of Esther's last supper is anchored by the most obscure details of her financial manipulations to falsify debts that Nucingen could be persuaded to pay (6:562–570).

But for all this imitation of Sue's and the roman-feuilleton's techniques, Balzac's narrative cannot disguise its differences. It is self-reflexive, aware of its own status as narrative, and self-subversive in a way that is more complex than Sue's relatively straightforward self-consciousness. "We're making prose" *(Nous faisons de la prose),* says

Herrera on the first page of the 1843 script (6:481): the implication, of sober factuality, is immediately belied by the following pages, which create the Gothic spectacle of Esther as romantic heroine immured in solitary splendour, a creature of the night guarded by savage beasts. She herself is a *stage* queen, existing in a world of artistic illusion. Balzac ensures that the reader is continually aware of the status of the story as fiction and of its intended context of a journalistic environment. The literary references to *Paul et Virginie* and to the *Mille et une nuits* are both signposts of convention and reminders of the fictional context. Herrera's Faustian pact with Lucien becomes not just a classic literary intertext but a specific reference to the journalistic motifs found in the faits divers or in the *Gazette des tribunaux:* "one of those infernal pacts you only see in novels, *but the frightening possibility of which has often been demonstrated at the Assises in celebrated courtroom dramas.*"[110] Nucingen's pastiche German accent acts as much a diegetic obstacle to the reader's comprehension as a mimetic device to aid characterisation: it physically slows the process of understanding the text, emphasising the very viscosity of the medium itself.

References beyond the implied narrative frame to a wider narrative known to the reader and the author but not to the in-story narrator, in particular implied references to other titles of *La Comédie humaine* (6:488, 533, 534, 539, 559, 563, 567), ensure that we differentiate author from narrator in a manner foreign to Sue. The creation of Esther's elaborate charade to fund Lucien's success out of Nucingen's lust is continually compared to the authorial process: "I am the author; you will be the drama," says Herrera to Lucien.[111] Different literary genres are explored, from the Shakespearean comic interlude (for example, Peyrade as pastiche English nabob; 6:654–660), to the Richardsonian epistolary narrative (6:600–604), to a prototype *roman policier:* "For the first time, these two artists of espionage [the two policemen, Contenson and Peyrade] came face to face with *an impenetrable text,* all the while suspecting a murky story."[112]

And, as befits a text paid by instalment, the narrative is constantly aware of its own status as a financial commodity. The central plot line is that of the iterative auction for Esther's favours, illustrating precisely how the value of Esther's story can be manipulated by Herrera as "author." Lucien's courtship of Clothilde equates fiction and finance: his false love letters themselves a literary echo of Julien Sorel's seduction of Mme de Fervaques for her millions in *Le Rouge et le noir*. "What is he living on?" *(De quoi vit-il?)* is the question on everyone's lips as Lucien's social ascent begins (6:509): it relates equally to his financial and fictional status as both in-story characters and readers are asked to assess his creditworthiness and credibility. Even the lumbering puns of the original chapter titles are used to carry metaphors of investment and return, as "A Hundred Thousand Francs Deposited in Asie."[113] And the central images that link narrative and money are, of course, those of the *courtisane* and of Nucingen, essentially two sides of the same coin.

The metaphor of the courtesan(e) serves Balzac in many purposes: as a commentary on the commoditisation of human relationships; as a challenge to social hierarchy; as moral commentary on the used and the user; as a means of contesting gender stereotypes; and not least as a titillating inducement to subscribers and readers. It also implies the deceptive prospectus that Esther will represent for Nucingen. A *courtisane* is different from a *fille:* the name implies, at least in Balzac's world, an illusory promise of something more, overlaid on the fundamental commercial transaction—love, a relationship, status. Balzac shows us time and again the bad faith on which this is based. Florine secretly mocks Matifat (5:375–377); Valerie Marneffe manipulates Crevel (7:331–337), just as Esther will play tricks on Nucingen (for example, 6:562–570). But he also is aware that the means by which the *courtisane* sells her proposition is exactly the same as the narrative device that drives acceptance of the fantastic: the punter's willingness to collaborate in his (or her) own deception.

The process is akin to a magician's trick in which the very denial of the fantastic ("look, no trickery") enhances its immanence. The audience understands it is being deceived, but colludes in anticipation of pleasurable mystification. It allows itself to be persuaded to ignore or discount the fantastic by devices that deflect attention or bewilder, while at the same time demanding more. An appeal to an outsider can act as illusory self-validation of the authenticity of the narrative. The narrative acquires a sense not just of its ability to describe deception but of its capacity to be the agent of the process as well.

Nucingen is proof of concept: arch exponent of the financial prospectus in *La Maison Nucingen,* here dupe himself. *La Maison Nucingen,* written and published contemporaneously with *La Torpille,* shows us the bridge between the prospectus as financial tool and as literary device. The common element is that the narrative must be capable of different interpretations in the hands of different recipients. As a financial fraud, Nucingen's third and final bankruptcy depends on Claparon shareholders and Nucingen depositors both believing that Claparon shares are at first undervalued, then overvalued, while he, Nucingen, knows they are the opposite. The Nucingen depositors must also believe that Nucingen's rumoured bankruptcy is real, while he knows it is not. Finally, Nucingen's partially informed associates, du Tillet and Rastignac, must behave with Claparon shareholders in respect of Claparon stock but with Nucingen in respect of Nucingen stock, choreographed to promote each in turn as the information they receive is manipulated. The same is true of the narrative itself. At the in-story level, Nucingen's prospectus is received and accepted as credible by his victims. At the level of the frame story, Bixiou's narrative tells the opposite story and posits the existence of a "discerning" reader able to penetrate and reveal the scam: the reader as investigative journalist or detective, with links to both literary genres. At the level of the reader of the text, we may reflect, as does Armine Kotin Mortimer, on how the process of deception works, on whether we have not ourselves just been victims of a narrative manipulated to postpone our own understanding through a process of obfuscation, and on the conclusion that Nucingen's skill ultimately lies as much in the manipulation of narrative as in that of securities.[114]

Is this narrative, therefore, also a false prospectus—not, or at least only in part, "du Sue tout pur," but instead a parody of Sue? Balzac gives us fair warning that all narratives are potentially deceptive, and he ensures that we are constantly aware of the text's status as narrative. In parallel with the "straight" reading of this part, the reader becomes progressively more aware that an alternative reading could take it as a pastiche.

Its very subject matter is ambivalent, capable of being read as a simple, unreflexive narrative or alternatively as a parody of the simplistic assumptions about audience reception inherent in Sue's text. It describes the construction of a series of deceptions: Herrera will con Nucingen out of his money using the illusory value of Esther's availability; he will use Lucien to dupe Clothilde into providing him with a position in society; he will trick the establishment into accepting his own series of false identities. In each case the mechanism is that of the Sue novel: the audience's own preconceptions and criteria are played back to them. Esther becomes—almost—the *courtisane* that Nucingen expects her to be. Lucien provides—almost—the proof of financial substance required of him by the Grandlieus. But, as Esther remarks, each flower has its worm (6:676), and we should perhaps take Balzac's hint to look closely. Herrera, superman and author of the fraud, fails at every hurdle. The market authorities, Peyrade and Contenson, are comically ineffective and, in Peyrade's case, melodramatically removed. But some of its recipients are able to see through its posturing: Derville and Corentin, literal readers of Lucien's backstory, are able to puncture the bubble of value.

The more we look at the detail, the more the fault lines appear. The opening section of the text is, as illustrated earlier, full of conventional devices of the roman-feuilleton designed to evoke predictable reader responses. Even here, we might notice a hint of cliché: the rather ham-fisted exoticism of Europe and Asie, the strained plausibility of Herrera's complete sequestration of Esther as the beauty in the tower. Even the original chapter heading as the scene is set seems to suggest an ironical detachment: "A Boring Chapter, as It Describes Four Years of Happiness."[115]

Gradually, however, Balzac seems to push the envelope. He is careful to introduce the shift slowly so that the reader only gradually becomes aware of it. A reader of *La Maison Nucingen,* for example, might notice that the Nucingen of *Esther* seems to share very little with his literary precursor: he may be called a "lynx," a *loup-cervier,* but what we see is a comically lovelorn Alsacien with a grotesque accent and a potbelly: this is more vaudeville caricature than credible banker (6:492–495). The moral code of the narrative is that of the financial markets. As Charles Bernheimer notes, Herrera has saved Esther not out of moral purpose but to enhance her market value: the heart of gold has investable value—the very opposite of Rodolphe's treatment of Fleur-de-Marie.[116] Motifs of substitution and masquerade—"the dandy, the forger, the courtesan"—mix with those of narration and rewriting: underneath each of Herrera / Vautrin / Jacques Collin / Trompe-la-Mort's disguises is another one until—but this will only come much later—we begin to doubt that there is a "real" character there at all.[117] Peyrade's introduction as "Old Canquoëlles" *(le père de Canquoëlles)* presents us with another caricature, from the unpronounceable name, which takes almost half a page to explain, to the bombastic excess of his description: "this old man swaddled in vices, calm as a Vitellius whose imperial belly was reappearing as if by palingenesis."[118] An original chapter headed "Les Mystères de la Police" seems to confirm suspicions of a parody of Sue.

The shift towards the implausible is mirrored by an increasing inability to handle realism, as demonstrated by fictional overload in the passage originally, and aptly, entitled "Fake *Abbé,* Fake Bills, Fake Debts, Fake Love" *("Faux abbé, faux billets, fausses dettes, faux amour"),* where the transaction by which Esther becomes the false debtor of false bills of exchange is so complicated as to lose even the most financially educated reader—and Balzac deliberately revises this passage in the Furne edition to introduce the completely new and immediately dropped character of D'Estourny to complicate the plot even further (6:563–564).

And could it be that Balzac reverts to what seemed inadvertent lapses in *La Torpille* to encourage us to see Herrera not as master criminal but as incompetent *auteur?* Small errors in continuity appear: Esther is brunette, not blond (6:554 vs. 461); Herrera forgets an address he already knows (6:635). More crucially, he has failed to do his homework in establishing Lucien's character. Derville and Corentin, the lawyer and the policeman, the market makers of narrative in *La Comédie humaine,* visit Angoulême and, within a few pages, are able to take apart Lucien's story. Herrera's own camouflage is pierced by one apparently trivial error in not disposing of a porter who has recognised Lucien: within a page, the "impenetrable text" opens for all to read (6:629).

Which way is up? The same themes of inversion that were first hinted at in *La Torpille* resurface. Herrera, characterised by the narrator as the literary personification of evil, is both author and lover of Lucien, described as half woman: does authorship then imply perversion?[119] Is Peyrade's secret vice, entirely irrelevant to the plot, simply an excuse for another Sue-esque excursion into the sordid but compelling shallows of human depravity, or is it a Balzacian commentary on the predictability of publisher or reader expectations? This narrative affords no definitive answer, perhaps because its need to remain a hybrid, a text that competes with Sue as well as a parody of his method, means that it cannot afford to. Its inflexion point is, symbolically, Esther's exchange of letters with Nucingen (6:599–604). On the one hand, it is the point at which she acquires her own narrative voice and an immediacy that greatly enhance the pathos of her death and the authenticity of Nucingen's grief. It is therefore an important device in securing narrative credibility. On the other, it is an equally striking parody of the implausibility of character construction in the roman-feuilleton, as the hitherto practically illiterate Esther suddenly acquires epistolary fluency. Exchanges of letters, *lettres échangées*, become bills of exchange, *lettres de change*, implying simultaneously the acquisition of real value by Esther as character and the suspicion that, despite her newfound plausibility, this is still a potential fraud on the reader.

Some contemporary critics seem to have agreed. Arthur de Gobineau reviewed the Furne version of *Esther*, published finally under the title *Splendeurs et misères des courtisanes* in September 1844 (which, it will be remembered, omitted everything after the renewal of Esther and Lucien's love affair; 6:481), in *Le Commerce* of October 29 and was clearly unimpressed: "In Esther, a story of unnecessary complexity . . . the plot picks its way with difficulty through laboriously constructed labyrinths, breaks down a thousand times during the trip and eventually, instead of arriving at a denouement, packs up for good without you being able to fathom why the book stops there." He delivers a forceful critique of all the clichés of the plot and characterisation: "Courtesans as models of chastity, convicts battling it out with the paragons of antiquity and modern times over levels of devotion and delicacy—we are accustomed to all these quirks which hold nothing out of the ordinary for us." And perhaps, unlike subsequent critics, he spots the parody: "So, all things considered, *Splendeurs et misères des courtisanes* might serve, like any other second-rate book, to introduce a system of indulgences for the roman-feuilleton. Here you might well ask: has this book actually appeared in the feuilleton slot of any paper at all? Our response is categoric: the fact is neither here nor there—enough that *Esther* carries clear traces of the intention."[120]

Lucien: *Deconstructing the Prospectus*

It is at this point, sometime between February and July 1844, that the story acquires its eventually definitive title, *Splendeurs et misères des courtisanes*. A letter to Mme Hanska on February 6 calls it *Les Amours d'un vieux millionnaire*, while one on July 16 refers to it by its current name in terms that imply a recent change.[121] The title seems at first to be rather Sue-esque with its implications of melodrama, investigative journalism, and voyeurism. But on closer analysis, an element of ambiguity creeps in. To which part(s) of the narrative do *splendeurs* refer? To which *misères?*

Which category does Esther's death fall into? How will bourgeois morality cope with resplendent prostitutes without bowdlerising the very excess that the title advertises? And where, indeed, have all the *courtisanes* gone? There are practically none in the final two parts of the book. Perhaps the title itself is an invitation to reread against the theme of deception. Received values, *splendeurs* and *misères,* turn out to be ambivalent, possibly inverted. Inversion leads to perversion as the underlying theme of sexuality resurfaces. Narrative itself becomes slippery, the medium of deception, perpetually self-questioning, multireferential. Successful narrative, Balzac seems to imply, requires excess—*splendeurs* and *misères*—to achieve melodramatic credibility, but the quest for intensity must inevitably end in failure as excess turns, at some unpredictable point, to over the top. And performing for money, creating predictable value for publishers, as the courtesan does for her (or his) clients, merely makes the inevitable happen sooner, as Esther's suicide has just proved.

The title appeared in between the publication of *Esther* in feuilleton form in mid-1843 and its reedition in book form in 1844, against the apex of Sue's popularity. *Le Juif errant,* acquired by *Le Constitutionnel* for a record-breaking 100,000 francs in an auction with the *Journal des débats,* took over from *Les Mystères de Paris* and ran from June 25, 1844, to August 26, 1845. Not to be outdone, the *Journal des débats* acquired the serial rights to Dumas *père's Le Comte de Monte-Cristo,* serialised in competition with Sue from August 28 to November 26, 1844, for the first part and, after a suspenseful break to encourage subscription renewals, from June 20, 1845, to January 15, 1846, for the second. Balzac seemed to struggle to find his niche in this new market. His output dropped from 100 feuilleton instalments in 1841 to 54 in 1842 and, although this picked up again to 109 in 1843, he was consistently unable to access the major titles and certainly could not compete with the rates commanded by Sue and Dumas.[122] The suspension of publication of *Les Paysans* was a watershed following which his publications in the feuilleton slowed to a trickle. But, as the short-lived craze for the *conte* had demonstrated, public tastes were fickle. Publishers tried to cash in: every newspaper had to have its feuilleton, and even the Dumas production line was unable to satisfy demand. Quality dropped: the critics were quick to pounce, and Balzac was recalled.[123]

The third part of *Splendeurs,* consisting of the story of Lucien's imprisonment, interrogation along with Vautrin, and suicide, was written between December 1845, when Balzac visited the Conciergerie, and May 1846, and appeared in fourteen feuilletons from July 7 to July 29, 1846, in the pages of *L'Epoque* under the title *Une instruction criminelle*. It was republished almost immediately in volume 12 of the Furne *Comédie humaine*, but under the title *Où mènent les mauvais chemins* and without chapter headings—one wonders how many readers bought both expecting a different story. Both the platform of initial publication and the speedy reissue indicate that, despite improvements, Balzac's financial position was not yet so assured that he could afford to ignore the successes of Sue and Dumas *père* and *fils*. He had made a more determined effort than ever before to reduce his debts, including repurchasing old letters of credit at discounts of up to 50 per cent of par on the strength of his own doubtful creditworthiness, and had at last squeezed a substantial sum out of Mme Hanska, but had then rather marred the result by overspending in true Balzacian style on the new house at rue Fortunée and investing in railway stock that promptly crashed.[124] The need to make money was still there, as was the dilemma about how to reconcile literary production for posterity to that for profit.

"The time has come when I need to produce two or three capital works to cast down the false gods of this bastard literature," Balzac writes to Mme Hanska on June 16, 1846. The context makes clear that he is thinking of a series of works including the two volumes of *Les Parents pauvres*: "For the end of July I need to have completed 150 printer's pages, 10 per day on average."[125] The *Lucien* narrative has been criticised as hastily constructed—Pierre Citron refers to "an excessively hasty composition" *(une rédaction trop rapide)* (6:747, note 1); Antoine Adam to lapses in style.[126] Prendergast describes the plot as "exotic" and "threaten[ing] to run out of control" from this point.[127] Brooks suggests that Balzac's attempts to reconcile "a world of representation and a world of signification that do not coincide and do not necessarily offer access from one to the other" drive him to ever-greater excesses of melodramatic hyperbole.[128] Perhaps it is more helpful to consider *Lucien* as an experimental text in which Balzac attempts to disassemble the mechanism behind "the false gods of this bastard literature" to find out whether it is possible to construct a narrative that mimics its effect whilst simultaneously laying bare the artifice of its creation.

The narrative is an allegory of the process of creating contemporary fiction. It is composed of two competing accounts of the same story, those of Lucien and of Vautrin, pitched to the magistrate Camusot, whose task is to decide which is true and which false, related by an opinionated and didactic narrator who provides a contextual overlay to his *récit*. He intrudes immediately and extensively, dominating the first thirty or so pages of the story in a series of tailgating digressions on the contemporary form of the Black Maria police van, *le panier à salade* (6:697–698), the judicial arrest and remand system (6:700–702), a guided tour of the Conciergerie (6:706–713), solitary confinement (6:715–716), the role of the *juge d'instruction* (6:717–718), and so on.

Why? What is Balzac's purpose in changing the narrative frame at this stage in the text? Eric Bordas suggests that these narratorial digressions provide a link to a wider context to which the reader can relate.[129] The wider context is, in practical terms, that of the roman-feuilleton within the typical layout of the contemporary newspaper page. The narrator is in the position of a journalist. Outwardly he is self-assured, with expert knowledge of legal procedures and prison operations, and positions the narrative as purported documentary providing enlightening and socially instructive content, with helpful, if a trifle patronising, explication: "But before we enter the terrible drama of a criminal interrogation it is indispensable, as I have previously mentioned, to have an understanding of how such a process usually works."[130] Beneath the objective exterior, we soon become aware that he is colluding with author and publisher to select information that sells newspapers.

The prison system provides a fertile source of such commercial material—voyeurism into the lower classes, exotic depravations, access to forbidden and criminal places—while simultaneously maintaining a defence against accusations of prurience. Explicit allusion is made to actual crimes with which the contemporary reader would have been familiar from, precisely, newspaper reports. The celebrated case of the murderer Edme-Samuel Castaing, guillotined in 1823 for poisoning the two sons of a rich notary to secure their inheritance for himself and, thereby, the hand of his socially superior mistress, is referred to twice in the novel (6:608, 746). The first, by Asie to Nucingen in *Esther* as she ramps up the price of access to Esther, is no more than an unnamed allusion to the lengths to which men will go to get a girl. The second, at the opening of Camusot's interrogation of Herrera in *Lucien*, refers directly to the crime "committed by Castaing," ostensibly as evidence of the psychological acuity of the magistrate, but indirectly as proof that the narrator's own investigative skills and access have created a text with commercial value, as he is at pains to point out: "This small detail might indicate, even to the least comprehending of people, how intense, fascinating, bizarre, dramatic and terrible is the battle of a criminal interrogation, unwitnessed but always recorded in writing."[131] It is difficult to imagine a more apposite description of the type of text a publisher could rely on for predictable reader response. The narratorial context provides a commercial backdrop to the rest of the narrative and a constant reminder that the text has to exist within a commercial framework whose objective is to sell subscriptions next week rather than create literary works for posterity. It purports to represent an objective reality that is, in fact, selectively edited to fit in with the publisher's commercial objectives. Everything, the narrator asserts, comes to be seen through the prism of the newspaper: "So, as we have seen, the most momentous life events are morphed into more or less accurate filler stories" *(de petits faits-Paris plus ou moins vrais).*[132]

"Plus ou moins vrais." Narratorial insouciance masks evidence of authorial concern. The opening of the *Lucien* story, so dominated by the narrator, gives way to a discourse on disguise. Asie borrows both costumes and identities as she visits Camusot, the Duchesse de Maufrigneuse, and Mme de Sérizy in her efforts to help Herrera and Lucien (6:733–745). The figure of the *marchande à la toilette,* simultaneously costumier, trader of identities, and procuress, is constructed from the essential building blocks of *Les Mystères de Paris:* mask, eroticism, social satire, the fascination of the upstairs-downstairs divide. But it also parodies the iterative hyperbole, the repetitive chase for intensity, of the Sue genre. Within a bare dozen pages, Asie transforms herself into a *baronne du faubourg Saint-Germain* sufficiently convincing to penetrate the Conciergerie at exactly the right moment to meet Herrera, yet is described in a manner that suggests more pantomime dame stuffed into her corset, "rudement sanglé[e]," than noblewoman (6:735). At what point, Balzac seems to ask, as Asie disappears down a staircase in pursuit of her lapdog, does the reader cease to respond as expected to the stimuli? The figure of the *marchande à la toilette* is an implicit challenge to narrative credibility. Asie moves effortlessly through society with no more than a change of clothes. If character is reduced to no more than clothes hanger, then how can the novelist ever construct a credible personality within the straitjacket of the rules of the roman-feuilleton? Is the *marchande à*

la toilette ever a credible character? Can the *marchand de phrases* ever become a "real" author?

The question is even more acute when applied to Herrera. The device of interrogation allows the separation of his story from that of
Lucien: the two narratives, of the same series of events, are thereby opposed and contrasted for the reader as well as for Camusot. From the
beginning of the *Lucien* narrative, his character takes on a disturbing
fluidity. "Nonetheless, Jacques Collin or Carlos Herrera (which name he
is given depends on the necessities of the situation) had long experience
of the ways of the police, prison and the judicial system": the implication that personality, as well as alias, might alter depending on situation leaves us wondering how this differs from the creation of an entirely new fictional character.[133]

The impression that we are watching an experiment in narrative
construction is reinforced when writing materials even emerge from
under his wig (6:717). Herrera's story (or is this Collin's?) is cast using
the traditional Gothic devices characteristic of Sue and intended to evoke
a predictable audience response: a convict disguised as an exotic Spanish
priest, a tale of his self-poisoning to escape interrogation and later resurrection, of his earlier escape from death by firing squad to explain
away his branding as a convict. But at every point, Balzac reminds us
that we are readers of fiction, makes us aware of the devices he is using,
and uses the process to debunk the character he is creating. "It must be
noted here that Jacques Collin spoke French like a Spanish cow, mum-
bling so as to make his responses almost unintelligible and to force his
listeners to ask him to repeat everything. Monsieur de Nucingen's Ger-
manisms have already studded these pages too much to want to include
other underlined phrases which are difficult to read and hold up a speedy
denouement."[134] Balzac's rejection of pastiche accent here serves to un-
derline his awareness of its effect in *Esther*. The original feuilleton chapter
titles are studded with the usual heavy puns and wordplay: Herrera is a
marked man and a remarkable man *(un homme de marque)* (6:746, note
a); pithy phrases are finessed: "Fin contre fin, quelle en sera la fin?"
(6:749, note *b*).[135] Perhaps the emblematic reference here is to the story
of the *vinaigre des quatres voleurs*, a tale of thieves who stole repeatedly
and with impunity from plague victims because they believed in the fiction that they would be protected by this vinegar (6:749). Some are able

to thrive on implausibility; for others, the merest hint of suspicion would be enough to undermine the most carefully constructed fiction.

Balzac, we feel, experimentally drives his narrative over the edge of plausibility to find out where it is. Herrera feigns death by poison and survives: this is a stock device of melodrama that fits a narrative convention accepted by both the in-story audience and the reader (6:748). He bluffs his way out of the discovery of his branding by a tale of disfigurement by firing squad that already causes suspicion amongst the in-story listeners and strains credulity at the reader level (6:747). And, finally, he is identified by a spinster from a previous story who recognises his chest hair (6:756). Even the in-story audience giggles at this point: the modern reader may reflect that narrative momentum and credibility have been severely damaged: peeling off one layer of disguise has revealed the underlying failure of the fictional skeleton.

Herrera / Vautrin is, as he has been since *La Torpille* and *Les Souffrances de l'inventeur,* the agent of narrative disruption. Even the physical characteristics of the text contribute. In the feuilleton version of the *Lucien* text, Balzac immediately establishes a new style of shorter chapters, typically addressing a single subject, such that the Furne text, which dispenses with chapter headings, can seem discontinuous and abrupt at times. Bordas suggests that the numerous digressions cause visible damage to the continuity of the text: "The Balzacian digression is the stylistic admission of a narrative paradox which appears to promote inclusiveness and coherence but which instead consistently reveals the rhythm of breaks, discontinuities and contradictions in the text."[136] The Herrera narrative forces us to consider whether its Sue-like carapace is not, in fact, a prospectus that is ultimately unable to deliver the value it promises.

If we assume for a moment that Balzac might have reached a similar conclusion, a natural response would be to try the experiment again in another genre to see whether the same result could be obtained. The story of Lucien's interrogation, involuntary inculpation of Herrera, and suicide from remorse does just this. It is, on the face of it, a romantic melodrama that has overt structural parallels to the conclusion of the preceding *Esther* narrative. The shift is heralded, appropriately enough in a chapter originally entitled "Enough," by the delivery to Camusot of Esther's last letter to Lucien. The epilogue to *Les Mystères de Paris* had been dominated by a series of increasingly tear-jerking letters describing Fleur-de-Marie's rejection of marriage and happiness, withdrawal to a convent, decline, and eventual death.[137] Esther's letter sets a similarly sentimental and clichéd tone: the image of her arranging herself on her funeral bed before taking poison (6:760) may even be reminiscent of George Cattermole's 1841 illustration of Little Nell's similarly composed death scene in Dickens's *Old Curiosity Shop*.[138] Esther's previous foray into correspondence with Nucingen had differentiated her from the stock Magdalene through the liveliness of her epistolary style. Here the movement is in the opposite direction: despite retaining a freshness of expression, she retreats back to the cliché of the dying heroine, as though whatever originality she possessed had been snuffed out by the requirement to conform to a literary stereotype: "The clock is striking eleven. I have said my last prayer; I shall lay myself down to die."[139] *Lucien* begins in a similarly clichéd vein, as Herrera describes its hero in Byronic terms: "a soul so young, so fresh, so magnificently handsome, a child, a poet."[140] But his credibility is sustainable in front of neither Camusot nor the reader, and Balzac carefully points out that it is the act of writing that demolishes both. The *procès-verbal* he signs confirms Camusot's penetration of his cover and simultaneously causes a surge of strength with which Balzac purports to justify a change of character so dissonant with anything with which we have associated Lucien that it merits a special narratorial explication. "With people of Lucien's character, as Jacques Collin had so accurately analysed, these swift transitions, from a state of complete demoralisation to a state of almost metallic strength, so tightly are human forces stretched, are the most explosive phenomena in the life of the mind."[141]

Narrative itself is the very medium of "the life of the mind," and the implication that Lucien's narrative credibility has just "exploded" is perhaps not entirely fanciful. The narrator dryly notes that Lucien's suicide reduces him to the status of a literary commonplace, "putting him in mind of the denouement of Romeo going to rejoin Juliette."[142] His will, two letters to Grandville and Herrera, and the formal retraction of his evidence (6:787–791) self-consciously echo Esther's three letters to Nucingen and farewell to Lucien, and represent not only the attempt to recreate similar narrative value by plucking the same strings but also its failure. His farewell letter compares Herrera to Pugachev, Robespierre, and Louvel.[143] We can only guess at the associations these three figures would have evoked in the mind of a contemporary reader, but it seems reasonable to assume that they would have been relatively one-dimensional: Emel'yan Pugachev the pretender; Maximilien Robespierre the architect of the king's execution; Louis Pierre Louvel the now-forgotten assassin of the duc de Berry in 1820. They represent people whose mention will create a predictable response from the audience because there is little else with which they are commonly associated.

And this, the narrative suggests, is the real depravity of contemporary fiction: to pretend that this cliché-ridden, formulaic system in which fixed correspondences exist independently of the reader's judgement and into which the artist can retreat without challenge can in some way represent valid narrative. "This is the poisonous plant of resplendent colours which fascinates children in the woods. This is the poetics of evil."[144] And its representative is the addressee of Lucien's letter, Herrera, the very agent of narrative perversion and author of this failed attempt to fix narrative exchange rates.

How, then, Balzac seems to ask, is the reader to sift the false from the real? To assess his competing narratives, Balzac proposes an in-story reader, editor, and valuer: the magistrate Camusot. Just as Herrera has acted as author, so Camusot functions as a metaphor for the publisher: a recipient of the narratives of others, an initial judge of narrative value, an intermediary in passing the narratives on to an audience that may have very different views of value or whose evaluations may be influenced by different external factors, and, most importantly, an editor, able to rewrite or even suppress the narratives told to him.

Like Balzac, he tries to disentangle real value from the values others wish to project. "Lovers of truth, magistrates are like jealous women: they deliver themselves up to a thousand suppositions, dig around in them with the dagger of suspicion like the sacrificers of old examining the entrails of a victim, then they stop not at the truth but at the probable, and end up with only a glimpse of the truth."[145] He compares narratives: Herrera's against Lucien's, police records against oral *récit*. He can dismantle received narrative hierarchies, in particular the misguided expectation that police files should be more truthful than oral testimony, comparing them ironically to the Bank of France's (poor) record of maintaining financial discipline (6:726). He is aware of the variable value of narrative and the difference that good editing can make—even to police files: "These boxes contain, in a way, the reverse side of the tapestry of crimes and their origins, almost always in unedited form."[146]

Camusot is conscious of his own role as reader and of the way in which his own reactions are manipulated by the narratives of others in ways designed to provoke a particular response, particularly through genre: Esther's suicide note to Lucien creates the intended spasm of jealousy but just as quickly represses it (6:763). He is also an editor, able to manipulate the texts of others, as his role in the redaction of Lucien's evidence illustrates (6:785). As publisher, though, he loses control of his own destiny to that of "the seven or eight publics which constitute the public," who seek to manipulate the narrative to their own ends.[147] His wife, the prosecutor general, Mme d'Espard, Mme de Sérizy, the Duchesse de Maufrigneuse, Herrera, and Lucien all seek to amend, suppress, or subvert the evidence. The implication is that narrative itself is unstable: one version may conform to a predictable value association, and then only within a defined readership, but multiple other actual or potential versions of the same narrative can exist simultaneously. The destruction of one variant simply allows another to take its place: the chapter ends with the forcible censorship of Lucien's incriminating *procès-verbal* by Mme de Sérizy and its replacement, symbolically, by trivia, "de petits faits-Paris plus ou moins vrais" (6:798).

What appeared initially as "an excessively hasty composition" seems on closer inspection to be a carefully constructed investigation of the mechanisms for creating narrative value in the contemporary market for literature. If so, its conclusions are fairly pessimistic. The search for predictable value leads towards narratives that, like those of Vautrin and Lucien, only work up to the point where their iterative search for intensity drives them over the edge of parody. Only a blissful lack of awareness of the parodic potential can confer any authenticity to this approach: the technique is simply not acceptable, Balzac seems to imply, for any author alert to it. Publishers are equally unreliable as guardians of literary value, as they have the power to misappropriate, rewrite, or substitute narrative in an effort to create an illusion of authenticity that the reader will buy. For the reader, no narrative is definitive; there is always another format, a pirate version of the text, a different edition, a censored copy, a version told by another, another version of the prospectus.

Vautrin: *Vautrin or* Vaut rien—*Who Decides?*

The title of the final part, *La Dernière Incarnation de Vautrin,* immediately echoes this theme of multiple narratives. It suggests both conclusion and confusion. Is this the last, or merely the latest, of Vautrin's incarnations? And what of Herrera, Jacques Collin, or Trompe-la-Mort? Do these aliases perish in a final incarnation as Vautrin, or do they survive in alternative, renamed, and distinct incarnations? Do they, indeed, become separate fictional characters? And why do all these questions arise, since the title also implies the agency of an author who appears to know from the outset that this is some sort of final version and who can therefore determine narrative direction? Does the title, in fact, imply the opposite of what it appears to represent: questions instead of answers, iteration instead of certainty, *misère* instead of *splendeur,* a false prospectus in a phrase—but this time targeted at the external reader?

There is evidence to suggest that the *Vautrin* narrative was written at a point in Balzac's life when some of the previous pressures had eased. The manuscript, which had been planned together with the *Lucien* story, was written during December 1846 and January 1847 and seems to have been finished around January 21, 1847. Eveline Hanska had agreed to marry him. His financial problems, thanks principally to her credit, were less pressing, although the house on the rue Fortunée remained a money sink. At the same time, *La Cousine Bette* was appearing in *Le Constitutionnel,* where from October 8, 1846, it alternated with Sue's competing title, *Martin, ou l'enfant trouvé,* which was serialised from June 26, 1846, to March 5, 1847. For the first time, Balzac seemed to have gained the upper hand. *Martin* had disappointed readers and publishers. "Sue is slipping" (*Sue dégringole*), Balzac writes on August 5, 1846, to Mme Hanska. "Everyone is saying the same thing about his work. Everybody thinks it is hideous, shaming—he's a goner."[148] Its failure, at least by Sue's previous standards, led to a revaluation, both financially and critically, of Balzac's work. *Bette* was an immediate success, and Balzac's stock rose. "The huge success of *La Cousine* got the papers all excited again; they'd all love something from me," is his typically modest commentary to Mme Hanska on October 24.[149]

Once again he had access to the major-circulation newspapers. *Vautrin* was quickly picked up by Girardin's *La Presse* when the publisher of *L'Epoque* hit financial difficulties, despite continuing rankles over the

1844 midstream cancellation of *Les Paysans*. In the spring of 1847, Balzac found himself publishing three novels simultaneously, in the pages of three different journals: *Le Cousin Pons* in *Le Constitutionnel* from March 18 to May 10; *La Dernière Incarnation de Vautrin* in *La Presse* from April 13 to May 4, and *Le Député d'Arcis* in *L'Union monarchique*.[150] Everything seems to suggest that Balzac had finally found a literary formula that reconciled the competing demands of the newspaper and the novel. There was even to be a sequel, another incarnation, depicting a final subterranean duel between Vautrin and Corentin.

The *Vautrin* narrative is, in many senses, a story of deception. It relates a tale of duplicity: Collin (to give him his prison identity) starts by convincing the other convicts to help him in maintaining his cover as Herrera; he exploits this to save the guilty Calvi by deceiving another convict, La Pouraille, into taking the blame for Calvi's crime; he blackmails the authorities into reinventing him as chief of police against the return of compromising letters that reveal the hidden natures of society ladies. This is a narrative that would not look out of place in any of Sue's works. It plays on cliché and received attitudes: the same fascination with the criminal classes that we have seen in earlier parts (6:822–844); the same revulsion in front of the machinery and method of execution (6:844–851, 856–859); the same curiosity in the face of an apparently unsolvable crime (6:851–856); the same titillation from the revelation of sexual depravity, particularly when related to class hierarchy (6:831–835, 901–903). It is an aggressive assertion of confidence in the ability to carry the reader through further and more extreme iterations in the search for a novel way of experiencing the expected.

It relies on a hierarchy of reader reaction every bit as established as the hierarchies it so carefully describes: the aristocracy of the criminal world, the *haut pègre,* the Grands Fanadels, and the Société des Dix-Mille (6:831–832); the aristocracy of high society, whose rules are set out by the duc de Grandlieu—"Before admitting anybody, one must know fully his financial situation, his family, all his antecedents"—and commented on by the narrator: "This phrase is the moral of the story, from the point of view of the aristocracy."[151] It is no coincidence that Balzac chooses to emphasise these hierarchies so clearly in the *Vautrin* narrative, nor that he links them to specific language codes that emphasise their relevance to its medium. The argot of the criminal world becomes a shorthand that immediately alerts the reader to setting, context, and emotional response

(6:828–830). The explicit nature of Diane de Maufrigneuse's correspondence with Lucien represents a transgression of the indirect and allusive mode of expression of the aristocracy, and its description in a further layer of circumlocution acts as a sort of linguistic veil to intensify the expected erotic charge: "So the duchess had kept these touching letters, as some old men keep obscene engravings, because of the hyperbolic praise of that which was least duchess in her."[152]

The reader will be able to follow the story to its most fantastic reaches without loss of credibility precisely because these rules of fiction specify that the more fantastic something appears, the more real it is likely to be: as Balzac's narrator observes, "The courage of truth allows combinations forbidden to art."[153] This is, self-consciously, the narrative of Vautrin, an assertion of the stability of identity notwithstanding multiple aliases; of the existence of rules on which an author can rely; of a system of fixed cultural, social, and emotional correspondences shared with a readership; and finally of a predictable financial exchange rate for the publication of narrative that will recognise the creative force of the author. It is the world in which genius can, reliably, thrive, since all the inconveniences and unpredictability of audience response based on free will have been eliminated. It is symbolised by *l'homme au secret*, the prisoner in solitary confinement, and the original title of the fourth chapter of the narrative, in which Vautrin is (re)introduced. His reincarnation, we are told, is a narrative inevitability after Lucien's death: "Once the little spaniel is dead, we ask ourselves if his terrible companion, the lion, will live!"[154] In this world where reader reaction can be determined before it has even happened, it is easy to postulate fixed correspondences. "In real life, in the world, deeds are so inevitably linked to other deeds that the one cannot exist without the other."[155] Without a reader other than the planted stooge, the artist can express his untrammelled talent without constraint, in echoes of *Séraphîta*: "Solitude is habitable only by the man of genius who can fill it with his ideas, the daughters of the spiritual world"[156]

But this is the world according to Sue. In a parallel universe, this cosy reliance on fixed exchange rates disappears. Balzac seems openly to subvert his own text. He sets up an opposition within which the reader has a stark choice: to subscribe to the prospectus, in the sense of "buying" Vautrin's conversion to civic worthy, or to tear it up and walk away empty-handed. The reader is, in effect, shown an avatar of himself or herself, a "mock reader," in Walker Gibson's terminology, in the process of "buying the story." Readers can decide for themselves whether they find the decisions of their avatars convincing.[157]

From the very first chapter, narrative is, again, confirmed as unstable. Themes of rewriting and rereading appear repeatedly in an opposition that echoes the theme of the title, *splendeurs* and *misères*. The section opens with depictions of both: Amélie Camusot redrafts her husband's interrogatories to suit alternative audiences (6:802), while Vautrin rereads Lucien's final letter, repeated verbatim to emphasise the focus now on the act of reading rather than writing (6:819–820). The original title of the first chapter, "The Two Robes," suggests both disguise and coexisting alternatives: whatever the provisional truth, it can be revised, as Amélie Camusot demonstrates. Even scientific fact is open to reinterpretation, as Balzac's digression on magnetism underlines by relating as fact opinions that readers in 1847 would have known to be a sham (6:810).[158] The act of rewriting calls into question the validity of any apparent narrative hierarchies. The protagonist's identity fluctuates according to label and milieu in a parody of conventional literary device: the Vautrin of the title is quickly discarded for "Jacques Collin, nicknamed Trompe-la-Mort in the prison world, and to whom we must now give no other name than his own" (though we may recollect with irony a similar phrase at 6:703 that limits the choice to Collin or Herrera), but, as if this confusion were not enough, the narrator reverts within three pages to calling him both Vautrin and Trompe-la-Mort.[159]

Carefully built suspense is sabotaged: the much-awaited confrontation between Collin and the convicts ends in bathos as Collin's mastery of disguise is exploded immediately, itself a commentary on the ease with which rewriting can be rewritten (6:841–842). The text itself becomes an obstacle to comprehension, illustrated by the use of argot as both a code requiring specific skills on the part of the reader and a parodic questioning of the value of acquiring such skills. Argot overload, together with translations in brackets, forms a visual and typographical barrier to comprehension that seems to draw attention to its role as a disruptive device and to act as a graphic parody of Sue's own use of convict slang (6:845–846).

The plot zigzags erratically. New characters—the convicts, Théodore Calvi and his entire entourage—appear with as little regard for narrative convention as Balzac accorded to Esther and Lucien in dismissing them from previous sections (6:851–865). Vautrin's conversion from master criminal to chief of police parodies any system of reader response that can think this a plausible development. By extension, a common critical reading of this switch as social satire, a Balzacian commentary on the lack of difference between the worlds of crime and high society,[160] is also undermined: implausibility robs the satire of its bite. Time and again the reader is asked whether he or she is prepared to accept yet another iterative round of excess as credible, *vraisemblable:* At what point, precisely, does the reader put the book down? What system of narrative conventions allows us to suspend disbelief as we read a scene in which Asie, stuffed into the costume of a marquise, is able to hold an entire secret conversation with Collin dressed up as a Spanish priest in front of assembled magistrates and police simply by adding random endings to French or argot words (6:863–865)? Are we so mesmerised by the notion that the fantastic is an indicator of intensified reality that we fail to consider that it might be simply preposterous?

Looking to readers for answers is a fruitless exercise. The in-story readers / recipients of the Vautrin prospectus—layers of magistrates, politicians, police, wives and mistresses, criminals—all fall into the traps and deceptions of the text with depressing predictability. Camusot vaunts his ability to develop reading strategies that unlock entire criminal plots from a single glance—but his own report still has to be rewritten by his wife (6:805). The audience is frequently untrustworthy, a stooge in a solitary cell, a policeman in disguise (6:851, 859–662). Reception does not imply comprehension: even the capacity to understand is mocked. Collin is able to plot with Calvi within earshot of the disguised Bibi-Lupin simply by talking in Italian (6:859). Balzac emphasises the connection by telling us that the conversation took place at reading speed (6:860). Calvi's crime is a sealed-room conundrum in which the eventual explanation, when revealed, is as obvious as it is improbable—and as improbable as it is obvious (6:861),[161] like the ape in Edgar Allen Poe's "Murders in the Rue Morgue."[162] The deal by which Collin persuades La Pouraille to take responsibility for Calvi's crime is so complicated that the reader, like La Pouraille, is left confused and with an ill-defined feeling of having been taken for a ride (6:865–872). La Pouraille's suspicions will, of course, turn out to be justified when Collin betrays him: just like the reader, he has been sold a false prospectus.

Increasingly, all that matters is the ability to project a story, irrespective of any underlying concern for plausibility. "Real-world achievements are nothing but sham: reality is in the mind," says Collin as he prepares his own prospectus as chief of police, a transaction that will be symbolically completed by an exchange of narratives: his rewritten biography for the letters of Lucien's three lovers, fantasy censoring reality (6:920).[163]

The final pages emphasise this point, if emphasis were needed. Mme de Sérizy is consoled by a letter from Lucien containing expressions of devotion that we as readers know to be fake (6:932–933). Collin's new position is based on evidence of Esther's and Calvi's innocence that, again, the in-story recipients believe to be genuine but that we know to be fraudulent (6:926–927). The conclusion itself, when it comes, is so perfunctory as to raise questions about whether Balzac cares at all about the reader's opinion (6:934–935). Readers, Balzac seems to imply, are simply not equipped to value a narrative which they lack the basic skills to decipher. Worse, there is no consistency of interpretation: every reader seems to produce a different interpretation, and there are as many interpretations as readers. The writer is caught in a vicious circle: if the reader, finding no value in the text, stops reading, then there is no point in writing. The reader who continues reading is, arguably, of value only to the publisher, never to the author.

Writing for a posterity that might bring a different set of values is the only option, and here again *Vautrin* incorporates its own answer. Trompe-la-Mort is the very emblem of posterity, the narrative that survives, the icon of perpetual reincarnation. But, asks Balzac, how credible is the pastiche reincarnation that Vautrin achieves? Is translation from Gothic outlaw to establishment functionary promotion or demotion? There is a sense in which Balzac's ending calls into question the entire value of writing: Vautrin or *vaut rien*, indeed.

So are we to take this as the final part of an experimental novel in which Balzac explores the contradictions between the demands of the marketplace and the qualities of viable literature, or simply as a failed example of Balzac trying too hard to write for a feuilleton readership? Both André Gide and Marcel Proust seem to suspect the latter, with Gide criticising Balzac's ham-fisted attempts at subtlety,[164] and Proust his servile adherence to a received social hierarchy.[165] Ultimately, it may be impossible to tell. But the mere possibility of the former means that, in a sense, Balzac himself becomes the chief protagonist of his own novel as literary explorer. We have followed the evolution of *Splendeurs* through all four episodes of its creation over a period of twelve years. Through each we have seen how Balzac first engages with the marketplace and then comes to challenge the literary straitjacket that it imposes. This final part of the text is, perhaps, an acknowledgement of defeat.

From the opening chapter, Balzac hints that the normal processes of narrative formation are breaking down. Camusot, a lawyer and thus of generic importance in *La Comédie humaine* as market maker and marketplace of narrative, returns in a state of *décomposition*. His wife tells him to start his story from the end (6:799). Inverted text signals inverted meaning, "the reverse side of the tapestry," just as his wife rewrites his manuscript (6:803). And inversion leads to the *inverti, l'homme au secret*—a man with a secret as well as a man ostracised from society. It is not, perhaps, until this final part of *Splendeurs* that we realise that the strongest and clearest impressions we take away probably relate to the erotic undertones—and if we find them pungent today, we can assume that they would have appeared even more so to a contemporary audience. Collin's reaction to Lucien's death confirms the strength of homo-erotic emotion in the bonds that linked them (6:818). There is a clear lesbian overtone in Diane de Maufrigneuse's seminude promenade in front of Mme Camusot (6:879). The salacious letters of all three of Lucien's lovers confirm what we have suspected for some time: that his own confused sexuality acts as a catalyst to release inhibitions in others, from Esther to Collin.

This theme, we now understand, has been gathering intensity throughout the work. What in isolation seemed like a bid for shock value now becomes part of a consistent pattern. Esther's sexuality is intensified by the contrast between her submissive facade and her training as a *fille*. Peyrade, clownish maestro of the instantly penetrated disguise and *père de famille*, saccharinely overprotective of his daughter Lydie, is also the Père Canquoëlle, sexual deviant with a penchant for young girls (6:534). Lydie herself, another of Lucien's lovers even if only from a distance, is kidnapped, prostituted, and finally driven mad (6:677–683). The criminal world is characterised by its gargantuan sexual appetites (6:833–834). As the novel advances through its four stages, so the Sue-esque concept of retribution for deviance weakens.[166] Peyrade may die, but Vautrin survives.

Other contemporary works show a similar degeneration into sensory excess. The description of the relationship between Pons and Schmucke, never explicitly confirmed as homosexual, is described in terms that

suggest a married couple—"joining their worldly wealth and their trou-
bles"[167]—and, one suspects, would have been all the more transgressive
to a contemporary audience by the very suggestion that this was
"normal." Remonencq's sexual appetite, driven by "the brutality of his
desires," leads to the murder of Mme Cibot's husband (6:655). Baron
Hulot, initially pillar of the establishment in *La Cousine Bette,* joins Peyrade in his taste for young girls (7:438). Valérie Marneffe, the obverse of
Esther's coin in exploiting sensuality rather than sentiment, ends in
physical and narrative disintegration: her bodily *décomposition* from disease introduced by Montès (7:329–430) is paralleled by the narrative disintegration introduced by Vautrin's return as chief of police (7:402).
The metaphor of disintegration, "le tout en morceaux," as Dällenbach
calls it, is picked up in the *Vautrin* narrative.[168] Collin goes to pieces in
the presence of Lucien's body: the image is compared first to oversmelted
iron, then to Napoleon's "dissolution" after Waterloo (6:821–822).

The plot and linguistic disintegration we have already seen are not
just clever devices to make a point about literary value: they are genuine impairments to the text, which suffers accordingly. If the in-story
audience is confused or finds its credulity stretched, then so do we as
readers. In contrast to previous sections, it is more difficult to engage as
a reader with this last part of *Splendeurs.* The central plot of Vautrin's conversion would defy credibility entirely were it not for the already shaky
characterisation of a Balzacian superhero who suffers from such a sur-
feit of aliases that we realise we have never been quite sure about who
he is anyway. The removal of the more one-dimensional major characters, Lucien and Esther, leaves a void that a plethora of lawyers and convicts barely fills. This is a damaged, limping script that Balzac seems by
the end to be in a hurry to get rid of. The promised sequel was withdrawn after its first mention. The false prospectus is, finally, revealed
for what it is. Perhaps we should not be surprised that, for all intents
and purposes, *Splendeurs* was Balzac's last major work.

Splendeurs is, I think, almost a secret diary of Balzac's struggle to
come to terms with the commercialisation of the publishing industry in
the 1830s and 1840s. It is unique amongst his works for its drawn-out
composition over the entire central portion of this period. It was evidently important to Balzac, as demonstrated by his repeated return to
the text. Its completion seems to have marked some sort of a turning
point in his life, since he wrote almost nothing more before his death

in 1850. It is a novel that critics have found problematic, since it tends to disrupt most attempts to make sense of the Balzacian universe, particularly those that take Balzac at his word in suggesting Vautrin as the "spinal column" of *La Comédie humaine*.[169]

I think it needs to be seen as an extended reflection on Balzac's experience of the emerging rules for the creation of narrative value, not by means of overt commentary but through the composition of the text itself. This is, literally, life writing. Balzac begins in a burst of excitement as his own ability to turn narrative into income is confirmed. Competition brings self-analysis, not just of why he is losing but of what it takes to become a wholly professional writer in terms of stylistic compromise. Self-analysis leads to parody, but neither readers nor publishers seem to notice, and satirical excess becomes, extraordinarily, a final burst of competitive and commercial triumph. In disgust, Balzac lays down his pen. In this autobiographical narrative of the commercialisation of literature, Balzac is both virtuoso and victim.

2

Dostoevsky:
Who Buys the Story?

"Isn't this, too, some sort of novel?"[1] asks Fetyukovich, Dmitry Karamazov's defence counsel. A few pages later the prosecutor responds, "We are accused of writing novels. But what is the defence doing, if not writing one novel about another?"[2] What, indeed, constitutes a credible narrative? Who decides? And is a single narrative adequate, or is iteration—a novel on a novel—an integral part of representation? I argue in this chapter that Fedor Dostoevsky's literary output, and in particular *The Brothers Karamazov (Brat'ya Karamazovy)*, evidences a continuing struggle between a desire to treat text as a prospectus-style medium for asserting an authorial view of its value and a recognition that the need to write a work of fiction with commercial value that would attract and retain readers imposed quite different requirements.

Evidence of Dostoevsky's preoccupation with reader reception is apparent even in his earliest works. His reengagement with the literary world of the early 1860s after his return from exile placed him in a situation in which almost all public texts became part of a wider polemic. The Great Reforms imposed new commercial, legislative, and judicial structures on a population that appeared to demand change but had little experience in how to handle it. The press copied the mass-market techniques of its English and French counterparts without having developed a mass market to address. Professional writers could not avoid becoming part of the polemic but needed to attract and retain subscribers for the periodicals in which they were published. Successful prose fiction demanded novelty to attract readers, yet had to be a predictable source of value for publishers. Dostoevsky's literary output reveals an unresolved tension between the economic need to tell a racy story that combined the staple commercial drivers of sex, money, and crime with a philosophical debate about morality and nationhood.

So this chapter proposes an "economic" reading of *The Brothers Karamazov*. Specifically, it addresses the issue of how the need to write for a commercial market, and the nature of that market, can be identified within the text through an examination of textual features that have economic effects. In particular, I think that Dostoevsky uses genre and iteration—in other words, the retelling of similar narratives in different styles or from different points of view—as an experimental technique to discover how changing the mode of delivery of a narrative can change its value to the reader.

My approach is of necessity interdisciplinary, involving aspects of economics, history, and culture, as well as literary analysis, so it intersects with the daunting body of critical literature on Dostoevsky at various levels without ever, I think, overlapping fully. It blends approaches taken by William Mills Todd III, who shows how serialisation affects the novelistic structure of Dostoevsky's works, with those of Robin Feuer Miller and Robert Belknap, who show how stylistic devices, such as interpolated or iterated narratives, affect the act of reading and reader reception.[3] It folds in those who have demonstrated the influence of changing newspaper formats and content on Dostoevsky's work. Leonid Grossman recognised as early as 1925 the importance of the commercial aspects of the literary market in which Dostoevsky participated and in particular the success of the boulevard newspapers and the content that drove their sales.[4] John Jones and Jacques Catteau have examined Dostoevsky's use of newspaper material, particularly crime reporting, in his novels.[5] Gary Saul Morson, Harriet Murav, and Irina Paperno, among others, have shown how *Diary of a Writer (Dnevnik pisatelya)* uses material from contemporary court cases, in particular those of Anastasya Vasil'evna Kairova and Ekaterina Prokof'evna Kornilova, in a more journalistic setting.[6] Igor Volgin's work on Dostoevsky as a journalist also highlights how his scope encompasses both the intellectual and the popular registers.[7]

My analysis starts, deliberately, from an economic rather than a literary critical or a philosophical perspective. So, for example, I look for economic motivation in a switch of genre: Does the new genre address a different reader demographic from the previous, and if so, why? Previous economic analysis of Dostoevsky's work has tended to focus on how he represents economic agents in his works. This has led to a "Dostoevsky as social commentary" approach, which draws attention to his depictions of the economic circumstances of his characters, from *Poor People (Bednye lyudi)* to Arkady Dolgoruky's ambition to "become a Rothschild" in *The Adolescent (Podrostok)*,[8] or alternatively to the way in which he represents money, again usually seen in opposition to the spiritual dimensions of his works. The role of the text itself as an economic agent, and of how Dostoevsky may have modified it to alter its commercial effect, has been less well addressed but is, to my mind, equally important.

The economic context is relevant as well. Both Bruce Lincoln's historical and economic account of the Great Reforms and Olga Maiorova's analysis of their cultural impact emphasise the feeling that Russia was in the middle of a gigantic experiment that would affect not just the political order in Russia but also its entire social, cultural, and economic structure.[9] Old certainties had disappeared, to be replaced by a new and experimental order, as Ekaterina Pravilova illustrates in her analysis of the concept and legal status of private property over the period of the Great Reforms and beyond.[10] The literary world was no different. All Dostoevsky's major novels of the period depict the instability of any moment of equilibrium, from Myshkin's pre-epileptic second of rapture to the fleeting solidarity of Stavrogin's bickering small-town revolutionaries. The novel becomes, at one level, a repetitive debate on how to deal with the conditions of its own production. Sarah Young represents the end of *The Idiot* as a fight amongst the characters and the narrator for control of the narrative.[11] John Jones suggests, memorably, that Dostoevsky was "writing the same book all his life" in different iterations.[12] Victor Terras speculates all too briefly that the novel may be a reflection on the art of writing a novel but never develops the thesis.[13] *The Brothers Karamazov* is Dostoevsky's most carefully orchestrated example of this technique of multiple, sequential, narrative bets. The very title suggests multiple perspectives around a family focus. Its plot is, in its barest essentials, a courtroom drama, a genre that depends on the competitive retelling of narratives. The accused's fate hangs not on facts but on narrative credibility. The issue of who has the "better story" is fundamental both to Dmitry's conviction and to the opposition between Ivan's Grand Inquisitor and Alyosha's Russian Monk. It matters how the story is told.

Genre has both philosophical and economic function: "flawed utter-ance," in Malcolm Jones's phrase, may indicate a fallen world but, more practically, may deter readers.[14]

I see Dostoevsky as a "speculative" writer, acutely conscious of the difficulties inherent in presenting philosophical and moral debate within the context of fiction without reducing its economic, aesthetic, or eth-ical value, strategically experimenting by retelling stories from different perspectives, or in different genres, to explore how altering the balance affects reader reception. The continuing critical polemic about Dosto-evsky's "meaning" or "message" in *The Brothers Karamazov* is testament enough to the unresolved struggle between text that seeks to assert a fixed value and that which relies on the vagaries of reader judgement.[15] Iteration, the planned and controlled return to the gambling table to try a new game theory or simply to hedge bets, the reversioning of a text to test a new mode of narration, becomes an obsessive inevitability. Spec-ulation is at once an accurate descriptor of Dostoevsky's narrative tech-nique, a reflection of his own character, and an emblem of the culture of his age.

Reform, Experiment, and the Novel

Dostoevsky's strategy is, in many ways, simply a response to the uncer-tainties of the world in which he lived. The Great Reforms overlaid a major social and political restructuring on an already weak economic foundation. With hindsight, it is perhaps unsurprising that it took a full two decades, and the whole of Dostoevsky's life after his return from Siberia, to work through the problems created by the combination. In the early 1860s there were many open questions but few satisfactory an-swers. The economic consequences of reform were, in effect, a lottery.

Russia's 1856 defeat in the Crimean War sounded an economic as well as a political alarm. The outdated muskets and warships that were overwhelmed by the modern equipment of the English and French forces attested to a chronically underinvested industrial base, a sclerotic civil service, and a labour market still based on feudal principles. The conflict sharply exposed the contrasts between Russia and the West. The Indus-trial Revolution in Russia's main European competitors was completed by the construction of the railway network; in Russia it marked the beginning. By the start of the 1860s, Russia had laid just 1,500 kilometres of track compared to 15,000 in England.[16] Russians who travelled abroad could see clear evidence of the economic gulf not just in transport but also in technology, entrepreneurial opportunity, and the availability of capital. Russia had hosted industrial exhibitions continually since 1829, yet Dostoyevsky's Underground Man chooses the 1851 Crystal Palace in London as his emblem of industrial progress.[17]

Why had Russia allowed itself to lag so badly? A series of wars dating right back to the Napoleonic invasion had depleted the state coffers. Printing paper money in response had caused a collapse of the paper rouble, the *assignatsiya*, in 1817, and heralded a century-long sensitivity to the discounted value of paper money to silver coin.[18] The sheer size and climate of the Russian territory impeded industrial restructuring. The industrial base itself was fragmented both geographically and structurally, with few large enterprises and many urban trades and rural crafts traditionally operated by sole traders. The Russian labour force became a byword for low productivity. Repeated social unrest in the West, particularly in France, also suggested a link between urbanisation, labour market reform, and political activism that the authorities were not keen to import. War in the Caucasus in the 1840s had further destabilized the budget and undermined the fragile economic gains of the previous decade. After the defeat in Crimea, the economic pressures to reform were, arguably, even stronger than the social and political drivers.

The social and political changes introduced by the Great Reforms were thus accompanied by a series of attempts to reform the economy. Mikhail Reitern, the finance minister to whom Alexander II entrusted the management of the economy from 1862 to 1878, was an educated and well-travelled man who had visited England, France, Prussia, and the United States. Indeed, he was known as an Americanophile and was even nicknamed the "Yankee."[19] His travels would have made him acutely aware of the extent to which the Russian economy lagged behind those of its Western competitors. His response was to introduce some of the economic liberalization that had driven growth in the West. State finances were consolidated and even made public from 1862. Some state interventions, such as the monopoly on salt, were abolished. Rights to collect taxes on alcohol were privatized, causing a sharp rise in alcohol abuse, which Dostoevsky records in *Crime and Punishment (Prestuplenie i nakazanie)*. Regulations governing private enterprise were eased: founding a joint stock company no longer required government permission, and almost all the new railway construction companies were privately owned and funded.[20] Plans were drawn up to simplify the tax system and move from taxing individuals to taxing income. Tariff barriers were initially lowered and imports of technology encouraged. In particular, real efforts were made to introduce a private credit system to develop greater access to capital. A new state bank was founded in 1860; private banks were introduced in 1863, and the state itself provided seed capital for key industries. By the mid-1870s more than forty new banks had been established. Alaska was sold back to the United States in 1867 for $7.2 million (some $123 million in 2017 dollars—still a bargain) and the proceeds reinvested in railway construction subsidies.[21]

The market took the hint. Between 1865 and 1875 over fifteen thousand kilometres of new railways were constructed. The line from Warsaw to Saint Petersburg on which Prince Myshkin arrived had been completed in 1862, five years before Dostoevsky wrote this episode. Demand for raw materials became a catalyst for growth in the coal, oil, and metal industries. Demand for workers stimulated reform in the labour market and in productivity levels. Capital flooded in, much of it from foreign sources, enticed by high rates of return and government backing.[22] A new class of merchant entrepreneurs emerged, providing local credit: Grushenka's successful investment career in *The Brothers Karamazov* illustrates, perhaps, how the demand for capital opened up new opportunities for different social groups to participate (13:281).[23] From 1870 to 1873, 259 new companies were formed with a combined capital of 516 million roubles.[24] Railway expansion opened up entire new economic regions, from iron and coal in the Donets Basin to cotton farming in the Transcaucasus.[25]

Yet these proved to be isolated successes. The Great Reforms contained within them, or at least within their implementation, the seeds of their own failure. Not until the 1880s and beyond would the promise of the reforms be translated into real economic growth. The labour market required a mobile workforce free of ties to the land and prepared to work in new industries for wages, yet the terms of emancipation tied peasants unprofitably to their old estates. Pravilova's work on property rights in nineteenth-century Russia traces the economically stifling effects of multiple poorly planned and executed changes, which created continuing uncertainty over property ownership. Land was redistributed, but a series of compromises left the former serfs with redemption obligations stretching over forty-nine years, labour obligations to former landlords, and illiquid assets in the form of a share of the output of the communes to which they were assigned.[26] Land values were inflated, based on a notional annual quit-rent income capitalized at 6 per cent, and compensation was 80 per cent underwritten by the state. So landlords had little incentive to modernize or rationalize, and every incentive to retain employees on their land in a state of permanent indebtedness.[27] Even in 1877, Leo Tolstoy's Levin still apparently requires a work quota from his former serfs, battles against their low productivity, and is resigned to renting out privately land formerly offered to the collective.[28] And the government's fear of political unrest still obstructed the concept of a fully mobile, urbanized workforce.

The very economic circumstances that had made radical reforms essential also conspired against their success. The financial foundations onto which emancipation was bolted were shaky. By 1862 the Russian state was on the verge of bankruptcy with over 2.5 billion roubles of debts. A wave of corporate bankruptcies had occurred and savings had dried up. An attempt to make the rouble convertible, at least against bullion, had been made in 1862 with the backing of a £15 million loan from the Rothschilds, but the loan proved insufficient, the currency collapsed, and convertibility was suspended in 1863.[29] Plans to reform the tax system towards income and land taxes, which might have helped align tax incentives with labour reforms, were shelved. In good times, foreign capital flooded in, but it withdrew just as quickly in the face of economic volatility and government intervention. As a result, the domestic capital market remained atrophied: as Sergei Antonov's investigation of lending habits as revealed by bankruptcy cases demonstrates, the private credit market tended to be based on personal connections, property transactions backed by landed estates, and unlicensed usury.[30]

The sheer complexity of introducing such massive changes across society itself seems to have caused a sharp drop in economic activity. Agricultural productivity remained stubbornly low until the 1880s and beyond. Industrial production initially shrank and investment dried up while uncertainty prevailed. Imports grew and the balance of trade deteriorated. Protectionism ensued and tariff barriers in many parts of the economy rose again after an initial attempt at liberalisation.[31] By the early 1890s a pound of sugar would cost three times as much in Russia as in England.[32]

Importing capitalism also meant importing its parasites, which found a supportive host in an already corrupt and opaque political economy. Speculation flourished, even though stock exchanges trading shares were forbidden until 1900.[33] The copy of the *Stock Exchange News (Birzhevye vedomosti)* in which Rogozhin wraps the 100,000 roubles he intends to pay for Nastasya Filippovna in *The Idiot (Idiot)* is indicative more of the growth of a trading mentality and the accompanying need for information than of any specific economic innovation (8:124). Railway barons abused government concessions and corruption remained endemic.[34] Substantial transfers of wealth from the state to the private sector occurred. When, in 1874, the European economic crisis that had followed the Paris Commune of 1871 finally hit Russia, the fragile financial system collapsed. The combination of recession, a stock exchange crash, the bankruptcy of a major bank, a run on deposits, and the subsequent Russo-Turkish War of 1877 undermined confidence and provoked a currency crisis and an exodus of foreign capital. Reitern resigned in 1878 and government economic policy, already returning to intensified state regulation, became increasingly intrusive and restrictive.

The two decades of the 1860s and 1870s stand out as an economic as well as a political and social experiment. Comparison with European competitors highlighted the need for change. But introducing Western capitalism to an economy just emerging from feudalism was an experiment that would take far longer to conduct, and prove far more complicated, than anyone could foresee. Dostoevsky represents economic change as a threat or a pipedream. The very process of transaction itself, of exchange and negotiation, is characterized as revolutionary, the age of the third horseman of Lebedev's Apocalypse, "the one that has the rider with scales in his hand, because in our age everything is weighed in the balance and settled by negotiation."[35] Luzhin's mercantile assessment of Dunya as an asset to be acquired in *Crime and Punishment* is both insistent and sinister (7:209–210). Arkady Dolgoruky's ambitions of wealth implied an impossible dream rather than a realisable aspiration (10:61). Even gifts are suspect: Myshkin's windfall legacy in *The Idiot* may enhance his credit, but the melodramatic inflation of his bank balance does little for his credibility as a fictional hero (8:128–129). The theme of economic change as threat recurs in Dostoevsky's journalism, from his critique of European greed in his essays on the bourgeois in *Winter Notes on Summer Impressions (Zimnie zametki o letnykh vpechatleniyakh;* 4:336–351) to his discussion of a feeling of social fragmentation or entropy, *obosoblenie,* in *Diary of a Writer* (11:346–349).

What was true in the wider economy was also true for the press. By the mid-1870s Russian literary culture had for decades tracked in parallel West European, and particularly French, publishing strategies without developing a comparable readership. As we have seen in Chapter 1, the French publishing market had begun to develop the periodical newspaper as the decisive tool with which to expand the readership back in the 1830s. The Russian market followed suit, even at times appearing to lead the way. Publishers in both markets realised almost simultaneously the power of innovative, cheaper formats to drive subscriptions to periodical literature. In 1834 the Russian publisher Osip Ivanovich Senkovsky set out to change the economics of the book trade by introducing the *Library for Reading (Biblioteka dlya chteniya),* the first of Russia's "thick" journals, at a subscription price of fifty roubles per annum, far lower than the equivalent output in book form. A full two years later, in 1836, Emile de Girardin introduced *La Presse,* priced at forty francs per annum, or half the norm for competing papers. But the Russian readership was tiny in comparison. When Léon Curmer published his enquiry into the French national character, *Les Français peints par eux-mêmes,* in 1840–1842, he was able to attract 22,700 subscribers. A very similar work published in Russia at the same time, *Nashi, spisannye s natury russkimi* (literally, *Our People, Painted from Nature by Russians*), attracted just 800.[36] Subscriptions to the *Library for Reading* peaked at around 5,000, and Senkovsky had ceased trading by 1845.[37] Subscriptions to *La Presse* peaked at 70,000 in December 1848, and the paper would go on to make Girardin almost 3 million francs in cumulative profits by the time he sold it in 1863.[38]

Writers discovered that narrative could have economic as well as literary value. The use of serialised fiction to promote subscriptions to an expanding periodical industry occurred more or less simultaneously in the mid-1830s in both France and Russia. In the absence of a mass readership, faster presses, cheaper distribution networks, or any of the other factors that would eventually transform the business of literature, it was considerably more efficient to distribute literary content bundled into journal form. Authors were paid up to ten times as much for periodical content as for books.[39] For the next half century, the publication of major prose fiction in serialized form, ahead of any eventual appearance, if successful, in book format, remained the norm in Russia as well as in France. But over that period, the French pool of literate readers over fourteen years of age grew from an estimated 7.3 million in 1801 to some 17.8 million in 1871.[40] Although literacy statistics for the period in Russia are suspect, in 1825 there were perhaps 50,000 "real" readers out of a nominally literate pool of no more than 5 per cent of the population, or 2.5 million individuals. By 1860 this might have grown to a book readership, of all types of books, of some 1 million.[41] Book titles published in France grew from 2,547 in 1814 to 13,883 in 1866.[42] In Russia 583 titles were published in 1825, of which almost half were by foreign authors, and 2,085 in 1860.[43] Investment in roads and railways had opened access to the French provincial reading public in the 1840s but would not do so in Russia until the 1870s. New printing technologies had increased capacity and reduced costs in France, but the same technologies would lag by almost half a century in Russia, at least in part because of concerns at the government level over the political risks in broadening the reach of the press.

By the early 1860s, the beginnings of a mass market with a readership spanning class and geography were discernible in France. Moïse Millaud's introduction in 1863 of the first representative of what we would now call the tabloid press, *Le Petit Journal,* is an evident response to these market trends. But the same happened in Russia, with the introduction in 1864 of the first boulevard newspaper, the *Petersburg Flysheet (Peterburgsky listok).* Even though some expansion of the readership into the military, the merchant classes, and lower ranks of civil servants had taken place in the wake of the Great Reforms, nothing remotely resembling a mass readership existed. The *Petersburg Flysheet*'s street sales were tiny: around 1,000 copies per issue in 1867, and still only 2,200 by 1880, even if many copies were passed around until they disintegrated.[44] It took several makeovers and changes of editor before the *Petersburg Flysheet* finally started to develop a broader readership from the 1880s onwards, perhaps indicating that its own evolution was dictated by the pace of that of its audience.[45]

Instead, the idiosyncratic Russian readership gave rise to its own unique format, the "thick" journal. Its omnibus content addressed a market too small, at least initially, to support more targeted periodicals. Its book-like format allowed for the relatively efficient delivery in a single compact package of a month's worth of reading, allowing journals to access the provincial market where timely receipt was impossible to guarantee. As few as two thousand to three thousand subscribers ensured breakeven but equally constrained what publishers could pay contributors. At the beginning of the 1860s, some eight to ten titles were sufficient to cover the available market. Reitblat estimates that the total print run of all the Russian thick journals, the major vehicle of serialised fiction, was around thirty thousand copies in 1860, rising to forty thousand in 1880. The most successful had subscriber lists of six thousand to ten thousand in the 1860s, rising slowly into the 1880s but offering little or no indication of the development of a mass reading public.[46] Dostoevsky's own *Diary of a Writer*, despite its extraordinary popularity, was capable of being run in its entirety from Dostoevsky's own home as a cottage industry by his wife.[47] By comparison, Emile Zola's *Nana*, published in book form in March 1880, the same year as *The Brothers Karamazov* appeared in book format, had a first-edition print run of fifty-five thousand copies and had reached its eighty-second edition by July 1881.[48]

French writers had enjoyed full access to the Russian literary market for almost the entire century: from 1875 to 1880, Zola even wrote a regular column for the Russian journal *Le Messager de l'Europe (Vestnik Evropy)*, while most Russian writers would remain more or less unknown in France until the 1886 publication of Eugène-Melchior de Vogüé's *Le Roman russe*.[49] Nikolai Strakhov, writing in his 1881 memoirs of Dostoevsky, attests to the influence of French literature on the literary society in which Dostoevsky moved: "Certainly, the outlook of this circle [that of Aleksandr Petrovich Milyukov, writer, editor, and host of a literary salon attended regularly by Dostoevsky] was directed by French literature."[50] One of the key imports from France was the format of the feuilleton. Through it, writers reflected and influenced public taste. The feuilleton posed as the reader's friend, acting both as a guide through the complexities of the Great Reforms and as a sympathetic echo of his or, increasingly, her frustrations. Katia Dianina argues that it played an important role in developing a broader audience, particularly in the growing broadsheet newspaper formats: "One way or another, the *feuilleton* always addressed the subject that interested the general readership most: their own tastes and opinions."[51] The need to appeal to a broadening audience dictated a wide range of content, from serious intellectual debate to populist entertainment. Dostoevsky, writing principally in the thick journals, where the feuilleton existed as a loose

stylistic designation rather than a literary context at the foot of a newspaper front page, took the device to heart: "Nowadays the *feuilleton*
is . . . is almost the most important thing. . . . This is what I think: that
if I weren't an occasional *feuilletonist* but one with a permanent position, on a daily basis, I'd like to turn into Eugène Sue, to write about
the mysteries of St Petersburg," his *feuilletonist* narrator writes in the
January 1861 issue of *Time (Vremya)*.[52] Vladimir Zakharov, reviewing the
range of Dostoevsky's output as a *feuilletonist*, remarks on how he uses
its breadth of content to cover travelogues, social commentary, national
promotion, and religious issues, as well as polemics with rivals and
more populist subjects.[53] Its breadth of genre also allows Dostoevsky to
experiment with a similarly wide range of diegetic registers, from fiction, the roman-feuilleton, to journalism, to feuilleton, *tout court*. The
flexibility afforded by the feuilleton format of *Diary of a Writer* allowed
him to shift from melodrama to diary, from confession to psychoanal-
ysis. And even though its physical broadsheet context may be absent in
the thick journal, Dostoevsky borrows from its original proximity to the
newsworthy by means of copious reference to topics that, in the French
context, were clearly broadening the newspaper readership. Catteau
calls him a "deep student of newspapers" and notes his use of the faits
divers not just as a source of novelistic plots but as evident hooks to retain reader interest with stories from the world of crime, the courtroom,
the lower classes, the sexual, the psychological—the very drivers of
French literature and journalism.[54]

Yet the readership at which these devices were targeted in France
barely existed in Russia. The most obvious audience consisted of a relatively narrow stratum of wealthy cosmopolitan society in Saint Petersburg and Moscow, most of whose members had received a European or
European-influenced education and were readers of foreign literature,
together with a small group of intellectuals and writers who provided
many of the publishers, editors, and critics for the commerce of literature. This group numbered perhaps twenty thousand at the beginning
of the 1860s, to which could be added a university student population
of some five thousand and a number, perhaps five thousand to fifteen
thousand, of self-educated women at home who were becoming an increasingly important part of the readership demographic. Since this was
the group from which Dostoevsky's social circle was largely drawn, and
which was also in a position to express its views through the medium

of journalism and salon culture, its responses were probably relatively easy to identify. A second group of largely provincial landowners and the upper echelons of merchant society, mostly self-educated and reading only in Russian, provided a further audience of up to 250,000 with secondary education, whose views Dostoevsky would have encountered in his years of exile but whose responses would otherwise have been muted by distance or class barrier. The final, and by far the largest, group consisted of the smaller landowners, the provincial merchant classes, and, increasingly, the more educated peasantry, into whose ambit Dostoevsky's works would barely have reached during his lifetime.[55]

The difficulty of reaching even part of this readership profitably imposed limits on what publishers were prepared to pay authors. S. Shashkov, writing in 1876, complains that despite a three- to fourfold rise in average literary earnings for a top-ranked writer between 1825–1850 and 1850–1875, most of the increase had been negated by rises in the cost of living.[56] We should remember that inflation in much of western Europe over the same period was more or less nonexistent, so by comparison Russian writers were even worse off.[57] Even this increase, Shashkov argues, was lower than for equivalent trades—median schoolteacher earnings, for example, had risen by 8.5 times between the 1840s and 1875—as a result of the exploitation of naive and unwary authors by unscrupulous publishers.[58] It is interesting that the one reason for authorial poverty that he does *not* advance is Russia's tardiness in developing a mass readership—almost as if the topic had not registered as an issue, despite the evidence from France.

As a professional writer who depended on the existence of a literary market to sell his work, Dostoevsky would have been acutely aware of the economic value of his work. In his lifetime he was variously journalist, novelist, publisher, editor, and press entrepreneur. His exchanges with successive publishers reveal an intimate familiarity with the worth of his literary output in terms of roubles per printer's page proof, as well as a developed sensitivity to his literary ranking against other writers expressed on the same scale. His financial position remained tenuous until the mid-1870s. "He had to write to the deadline. . . . The reason was that he lived only from the income from his literary work and . . . except for the last three or four years of his life, he was in great financial need," writes Nikolai Strakhov.[59] The eventual stabilisation of the family's finances owed much to Dostoevsky's good sense in marrying one of Russia's first professional secretaries (and stenographer to boot, illustrating the introduction of new skills), who took over many of his business dealings. Maximizing current revenue meant producing content that contemporary readers would pay for in the shape of subscriptions to the periodical that carried them. It also meant becoming part of his publishers' sales strategies, which not only dictated serial publication but also timed the appearance of highly rated content to maximise subscription renewals. In addition, it required sensitivity to political winds to avoid censorship.

Determining the value of literary production involved a delicate judgement between writing for a contemporary readership that paid the bills and for a future mass readership that was clearly developing in West European markets but was still in its infancy in Russia. Just like the Great Reforms, this prospect opened a new landscape but gave little guidance on how to reach it. The reforms themselves created a proximate incentive to reading: the decrees were distributed widely in printed form as well as being read aloud in churches, the process of transferring land required a significant amount of paperwork, and participation in the new *zemstva* even more.[60] Although the boulevard newspapers and "thin" periodicals would not attain their peak popularity till the 1880s and 1890s, their subscriber base was already growing fast.[61] The railway network was, as we have seen, finally expanding.[62] New bookstores were opening to serve the growing readership and to provide distribution outlets for the rising number of periodicals that flourished following the relaxation of censorship in the new press laws of 1865. The number of periodicals and newspapers published rose from 170 in 1860 to 485 by 1880.[63] New formats, such as the boulevard newspapers, and new literary genres, such as the detective story, were being invented to address this nascent readership. The *Intermediary (Posrednik)*, a periodical launched in 1884 to address this market, achieved copy sales of four hundred thousand by the end of its first nine months.[64] Over the final quarter of the century, increasing urbanisation would finally create a mass readership across all social classes. Russia's first census in 1897 still reveals overall literacy at only around 21 per cent, or 26.5 million readers, compared to over 90 per cent in England and France, but the process towards broader literacy across the population was under way.[65]

Dostoevsky's works can be seen as a mirror of the economic context in which he lived. The economic ramifications of the Great Reforms represented the greatest experiment with the structure of the Russian economy in the entire nineteenth century. The outcome of that experiment was far from clear at the time of Dostoevsky's death, and twenty years later Anton Chekhov would return to many of the same questions about the eventual consequences of emancipation in works like *The Peasants* (*Muzhiki,* 1897) and *In the Ravine* (*V ovrage,* 1900). During the last two decades of his life, Dostoevsky had experienced a switchback series of policy initiatives, partial successes, defeats, and relaunches. The literary economy had followed suit as it copied developments in western Europe. But whether either would prove capable of developing solutions suitable for the Russian context, with its different history and culture, remained unclear. Dostoevsky had evidently gone some way towards merging Russian and French formats, content, and genres in an attempt to create a literature that might have value both in the contemporary literary market and to posterity. But ultimately, writing for this unknown but obvious future audience could be based on nothing much more than guesswork about what its tastes might be. A strategy of multiple iterative texts, speculating on the value a future and broader readership might attach to each, is a logical response.

Considering narrative as a commodity with a clear economic function as well as a proven link to speculation also seems justified in terms of Dostoevsky's own economic circumstances. As Joseph Frank's biography records, from his days as a student, his correspondence reveals an almost continual lack of money fuelled by spending habits regularly in excess of whatever income was available. Advances from publishers regularly fed his gambling habit during his travels in Europe in 1867–1868—a voyage in part taken to escape domestic creditors.[66] A misjudged and highly speculative contract with Fedor Timofeevich Stellovsky almost led to the surrender of rights to his pre-1867 output when he narrowly avoided failing to deliver the manuscript of *The Gambler* (*Igrok*) on time.[67] His own experience with publishers, from the initial impact of *Poor People* and the unexpected success of *Notes from the House of the Dead* (*Zapiski iz mertvogo doma*) to the critical rejections of *The Double* (*Dvoinik*) and *Notes from the Underground* (*Zapiski iz podpol'ya*), had illustrated the variable value of his own output, and the several interventions by the censor, or by publishers acting—justifiably or not—as censors, had indicated the extent to which value could be changed through external forces.[68] Developing methods of hedging against volatile valuations by the various recipients of his output is a logical authorial insurance policy.

Dostoevsky's awareness of the economic function of narrative is evident from his earliest works. *Poor People* openly discusses how literary value is created. The epistolary form itself draws attention equally to the act of writing and to that of reception. Repeated intertexts with, in particular, Aleksandr Pushkin and Nikolai Gogol emphasise its own claims to literary worth (1:47–49). Makar Devushkin is a copyist, the lowest rung of literary creation, where innovation is forbidden: all that is possible is for him to subtract value from a text by omission or error. But he is obsessed with the nature of literary value creation. At times it appears quite arbitrary and inexplicable, epitomised by a copying error that lands him one hundred roubles instead of a reprimand (1:71–73) At other times it seems formulaic and predictable: he accurately identifies Ratazyayev's use of different genres to enhance the value—expressed in roubles per printer's sheet—of his production capacity and contemptuously dismisses these as indicators of commercial, rather than literary, value. "Just look at how even that Ratazyaev pulls it in! What effort does it cost him to write a sheet? And some days he's even written five, at 300 roubles a sheet, so he says. Some trivial anecdote or other, or some odd titbit—five hundred, take it or leave it, don't argue, pay up."[69] And we, the external readers, are left wondering what qualities of the text keep us reading—the commercial mixture of sentimental romance, melodrama, and voyeurism, or the intellectual debate about literary worth into which we are none too subtly nudged by Dostoevsky? Morson argues that as early as 1847, Dostoevsky was already using his *Petersburg Chronicles (Peterburgskaya letopis')*—his own feuilleton in the *Saint Petersburg News (Sanktpeterburgskie vedomosti)*—to illustrate how the writer ends up relating not the story but the process of reading the story, and suggests that this metaliterary play is already a literary convention associated with literature in a journalistic context.[70]

At some level all of his works can be seen as an exploration of ways of creating (or, at times, destroying) narrative value. Even *Notes from the House of the Dead,* self-evidently Dostoevsky's own convict memoirs but dressed up as the fictional recollections of Aleksandr Petrovich Goryanchikov, forces us to consider whether the text somehow has a different value if considered as fact or fiction. *The Double*, written in a first (1846) version before Dostoevsky's exile, received a poor critical reception and was substantially revised for republication in 1866. It is a text quite literally retold, at a distance of twenty years, to improve both its commercial and its literary value. The revisions pared down the original text to focus on the underlying iteration of the motif of the double—if both original and double are fiction, the story seems to argue, what makes the reader able to tell one from the other any better than its poor, confused hero? *Notes from the Underground* is rarely analysed from a commercial perspective but contains many devices whose function is as much economic as psychological or philosophical. The narrator's trick of simultaneously repulsing the reader and seeking his or her sympathy as an underdog is a skilful way of ensuring that readers attracted by either trait keep reading. The narrative is self-reflexively aware of its status as narrative and conscious of the irony of a narrator writing a private memoir that the author will publish: "But are you really so credulous that you think I'm going to publish all this, let alone give it to you to read? And another problem: why am I calling you 'gentlemen,' why am I treating you as if you really were readers?"[71] The narrator's ability to assert value may appear to be undermined by his representation as dysfunctional, but his narrative is itself a highly functional construct designed to ask questions about how readers place value on fictional discourse. Its shifting genres, from diary, through confession, philosophical dialogue, and newspaper reportage, to mock-sentimental melodrama, make us acutely aware of the narrative medium and force us to consider how each genre affects our reception of the text.

In *Crime and Punishment* Dostoevsky turns to the new commercial genre of the detective story, itself a relatively new introduction to the European roman-feuilleton readership popularised by Edgar Allen Poe's works. Dostoevsky had already published translations of three Poe stories in his own periodical, *Time*, in 1861, suggesting that he recognised the commercial as well as the literary potential of Poe's writing.[72] His inversion of the genre from "whodunnit" to "whydunnit," which many critics have noted, is at least in part an effective commercial device designed to keep readers searching for an answer which ultimately never fully comes. His choice of subject comes closer and closer to that of the boulevard newspaper: two, possibly three, gruesome murders, a fatal traffic accident, a cat-and-mouse police investigation, sexual perversions, a suicide. Combined with these commercial drivers is an active engagement with contemporary ethical, social, and philosophical concerns: criminal motivation, social deprivation, natural justice, perhaps reflecting the typical spread of content of the thick journal. Once again the narrative is aware of its own status and effect: Oliver Ready's introduction to his translation talks about "the complicit and complicating role of literature itself. . . . Raskolnikov has blood on his socks and ink on his fingers."[73] The emergence of the newspaper and periodical industry as the key economic driver of the commercial publication of prose fiction during this period creates an inevitable tension between the requirements of publishers for texts that will drive the growth of the reading public into new demographic areas, and those which satisfy an authorial ambition for intellectual content.

Dostoevsky himself appears to recognise the tension when he writes to Strakhov in 1869, in a much-quoted phrase, "I have my own particular take on reality (in art), and what most people would call quite fantastic and unrepresentative is sometimes for me the very essence of the real."[74] Time and again Dostoevsky asks us, as readers, to consider the difference between the narration of reality and reality itself. His concept of realistic representation is explicitly associated with its newspaper context: "In every edition of every newspaper you will find *reports of* facts [my italics], from the most mundane to the most far-fetched. To writers here they seem fantastic, if they are noticed at all; but in the meantime they constitute reality precisely because they are *facts* [Dostoevsky's italics]."[75] The facts Dostoevsky refers to are, in all probability, those of the faits divers, thus facts that have been preselected by journalists and editors for their commercial impact and that define the genres that sell newspapers. This is, perhaps, less of a definition of realism than a commentary on the role of journalistic writing in re-creating a story that readers would buy, both metaphorically and literally.

The novels become experimental—or possibly accidental—test beds for assessing how readers discover value. *The Idiot* is a narrative *about* the value of narrative. Dostoevsky's correspondence and notes indicate a clear desire to use the text to convey values defined by the author in the shape of his presentation of Myshkin as a type of moral ideal. "The main idea behind the novel is the representation of a perfectly good man," he write to his niece Sofya Ivanova in January 1868, before admitting that, having written the first part, he has no idea how to continue.[76] Myshkin puts the theory to the test by offering narratives to the other in-story characters: this is a form of narrative auction in which Myshkin's fictional credibility will be established by the reception he is given by the recipients of his narratives. He is an outsider with neither family nor fortune to rely on, so the results of the auction determine both his credibility and his credit balance. The very terms in which the debate is framed suggest an intrinsic conflict. Dostoevsky offers his perfectly good man to the reader through a form of prospectus narrative based on fixed values asserted by the author through his character. But the very concept of the good man depends on the establishment of an alternative, nonfinancial concept of exchange based on ethical or emotional criteria such as goodness, respect, or love.[77] All Myshkin's attempts to establish such a basis of exchange fail. He is trumped by Rogozhin's cash in his offer for Nastasya Filippovna. He fails to win Aglaya. Even his offer of reparations to Burdovsky is spurned. Dostoevsky provides in-story yardsticks, in the shape of the reactions of Nastasya Filippovna and Lisaveta Prokof'evna, by which his slow-motion failure is recorded. The narrative structure itself is forced to rescue Myshkin by the intrusive device of an unexpected legacy when his credibility is threatened (8:128). The internal logic of the prospectus has been replaced by pure randomness: the *skandal* of the auction for Nastasya Filippovna is as much to do with the shameless attempt to subvert the plot as with perverting the heroine. Unsurprisingly, Myshkin's financial substance is only restored at the cost of his fictional credibility. Narrative is revealed as more speculation than prospectus or auction, as Dostoevsky's own analogy reveals: "I chanced it, just like at roulette: 'Maybe it will develop as I write!'"[78]

Narrative devices hint at implied values that seem to contradict those asserted on the surface of the text. Myshkin's extended encounter with Rogozhin at his house represents an extended moral debate on the nature of faith, with Myshkin asserting a strongly Christian ethical position (8:155–169). It is no coincidence that this episode is described in the genre of Gothic melodrama, announced by the symbol of Rogozhin's burning eyes.[79] The implication that prose fiction is only capable of sustaining serious moral or philosophical engagement in a genre characterised by excess, hyperbole, and the fantastic is profoundly damaging to any suggestion of the viability of prospectus narrative. Indeed, the theme of the failed transaction, not just the failed gift, is central to *The*

Idiot: the auction for Nastasya Filippovna fails, Burdovsky's claim against Myshkin fails, Ippolit fails to commit suicide. All completion risks failure. Better, perhaps, to avoid defining value, or to revalue at a moment's notice, as the behaviour of Lisaveta Prokof'evna and Lebedev demonstrates. The motifs of *The Gambler*—iteration, rolling the dice again, speculation on constantly shifting values with unpredictable results—again become at once the hallmarks of credibility as a character and the foundations of narrative structure.

The Idiot bears the hallmarks of impetuous experimentation, from the failure to plan beyond the first book to the repeated problems in establishing the credibility of Myshkin's character on a consistent basis. *Diary of a Writer* is a more considered response to the dilemma. Its format explicitly allows prospectus text, where the author is able to assert and promote his own values, and ensures that the result is not capsized by the need to support a superstructure of fiction. It must, however, prove itself commercially by attracting subscribers, so it cannot divorce itself from reader reception, as the prospectus in miniature at the end of each issue reminds us. Despite the diary format, it can still publish prose fiction, just as its competitors do. Morson suggests that the ongoing nature of the debate from issue to issue is a form of response to the dangers of premature completion identified in *The Idiot*. The reader's approach to the text, "harvesting" items that catch his eye rather than proceeding sequentially from start to finish as in a single work of prose fiction, is also better able to reflect the discontinuous nature of observed reality.[80] But it is nonetheless clear that Dostoevsky enjoys a vehicle that allows him to assert his own values without direct contradiction or editorial intervention. Indeed, his position as his own editor places him above the discontinuity of which he writes, as the *déchiffreur* of society.

As a successful commercial venture, *Diary of a Writer* gives us some indication as to what readers valued—or at least as to what Dostoevsky thought readers valued—in the mid-1870s. In terms of subject matter, there is a clear concentration around the genre of the *fait divers*. The themes appear in both factual and fictional contexts, illustrated by the retelling of the Kornilova murder case, on which Dostoevsky comments at length in the October 1876 issue, as the story of "The Meek One" ("Krotkaya"), published in November.[81] This suggests that Dostoevsky assumed that in this respect the growing Russian readership would behave like that in France, where the importance of these themes as com-

mercial drivers had long been established, as much in Zola's contemporaneous novels as in the columns of the Parisian boulevard newspapers.
A further common ground appears in the fascination over issues of national identity, expressed throughout *Diary of a Writer* as Dostoevsky's
belief in the otherness of the Russian psyche and destiny.[82] The irony of
Dostoevsky using a theme so common in western European literature
to assert the distinctiveness of Russian culture simply serves to highlight
the hybrid nature of Dostoevsky's creation. The intellectualisation of
these themes, often through Dostoevsky's use of a narrator or protagonist whom he dubs the "paradoxalist" and whose role highlights the discontinuities of contemporary life, can also be seen as a recognition that
his two thousand to three thousand actual subscribers (perhaps six
thousand to seven thousand including newsstand sales) expected a hybrid diet of melodrama and intellectual debate. But Dostoevsky's paradoxalist is also a virtuoso debater who is demonstrably able to argue convincingly from any point of view.[83] The reader can never be quite sure
whether Dostoevsky is arguing for something he genuinely believes in
or simply replaying the reader's own prejudices to him or her as a commercial device. His defence of the alleged murderess Kairova, on the
grounds that the intention of another person is never fully knowable,
shows how this intellectual point of view can be combined with a prurient topic to create a fusion of the philosophical and the commercial.[84]
The success of *Diary of a Writer* demonstrated that this combination
worked within a journalistic format. Whether it would work as well in
the extended format of the novel was less clear. *The Brothers Karamazov*
is, I suggest, Dostoevsky's way of finding out.

How to Write a Novel?

Even in its preface, *The Brothers Karamazov* advertises its own status as
narrative. The very title of the preface, "From the Author" ("Ot avtora"),
reminds us of its creative origin. It takes the form of a direct address to
the reader. It lays claim to a format and a hero: a fictional biography *(zhiz-
neopisanie)* of Alyosha (13:7). It describes the work as a multiple narrative, two novels in one, "two stories 'within the essential unity of the
whole'": parallel biographies of this hero at different times of his life.[85]
The title of the novel itself echoes this sense of multiple narratives, of
brothers, plural. And the preface also forces us to engage with the text

as literary artefact. Who is this tongue-in-cheek "author" of the preface? Is this really the author at all? It serves to remind us that the reader has an active role in deciding textual value and, as the "author" admits, the ultimate sanction of closing the book: "Of course, nobody's obliged to do anything, you can always just close the book two pages into the first story and never open it again."[86] The story is offered, in part, as a discussion of the structural issues addressed in its own creation.

Its plot, too familiar to warrant much recapitulation, interweaves a series of stories in sharply contrasting genres. The locomotive is the courtroom drama of the murder of Fedor Pavlovich and the arrest, interrogation, and trial of his son Dmitry, at war with his father over his claimed inheritance and the entrepreneurial peasant girl they both covet, Grushenka. Alongside the courtroom drama runs the story of Dmitry's younger brother Alyosha, whose status as novice monk both links him to the traditional Russian literary genre of lives of the saints and simultaneously allows him to travel effortlessly among all the social classes of the provincial town where the drama is played out. His links to the local monastery and, in particular, to its most famous elder, Zosima, create an ethical and religious perspective within the narrative and allow Dostoevsky to explore the moral implications of the life choices that his characters make, including those of the monks themselves. The third brother, Ivan, adds a layer of psychological drama as his attempts to rationalise his relationship with his dysfunctional family and a world he sees as equally dysfunctional gradually fall apart. Finally, the story of Smerdyakov, the half brother to Fedor Pavlovich's three other sons, introduces elements of popular journalism: voyeurism as his upbringing as a servant provides an "upstairs-downstairs" perspective, mystery as his behind-the-scenes machinations unfold, and crime as the identity of the real murderer is eventually revealed.

Serialisation, too, creates multiple narratives. Publication took place in Mikhail Nikiforovich Katkov's *Russian Herald (Russkii vestnik)* in sixteen instalments over a twenty-three-month period from January 1879 to November 1880.[87] Four books (5, 8, 11, and 12) occupy two instalments. Breaks of a single month occurred in March, July, and December 1879; two-month breaks intervened on either side of the publication of book 10 in April 1880. Dostoevsky began writing in July 1878, and it is clear from the chronology of the notebooks for each chapter, as well as the records of composition from his correspondence, that composition and publication were broadly aligned, with each instalment being written shortly, sometimes very shortly, before the publication deadline.[88] Todd notes that each instalment was intended to be an artistic whole, with little recourse to the normal serial writer's devices of surprise or suspenseful endings.[89] The first instalment, in January 1879, is the only one to contain two books and the preface, and in doing so ensures that Dostoevsky's entire exposition of the creative process is uninterrupted.

The notebooks indicate a more orderly planning process than, for example, that of *The Idiot*. Belknap's analysis of the genesis of the novel reveals both how far some of its themes can be traced back through Dostoevsky's life, work, and reading and how developed the plot seems to have been by the time Dostoevsky came to write each book.[90] The notebooks are, by and large, not used to develop the overall shape of each book, as for earlier novels, but much more to work out individual scenes or fragments of dialogue that fitted into an overall canvas which, evidently, Dostoevsky saw no need to record. Nor are there many significant changes between the published text and the notebooks, with the exception of some omissions, generally to prevent the reader from solving the crime too quickly, a technique already developed in *Crime and Punishment*. The impression, reinforced by evidence of planning from Dostoevsky's correspondence, is that he had a fairly clear idea of the overall shape of the narrative before putting pen to paper, even if some of the detailed development and research had yet to take place. If, as I think, *The Brothers Karamazov* is in part an experiment in the creation of literary value, then it seems to have been a carefully planned one, and its architecture does indeed suggest just that.

The first serial instalment consists of a series of converging narratives in contrasting genres. As the preface advertises, the first book begins as a biography of the Karamazov family, describing origins and relationships in a relatively conventional manner that would not look out of place in a novel by Balzac or Dickens. Each brother comes equipped with his own genre. Dmitry's is the romantic, emphasised both in the biographical details given to us by the narrator in the first book and following his dramatic entry in the second. He is initially represented by the narrator as a stock romantic hero, complete with Lermontovian tags of soldierly derring-do in the Caucasus, duels, debts, and women (13:13). Fedor Pavlovich describes him as a character from Friedrich Schiller's

Die Räuber (13:61). Zosima's bow to him in the second book creates an aura of romantic mystery.

Ivan introduces a new genre, that of the intellectual essay in the pages of a Russian thick journal, when he summarises his arguments on church and state. It is easy for a modern reader to overlook the fact that the physical context of this instalment was the January edition of the *Russian Herald,* which contained essays on subjects as varied as the importance of woodland in classical mythology, the Eastern question, and student life in Germany, along with a poem by Maikov, a short story, and a play in four acts about a marriage arranged for money, in addition to the first part of *The Brothers Karamazov.*[91] The genre of Ivan's discourse, which we are even told he has previously published as an article in a similar periodical, must have been obvious to a contemporary reader.

When the narrator's biographical focus shifts to Alyosha, his entry into monastic life is also the cue for a genre shift towards hagiography, introduced through a chapter on the role of the church elders and pursued in the anecdotes from Zosima's life. The narratives converge on Fedor Pavlovich, who has his own genre, to which we shall return.

The main characters and genres are linked by two common themes: belief and inheritance, or, to rephrase in more literary terminology, credibility and posterity. The impetus to rephrase comes from the narrator himself. His role has been the subject of critical interpretations without end, too numerous to summarise here. Most overlook the simple fact that he reminds us that we are being told a story. His viewpoint, from local diarist limited by his own knowledge to omniscient author able to reveal the deepest feelings of his characters, shifts with growing frequency over the course of this first instalment. The shifts, which pass unnoticed at first but become more insistent at each iteration, have the effect of making the reader more aware of the diegetic medium.[92] His frequent references to literary intertexts—Shakespeare's Ophelia appears on the very first page (13:9)—to the fact that he is writing a novel, and to the existence of his readers (for example, 13:18) constantly remind us of the fictional frame. Narrative reality, he seems to imply, is the only sort that matters. "Dmitry Fedorovich hasn't yet come into existence" is the literal translation of Fedor Pavlovich's answer to a question about whether Dmitry has yet arrived: the phrasing of the response seems to be as much a commentary on his fictional realisation as on his observed presence.[93] The narrator continually asks us, at times even directly, to reflect on how the story is being told, on whether we find it credible, and, if so, on why we believe it.[94]

Belief and credibility are two sides of the same coin. The multiple narrative threads and different genres compete for credibility and insure the writer against the failure of any one. The gradual accretion of different modes of narration slowly makes the reader aware that the issue of determining credibility, or establishing a hierarchy of value, rests with him or her. To make the point clear, the narrative illustrates the difference between belief and credibility. The chapter describing the church elders illustrates belief by assertion, pure prospectus narrative. It depicts a society governed by values asserted by the elderhood: even the burial of a saint is impossible without his elder's permission (13:26). Narrative authority is absolute: this is Mikhail Mikhailovich Bakhtin's "authoritative word" in its purest form, and in Karamazovian terms Bakhtin even describes it as "the word of our fathers."[95] This form of belief is utterly secure in its assessment of its own value and seeks no external validation.

But it only attains credibility when validated by the recipient. The possibility of doubt implies the agency of the receiver in assessing a narrative. In an image that will recur when Ivan meets his devil, almost as a frame to the entire novel, the narrator evokes the figure of Doubting Thomas, who "believed only because he wanted to believe."[96] The two modalities are directly contrasted in the titles of the third and fourth chapters of book 2: "Peasant Women Believers" ("Veruyushchie baby") and "A Lady of Little Faith" ("Malovernaya dama"), which oppose the unquestioning faith of the peasants to Mme Khokhlakova's belief contingent on a verifiable return, prospectus value against auction value (13:41, 46). Ivan proposes a further alternative: belief based on a process of Euclidean logic, which recruits the power of reason and intellectual argument to render the process of belief credible, but here the archaic, biblical resonances of the title of the chapter, "It Will Be, It Will Be!" ("Budi, budi!"; 13:52), seem to imply, ironically, that this is simply a different kind of asserted value. This first instalment insistently asks the reader to reflect on whether any belief is genuinely independent of its reception, thus of the medium by which it arrives at the receiver. Or, in literary terms, does the way in which the story is told affect its credibility, and, if so, how?

Lasting credibility creates inheritable value in the shape of memories and narratives that travel between generations. In its simplest form, inheritance, financial, doctrinal, and artistic, is the basis of the plot of the novel. The Karamazov family has gathered at the monastery to find an environment in which it is possible to have a serious debate about Dmitry's inheritance claim. The narrative credibility of Dmitry's claim is thus measured in terms of its posterity value: the more credible the claim, the more it should be worth in securing his future. Its credibility is intimately linked to the mode of its expression: its value, the narrator tells us, has already been affected by the manner in which Dmitry has asserted it and the reception Fedor Pavlovich has accorded it (13:13). As readers, we are given too little information to form a view based on fact, so our own perception of right and wrong is swayed by the way in which the story is told. The notion that the best story, rather than any measure of factual accuracy or observed reality, will win the contest for lasting value is fundamental to the construction of *The Brothers Karamazov.*

Other forms of discourse are also shown as having enduring worth. The word of an elder has value literally beyond the grave (13:26). Zosima is represented as on the verge of death and capable of creating a lasting heritage for his monastery (13:26). The narrator implies that Alyosha's faith is linked to his mother's memory (13:19). Belknap makes the case for the importance of memory as a form of inheritance in the novel generally.[97] Literary devices themselves can indicate inheritance: quotations and literary intertexts are both expressions of posterity value through memory. Nina Perlina's examination of the role of quotation in *The Brothers Karamazov* goes even further in suggesting that Dostoevsky's system of quotation establishes a hierarchy of asserted narrative value in which the word of the Holy Writ takes precedence.[98]

And yet throughout this first instalment runs a challenge to all asserted values and hierarchies. It is represented by Fedor Pavlovich and by the genre of the commercial boulevard newspaper. It is as much a challenge to how the story is told as to what the story tells. It is expressed by the disruption of the narrative itself. The theme first appears as part of the plot. Fedor Pavlovich is depicted as an agent of disruption within his own community and family, as the narrator lingeringly describes over the first four chapters. His disruptive behaviour, though, is ironically a crucial part of why readers keep reading. The themes of commercial fiction, sex, crime, and money dominate his biography. The narrator's juicy scandal-mongering and speculation is both a biographical detail and a commercial device to persuade readers not to put the book down, as the author of the preface had feared.

Fedor Pavlovich's representation is full of disruptive devices. He is described as a clown *(shut)*, a traditional figure of disruption, which Bakhtin associates with the concept of the testing of an idea and its carrier (13:34).[99] He forces the reader to recognise that narratives can lie. "I made it up to spice up the story," he admits, in yet another reminder that narrative credibility has nothing to do with truth or authenticity.[100] He drives a wedge between belief and credibility. Why should we believe in hell, he asks, if the devil can't even get his story right? If sinners are hung on hooks, then there must be a ceiling to hang them from, yet none of the stories about hell mentions the ceiling (13:24). His discourse jettisons both Ivan's logical progressions and Zosima's scriptural assertions in favour of a narrative that relies on graphic imagery, shock value, and an appeal to a common denominator of public taste.

In short, they are fictional faits divers, often referring explicitly to sources in the newspaper journalism of the boulevard newspapers. He twice calls Maksimov by the name von Sohn (13:33, 75): the two episodes bracket the second book and stand as an emblem of this compulsive vein of narrative. We eventually find out that a newspaper article had reported the murder of a man named von Sohn whose body had been sent in the luggage van of a train from Saint Petersburg to Moscow in a crate. "And while they were nailing him down, exotic dancers sang songs and played on the gusla, or rather the fortepranco."[101] The relevance of the anecdote to Maksimov is never established. But the combination of newspaper fait divers, the criminal, the ghoulish, the exotic, and the comic failure of the pun, in Russian as well as in my translation, requires the reader to focus on the mode of transmission of the narrative. This is a commercial register, as the quotations and imagery from the newspaper world confirm, which offers a different bill of fare to its readers. It challenges established concepts of literary value and disrupts conventional hierarchies of literary merit, just as its content disrupts hierarchies of belief. It is explicitly represented as a literature of the future, the publishing world that Ivan expects Rakitin to join, rejecting his monastic novitiate in favour of the editorship of a thick journal. Ivan's sarcastic formula for Rakitin's commercial success, introduced in this first instalment but heralding a theme that will follow the novel throughout its length, is to play back the readers' own values to them, publishing the journal, once he had obtained control of it, "definitely from a liberal and atheist standpoint, with a bit of a socialist tendency and even perhaps a lick of socialism proper, but keeping an ear to the ground, which really means keeping a foot in both camps and one step ahead of idiots."[102] Literary values, it implies, may be changing.

The "scandal" scene with which the second book ends is thus not merely chapter title and plot description; it is also a challenge to conventional literary judgement. It asks the readers of this serialised instalment to consider whether they buy the story, to examine how they assign value to text, and to question the relevance of received methods of valuation. It implants a suspicion that the compulsion of the commercial narrative vein that has kept the plot moving to this climax could also be a potent challenge to a new generation of readers' tolerance of sustained intellectual debate of the sort represented by Ivan and Zosima. It suggests that, beyond the reach of the thick journal that carries the story, a new readership may be developing, that of the boulevard newspaper, which may have quite different criteria. It seems significant that Dmitry's melodramatic irruption into the text and the narrative disruption that Fedor Pavlovich symbolises have so much in common. Perhaps Dmitry's real inheritance from his father will prove to be literary rather than pecuniary?

The Novel as Prospectus

The first serial instalment had implicitly posed a series of fundamental questions about the type of narrative that contemporary readers would buy, both literally and commercially, and about whether future readerships would react in the same way. Novels clearly had to be commercially viable, not just for the good of the writer but because this was likely to be the only way to persuade publishers to target a mass readership. But "dumbing down" to reach a broader readership was an unnecessary price to pay, as Dostoevsky's commercial success with *Diary of a Writer*'s idiosyncratic blend of intellectual debate and populism had indicated. Achieving the same success in a work of fiction required a different approach but offered the prize of far greater posterity value than the ephemeral impact of journalism. The remainder of the novel is, I think, a series of carefully orchestrated experiments in varying the proportions and natures of the commercial and the intellectual to discover whether a point of equilibrium exists that could maximise both current and possible future value. This is, indeed, a novel about how to write a novel.

The starting point is to establish whether any form of asserted value is compatible with the novelistic format. Dostoevsky chooses a series of genres traditionally associated with the transmission of a message from author to recipient and, over the course of four entire books, explores whether any of these can coexist with a commercially viable work of fiction. The "headline" genres he selects are confession, a traditional vehicle for the assertion of personal belief; melodrama, which relies on predictable audience reception of hyperbolic emotion; parable, where the narrative is expected to carry a message; and hagiography, which assumes a shared set of beliefs between author and recipient. In their different ways, all are experiments in "prospectus" narrative. The narrator of each asserts the value of his story as something that can validly be determined by him, even if others do not accept his view. Narrative structure and content combine to form an extensive and multifaceted investigation of the novel's ability to function as prospectus while at the same time retaining the ability to tell a compelling story.

Each experiment forms the central part of a separately serialised episode in the *Russian Herald*. The confessional genre is represented by Dmitry's confession to Alyosha in book 3, "Sladostrastniki," usually translated as "The Sensualists" or "The Voluptuaries." It appeared as the second episode in February 1879, followed by a one-month pause. The various stories grouped under the title "Nadryvy," or "Lacerations," in book 4 experiment with different levels of melodrama and appeared in the April edition. Ivan's philosophical exchange with Alyosha in book 5, "Pro and Contra" ("Pro i Kontra"), uses stories of the suffering of children and Ivan's legend of the Grand Inquisitor as parables to investigate the authority of asserted narratives. The book, which was divided into two parts with "Rebellion" ("Bunt") in the first and "The Grand Inquisitor" ("Veliky Inkvizitor") occupying the whole of the second (in a single, immense paragraph as the result of a printer's error), appeared in the May and June editions, again followed by a one-month break. Finally, Alyosha's life of Zosima in book 6, "A Russian Monk" ("Russkii inok"), is an experiment in hagiography and was printed in the August issue. So for seven entire months the readership was required to follow Dostoevsky through his laboratory of narrative value.

A key image that helps to illustrate Dostoevsky's investigative technique occurs at the opening of "Rebellion." Ivan refers to the story of Saint John the Merciful *(Ioann Milostivy)*, celebrated as a reformed parricide who ended his life atoning for his crimes by acts of great contrition and self-abasement: "I read somewhere that some saint or other, called St John the Merciful, when a famished and frozen traveller came to him begging for warmth, lay down with him in bed, wrapped him in his arms and started to breathe straight into his mouth, which was festering and foul from some terrible disease."[103]

Terras notes that the image probably comes from Gustave Flaubert's *St. Julien l'Hospitalier,* translated into Russian by Ivan Turgenev in 1877, the same year as its publication in France.[104] Like the two other stories of Flaubert's *Trois contes,* the narrative is as much about the interrelationship between genre and credibility as it is about the moral issues raised by the tale.[105] Flaubert's image, derived from a stained-glass window in a local Normandy church, depicts a saint, reformed from a childhood of sadism, butchery, and the eventual murder of both his parents, achieving epiphany by embracing and warming with his own body a dying leper who turns into an image of Christ:

> Julien removed his clothes then, naked as on the day he was born, lay down again in the bed. Against his thigh he felt the leper's skin, colder than a snake, as rough as a rasp. . . .
> [He] covered the entirety of the leper's body, mouth to mouth, breast to breast.
> Then the leper gripped him tight; eyes shining with the clarity of the stars, hair splaying into rays of sunshine; breath sweetening with the perfume of roses. A cloud of incense rose from the fire, the waves sang . . . the roof disappeared, the firmament unfurled itself, and Julien rose towards the blue void, face to face with Our Saviour Jesus Christ who was taking him to heaven.[106]

The image contains almost all the themes Dostoevsky investigates. It is part hagiography by virtue of its received religious interpretation, which presumes predictable reader responses. It raises key philosophical and theological issues of the "cost" of sin and the "price" of redemption. It explores the limits of melodrama in figures of polarisation and hyperbole, as well as the registers of pathos and sentimentality. And finally it employs all the commercial techniques of the fait divers in its outright sensationalism, shock value, and voyeuristic titillation. Flaubert's description of the embrace is meticulously constructed, grotesquely detailed, and sexually compromised.

It is also a typically Flaubertian experiment in narrative subversion. It employs devices of conventional religious hagiography. At the same time, it seems to push the graphic excess of its description as if to test the limits of reader tolerance. At the diegetic level, it asks whether the reader is still able to believe the story when pushed to these limits. Are we repulsed by some unwritten infringement of literary taste in the sexual prism through which a traditionally religious image is viewed? Or is this justified by an appeal to codified religious symbolism, where the signification of the symbol overwhelms any digressive signal from its mode of representation? At a philosophical level, it asks whether the ethical and moral issues are in some way linked to a genre of excess: does the reader's ability to engage with a moral debate depend on the mode of its representation? And if the fictional narrative depends on excess to facilitate the process of suspending disbelief, does this undermine in equal measure the relevance of the ethical debate to a more everyday representation of reality? The image is simultaneously moral ideal and compulsive viewing, situated so precisely on the border where compulsion meets repulsion as to call both its philosophical and its commercial value into doubt.

Dostoevsky seems to experiment, similarly, with different "strengths" of fiction in his four experiments. In each case he seems to be asking at what point the credibility of the narrative as fiction breaks down. The concept of "excess" is one to which he had returned time and again, in the tipping point between reason and fantasy in *The Double,* in the philosophical hamster wheel of the underground man, in Svidrigailov's dream and subsequent suicide in *Crime and Punishment,* in the point at which small-town posturing leads to murder and suicide in *The Devils (Besy),* in the metaphysical confluence of Myshkin and Rogozhin when in the Gothic reaches of the latter's house. In *The Idiot* a point of equilibrium does seem to be achievable within which narrative can expand to encompass a rich philosophical vein. But, as we have seen, this seems to coincide with the point of maximum fictional "strength," the furthest extent of Gothic melodrama, as the two meet over Nastasya Filippovna's murdered body in the cell-like alienation of a Gothic set. The implication is that the medium of fiction can only carry the kind of intellectual weight Dostoevsky seems to crave when its method of transmission is least suited to such an attempt.

The link that so fascinated Dostoevsky between the content and style that sold newspapers and the intellectual weight they were able to sustain was not a new subject. The story of the French murderer Pierre François Lacenaire, the archetype of the educated criminal who wrote his memoirs while awaiting execution, recurs as both a model for Raskolnikov and a point of reference for Ippolit in *The Idiot* (8:317). It illustrates the point that apparently incompatible genre and content did not necessarily lead to reader rejection and could still form the basis of serious psychological analysis. Alex de Jonge comments thus: "[Lacenaire] wrote in a stilted, old-fashioned rhetoric of sensibility, which would have rendered his work perfectly comprehensible to a contemporary of Rousseau. Lacenaire uses this utterly inappropriate code to provide the most matter-of-fact account of his crimes"—but that had clearly not impeded either the commercial success of Lacenaire's memoirs or their relevance as an intellectual discussion of the motivation of murder.[107]

In the October and November 1876 editions of *Diary of a Writer*, Dostoevsky reports, comments on, and then fictionalises the story of a destitute seamstress who has committed suicide by jumping from a window while holding an icon.[108] The process is revealing. Dostoevsky's initial journalistic commentary highlights less the religious conundrum of a suicide holding an icon than it does the compulsive, and commercially powerful, recurrence of the image in his memory. The account in "The Meek One," which occupies the entire November edition, is an expression in prose fiction of this recurrence in recognition of the fact that it can, on its own, sell an entire journal issue. It, too, explores the limits of reader reception. The story imagines the suicide from the point of view of her husband, justifying to the reader his abusive behaviour, which had led to her suicide. Dostoevsky, writing the preface to the story, calls it a "fantastic tale" *(fantastichesky rasskaz)* and explains that the fantastic comes not from the content but from the unusual and innovative position of the narrator: "And so it is this assumption of a stenographer recording everything (and whose account I simply polished) that I call the fantastic element of my story."[109] The novel narratorial perspective is vital to the commercial success of the story, where it serves to distinguish this version from the previous reportage and to create a new hook by exploiting the reader's reaction to the husband's attempts to justify himself. At the same time, it broadens the psychological and ethical debate by exploring the link between domestic abuse and suicide. It appeared that combining commercial drivers with intellectual content could, under the right circumstances, be made to work.

Confession

Dostoevsky was familiar with numerous variants of the genre of literary confession, from Nikolai Mikhailovich Karamzin's short story "My Confession" ("Moya ispoved'") to Jean-Jacques Rousseau's *Les Confessions.* Confession is a complex genre, as Richard Terdiman points out in his introduction to an article on Alfred de Musset's *Confession d'un enfant du siècle.* If it is considered as an act of expiation, then the very process of narration immortalises that which it seeks to expunge. A liturgical process becomes an act of literary performance. The effect of this, he argues, is to relativise the sacramental role of confession, implying that an assertion of faith is only as good as the skill with which it is told.[110] Miller's analysis of the influence of Rousseau and *Les Confessions* on the character of Stepan Trofimovich in *The Devils* points up the link when she talks about how Dostoevsky combines "men and literary characters . . . begotten from ideas" with narrative devices reliant on sexual taboos and voyeurism.[111] How the story is told is what matters. Dmitry's confession highlights precisely the importance of the means of narrative delivery. The confession is divided into three chapters that contrast three narrative approaches, identified by chapter titles that refer directly to literary registers or devices and that together become a formulation of an authorial strategy for the subsequent role Dmitry plays in the novel.

The first, the "Confession of a Burning Heart. In Verse" ("Ispoved' goryachego serdtsa. V stikhakh"), invites us to consider Dmitry's confession from the perspective of a discourse in literary language. His performance, a borrowed mix of romantic poets and biblical imagery, parodies his attempt to lay claim to the genre. From the very start, the novelistic contrivance of Dmitry's coincidental meeting with Alyosha suggests that his confession, too, may be more artefact than accident. His narrative starts off as a rambling, drunken circumnavigation of the point: "Well, you can see for yourself how this could all end up as some sort of natural disaster. I'm here in secret and I've got a secret to keep. I'll get to the explanation, but because it's a secret I suddenly start talking all secretively, like some sort of whispering idiot, for no reason at all."[112] Unable to express himself adequately, he borrows the philosophical and emotional vocabulary of others in quotations (and misquotations) from Nikolai Alekseevich Nekrasov, Pushkin, Goethe, the Bible, and, at length, Schiller.[113]

Even the most apparently intense moments of this confession are ambiguous. Is this a credible literary character speaking, or the novelist's own ideas in the mouth of a *porte-parole?* "And right in the middle of this disgrace I suddenly strike up a hymn. I may be cursed, I may be base and vile, but let me kiss the hem of the mantle which envelopes my God; though in the same moment I consort with the devil, yet am I thy son, O Lord, and love thee and experience that happiness without which the world can neither exist nor continue."[114] Dmitry's character is too little developed by this point in the novel for the reader to resolve the ambiguity definitively. When Dmitry finally comes to the point, which he expresses through a complicated analogy to a warring alliance of Sodom and the Madonna, both the reader and Alyosha have difficulty in understanding what he is getting at, partly because he has not yet explained the context of the various religious allusions he makes, and partly because we still have no means of knowing whether this is genuine profundity or the wisdom of a drunk and, if the former, Dmitry's own words or an author putting an argument into the mouth of a character unsuited to the role.

Alyosha, as perpetual recipient of the narratives of others, stands proxy for the reader. As the novel progresses, his role as reader will become more complex, since he will not only receive narratives but also transmit them onward. The process of onward transmission transforms his role from that of reader to that of an actual editor, in ironic juxtaposition to Rakitin's so far unrealised ambitions to edit a thick journal in Saint Petersburg. The edited narrative, of necessity, will assume its own identity, separate from the original, introducing the possibility for ambiguity in even as apparently trustworthy and transparent a vessel as Alyosha. Just as Karamazov blood places him in a hierarchy that ultimately leads to the excesses of Dmitry, even if on the bottom rung, so his participation in the process of narrative will eventually implicate him in the failure of the "authoritative" word, the ability of narrative to carry a single meaning, prospectus.

For now, though, Alyosha is simply the recipient of Dmitry's narrative, in the same position as the reader. His status as a novice monk, and Dostoevsky's presentation of his character thus far, inclines us to consider his critical verdict seriously. His reaction to Dmitry's Schillerian rapture is complete silence. The jury is out, but the possibility of incipient reader indigestion remains on the table. The swift shift to a more contemporary short story format, styled a confession "in anecdotes," suggests that Dmitry's pretended kinship to the romantic heroes of Schiller, Pushkin, and Mikhail Yurevich Lermontov is as suspect as his attempt to borrow their genre.

Dostoevsky calls the second chapter a confession "in anecdotes" *(v anekdotakh)*. The genre takes us back to Fedor Pavlovich's method of narrative progression, as well as to the narrative register that opens the third book. Its subject is a commercial transaction—the exchange of Katerina Ivanovna's honour for her father's rescue from financial misappropriation. Readers are attracted not by intellectual debate but by a titillating mix of sexual and financial indiscretion, combined with a voyeuristic fascination with the lower classes in the story that opens this book of the rape of Lizaveta Smerdyashchaya, made all the more alluring by overtones of religious mania. This suddenly sharper, more pacy style, with its contemporary intertexts to Paul de Kock (13:93) and its focus on sex and money, relies on the use of narrative and plot devices well understood by readers and carefully signposted by these genre markers, which appear to act as interpretative instructions. The 5,000 rouble bill of exchange that is to pay for Katerina Ivanovna's honour is hidden in a French dictionary—a pointer to the values of Balzac and the roman-feuilleton.[115] Dmitry's fluency as a narrator contrasts pointedly with his inability to express himself in the preceding chapter and suggests that this prose genre is far better suited as a mode of transmission for his narrative to the reader. Significantly, Alyosha listens "extremely attentively."[116]

As we are already beginning to realise, whenever the narrative returns to Dmitry from now on, it will assume "commercial" characteristics—pace, sensation, melodrama. The title of the final part, "Head over Heels" ("Vverkh pyatami," perhaps better translated as "Upside Down" or "Topsy-Turvy" to avoid the English-only implication of ". . . in love"), suggests that uncertainty and suspense are part of this genre too. Katerina Ivanovna has suddenly become rich, by a novelistic inversion characteristic of the plots of Eugène Sue, Paul de Kock, or, indeed, Dostoevsky himself, who likens it to something from the *Arabian Nights*.[117]

She may or may not love Dmitry, or Ivan (13:9). Dmitry may or may not have intended to defraud her but his status as romantic hero is clearly compromised (13:101). He may or may not be serious about murdering his father and rival for Grushenka (13:103). Dmitry may not inherit financially, but he is already the legatee of his father's narrative leitmotif in the shape of this commercially tagged, disrupted narrative. Alyosha begins at last to show some emotion in his responses.

The implication is that confession has had to be recast as a genre. Its traditional incarnation as a romantic expression of individualism has been reinterpreted as a more contemporary variant in which the commercial drivers of the boulevard newspaper have all but overwhelmed its ability to convey the message of high moral purpose with which Dmitry starts out. The theme of inversion and challenge is repeated in Smerdyakov's story, which follows. He too rejects the literary heritage that he is offered, in the shape of classics from Fedor Pavlovich's library (13:105–106), just as he goes on to reject the standard biblical interpretations of the nature of belief (13:109). Traditional values can no longer be accepted without question: even Ivan and Alyosha's dispute about the existence of God and everlasting life degenerates into a sterile "does / doesn't" exchange that mocks the very possibility of intellectual debate (13:113) and, inevitably, ends in fisticuffs (13:117) and a catfight (13:127). As Alyosha returns to the monastery, even the monks are shown inventing fictitious confessions (13:132). Received values can no longer be relied on, but the new genre of action, sexual tension, and money certainly maintains narrative momentum.

Melodrama

Book 4, "Lacerations," was published in the April edition of the *Russian Herald* after a one-month pause. During this gap, the first reactions to *The Brothers Karamazov,* both critical and commercial, were becoming apparent. Dostoevsky writes to Viktor Feofilovich Putsykovich on March 12, 1879, "*The Brothers Karamazov* is causing a furore here—at court, with the general public, at public readings, as you can see, by the way, from the papers (*The Voice, Rumour,* etc.)."[118] Invitations from the imperial family and public readings followed.[119] Not all the papers shared the same view, though, and as serialisation progressed, it would become more and more apparent that popular success did not imply universal critical acclaim. Both Todd and Terras make the point that these contemporary critics were hardly judging the novel on its own merits. "In summary, then, contemporary reviewers sought to find in Dostoevsky's novel no more and no less than a confirmation of their own views. Few of them were satisfied," is how Terras puts it.[120] It would rapidly become evident that the commercial value of the text was less volatile than its critical value, a situation that probably still holds true today. It would also become apparent that the early critics looked more for reflections of their own views in the text, rather than at what the text actually said, a situation that is frequently also true today.

So the fourth book, and first instalment of part 2, can be seen as a continuation of the process of experimenting with different registers of narrative that we have seen in the first part. Its Russian title, "Nadryvy," has been translated as "Lacerations," "Heartache," "Crack-up," and "Strains."[121] In the text the word is also translated as "hysterics." Belknap's sensitive analysis of this book suggests that *nadryv* is strongly allied, in its drive towards excess, to the concept of buffoonery, which characterises Fedor Pavlovich, but with an overlay of authenticity that inverts buffoonery's tendency to the base into a quest for dignity.[122] The concept of the exploration of excess, symbolised by the legend of Saint John the Merciful, is intimately linked with its role in genre. The different translations of the title of the book suggest at least four different registers, from the potentially tragic ("lacerations"), through the sentimental ("heartache"), to the psychological and possibly even comic ("crack-up" / "hysterics").

The common theme is that of melodrama, a genre that enables excess to play both a commercial and a philosophical role. Christopher Prendergast argues that melodrama uses its hallmark polarisation of virtue and evil to create a more legible universe in which cause and effect become easier to anticipate.[123] His argument could be extended into a discussion of the commercial attractions of the genre as one that generates predictable reactions from readers and, thereby, reliable subscription income for publishers, as Sue had effectively demonstrated with his *Mystères de Paris*. Peter Brooks suggests, in his analysis of Balzac's use of melodrama, that in a desacralized world where all received readings are open to challenge, this legibility, revealed only at the apex of excess, provides fleeting moments where signification is restored and, by implication, the moral compass can relocate true north. "Melodrama is a necessary mode of ethical and emotional conceptualisation and dramatization in the forms and for these writers [Balzac, Dickens, Dostoevsky, and Henry James], and only in direct, unembarrassed confrontation of the melodramatic element do they yield their full ambition and meaning."[124] But just this experiment had previously led to narrative failure in *The Idiot,* where melodrama did indeed create an atmosphere in which an ethical message could be suggested in the Gothic sanctum of Rogozhin's house, but where the very dissociation of this setting from the remainder of the action of the novel created a dislocation that affected the integrity of the novel's construction and the relevance of the ethical proposition in equal measure.

We can, perhaps, view this book as an investigation into the literary role of melodramatic excess, this time in carefully moderated doses. The series of anecdotes that constitutes the chapter all represent excess in various guises. Ferapont tries to cast out devils only he can see. Ilyusha, overreacting to playground humiliation, bites Alyosha's finger. The Khokhlakov family provides comic relief in a permanent state of near hysteria. Katerina Ivanovna pledges herself to Dmitry while, we are given to understand, secretly loving Ivan. Snegirev tramples charity underfoot. All of these individual narratives frame more serious discourses. Ferapont's rantings accompany Zosima's last sermon; Ilyusha's stone throwing finally gives Alyosha a voice; Lise's "natural" love for Alyosha is compared to the self-centred attachments of Katerina Ivanovna; Snegirev's tantrums highlight Ilyusha's suffering. It is as though Dostoevsky is trialling various blends of melodrama with different weights of intellectual content. Here intellectual content is suggested, rather than brought to the foreground, and is the more effective for being better integrated. The narratives incorporate many commercial features: they are fast paced and vivid, and they avoid significant digression or expansion. They serve to build tension in expectation of a crisis to come: as the title hints, these are lacerations, not yet murder.

By and large, the combination seems to work at this moderate level of intensity. There are some hints, though, that the conflict has not been entirely resolved. All the stories are told to either Alyosha or Mme Khokhlakova, or both, who sometimes also participate in the action, and sometimes simply listen. Their responses are an interesting guide. Alyosha, our narrative barometer, has trouble remembering all of Zosima's sermon (13:135), whereas he has no difficulty recalling the events of Ferapont's appearance (13:141). The chapter title, "Father Ferapont" rather than "Zosima's Last Sermon," suggests that Dostoevsky also suspected which track his reader would follow.

Mme Khokhlakova, an avid consumer of the emotional excesses of others, rejects any attempt at intellectualisation, simplifies everything, and categorises events repeatedly into genre buckets of comedy or tragedy (13:150). Both listen to Katerina Ivanovna's agonising between Ivan and Dmitry. Alyosha responds to the substance of her dilemma and offers his reading of the situation (that she secretly loves Ivan, not Dmitry; 13:159). But excess confuses him and, ironically, upsets rather than confirms his moral compass: "He couldn't love passively, and once involved he immediately set about trying to help. . . . But instead of a fixed objective there was nothing but murk and mess. 'Hysterics, heartache'—that was the word which had just been uttered. But what on earth was he to make of these hysterics and heartache? He didn't even understand the first word in the whole tangled mess."[125] His asserted judgement is certainly rejected by Katerina Ivanovna and by Ivan, even if the reader may suspect that Dostoevsky would like us to take it as a perceptive prophecy. Mme Khokhlakova, by contrast, responds to the symptoms, visibly enjoys Katerina Ivanovna's emotional distress, and generally reacts as the reader of a boulevard newspaper might, seeking the voyeuristic pleasure of a good read about other people's problems. Katerina Ivanovna has *nadryvy;* Mme Khoklakhova calls them *isterika* (13:159 versus 161). There seems to be a clear sense not just that different readers find different things in the same narrative but that the narrative must also find a way of coping with all these different requirements.

Judging the impact of narrative can, however, be difficult. The story of Snegirev and his son begins an experimental journey into another form of melodramatic excess, that of the sentimental. It seems to ask whether intensifying the level of melodrama, of excess, leads to greater predictability of reader reaction. Dostoevsky forces the pathos, to the extent that the latter parts of this episode begin to resemble scenes from *Insulted and Injured (Unizhennye i oskorblennye),* such as that in which Nelly, like Snegirev, also refuses charity (4:219–220). He labels Snegirev with a leitmotif of excess in the shape of his straggly beard, described as a washrag *(mochalka),* which Dmitry has earlier pulled and which now encapsulates the extent of his debasement and humiliation (13:164, 165, 169). The very point of the leitmotif is that it depends on a preprogrammed reception, capable of being repeated on command by the author. On one level this clearly works: Snegirev's character is pitiful and rebarbative in equal measure and uses the proven technique developed in *Notes from the Underground* to pique the reader's curiosity by the volatility of his responses. The more unpredictable the character, it seems, the more predictable the reader response.

There is, though, a parallel sense that at another more reflective level, conventional expectations of reception are not to be trusted. Snegirev accepts, then repulses, Alyosha's charity, but he does so in a way that leads Alyosha to think that he is simply paving the way for later acceptance (13:175). But is Alyosha's conclusion right, or just a rather smug presumption about the acuity of his perception? Snegirev may, indeed, later accept the money, but his actions do not seem to us as premeditated as Alyosha assumes. And are Alyosha's motives pure, or is he, too, trying to buy off trouble for his brother? For readers of detail, Alyosha's credibility has already come under suspicion. He tells Snegirev that the 200 roubles he is offering come from Katerina Ivanovna and have nothing to do with Dmitry. This is not, in fact, strictly true. Dmitry has lent 5,000 roubles to Katerina Ivanovna. When she inherits, she repays him in total 4,800 roubles. She needed only 4,500 roubles to save her father, so repaid 300 roubles immediately to Dmitry out of the 5,000 roubles bill of exchange, net of 200 roubles negotiation fees, and the remaining 4,500 roubles on receiving her inheritance. The outstanding 200 roubles were apparently never repaid so, ironically, in a sense the money Alyosha offers to Snegirev did come from Dmitry, despite Alyosha's denials. Whether consciously or not, Alyosha is not always as dependable as he seems, either as a reader or as a projector of narrative.

"Lacerations" seems experimentally to anticipate the response of the contemporary literary market. The commercial characteristics of this series of experiments in melodrama appeal, on a broadly predictable basis, to any readership represented by Mme Khokhlakova. Alyosha's reactions suggest that not only is he also swayed by the same textual devices, but when he engages with the more intellectual or philosophical dimension of the narrative, his responses are less trustworthy.

Parable

The combination of an enthusiastic public reception and the suggestion in book 4 that some sort of equilibrium between the commercial and the intellectual might be attainable seems to have encouraged Dostoevsky to push the experiment to a new level. Book 5 proposes a narrative that dramatizes a philosophical debate, through Ivan's "Rebellion" and "The Grand Inquisitor." The title of the book, "Pro and Contra," implies the context of a debate and a trial. Dostoevsky's intentions, as expressed in his correspondence, appear consistent with the idea that this is some sort of experiment in the ability of fiction to carry a significant philosophical charge. A letter to Nikolai Alekseevich Lyubimov in May 1879 describes its concept in terms of the depiction of abstract ideas—atheism, anarchy, and social disintegration: "The thought behind [the book], as you will see from the text I've sent you, is to portray out-and-out atheism and the concept that the modern age in Russia is being wrecked by a younger generation completely detached from reality, and anarchism alongside the atheism."[126] A further letter in June describes the structure of a response, in the shape of Zosima's last words.[127] At the same time it was becoming clear that the scale of the experiment was greater than originally envisaged: book 5 stretched over two instalments, in May and June; book 6 would not appear until August; and in early July Dostoevsky writes to his editor to give him the news that the entire novel will now extend into the whole first quarter of 1880.[128] The need to keep readers on board for an extended period was becoming more acute.

The power of Ivan's argument, on which critics agree who rarely see eye to eye elsewhere, owes much to the manner of its transmission. Dostoevsky carefully blends intellectual argument with commercial device. Like Dmitry's earlier confession, Ivan's confession to Alyosha in "Rebellion" is couched in a series of anecdotes that take the form of parables by virtue of their association with a projected philosophical or ethical viewpoint. The subject matter of the six anecdotes is all related to suffering inflicted on those who cannot defend themselves, in particular children: atrocities inflicted by Turkish soldiers on enemy children; the execution of a murderer after his conversion to Christianity and repentance; a tale from Nekrasov about a peasant beating a horse; two stories about parental child abuse; and a final anecdote that Ivan remembers as being from an old archival collection but that had actually appeared much more recently in the very periodical in which *The Brothers Karamazov* was being published, about a boy hunted down for sport by dogs (13:197–201).[129] They recall the similar series of interpolated narratives in *The Idiot* with which Myshkin stakes his claim to fictional substance and take the form of a similar claim by Ivan, who has so far featured hardly at all in the narrative since the second chapter, to literary credibility.[130] The very presence of the anecdotes in the text seems to be a literary contrivance, a set-piece scene engineered to raise key philosophical or moral issues. They are literary artefacts and are framed by allusions to this status.

The reference to Saint John the Merciful, and intertext to Flaubert's *St Julien,* introduces them and, as I have previously noted, opens an enquiry into the role of excess in attracting or repelling readers. In contrast to Dmitry's borrowings from the romantic canon, Ivan borrows from newspapers, and openly admits as much (13:199). Dostoevsky's correspondence explicitly refers to this as a device to enhance the relationship between abstract argument and reality: "Everything my heroes say in the text I sent to you is based in reality. All the stories about children really happened and were reported in newspapers—I can even show you where. I didn't invent any of it."[131] But despite this apparent abjuration of authorial manipulation, Ivan's anecdotes use the familiar stylistic tricks of the press to create impact—sentimentality, sensationalism, iteration, hyperbole, melodrama. John Jones calls Dostoevsky's handling of the source material "parajournalistic" and points out how he has revised the story of the hunted boy to focus on the boy rather than his mother, as the notebooks indicate.[132] The simplified rhetoric of the journalistic anecdote, the immediacy of the fait divers, and the appeal to emotion over intellect prove to be powerful tools in asserting Ivan's prospectus. Dostoevsky's notes for the chapter refer to a quest for the sensational in literature and cite a potent literary precedent: "bestial depravity, with all its consequences, to the point of cruelty, to the point of crime, to the point of the Marquis de Sade."[133] The power of the narrative lends force to Ivan's argument and shows how a deft combination of journalistic technique and ethically charged material can, at one level, support a philosophical proposition.

Such intertexts, however, are not just an indication of Dostoevsky's desire to dramatise a philosophical debate. They reveal an underlying ambiguity. Just as they create a sense of narrative drive, so, in equal measure, they become an ironic commentary on Ivan's need to resort to these devices of excess and melodrama to convey an intellectual point. The reader—or at least this reader—continually asks whether the com-

pulsion to keep reading does not stem more from the strength of the anecdote than from any engagement with the moral debate. Fiction—at
least in this genre—simultaneously transmits and infects philosophy.

Dostoevsky seems to be well aware of this conundrum, as he exploits
it himself in Ivan's self-reflexive analysis of narrative value in "The
Grand Inquisitor." Ivan's presentation emphasises its claims to literary
status: the narrative is labelled a *poema,* and he adds a genre signpost
and claim to literary value by comparing it to the opening of Victor Hugo's *Notre-Dame de Paris* (13:204). Even his dismissal of the story as "the
stupid work of a stupid student,"[134] and his introduction, which highlights its pretentiousness and derivative origins, have the opposite effect:
his self-deprecation is contradicted by the scale and evident importance
of the encounter in the novel (13:204–205).

In contrast to the authentic prospectus of Ivan's rebellion, this is an
experiment in promoting a series of false prospectuses. The Grand Inquisitor himself knows that his projected altruism conceals covert tyr-
anny (13:212). For both Ivan and the Grand Inquisitor, therefore, the
credibility of their narratives to the intended recipients is crucial. A key
plank of the Grand Inquisitor's argument is that man follows credible
stories, not real religion: "If man once rejects miracle, he will simultaneously reject God, for man seeks not God but miracles."[135] The Grand
Inquisitor plans to achieve power through a projected narrative of such
strength as to convince the majority of humanity, even though he is
aware of its falseness. Ivan also tries to convince Alyosha by the power
of narrative, despite his reservations about the effectiveness of the medium. Dostoevsky, too, is experimenting with a new narrative variant
as a vehicle for a far more dense ethical debate than he has previously
attempted in the novel, and the genre he chooses for his experiment is
that of full-strength melodrama.

The three qualities that, the Grand Inquisitor claims, underpin his
philosophy are precisely those of successful melodrama: miracle, mystery, and authority, or, to retranslate in more literary terminology, fantasy, suspense, and authorial control. Dostoevsky is simultaneously
writing a narrative describing the attempt by the Grand Inquisitor to
seize control of his fictional universe and exploring whether the same
techniques work on his own readers. He starts by setting the scene in
the traditional manner of melodrama. The location of the Grand Inquisitor's narrative is a chiaroscuro dungeon on a "dark, hot and 'breathless'

Seville night" smelling of lemons and laurel,[136] amid the fabled brutali-
ties of the Inquisition (13:189). The story is segregated from the remainder of the narrative at every level: the setting is remote in time;
the country is far from Russia; the Grand Inquisitor meets Christ at night
in a prison. In the frame narrative, Ivan and Alyosha converse alone in
a partitioned room of an inn. Even the text is physically segregated as
a separate chapter. Within this isolated fictional world, the normal
laws of credibility seem to be temporarily suspended, as happened in
Rogozhin's house, in anticipation of a moment of revelation.

The subject of his tale is authorial control. The Grand Inquisitor's
route to narrative credibility relies on the threat of coercion to suspend
disbelief: the very metaphor of the Inquisition implies as much. Ivan suggests that the author of a successful prospectus narrative, which can
create, manipulate, and sustain predictable recipient response and
thereby control its audience, is equivalent to a successful dictator. The
Grand Inquisitor's concept of the perfect state is one in which all responses are controlled and predictable. "Yes, we'd make [people] work,
but in their free time we'd arrange their lives just like a children's game,
with children's songs sung in choirs and innocent dances."[137] Even experience beyond life can be controlled: "In peace will they die, in peace
will they expire with your name on their lips, and beyond the grave they
will find only death."[138]

But the very isolation that encourages fantasy also threatens it. The
setting referred to earlier could be the opening of a chapter from *Melmoth,* where Charles Maturin's "Tale of the Spaniard" is set at the time
of the Inquisition and occupies over a third of the entire work.[139] The
intertext with a work that played a significant role in establishing the
Gothic Romance as a cornerstone genre of popular literature is ironic in
the context of a narrative laying claim to philosophical weight. Dostoevsky, rather than Ivan, seems to be asking whether authorial control
within a genre so far removed from reality is not, in fact, self-defeating.
Samuel Taylor Coleridge raises similar doubts about the ability of Gothic
fantasy to support a moral argument in his review of Matthew Lewis's
Monk: "All events are levelled into one common mass, and become almost equally probable, where the order of nature may be changed wherever the author's purposes demand it. . . . The writer may make us
wonder, but he cannot surprise us. For the same reasons a romance is
incapable of exemplifying a moral truth."[140] The issue raises precisely

the Flaubertian questions about the links between narrative control, excess, and philosophical credibility that Dostoevsky had himself introduced at the very start of the scene with the reference to Saint John the Merciful. Is Dostoevsky planting the seeds of failure of the Grand Inquisitor's philosophy by his choice of mode of narration? Or does it have more to do with a general incompatibility between philosophical discourse and narrative fiction, as he had discovered in *The Idiot?*

Dostoevsky's correspondence, as we have seen, suggests that he is depicting a point of view with which he has little sympathy and that his intention is to show its failings.[141] But the text itself is more ambiguous, at all levels. The Grand Inquisitor's argument in favour of despotism is itself presented as a response to the unpredictability of narrative credibility. If audience reaction is incapable of being programmed, chaos will result, he claims to Christ: "Instead of the fixed law of old, man in future has to decide freely for himself what is good and what evil, with only you as role model—but surely it must have occurred to you that in the end he would challenge and question even your model and your truth if you saddled him with such a heavy burden as freedom of choice."[142] Prospectus, an assertion of "true" worth, is the only way to ensure the value of narrative but is immediately invalidated as a lie. The audience response within Ivan's narrative itself implies rejection: the Christ figure remains silent.

At the level of the frame story, Alyosha responds by questioning the credibility of Ivan's entire narrative—he describes the story as a "wild fantasy," states bluntly that the Inquisitor is not credible as a character, and seems to imply that the text has trouble dealing with the philosophical weight put on it: "What's more, such a fantastical character as your inquisitor clearly couldn't have existed. What are these sins of men that they take on themselves? Who are these keepers of the mystery who have assumed some sort of curse for the happiness of mankind? When were they ever seen?"[143] By the end of the story, Ivan is even losing his claim to authorship: the phrase most closely associated with his philosophy, "all is permitted" *(vse pozvoleno)*, turns out to be Dmitry's, and Alyosha plagiarises the kiss that Christ gives to the Grand Inquisitor (13:218). Creating a credible narrative that can sustain real intellectual weight turns out to be more difficult in the context of a novel than it had been in the more flexible but less enduring context of *Diary of a Writer.*

It is easy to forget Smerdyakov. His status is never defined—a possible by-blow of Fedor Pavlovich, so a possible half brother to the three legitimate sons. His story has so far been tucked into corners dominated by others. His birth is described not together with the stories of the other brothers but at the opening of a book dominated by Dmitry's confession. His education and ideas preface Ivan's exposition of his own philosophy in "Rebellion" and "The Grand Inquisitor." And his suggestion to Ivan that, by faking an epileptic fit, he can put himself in a position to manipulate Fedor Pavlovich's fate forms a curious coda to the same book.

Initially his story acts as a commentary on the value of the narratives of others. The numerous parallels that many critics have identified between him and the other sons turn his story into a partial renarration of their own. William Leatherbarrow characterises him as the composite double of all the other brothers, part person in his own right, part travesty, and notes how even his linguistic register is polluted by idioms copied from his siblings.[144] The genre of his genesis, in the boulevard newspaper voyeurism of his birth and mother's death, sharply separates him from the genres associated with his siblings: the formulaic discourse of scripture associated with Alyosha, the dated romanticism that introduces Dmitry, and the Gothic fantasies of Ivan's imagination. The interpolation of parts of his story throughout the confessions of the other sons ensures that they act as a running commentary on the many ways in which their attempts at prospectus narrative can fail. The sophistry of his philosophical argumentation, acquired under Ivan's tutelage, interrogates the sophistication of Ivan's own proposals. Smerdyakov's own life story denies all forms of asserted values, from the class structure that denies him social standing and inheritance rights to the received wisdom of the scriptures. The captured soldier in Smerdyakov's anecdote of the prisoner forced to recant his faith to avoid torture can—indeed, should—abjure his religion to escape the consequences: no values are permanent and narrative can, if necessary, be twisted to legitimise each new position (13:109).

There is, however, one set of values that Smerdyakov does claim to control: that of a commercial author. Diane Oenning Thompson notes his role from childhood in corrupting what she calls the collective sacred memory—he holds a mock religious ceremony over a cat he had killed, he challenges the story of Genesis, he casuistically distorts the parable of the mustard seed—but perhaps these should also be seen as early and unconscious attempts to rewrite received narratives.[145] It is not until the scenes after the Grand Inquisitor chapter that he proposes himself as surrogate novelist. His epilepsy both prequalifies him, in the Dostoevskian value system, and provides his creative inspiration. He suggests faking an epileptic fit, which, we and Ivan are pushed to speculate, would allow him to murder Fedor Pavlovich while throwing suspicion onto Dmitry (13:224–225). His proposal to Ivan is, effectively, to allow him (Smerdyakov) to take over as the author of the story by arranging that most novelistic of devices, a coincidence, to take control of the narrative line.

The narrator reports that Ivan is unable to deal with coincidence: "Ivan Fedorovich would have tried 'not to think' but even that wouldn't have helped. What was really annoying and irritating about this depression was that it felt almost coincidental and had nothing to do with him."[146] Smerdyakov, though, can. He is, he points out, in a privileged position to see all the plot lines through his possession of the admission codes to the crucial location, the sequence of knocks that will gain access to Fedor Pavlovich's house. He can rewrite the story by faking illness. He understands the importance of proper preparation and research, and can exploit his own personal experience to make his narrative realistic. He is aware of the role of literary device and understands how to use coincidence, one of Dostoevsky's own favourite devices. As his narrative develops in his own eventual confession to Ivan, we discover that he even thinks like the novelist of a courtroom drama: if he removes the money he has stolen from Fedor Pavlovich from its envelope, he muses, that will throw suspicion onto suspects who needed to check its contents—whereas he, Smerdyakov, would have known what the envelope contained (14:222). And finally he proposes a rational method for valuing this narrative: he will deliver it to the person who he believes will value it most highly based purely on financial criteria, in the shape of Ivan, who would be the chief beneficiary if Fedor Pavlovich were to die ostensibly at Dmitry's hand before marrying Grushenka, since the inheritance would then be split between two brothers rather than three (13:225–226).

The interposition of his narrative immediately after the story of the Grand Inquisitor is significant. It debunks the grandiose claims of Ivan's hero to authorial control in the interests of a philosophical ideal. It serves to highlight Ivan's own state of intellectual paralysis. Low cunning, it implies, is just as effective as Gothic fantasy and creates a far more convincing story to boot. Melodrama, *pace* Coleridge, may be able to carry more intellectual baggage but is hardly needed if Smerdyakov's pragmatic subterfuge works. The Grand Inquisitor's benevolent dictatorship appears even more fantastical when confronted by Smerdyakov's slippery, down-to-earth self-interest. And the narrative register of Smerdyakov's proposition is that of a future generation of readers to emerge in Russia, barely visible when Dostoevsky was writing these pages—the aspirant urban member of the lower classes seeking to better himself and dreaming of moving to the city to open a restaurant (13:186). It suggests the ability to take control of one's own destiny, but with limited and modest aims. In careers as in narrative, it seems, aiming too high deflates the credibility of the proposition.

Hagiography

Notwithstanding Smerdyakov's intervention, Dostoevsky's own commentary suggests that he saw both "The Grand Inquisitor" and the following book, "A Russian Monk," as part of a wider discussion of how to create this new genre of "philosophical fiction" within a commercial environment. In a letter to Konstantin Petrovich Pobedonostsev, he voices concerns that the need to stay in character will prevent him from offering a direct refutation of Ivan's position in both "Rebellion" and "The Grand Inquisitor":

> So I had intended this sixth book, 'A Russian Monk,' which is coming out on 31 August, to be the answer to all this negativism. But now I'm afraid, in the sense that it might not be an adequate answer. The more so in that it's not a direct answer, in terms, to the propositions already set out (both in 'The Grand Inquisitor' and earlier), but more an oblique response. . . . And on top of that there's the artistic imperative: the character needed to be portrayed as humble and majestic, while life is full of comedy . . . so willy-nilly, for artistic reasons, I had to touch on even the most mundane sides of my monk's biography so as not to harm its artistic realism.[147]

A slightly earlier letter, also to Pobedonostsev, refers to the wave of commercialism that Dostoevsky found on his return to Bad Ems in Germany (and that he attributes, unattractively, to a Semitic invasion) which he describes in quasi-literary terms as the "spirit of speculative realism."[148] To Putsykovich he voices concern that the process of serialisation, and in particular interventions by his publisher Katkov, would prevent the exposition of more sides of the argument: "That's not the only thing: in the novel I had to put across several ideas and points of view which I'm afraid won't go down well at all with him [Katkov], particularly as right up to the end of the novel you could end up with the wrong end of the stick on all these ideas and propositions."[149] Taken in this context, "A Russian Monk" can be seen as an experiment in the hagiographical genre, to determine whether it could provide the philosophical refutation of Ivan's propositions that Dostoevsky seems to have intended, whilst at the same time maintaining both commercial momentum and aesthetic integrity.

Dostoevsky is very specific about the status of this text. The narrator tells us, in an extended ellipsis, that it is a collage formed of recent memories of Zosima's last conversations to which, the narrator speculates, Alyosha may have added recollections of previous teachings to form a composite and uninterrupted whole (13:235–236). He makes the point that these were conversations that were not seen as specifically important in themselves but which acquired value subsequently by virtue of Zosima's death—a direct representation of the process of creating posterity value. Although the text is thus clearly coauthored by Zosima and Alyosha, their authorship has entirely different functions that differentiate the value of Alyosha's text from that of Zosima. Zosima's teaching is, effectively, a gift, an exchange from master to pupils without a discernible expectation of reward and without attempt to attach especial value to the words. In Marcel Mauss's spectrum of the relative disinterestedness of gifts, the episodic and fitful nature of the teachings seems to downplay their claim to a return—although the reader may remember from the very first book that the status enjoyed by the elders derived from their imparted wisdom, so the transaction may not be not entirely altruistic.[150] Alyosha's hagiography is, just as evidently, an attempt to create posterity value by the acts of compilation, editing, and publication. If we accept this distinction, we have, perhaps, a useful tool to differentiate the two widely differing modes of reception that have characterised this chapter. Those who focus on the religious substance of Zosima's teachings ascribe value to the message while either ignoring the medium or allowing their perception of the value of the teachings to influence their judgement of the way the story is told.[151] Those who note the flaws in the medium tend to assume that this reflects flaws in the message, which thereby becomes an unsatisfactory refutation of Ivan's case for the opposition.

Differentiating medium from message allows us to give weight to a characteristic that Alyosha has, in fact, demonstrated for some time but that is only now coming to prominence. The early parts of the novel show him primarily as a reporter, using his station as novice monk to move freely between the monastic and secular societies of the town as an observer trusted by all, spectating but rarely commenting. As the plot develops, so he gradually acquires his own story and voice. In doing so he discovers, to his evident surprise, how the process of communication can produce unplanned and quite speculative results. He thinks he has convinced Snegirev to accept Katerina Ivanovna's charity, but Snegirev abruptly changes tack and rejects the proffered money (13:175). Lise mocks his clumsy postrationalisation (13:179), and her own irrationality is a sarcastic commentary on his expectations of predictability. Mme Khokhlakova, talking about Lise, points out in terms how language can behave in unpredictable ways: "The great thing about her is her little turns of phrase and expressions, really surprising expressions, the sort of thing you'd never have expected, but which suddenly seem to jump out of her mouth."[152] Throughout the love scene between Alyosha and Lise, which forms the first chapter of the book that contains Ivan's "Rebellion" and "The Grand Inquisitor," her flighty inconsistency is contrasted with Alyosha's expectation of logic and meaning. Narrative is suddenly made to appear speculative, unpredictable, random. Ivan's philosophical exposition in "The Grand Inquisitor," which depends on an assertion of authorial control, is framed on one side by Alyosha and Lise's demonstration of the difficulty of controlling language and, on the other, by a theft of authorial control as Smerdyakov takes control of Ivan's narrative. It is difficult to imagine a more ironic commentary on the ability of any author to assert a prospectus narrative.

And yet this is precisely what Alyosha tries to do through his hagiography of Zosima in "A Russian Monk." Indeed, the very choice of the hagiographic genre implies as much, since its essence is the projection of biography as exemplum, a measure of unchanging value by which others can assess themselves. Alyosha's voice, though, is barely developed. So Dostoevsky puts him through a series of experiments with different styles, mirroring his own authorial experience in Alyosha's education as a writer. In fact, in another of the ironic twists in the novel,

Alyosha borrows from his brothers. He tells three anecdotes, echoing Dmitry's three confessions, the Grand Inquisitor's three temptations, and the narratives of the three brothers. The first is the story of the short life, spiritual transformation, and ecstatic death of Zosima's elder brother Markel. It explores the voice of romantic sentimentality. It echoes, as many readers have noticed, the story of Alyosha's memories of his own mother (13:19), as well as Ivan's hankerings after a Rousseau-esque return to nature (13:190). In repeating these motifs, Alyosha also intensifies the emotion: the casual tragedy of his mother's death becomes rather cloying pathos as Zosima's brother expires. The repetition and intensification seem to raise the issue of whether this borrowed style turns to cliché if pushed to excess. Alyosha abruptly curtails his own narrative— "And there was a whole lot more which I can't remember and shan't include"[153]—and switches style.

The next anecdote relates episodes from Zosima's early secular career as an army officer, in which he misbehaves in the manner expected of literary army officers, repents after abusing his servant, abandons a duel with an opponent he has wronged, leaves the army to become a monk, and undergoes a moral rebirth. It borrows a voice that we associate with Dmitry's upbringing. Zosima is shown as a romantic hero, with intertexts to Lermontov's Pechorin (to whom he has already been compared: 13:114), a host of Byronesque precedents, and, of course, Dmitry's own confession in verse, which had earlier seemed so dated. Zosima's moral awakening echoes Dmitry's own, as well as recalling a plotline from Pushkin's *Shot (Vystrel)* that is so strikingly similar as to be immediately recognisable to a contemporary Russian readership. We might, indeed, remember that Ivan jokingly accuses Alyosha of plagiarism when the latter copies Christ's kiss from "The Grand Inquisitor": the association reminds us that this is still an assumed, experimental voice. This anecdote reveals different tensions. It is pacy and melodramatic: in the space of a few pages, we have a love affair, a duel, and a theatrical religious conversion. It contrasts sharply with the immediately preceding interpolation, dealing with the importance of Holy Writ in Zosima's life, and seems to acknowledge that readers might appreciate a return to action to carry the narrative forward. But it is equally evident that this experiment is only of temporary assistance: Zosima's conversion implies that this style has to be left behind, along with his life as a soldier. Alyosha is forced to change voices once again.

The third anecdote tells the story of the mysterious visitor Mikhail, who discloses to Zosima the secret that he had murdered a girl who preferred another suitor and pushed the blame onto a servant who had subsequently died while under arrest. Zosima convinces him to accept responsibility for his crime and to own up. The story experiments with psychological melodrama in a genre that seems to mix Poe and parable. Caryl Emerson puts it thus: "Much in Mikhail's conflated character seems an awkward graft of sensational crime to saintly prototype."[154] Alyosha—and Dostoevsky—seem yet again to be experimenting with how to blend commercial device, which ensures the reader keeps reading, and hagiography, which encapsulates the message. And once more there are issues. The subject of the story is, explicitly, the ability of narrative to mislead: the credibility of Mikhail's false story led to the conviction of a servant for a murder that Mikhail had himself committed, and he is now left with the problem of convincing his reader— Zosima—of the credibility of its contradiction in the shape of his confession. One story may conceal its own opposite. The reader is left with the uneasy feeling that the reason he or she has kept reading is more the "courtroom drama" urge to find out which narrative prevails, coupled with the pull of the sensational and prurient, rather than the appeal of confession and moral salvation. And just as the previous narratives have drawn on family intertexts, so this is perhaps Alyosha's imitation of Smerdyakov's voice: Mikhail's story will turn out to be a template for Smerdyakov's concealed murder of Fedor Pavlovich, transfer of suspicion to Dmitry, subsequent backstage confession to Ivan, and ultimate extinction along with the proof of his involvement. It suggests that narrative value derives more from the representation of a miscarriage of justice than from the parable of the repentant sinner.

The final chapters of the book are, in hagiographic tradition, the teachings of Zosima. Even here there is an incipient conflict between medium and message. Alyosha's narrative is that of pure prospectus, asserted value in the expectation that the reader will accept and share the same system. Zosima's teachings, by contrast, focus on passivity, humility, a refusal to judge, and an acceptance that others have different value systems by which they choose to live. Given the earlier problems with his previous experimental voices, it is perhaps understandable that Alyosha, as Zosima's life writer, should give up on fictional devices and revert to a pure hagiographic style.

Hagiography, though, is no less experimental in the context of a novel. It may be a long-established literary genre as a separate format, but it is not a conventional part of a work of prose fiction. Todd makes the point that Dostoevsky is here joining a topical cultural controversy that was being aired in contemporary thick journals.[155] Monasticism had grown substantially over the second half of the nineteenth century in Russia: debate over its role as an institution and about the nature of monastic observance was a current subject of interest, at least amongst a portion of the readership of the *Russian Herald,* which, as Todd notes, published three further life stories of prominent monks during and in the year following the publication of *The Brothers Karamazov.* Contemporary reactions seem to indicate that readers responded actively to the theological positions that Dostoevsky represents—Todd sees Konstantin Leont'ev's portrayal of Father Kliment in the November and December issues of the 1879 *Russian Herald* as a refutation of Zosima's doctrinal approach. Perhaps we should see these chapters more in the light of journalism than of hagiography. Dostoevsky's own correspondence clearly acknowledges a necessary polemical role for these chapters in refuting the arguments of those closer to Ivan's position.[156] If so, then this is further evidence of the experimental nature of Dostoevsky's search for new ways in which to engage with a specific section of his readership that would respond to the cultural debate rather than to its qualities as fiction.

For those less willing to overlook the fictional context, however, these chapters have posed a real obstacle. Some critics have taken the position that Dostoevsky's theological proposition is itself so powerful that no narrative device is required for its credibility, but the implication that *The Brothers Karamazov* can only be properly appreciated from a Christian believer's perspective seems unnecessary and in any case impaired by the realisation that Dostoevsky, as his contemporaries appeared to recognise, is presenting a partisan view of Christian doctrine.[157] As we have already seen, Dostoevsky himself questions whether the Zosima response is adequate given the requirements for artistic authenticity. Other critics have assumed that this is simply an instance of an artistic failure by Dostoevsky. "The writing is pallid, abstract and lacking in drama. . . . The fragments are amplified, but the amplification is that of exposition and not of drama," writes Edward Wasiolek.[158] Morson is blunter: the problem with utopias, he says, is boredom. "One might ask, as critics of utopias frequently have, how narrative art is possible at all without conflict and change; for what, if not change, could be narrated? In a curious way, the question about theodicy—if God is all good, how can evil exist?—re-emerges as an aesthetic question for utopia: if heaven and the Republic are perfect, how can there be narratable events?"[159]

A further possibility, particularly in the light of Dostoevsky's insistence to Pobedonostsev on the need to maintain artistic integrity, is that this is more a reflection on Alyosha's ability to tell a story than on what he is trying to communicate. Alyosha is trying to find a way to create posterity value through narrative. His attempts to do so using borrowed voices from his brothers have all foundered on inherent contradictions between genre and the object of its representation: sainthood sits as uneasily with sentimental cliché as with romantic heroism or psychological drama. His reversion to the traditional record of the saint's teachings is an admission that he has not yet found the right medium to convey sanctity credibly. The nonfictional nature of the text in the middle of a work of fiction serves to emphasise this dislocation. The journalistic overtones ironically compare Alyosha to Rakitin—who is about to reappear in the opening chapters of the next part—as a manipulator of words and simultaneously emphasise how far this takes Alyosha out of his narratorial comfort zone. The narrator's intervention at the end of the chapter to repeat that Alyosha's text is incomplete and fragmentary reinforces the impression of a failure. He rapidly dusts off the parked plot and deals with Zosima's death in a single paragraph. As importantly, he signals a return to commercial values by creating a swift cliff-hanger ending promising something so unexpected in the next chapter that the town was still talking about it (13:266).

His reference, of course, is to the premature decomposition of Zosima's body in the first chapter of book 7. A chapter that had begun as Alyosha's attempt to create posterity value for Zosima's life and teachings ends in a representation in the crudest of terms of his failure to achieve immortality, and in front of the in-story readers for whom Alyosha's words would have been intended. Even more ironically, in a celebration of the power of memory to create lasting value, the narrator implies that the one memory of Zosima that will persist in the minds of the townsfolk is the tabloid scandal of his corpse. If this attempt to create a narrative of lasting value through the assertion of the worth of a character whose entire life has built towards this point has collapsed, then prospectus narrative has indeed failed.

The Rejection of Prospectus

Book 7, entitled "Alyosha," was serialised in the September 1879 issue of the *Russian Herald*. By this time it was already obvious that the novel was a considerable commercial success, even if reactions from professional critics continued to be more variable. Dostoevsky records its extraordinary reach, even amongst the youths who might have been deterred by the unflattering portraits of the young revolutionaries in *The Devils*, in a letter to Pobedonostsev at the end of the summer of 1879.[160] But for all its success it remains an experimental text: the same letter refers to Dostoevsky's doubts that the novelistic format will allow him to convey properly his refutation of "The Grand Inquisitor" and suggests that such polemics are more easily expressed in the "firm, fearless voice" of a format like that of *Diary of a Writer*.[161] From now on the novel's focus will shift more towards a representation of the external, commercial world outside the gates of the monastery. To Lyubimov, in a letter accompanying the first three chapters of "Alyosha," he indicates that he is now done with the monastery, about which there would be nothing more.[162] The change of representational focus is mirrored by a similar switch towards an investigation of the commercial characteristics of fiction. Joseph Brodsky, writing about Dostoevsky in a 1980 article, notes the trend: "Every writing career starts as a personal quest for sainthood, for self-betterment. Sooner or later, and as a rule quite soon, a man discovers that his pen accomplishes a lot more than his soul."[163]

The narrative structure of the novel follows a similar curve. Books 1–2 set out the bones of the narrative problem. Books 3–6 have tested to destruction the ability of different genres to represent philosophical, ethical, and theological convictions while keeping readers on the hook. Books 8–12 will chart the ascendancy of the commercial possibilities of narrative along with increasing problems of controlling it. Book 7, sandwiched between the end of Zosima's spiritual quest and Dmitry's desperate chase for money, is the pivot around which this change of narrative direction occurs.

It starts with a parody of the Grand Inquisitor's recipe of miracle and mystery in a series of anecdotes that are open to quite different interpretations if seen as spiritual or secular narrative. The conflict of two apparently stable interpretations destabilises both. The rot, literally, begins with Zosima's death: the report of his decomposing body questions whether he qualifies for the expected miracle and is precisely the mystery the boulevard press would seize on (13:267–276). Dostoevsky insists, in correspondence with his editor, that the coarse verb *provonyal* (stunk), which he puts in Ferapont's mouth to describe the process of Zosima's putrefaction, should not be adulterated: the shock value of language is an inherent component of the linguistic register he is seeking to achieve.[164] Journalism meets hagiography, just as Rakitin, proto-journalist, meets Alyosha as he leaves the monastery (13:278).

The clash of expectation and result causes Alyosha's faith to wobble. Just as importantly, the contrast between the hagiographic subject and the sensationalist reportage forces the reader to reexamine how narrative value is created. The two succeeding anecdotes are open to equally conflicting interpretations. Alyosha's visit to Grushenka is, alternatively, the beginning of her miraculous spiritual redemption or the attempted seduction of a novice monk by the town tart, procured by an aspiring reporter in the shape, once again, of Rakitin. The narrator lingers over the description of Grushenka's commercial acumen (13:281), allowing her subsequent redemption to be interpreted at one level as a rejection of commercial values—but simultaneously using the very description of her prowess to create a narrative with powerful dramatic and commercial characteristics. Grushenka's story of the wicked old woman and the onion similarly serves two purposes. On the one hand it is a parable of salvation. Kate Holland interprets it thus: "The onion narrative offers two different conclusions: in the legend the old woman fails the moral test set by her guardian angel, but in the novel itself Grushenka takes the onion, refuses to seduce Alyosha, and thus begins her moral regeneration."[165] Yuri Corrigan sees it as a key step in Alyosha's journey towards "a transcendent source or a life-principle at the core of self."[166] But it is also a story that appeals on a much more immediate level to readers: as Grushenka says, "It's just a fable, but it's a good story—when I was still a small child my Matryona, the one that works for me now in the kitchens, used to tell it to me."[167] It is, indeed, a good story, and we should not overlook its commercial role as a device that slots neatly into at least two categories associated with defined reader responses. That of "fable" *(basnya)* links it to a long tradition of simple, folkloric morality tales and thus to an expectation of an asserted moral value. That of the nursery tale, passed down from, presumably, Grushenka's nurse, links it to a recurring literary theme and particularly to Pushkin's evocation of romantic domesticity in Tatyana's exchanges with her nurse in *Evgeny Onegin*, or in his descriptions of his own nurse, Ariona Rodionovna, in, for example, the poem *A Winter's Evening (Zimnii Vecher)*. Why, the text seems to ask, do we keep reading? Is it the compelling nature of a tale of moral resurrection, or is it the impetus of a good traditional folktale in a slightly salacious context?

This querying of reader motivation continues, I think, in Alyosha's dream of Cana of Galilee, which Dostoevsky himself sees as "the most essential chapter of the book, and perhaps of the whole novel" (although we might note he said the same of the chapter "A Russian Monk").[168] Once again, the text physically juxtaposes a narrative allied to an established reader response—in this case the biblical text, quoted verbatim, of the miracle at Cana—to Alyosha's own epiphany. The biblical narrative is spare and factual, relying on established interpretation to provide emotional and intellectual stimuli. The description of Alyosha's experience uses, by contrast, images of romantic excess: a vision of Zosima, a message from beyond the grave, a mystical communion with nature and the universe, the suggestion of a spiritual revelation. The voice is not that of Alyosha but that of an omniscient narrator able to see into Alyosha's deepest thoughts. Yet despite this ability, neither he nor Alyosha can describe this experience in other than the vaguest terms: "Some sort of idea, or something along those lines, rose to power in his mind," is how the narrator describes it, while Alyosha in his own words is even less specific: "Someone visited my soul at that moment."[169] No matter how much we want to believe in Alyosha's spiritual transformation, the text forces us to contrast the biblical description of a "real" miracle, grounded in received reception, with the excess and lack of specificity of Alyosha's experience. Petr Mikhailovich Bitsilli compares this passage to Prince Andrei's epiphany after the Battle of Borodino in *War and Peace* (vol. 3, pt. 2, chap. 37) and uses the contrast to illustrate how easily Dostoevsky's version slips into cliché.[170] Yet again Alyosha is associated with a narrative mode that seems to question its own ability to deliver a text matching its apparent intentions. In some circumstances, particularly in asserting faith-based prospectus values, authorial control may be more difficult to manage than the Grand Inquisitor seems to assume.

Auction: The Return of Commercial Value

If prospectus narrative has failed because the recipient of the narrative cannot be relied on to accept it in the way the author intended, then how can an author convey his message to the reader? One answer is evidently to investigate which values do generate predictable reader responses and to see whether those can be combined in some way with the author's intellectual and philosophical concerns. This approach uses the techniques of the auction, in that it assumes consistent enough responses from buyers of the text to generate an approximate theory of how recipients determine value, while recognising that the offeror cannot independently assign value to the text.

So it is, perhaps, unsurprising that the narrative changes character from this point. Through books 8 and 9, "Mitya" and "The Preliminary Investigation" ("Predvaritel'noe sledstvie"), the plot moves ahead more rapidly as the murder investigation unfolds. Digressions (other than the story of the children, to which we will return) almost disappear. The narrative describes a series of attempted commercial transactions, in Dmitry's attempts to get money, in his shopping at Plotnikov's, in his consumption at Mokroye. The frequency of occurrence of the motif of 3,000 roubles rises dramatically, as Dmitry dashes headlong from Samsonov to Lyagavy, to Mme Khokhlakova, and on to Mokroye. Perhaps in recognition of this, the theme of money takes on a new importance in the second half of the novel. References to it in the third and fourth parts of the novel occur almost four times as frequently as in the first two parts.[171] Between the second and third parts, the increase is even higher. Relationships, people, and motives are reducible, ultimately, to monetary values. Katerina Ivanovna's honour is set at 4,500 roubles. The auction for Grushenka establishes her value at 3,000 roubles. Family relationships are reduced to disputes over inheritance monies. The object of the murder is money. The evidence that convicts Dmitry relates to how much he had previously stolen from Katerina Ivanovna.

Much has been made of the relentless drumbeat of the sum of 3,000 roubles throughout the novel. Boris Christa notes Dostoevsky's habit of referring repeatedly to specific sums of money and argues that he uses a technique of "trial by money" to demonstrate the moral and spiritual worth of his characters.[172] Brodsky cites Elizaveta Shtakenschneider's assessment, recorded in her 1880 diary, as evidence of Dostoevsky's ability to connect with his readers on a level they understood: "But [Dostoevsky] is a petit bourgeois. . . . He bears himself with dignity, and yet the petit bourgeois in him trickles through. It can be spotted in certain traits, surfacing in private conversation, but most of all in his works. . . . In his depiction of big capital he will always regard 6,000 rubles as a vast amount of money": this colossal sum, she implies, could genuinely represent colossal emotional expenditure and create colossal literature.[173] Perhaps not entirely coincidentally, 6,000 roubles is also the sum Fedor Pavlovich has paid to Dmitry in an attempt to impose a final settlement on Dmitry's inheritance claim (13:95).

The motif of 3,000 roubles does indeed recur repeatedly. It is, variously and possibly not even exhaustively, Dmitry's residual claim on Fedor Pavlovich for his mother's estate (13:102); the amount Katerina Ivanovna asks Dmitry to send to her sister in Moscow (13:101); what Dmitry allegedly stole from Katerina Ivanovna and spent on Grushenka during his first visit to Mokroye (13:101); the amount he tries to borrow from Samsonov (14:13), Lyagavy (14:19), and Mme Khokhlakova (14:27); what he is alleged to have spent during the second visit to Mokroye (14:37, 43, 49); the amount he offers to the Poles for Grushenka (14:61); the price offered by Fedor Pavlovich for her (13:102); and hence the amount in the envelope stolen by Smerdyakov and passed to Ivan (14:217); the difference between Maslov's and Gorshkin's offers for Fedor Pavlovich's wood, which Ivan was to have negotiated at Chermashnya (8,000 roubles versus 11,000 roubles, respectively; 13:230); and the fee paid to the lawyer Fetyukovich for Dmitry's defence (14:171).

At one level this clearly comments on the commercialisation of life, the reduction of human emotion to commercial values, the opposition of the commercial to the spiritual dimensions of the Russian character, and similar social issues, as Sophie Ollivier argues.[174] But such a theme was not new—writers from Balzac to Dickens and Gogol had used it as a recurrent characterisation of the nineteenth century. Nor does it explain fully the choice of a fixed value when any measure of monetisation would have done.

The figure of 3,000 roubles is perhaps best seen as the emblem of an emerging approach to narrative. At a superficial level it signifies a genre and a narrative tempo associated with sensation and action. Through iteration it acts as shorthand for "readability," for that particular register of easily recognised commercial fiction based on the representation of sexual and financial greed that is the key motive force of the plot. The combination of iteration and stable signification creates a predictable reader response, or at least the anticipation of one. Repetition also conveys a sense of inevitability: just as the lives of the characters revolve directly or indirectly around money, so the text must return frequently to its commercial roots if it is to maintain the reader's attention. The figure of 3,000 roubles is just as much a reminder of the commercial value of narrative as it is a symbol of the in-story commercial motives of the characters. Its iteration, significantly, also shows how cliché is born, through the repetition of a fixed association until the original signification is dulled into banality.

Not all monetary values are fixed, and deviations from the 3,000 rouble gold standard are particularly noteworthy and usually act as signals of submerged currents that undercut the apparently stable equivalences of the surface. The diminishing credibility of Dmitry's narrative is signalled by the serial rejection of his loan requests from Samsonov, Lyagavy, Mme Khokhlakova, and eventually the Poles. The purse *(ladonka)* that Dmitry claims he hung around his neck, supposedly containing 1,500 roubles and therefore both half full and half empty, becomes a symbol both of the possible reflation of the value of his defence narrative if his alibi has value and of its terminal deflation if not. Since the alibi cannot be proved, the purse becomes a symbol of speculative value, the more so as the very existence of the purse itself is called into question as Dmitry fails to offer a credible narrative for its provenance. Even the external reader, who would like to believe Dmitry but is as dismayed as the prosecutor is sceptical at the flimsiness of his alibi, is forced to participate in the experience of the value of Dmitry's narrative fluctuating wildly each time he is asked a new question about the purse.

This mutation of an apparently fixed value into something more speculative or factitious is nothing new. Dostoevskian money often pointedly fails to establish value or to translate into real spending power. Makar Devushkin's copying mistake, as we have already seen, brings him 100 roubles—the logic is as arbitrary as the sum (1:71–73). Raskolnikov fails to use the famously precise 317 silver roubles and 60 kopecks he steals (7:367). The eleventh-hour arrival of Myshkin's legacy makes us realise how artificial his fictional construction is (10:128–129). And in *The Gambler*, the arbitrariness of monetary values that rise and fall at the throw of a die is mirrored by human relationships that couple and uncouple with an equal lack of consequentiality. Fictional identities follow suit: Mademoiselle Blanche acquires a surname complete with aristocratic particle and a mother, Madame *veuve* Cominges, at the moment she teams up with the Marquis des Grieux, whose name is not only derived from picaresque fiction *(Manon Lescaut)* but whose title and very existence turn out to be fictional (6:254–255). The hero of *The Gambler* sums it up: "The point here is that one spin of the wheel changes everything. . . . What am I today? Zero. What could I be tomorrow? Tomorrow I could come back from the dead and start a new existence."[175] But whether a new existence would be more or less credible than the old as a fictional construct remains, itself, a matter of speculation. Mere intention is insufficient to guarantee results. Dostoevsky's own gambling habit, which had dogged him through much of the 1860s, must have shown him how the good intentions so repeatedly expressed in contrite letters could evaporate in a few moments.[176]

And so with the construction of novelistic value. The apparently fixed exchange rates that allow predictable exchange values, in the shape of reliable reader reactions, to be established, do work some of the time. But they are not consistently reliable. As Alyosha has found out, the unintended, the unforeseen ambivalence and slipperiness of language, perverts meaning and impact. Iteration acts as a kind of reset button, allowing a reversion to the initial assumption of fixed values. Yet the expectation of distortion, of an outcome produced by speculation rather than intention, lurks behind every repetition.

The 3,000 roubles is thus also a motif of incipient failure. What is common to all of the transactions in which it figures is a failure to complete. Dmitry does not collect his inheritance, nor does he send the money to Katerina Ivanovna's sister, nor does he spend the full 3,000 roubles on Grushenka at Mokroye, at least on the second occasion, nor does he succeed in borrowing it from any of his potential lenders. Fedor Pavlovich never succeeds in acquiring Grushenka, and the amount in the envelope is unverifiable by the time it reaches court in Ivan's possession. The deal for the wood is never completed. Dmitry never pays the Poles who convert the sum into the amount they want to be paid to go away and, ironically, reduce it over time from 3,000 roubles to one rouble as the value of their narrative evaporates. And, finally, Fetyukovich's defence of Dmitry fails.

So, with some irony, this fixed sum becomes a sign of the failure to establish stable relationships between the commodities for which it is exchanged. We are led to believe that a relationship might exist by the coincidence of identical value, or by equivalences that turn out to be valid only incidentally, but eventually we realise that its own inflexibility simply provides a common currency against which the fluctuations of the value of other commodities can be measured. Belknap seems to describe, in different terms, exactly this process when he argues that Dostoevsky converts financial relationships into far more volatile emotional ones.[177] And since other commodities, as we have seen, are often expressed in their own narratives, it becomes a measure of the instability of narrative value. Grushenka's Poles write florid letters to demand money, implying that a grand style should bring a grand reward, only to find that their narrative currency is swiftly devalued to worthlessness (14:170).

The mere mention of the fixed sum of 3,000 roubles eventually becomes an authorial signpost for speculative value. The amount itself is of a size to be credible in almost all the instances where it is used: Dmitry defends his inheritance claim as proportionate to the profits Fedor Pavlovich has made from investing his first wife's dowry, while his father's offer for Grushenka is equivalent to the profit he expects to make on a sale of timber (13:102). John Jones rightly notes that this attention to small, tactile details is a cornerstone of Dostoevsky's approach to realism.[178] But in other instances the claimed value vanishes. Dmitry may, or may not, have spent 3,000 roubles at Mokroye. Smerdyakov produces the actual 3,000 roubles stolen, yet Ivan cannot prove their validity. Fetyukovich, as counsel for the defence, argues that they never in fact existed, while Ippolit Kirillovich, as prosecutor, maintains that they were indivisible, so while the entire 3,000 roubles must have existed, a separate 1,500 roubles could not have (14:280). Signifier and signified become gradually detached, just as the face value of contemporary paper money deviated from its exchange value. Iakov Zundelovich expresses this process of adjustment in quasi-mathematical terms as a "conundrum facing the writer who has—as he imagined—carefully distinguished clear positives from clear negatives in his mind's eye, but who, when he comes to give artistic expression to these intellectual constructs, discovers painfully that his positives are not at all as definitive as he had thought, and that his negatives have shades and gradations which do not allow him to take them out of brackets."[179]

Narrative value follows the same pattern. The established conventions and hierarchies of genre create an architecture of fixed relationships that the author cannot ignore if he cares about the commercial success of his output. But the speculative nature of communication perverts and distorts these established relationships in an unpredictable manner, leading to potential interpretations that, as with Flaubert's *St Julien l'Hospitalier*, challenge both the received interpretation and the reader's own methods of measuring narrative value. In an effort to cling to established commercial value, the novelist may frequently revert to the commonplaces of genre, to sensation and melodrama, but each iteration may require greater excess, to the point where credibility is lost, or may alternatively lead to cliché through the simple process of repetition. Even maintaining a formula dilutes its effect, as Sue had discovered in the process of trying to repeat the success of *Les Mystères de Paris*. Excess and cliché become the Scylla and Charybdis on which the plotted narrative course founders, and the rules for avoiding the rocks are self-defeating since avoiding cliché requires ever-greater excess.

The courtroom drama, with its hidden central trunk of "what really happened" surrounded by a forest of alternative versions, is the perfect genre to allow the author to maximise the commercial potential of the novel. Its essence is the assumption that the author will offer multiple possible narratives in such a way that the value of each is deliberately uncertain, hidden, or open to misinterpretation. Dostoevsky's notebooks offer clear examples of detail subsequently suppressed in the final text to obscure motive and maintain dramatic tension: for example, Ivan's awareness of the involvement of Smerdyakov in the murder of Fedor Pavlovich is present in the notes but is suppressed in the novel, evidently to maintain dramatic tension on this point.[180]

Value discovery happens by the techniques of the auction room, where objects are serially presented to buyers for valuation by competition. Dostoevsky shows us how the in-story characters participate, with different values being assigned to the same narrative by different recipients. How much did Dmitry spend at Mokroye on his second visit? He says less than 1,500 roubles (14:109). The innkeeper swears to double, perhaps even 6,000 roubles over the two visits (14:117–118). The Poles confirm that Dmitry offers them a 3,000 rouble bribe (14:119). What figures Dostoevsky gives us, the readers, for Dmitry's expenditure add up to a total of 1,266.40 roubles (14:102).

Competitive tension arises both between reader and author over whether the reader can spot the false trails laid by the author, and between reader and in-story characters over the consequences of mismatched levels of information. The narrator assumes multiple identities, switching from an ability to see the innermost thoughts of his characters to professions of ignorance of anything beyond his own direct knowledge in such an overt way that the reader cannot help but notice the trick. The techniques act as a kind of novelistic laboratory where each iteration allows the author to test its value on the in-story audience and to take the results into account in formulating the next iteration, and eventually in presenting a completed episode of the serial to the external reader.[181] Breaking the narrative into discrete component parts also allows the author to rely on the cumulative experience of all past iterations in formulating the next, just as an auctioneer relies on precedent to estimate the value of new goods for sale.

Over the remaining five books, Dostoevsky will propose no fewer than eight full and thirty partial retellings of the central story, which itself is never wholly revealed.[182] Some are presented as within the direct knowledge of the narrator himself, others as dramatized scenes in which he is able to reproduce accurately the dialogue of others in direct or indirect speech, and at times even the thoughts of the characters involved. They span the gamut of genre from detective story and courtroom drama (the police investigation and trial) through confessional (Smerdyakov) and journalistic (Rakitin) to epistolary (Dmitry). The changing focus, literary medium, and apparent variability in the narrator's powers of memory jolt the reader into awareness of a process of narrative manipulation. The narrator begins with his own full version of the murder scene. Narratives two to six are Dmitry's subsequent variants of the story as told to Fenya and Perkhotin, Perkhotin's further speculations when Dmitry leaves him, and Dmitry's own reflections at Mokroye and when he is arrested. Seven and eight are Fenya's and Mme Khokhlakova's interpretations to Perkhotin. Nine is the full initial police version of events as reported by the narrator. Ten is the record, again supplied by the narrator, of Dmitry's full interrogation. Eleven to fifteen are supplied by the witnesses interviewed in the police investigation at Mokroye (the landlord and his staff, Kalganov, the two Poles, Maksimov, and Grushenka),

The sixteenth, and a key full variant, is the tabloid report of the crime written by Rakitin in the Petersburg boulevard newspaper *Rumours (Slukhi)* and retailed by Mme Khokhlakova to Alyosha, who subsequently gives his own interpretation of guilt to Ivan in the seventeenth narrative. Smerdyakov's confession, a full account in three extended sections, is interpolated with three contradictory indications culminating in the letter from Dmitry to Katerina Ivanovna, reported verbatim, and another full account, which directly conflicts with Smerdyakov's confession. These four narratives form iterations eighteen to twenty-one. Ivan's decision to confess, as reported to Alyosha after the devil scene, is the twenty-second. Finally, the factual and expert witnesses at the trial—Grigory, Rakitin, Snegirev, the landlord, the Poles, Alyosha, Katerina Ivanovna, Grushenka, and Ivan, together with the three doctors—add twelve more accounts and raise the total to thirty-four. The speeches of the prosecutor and defence counsels at the trial add a further two full versions. Dmitry's final plea is the penultimate repetition. The jury verdict, as interpreted by the narrator, could be said to provide the final, thirty-eighth, variant.

Iteration is a novelistic device with proven commercial function. Balzac had used characters who returned in subsequent novels to encourage his readers to follow the trail across different publications. The success of *A Christmas Carol* led Dickens to produce regular Christmas stories. Zola's *Les Rougon-Macquart,* subtitled *Histoire naturelle et sociale d'une famille sous le Second Empire,* follows a single family through the iterations of its genes. Dostoevsky would have been well aware that Zola had succeeded almost singlehandedly in changing the economics of the French publishing market with the 1877 publication in book form of *L'Assommoir,* which ran through thirty-eight editions in its first year, seventy-three by 1880, and became one of the forerunners of modern best sellers with huge print runs.[183]

The Brothers Karamazov had been a commercial success from the outset, and Dostoevsky proved able to maintain the commercial value of the text consistently over ten episodes of serialisation, from the end of book 6 to the epilogue, spanning fourteen months, from September 1879 to November 1880, with three gaps totalling five months. One of these gaps occurs in December 1879, when he publishes an apology for the delay of the expected episode. Book 8 ended in November 1879 with the cliff-hanger of Dmitry's arrest: the delayed book 9 would deal with the police investigation. December is an important month for subscription renewals: delaying book 9 to January looks suspiciously like a publisher's ruse to encourage subscription renewals, despite Dostoevsky's denial of such tactical manoeuvres. "In the papers, I've read with my own eyes on three occasions already accusations and insinuations against the publishers of the *Russian Messenger,* to the effect that they have deliberately (for some mysterious reason or other) spun out novels (Leo Tolstoy's and mine) over two years."[184] The same correspondence again makes clear that Dostoevsky is well aware of the commercial success of the novel: "The novel is being read everywhere, people are writing me letters, young people are reading it, the same in high society, the critics either love it or hate it and from the impressions it produces all around I've never yet had such a success."[185]

But for all this, finding a readership that was able to accept intellectual weight along with the murder mystery remained elusive. Dostoevsky even, perhaps, describes the newly emerging readership. Mme Khokhlakova, subscriber to her Petersburg gossip sheet (14:175), recipient of Perkhotin's melodramatic account of the murder of Fedor Pavlovich (14:75), butt of Rakitin's vindictive doggerel (14:189), and listener at keyholes (13:181), is perhaps a representative reader of the developing mass market in commercial fiction, just as Rakitin is the representative of a new breed of commercial journalists. She is a woman living in the provinces, of independent means, literate and educated to a point, and so a member of a relatively new demographic for the Russian market of the late 1870s. She is fashion conscious and aware of her sexuality: Alyosha suspects her of compulsive flirting (14:174). She is fascinated by criminality and legal procedure, although her views on the new, postreform courts are amusingly simplistic (14:179). It is no accident that she is the means by which Rakitin's sensationalised article on the murder reaches us, nor that she is represented as trivialising intellectual ideas, as she does with her notion of how a plea of temporary insanity *(afekt)* works (14:179). She is by her own admission an avid consumer of gossip, where she finds Rakitin's version of the murder: "Here it is, in the paper, in *Rumours,* the Petersburg paper. It came out earlier this year, this *Rumours,* I just adore gossip so I subscribed, and look what I've brought on my head, that's gossip for you."[186]

By the time the contemporary reader had reached this description, at the beginning of the penultimate book of the novel, published in July and August 1880, he or she might have realised that for the past nine months Dostoevsky had been producing material apparently directed at just these tastes. The final four books are dominated by motifs from the popular press that would barely look out of place in the faits divers columns of the boulevard newspapers: murder, theft, sex and a wild party, a police investigation, arrest, trial, and punishment. Terras notes the parallels with the Zaitsev murder case, spectacularly reported in the Petersburg newspapers in January 1879.[187] In laughing at Mme Khokhlakova's foibles, we are reminded that what has driven our own engagement with the text is perhaps not so different.

But what consequences, then, must an author draw if Mme Khokhlakova is representative of the new generation of mass readers? She sees the world around her in terms of her own tastes and simply rejects anything that does not conform. Like Mme Epanchina in *The Idiot*, she is, in André Gide's phrase, *inconséquente* to the highest degree.[188] She and readers like her may respond consistently to some textual stimuli. The author may even be able to manipulate audience reactions in a mostly predictable manner, and to exploit its own desire to be manipulated, in the manner of a crowd responding to a magician. Dostoevsky's ability to do so within the confines of a courtroom drama had been amply demonstrated over the course of books 8 and 9. He had, arguably, proved the success of the auction approach to narrative. But he had also, inadvertently, shown its shortcomings. The price was a commercially successful text that found itself quite incapable of including the kind of intellectual weight that the earlier books had so clearly sought. The "Mme Khokhlakova problem" was neatly demonstrated in real life when one of his readers, a Mme Lebedeva, wrote to ask whether Dmitry was guilty of the murder. Dostoevsky's testy reply shows he was sure that he had left enough clues for an intelligent reader not to be fooled: "It's not just the subject of the novel which is important for the reader, but also that he should have some understanding of the human mind (of psychology): every author has a right to expect that of his reader."[189] But, evidently, neither Mme Lebedeva nor, in all probability, Mme Khokhlakova could be relied on to bring such intelligence to the table. Unhelpfully, the Grand Inquisitor turns out to have been right: fantasy, suspense, and authorial control are very effective at controlling an audience but may be poor tools for intellectual dialogue.

Speculation

For the space of two entire books (book 8, "Mitya," and book 9, "The Preliminary Investigation"), representing three serial instalments covering a four-month publication period from October 1879 to January 1880,

Dostoevsky had concentrated on the murder and the investigation to the exclusion of any digressions, interpolated narratives, or philosophical debates. The narrative describes, in a tightly controlled fashion, the process by which a murder investigation itself runs out of control. This combination of diegetic control and mimetic unravelling is a highly commercial device that was clearly successful in keeping readers hooked.

But for the writer, simply being the virtuoso creator of courtroom drama may not be enough. The next two books, 10 and 11, seem to experiment with the return of different forms of intellectual content, represented by the renewed focus on Alyosha and then Ivan as the central characters of the respective books, within different genres. Both characters had earlier demonstrated how any attempt to project value through prospectus narrative had been undermined by a failure in the mode of transmission, which resulted in an entirely unpredictable outcome, like the spin of a wheel at roulette. Both books now investigate how this loss of control arises and its implications for narrative value.

Dostoevsky seems deliberately to disrupt his own text to jolt it out of its commercial rut. Jean Genet puts it in terms that might have appealed to Dostoevsky himself, or at least to Ivan Karamazov: "Is my reading of *The Brothers Karamazov* incorrect? I have read it as a joke. . . . Having read the book in this way, it now seems to me that any novel, poem, painting, or musical composition that does not destroy itself—by which I mean, that is not constructed as a blood sport with its own head on the chopping block—is a fraud."[190] Images of excess start to appear, recalling the still unanswered questions posed by Ivan at the beginning of his "Rebellion" by his evocation of the figure of Saint John the Merciful / Saint Julien l'Hospitalier. The disruptions are both figurative and structural and open a debate about the author's ability to control his own text that will continue throughout the remainder of the novel.

Representations of loss of control are a consistent theme in the novel, but one of which we only become aware gradually through iteration. We have already investigated how Alyosha loses control of his narrative in his hagiography of Zosima, only to be followed by a parallel loss of control of his own emotions in "Cana of Galilee." The image of loss of control is inherently ambiguous, and Dostoevsky is able to exploit its contradictions to the full. On the one hand, it becomes a metaphor for the entropic vision of the world he describes, in which discontinuity, disintegration, and fragmentation affect so many lives. He discusses this on several occasions in *Diary of a Writer:* "Indeed, I keep thinking that we have begun the epoch of universal 'dissociation.' All are dissociating themselves, isolating themselves from everyone else, everyone wants to invent something of his own, something new and unheard of. . . . Meanwhile, there is scarcely anything about which we can agree morally; everything has been or is being broken up, not even into clusters but into single fragments."[191] On the other hand, it is at times an ironic reminder that only an author in control of his text can describe loss of control so effectively. But as the novel progresses, there seems to be a shift from a discussion of loss of control to the sensation that it may actually be happening in real time. Fedor Pavlovich proposes the theme in the very first book and asks how the novel will deal with both behavioural disruption and narrative discontinuity. The representation of Dmitry shows how closely the author can stay in control diegetically while describing an escalating loss of control at the mimetic level. To make sure the reader does not miss the point, Dostoevsky even incorporates a description of the process into the narrative: Smerdyakov fakes loss of control in his pretend fit to show how an author figure can remain in charge while depicting dysfunction—but then is ironically dethroned by the real epileptic seizure that follows.

Dostoevsky concludes his description of the preliminary investigation in book 9 with a description of Dmitry's dream of a starving child, *ditë*, in a burnt-down peasant village (14:122–123). In this penultimate chapter of the book, the narrator refers three times to the novelistic qualities of Dmitry's story. In the first instance, Dmitry's experience on the night of the murder is called a "novel," in quotation marks (14:118). In the second and third, the investigator is described as shying away from the more "novelistic," or possibly "romanesque" *(romanichesky)* aspects of the case—specifically Dmitry's relationship with Grushenka—in favour of the financial details (14:119, 121). The effect, I think, is to sensitise the reader to the novelistic qualities of the text itself and, in particular, to prepare the ground for Dmitry's dream. The passage of the dream stands out from the preceding text by virtue of the intensity of its fiction, as Dmitry passes voyeuristically through a landscape of destitution, destruction, and misery. It has been interpreted as the beginning of his spiritual redemption.[192] But it is also a striking image of loss of control. As Dmitry loses control of his own senses in this dream with overtones of madness, so the text itself seems to require the reader to notice its own incipient loss of control. The authorial viewpoint switches abruptly from that of third-party police reporter, assiduously documenting the preliminary investigation, to a poetic standpoint within Dmitry's own consciousness, able to accompany Dmitry to the edge of madness without compromising the writer's own lucidity. Is this the reporter simply showing off his powers after a boring day in the police department, or is it a sign that the text itself can go off the rails as easily as Dmitry?

The theme of loss of control is taken up in the very next book. The story of the Snegirev family has already registered as a significant change of narrative direction and genre in book 4. Its continuation in book 10, "The Boys" ("Mal'chiki"), intervenes equally abruptly in the buildup of the murder narrative. As if to emphasise its experimental nature, the book is isolated in time by the circumstances of its publication. Book 9 had appeared in the *Russian Herald* in January 1880; book 10 did not appear till April. After its publication, a further two-month gap intruded before the appearance of the first part of book 11 in July. Dostoevsky evidently saw it as a rather different narrative thread. "By the way," he writes to Lyubimov, "I'm very pleased that the book 'The Boys' . . . is so separate and episodic: the reader won't fuss nearly as much as if I'd broken off at a quite unfinished point and stuck in 'to be continued'"— and points out in addition that the further delay would also help the novel's commercial prospects as reader numbers typically rose over the summer months.[193]

The reader, forewarned perhaps by the way in which the preceding book had just been concluded, is forced to stop and ask why the author is embarking on this new experiment. Despite the many echoes of the main text, the book is quite different in both content and genre from the surrounding narrative of Dmitry's trial. Some of its episodes, such as the touching vignette of Kolya's care for the "bubbleheads" *(puzyri)*, the two children of a single parent in the neighbouring apartment (14:131–135), seem to have almost no relevance to the remainder of the plot and disappear as swiftly as they arrive. "I know, I only said it because it sounded good," says Kolya to the children, and Dostoevsky's selection of some of his material gives the impression of having been based on the same criterion.[194] Its highly charged emotional content makes it easy for the reader to be swept along by the Dickensian pathos of the story of the dying Ilyusha. This momentum makes it an undeniably successful commercial narrative. But simultaneously the sentimentality of the genre, reminiscent of *The Insulted and Injured,* makes us wonder whether this is not another experiment in Flaubertian excess. At what point, Dostoevsky seems to be asking, does the author's apparent control of this narrative slip into something with far less predictable results?

Alyosha's encounter with Kolya shows how easily this can happen. Kolya is to Alyosha what Alyosha was to Zosima in the early books: acolyte, novice, pupil. The gang of boys plays the role of monastic congregation. Kolya, though, trivialises Alyosha. Instead of wisdom, he learns precocity. His version of Alyosha's scriptural heritage is fragments from the supposed humanist canon—Smaragdov, Pushkin, Belinsky—parrot-learned and asserted with a bravado that mocks not just Ivan and his ideas but Alyosha's own attempts to project a narrative. He is the purveyor of illusion, unashamedly and ironically borrowing the Grand Inquisitor's recipe of miracle and mystery to ensure his in-story audience accepts his values, that Ilyushka believes the dog Perezvon is not Zhuchka, that canny peasants will be taken in by his swagger. Alyosha responds not with wisdom but with banality. "Don't be like everyone else; even if you are the only one to stay out, don't be like everyone else," is Alyosha's version of Zosima's last sermon.[195] "You are a prophet" (Vy prorok), responds Kolya a few lines later; the accolade from his mouth suggests the opposite.

And in the lines between the two quotations, an ambiguous exchange occurs in which Kolya declares his love for Alyosha (14:163). Alyosha's handsomeness has previously been noted (14:142), and Kolya starts blushing. There are no signposts as to whether this is due to the overcharged emotional atmosphere, or whether another homoerotic explanation is possible. Susanne Fusso points out that Dostoevsky must have been aware of homosexuality from his own environment, so a completely naive reading appears unlikely.[196] But the mere possibility of the suspicion suggests a wayward and speculative narrative that is less tightly under the control of the author than we had previously suspected.

This is a narrative that ultimately seems to trip itself up. As Miller argues, at one level it is finely constructed with a web of intratexts and mirrorings that tie it into the remainder of the novel. At another it is indeed a "narrative *tour de force*" that she acknowledges as her favourite book.[197] But I would argue that it seems to achieve a series of perverse outcomes. What begins as an apparent satire on Ivan's philosophy ends up as a debunking of Alyosha's putative conversion into seer. It shows how iteration, in the shape of a retelling of the main themes of the work in a different genre from a different perspective, with children playing the role of adults and parodying their behaviour, turns from repetition into a commentary on inauthenticity. The process of retelling itself seems to encourage a flight to excess, in this case of melodramatic pathos, in which the very exaggeration that can guarantee specific reader reception in one plane seems to undermine its own effect on another.

Book 11, "Brother Ivan Fedorovich" ("Brat Ivan Fedorovich"), turns out to be a further examination of the implications of loss of control. It chronicles Ivan's destructive influence on those around him and his descent into madness. There are obvious parallels and contrasts with Dmitry's progression towards his own loss of control in book 9, and with Alyosha's ambiguous epiphany at Cana, as well as his more recent deflation at the hands of Kolya. And just as the story of Ivan's rebellion in the previous book about him, book 5, "Pro and Contra," had begun with an image of excess in the shape of Saint John the Merciful, so this book, which bears Ivan's name as its title, opens with an image of excess in the form of Lise's dream of the pineapple compote (14:184). Alyosha visits Lise, who is ill, capricious, and plotting to transfer her affections to Ivan. She recollects a crime story in which a four-year-old boy had been mutilated and crucified by a Jew who then claims in mitigation at his trial that the boy died within hours. Lise imagines that she was the perpetrator and would then sit in front of the crucified boy eating pineapple compote.

Belknap links the images of Saint John and the pineapple compote as creating an awareness in the reader of "an over-arching evil existing in some sense outside of both Ivan and Lise," but they may also act in a much more direct way as indications of an inner battle within the text.[198] The image of the pineapple compote is itself one of uncontrolled excess and is used to suggest a loss of control in Lise, who is represented as on the verge of a breakdown. It operates on the reader at an initial level through commercial compulsion, in much the same way that a horror movie or the tabloid reporting of a gruesome murder does—we are even told that its source is "a book I read about some trial or other," probably an almanac of sensational crimes.[199] The context also has the effect of overwhelming the alternative debate that the image seeks to prompt on the moral issues of child suffering and anti-Semitism, partly because this lead is simply hijacked by the competing narrative and partly because its seriousness is undermined by the sensationalised genre of its presentation, which suppresses the intellectual in favour of the emotional.

The reference to pineapple compote, with its overtones of the exotic, the exclusive, and the fashionable, reinforces the dominance of the trivial over the intellectual but also sets up a jarring note that references Lise's possible mental state at one level and, at another, the possibility that, once again, the experimental disruption has caused a fundamental loss of control within the text itself. The chapter in which this scene occurs pits Lise's emotion against Alyosha's lack of it. After the stylistic excess of his Cana epiphany, he seems to have reverted to his former inarticulacy. His answers to her intense questions are monosyllables, repetitions of her queries, or short statements—no answer in the entire chapter extends to more than two lines of printed text. The epithets used to describe his reactions are lacklustre:

> "Alyosha, why don't you love me at all?' [Lise] concluded in a frenzy.
> "I do love you!" replied Alyosha warmly.[200]

His profession of love for Lise is expressed in Russian in a single word. Alyosha's lack of conviction as a red-blooded lover seems to deliver another knock to his credibility. As with Prince Myshkin, the credibility of the "beautiful man" *(prekrasny chelovek)*, which Dostoevsky seems to have wanted to portray, turns out to be much harder to deliver than envisaged.[201] Is Alyosha, we ask, really the hero of the novel as the preface would have us believe, or has the author in fact lost control of his text in a far more fundamental way?

Images of narrative loss of control intensify throughout book 11. Alyosha's visit to Lise provokes the image of the pineapple compote, perhaps the point at which the exploration of excess derails. Dmitry, pursued by his own hallucinatory image of excess in the shape of his dream of the abandoned baby, talks of symbolic escape, of breaking the controls of the body politic (14:193). Once again Dostoevsky uses Smerdyakov as the in-story author of his own narrative to show how the process works. His confession in three parts to Ivan is a virtuoso display of how iteration can be used to manipulate an in-story audience by allowing glimpses of a truth that is not revealed until the final episode, in ways that contrive to throw doubt on the denouement until it finally arrives.

Just as he misleads Ivan, so Dostoevsky toys with his readers, who suspect the outcome but still need it confirmed "in writing": the act of inscription of the narrative constitutes reality. Dostoevsky calls him a "storyteller" *(rasskazchik;* 14:221), a word only used once elsewhere in the entire novel, and then, in ironic contrast, to refer to Dmitry's confession to the prosecutor (14:92), in which he entirely fails to manipulate his stolid and unimaginative police audience. But Dostoevsky then illustrates how even Smerdyakov's ability to control narrative fails. His control over the events of the murder is destroyed by that most random of external interventions: a real epileptic fit, just as Dostoevsky's own creative process was repeatedly disrupted. And over the course of his three interviews with Ivan, the narrative that for so long he has tried to hide forces its way out of his deteriorating body. Narrative, even more so than murder, will out, and not even its own author can ultimately control it.

There seems to be a fundamental contradiction between the figure of Dostoevsky as *rasskazchik,* the confident professional storyteller, the auctioneer of narrative able to manipulate the reactions of his buying public, and the intellectual whose attempts to combine fiction with a serious discussion of major issues of faith and ethics have been repeatedly deflected back to the common denominator of what works commercially. The impression is reinforced by Rakitin's journalistic retelling of the story of the murder, which Mme Khokhlakova retails to Alyosha, to which I have already referred in suggesting Mme Khokhlakova as the representative of a new reader demographic. It shows how quickly and completely a narrative can spin out of control. The murder, it suggests, was committed by Dmitry for money to free himself from the attentions of a barely anonymised Mme Khokhlakova, who was trying to persuade him to run off with her to seek his fortune in the Siberian gold mines (14:176). This retelling, in conflated form, of a series of narratives that the reader has previously encountered acts to expose the manner in which the commercial imperative can deform the original story. The article bears almost no resemblance to the original truth, but every reader will understand why it is compulsive reading. Even the name of the town, Skotoprigonevsk—perhaps "Cowbothy" gives a sense—which surfaces for the very first time in this medium, plays to the urban reader's urge to mock provincial antics. The process serves as a revealing vignette on the way in which Dostoevsky himself has used commercial devices to ensure he retains reader attention, and hints that readers should be alert to signs of similar narrative distortion.

The culmination of this exposition of loss of control is Ivan's nightmare. Its very form questions whether loss of control applies to the narrative itself, rather than just to what it describes. Its subject matter deals with the unreliability of the method of transmission. Ivan cannot tell whether his devil is "real" or a hallucination, as Dostoevsky confirms in a letter to Lyubimov: "Even as he [my hero] denies apparitions are real, as soon as one disappears he insists on its reality."[202] For Ivan, a real distinction exists. For the reader, both are simply variants of a fictional narrative. At the mimetic level, we are invited to participate in Ivan's struggles to distinguish reality from fiction; at the diegetic, all is fiction: which story to believe? The unusual detail of the description of the devil appears to anchor him in reality but simultaneously, and precisely because the level of detail is unusual, puts us on notice that we are being told a story.

The recipient, for whom everything is part of the story, can never know whether what he or she sees or understands is underlying "truth" or simply an artefact of novelistic transmission. Recipient response is therefore no real guide to narrative value. As Ivan will discover, there are no intrinsic markers that distinguish one narrative as "real" and another as "fantasy": it depends on the response of the recipient, and recipients, even when not suffering from fever, are unpredictable and unrepresentative. The devil, with calculated irony, cites the same example of the apostle Thomas as the narrator used to describe Alyosha's instinctive belief in the first book: "Thomas believed not because he saw the risen Christ but because, even beforehand, he wanted to believe."[203] The very argument that appeared to reinforce the primacy of recipient response in its earlier incarnation is now used to suggest that the individuality of each response destroys its value as a tool for the author.

Just as he has done with Smerdyakov, Dostoevsky now sets up the devil as temporary author. At the level of the lowest common denominator, a form of predictable response does exist—"your earthy realism [where] everything is defined, formulaic, geometrical"[204]—but only in the shape of the overweight merchant's wife, whose preprogrammed beliefs the devil longs to be able to accept without question, or of a smallpox vaccine, with its reassuring certainty of cause and effect (14:228–229). The effect is independent of genre and works just as well

in the realms of melodrama, where an axe in space ceases to be fantastical and has its orbit plotted by astronomers and recorded in commercial almanacs, a staple of the trade in popular literature (14:230).

But beyond this the system breaks down. The artist has no special
powers of discernment—"Such dreams are sometimes seen not by
writers but by quite ordinary people—civil servants, journalists,
priests"[205]—so cannot act as seer. Much like Dostoevsky in the broader
landscape of the novel as a whole, the devil keeps "philosophising" (*fi-
losofstvovat;* 14:230, 231), as Ivan sarcastically complains, but ends up be-
moaning his own inability to mount a coherent argument (14:232). Indeed wisdom itself is compartmentalised and trivialised: Gogolesque
doctors specialise in diseases of the left nostril, cures happen not by science but by accident (14:231). The devil's role is reduced to that of defining himself by opposition, critic rather than author, "x in an indeter-
minate equation."[206] Straightforward answers do not exist in an
environment where even framing questions is tricky: "Je pense donc je
suis, that I'm sure of, but as for everything else around me, all these
worlds, God, even Satan, it remains to be proven whether they really
exist independently or are just a figment of my imagination."[207]

If there is no separately identifiable "reality," then all is, effectively,
story. To make the point, the devil tells an anecdote, the story of the
atheist who continues to reject life after death even when offered it after
his own death, is condemned to walk a quadrillion kilometres before
the heavenly doors will open for him, finally does so, and becomes a
believer on the instant. The devil corrects himself—the story is, he says,
more a "legend" than an anecdote (14:232–233). The distinction is important: legends are a type of prospectus narrative existing within a cultural tradition that provides a framework for a received interpretation
of the narrative. It has a fixed exchange value: "I sold it for what I paid
for it," says the devil, to use a literal translation of the Russian.[208] But
reader reception is no longer so reliable. The devil himself, as raconteur,
notices that the denouement is a little too pat to be credible (14:234).
Ivan, prefiguring Roland Barthes, argues the nonexistence of the devil-
as-author since he can reinterpret the devil's narrative wholly in terms
of his own personal experience. The devil's satirical plagiarism of
Ivan's previous arguments is, with equal plausibility, a demonstration
of Ivan's loss of control of his own narrative. Arguments degenerate
into absurd wordplay, Jesuitical casuistry, or both together, as a friar

reassures a noseless marquis that at least he will no longer have to suffer his nose being put out of joint (14:235).

Like a model of the novel in miniature, attempts to introduce philosophy end either in excess or in trivialisation. The noseless marquis commits suicide, but this is not the suicide of *Diary of a Writer,* where Dostoevsky can debate the topic over four issues, interweaving newspaper reportage with fictional correspondence, a novella about a suicide, and eventually the exposition of an ethical position on the matter.[209] Here the suicide supervenes in one line, without explanation. The bald statement, "The unfortunate young man returned home and shot himself that very night: I was with him right up to the very last moment," implies an expectation that reader reception is no longer material, that details like rationale and narrative continuity are irrelevant, presumably because the reader is no longer considered able to judge anything but trivia.[210] As if in response, suicide is followed by a juicy titbit of sex and the clergy in a clichéd anecdote of the *blondinochka* that can trace its provenance back for over a century.[211] Just as the novel itself shows that the attempt to combine successful fiction with intellectual debate continually slides off into excess or cliché, so the novel in microcosm of Ivan's dream parodies the process.

Only the commercial is predictable. All other narrative is, by definition, speculative given the vagaries of reader response. Smerdyakov's suicide even leaves two narratives. The story of his death circulates, newspaper-fashion, by word of mouth round the town, carried by Alyosha the reporter. The alternative narrative of his part in the murder is inherited by Ivan, who is now ironically referred to as the *romantik* (14:241)—both romantic and narrator of romances—and will turn out to be of speculative value only in the trial. And the ultimate test of narrative, by gladiatorial combat, will come in the trial itself, the random outcome of which Dostoevsky signals right from the outset in its title: "A Miscarriage of Justice" ("Sudebnaya oshibka"). This, the twelfth and final full book of the novel before the epilogue, was serialised in two parts in September and October 1880.

The trial scenes are a dramatic exposition of the speculative nature of narrative. Both counsel, Ivan Kirillovich for the prosecution and Fetyukovich for the defence, present prospectus narratives, which assert the value of their arguments over all others. Both retell the story in words that make it clear that what is at stake here is a literary contest between two narratives rather than an attempt to reveal some notion of truth or reality. The prosecutor's "factual evidence" turns out to be another narrative variant, since he uses "facts" that the reader knows not to be true.[212] Fetyukovich even tries to argue that the very facts themselves, the money, the robbery, and the murder, did not exist (14:303–313).

Both explicitly refer to the presentation of evidence as akin to the process of writing a novel. The prosecutor accuses Dmitry of poor authorship because, he claims, Dmitry has overlooked crucial details in making his story realistic: "The main thing there is that a triumphant novelist can be undermined and brought crashing down by details, just those details reality is always so rich in, and which are always overlooked as completely meaningless and unnecessary trivia by those unfortunate and accidental authors, to whom they don't even occur."[213] The defence retorts that melodrama and plausibility are unlikely bedfellows: "It was just that idea which lay behind the prosecution's suggestion that the money was hidden somewhere in a crevice at Mokroye. And why not in the dungeons of the Castle of Udolfo, gentlemen of the jury? Isn't the suggestion fantastical, straight out of a novel?"[214]

We may admire their evident skill in renarrating the evidence to such opposed conclusions. By extension, we may also applaud Dostoevsky's own skill in creating and controlling these two contradictory narratives. But prospectus narrative once again fails to produce anything other than an apparently random outcome. The narrator suggests that the public has made its mind up along gender lines before hearing any evidence at all (14:248). The presiding judge favours a sociological interpretation. Rakitin, emerging as a full-fledged journalist, imposes a political interpretation (14:252). As many critics have noted, the prosecuting counsel is wrong for the right reasons, while the defence counsel is right for the wrong reasons.

But just as the trial scenes disprove the value of narrative at one level, so they assert it on another. This is a gripping courtroom drama, a commercial narrative genre that relies on established literary devices to create predictable effects. Its subject matter is sex, money, and crime. The narrator is, literally, a court reporter able to produce a quasi-stenographic record of proceedings. He sees the courtroom audience in terms of newspaper demographics and reports separately the responses from the male and female segments (14:244). Sudden plot inversions maintain suspense: contradictory facts, such as Dmitry's confessional letter to Katerina Ivanovna, which is new to the court though not to the reader, are introduced to challenge received assumptions. The break in serialisation comes not at the point where the prosecution hands over to the defence but at the end of chapter 5, when the contradictory testimony of Ivan, who offers Smerdyakov's story and the envelope containing the stolen 3,000 roubles, and of Katerina Ivanovna, who produces Dmitry's letter, creates a dramatic climax (14:269). Dr. Herzenstube demonstrates the power of the story by his vivid and sentimental anecdote of Dmitry and the pound of nuts (14:258).

Both prosecution and defence counsel acknowledge the role of the commercial press. Ippolit Kirillovich, reflecting on Russian society, acknowledges that the modern press has been responsible for bringing the graphic immediacy of criminal acts to the public (14:274). His psychological argument about the contradictions of the Karamazov nature is also a literary argument about the credibility of the polarisation and hyperbole that underlie melodrama (14:279). Fetyukovich repeatedly uses illustrations of crimes from popular newspapers to illustrate his points and, implicitly, to keep his audience hooked by journalistic stories that have previously demonstrated their value (14:316).

"After that everything descended into the most awful chaos."[215] The jury's apparently perverse verdict, contrasted with the reader's own superior knowledge of a different narrative of the crime, is a spectacular demonstration of the subjective nature of narrative reception. Readers, it seems, react not to the narrative offered by an author but to another, parallel discourse of their own invention that can be influenced by unrelated external circumstances, such as gender stereotypes or class distinctions—the narrator records that the men in the courtroom were pleased with the verdict while the women were upset, and attributes the verdict to the reactionary reflexes of the peasantry (14:323). And yet Dostoevsky has successfully led his reader through almost two years of serialisation, from January 1879 to November 1880. His strategy of iterative experiment has paid off if the reader has followed to the end of the story. Multiple retellings of the same narrative allow an author to vary almost every parameter of the text—genre, narratorial position, intellectual weight. The extent and variety of subsequent critical commentary is evidence of the text's ability to support multiple and contradictory reader interpretations.

So the epilogue, published in November 1880, only two months before Dostoevsky's eventual death, stands in some measure as Dostoevsky's envoi to his contemporary reading public and to the future
mass audience he seems to have anticipated in Mme Khokhlakova. Its
subject is the enduring value of memory, or, in different terminology,
the perpetuity value of stories. As early as April 1880 he writes of "Ilyusha's burial and Alexei Karamazov's funeral oration to the boys, in
which the meaning of the whole novel will to some extent be revealed."[216]
This is, apparently, a reversion to the prospectus narrative of the first
half of the novel, in which the ability to manipulate text is equated to
the ability to manipulate reception.

The evidence of Dostoevsky's contemporary correspondence clearly
suggests an intent to project a Christian point of view. In the month
following the publication of the epilogue, he writes to Blagonravov,
"But a new intelligentsia is coming. They will want to be at one with
the common people. The first sign of an unbreakable fellowship with the
people is a respect and love for that which the great mass of the people
honour and love more and higher than anything else in the world—that
is to say, their God and their faith."[217] A Christian interpretation of Alyosha's speech at the stone would indeed see it as an encomium to faith
and community through the power of narrative to provide continuity.
The novel's biblical epigraph about the grain of wheat that must die to
bear fruit suggests the ability to harness experience to create posterity
value.

Miller argues that the way in which the book links many of the previously more separate strands of the novel demonstrates the power of
this shared dialogue to create its own perpetuity value through common
memories.[218] The speech at the stone not only perpetuates the memory
of Ilyusha but also affirms Alyosha's ability to combine inheritances
from both the Karamazov psyche and Zosima into a transformed ar-
ticulacy that allows him to create lasting prose. Dostoevsky's 1880
Pushkin speech shares the same theoretical platform. It depicts Pushkin
as the descendant of a line of Russian chroniclers and the creator of a
Russian eternal feminine in Tatyana, and suggests that the validation of
a future set of readers, of which Dostoevsky is the chief representative,
should result in a reassessment of both Pushkin's posterity value and
Russia's destiny: "I am speaking merely of the brotherhood of people and
of the fact that, perhaps, the Russian heart is most plainly destined,

among all the peoples, for universally human and brotherly unity; I see traces of this in our history, in our gifted people, in the artistic genius of Pushkin."[219]

But the epilogue, like all other prospectus narratives, refuses to behave as apparently intended. Underneath the theme of spiritual redemption lurks a mistrust of just the sort of prospectus narrative represented by Alyosha. The novel's epigraph, after all, implies that the attainment of posterity requires a change of status so fundamental that all memory of a prior state would be lost. The epilogue depicts a series of attempts to create future value by means of a return to the past. Dmitry imagines his future as a fantastic land full of redskins, the 1750s America of James Fenimore Cooper and the last Mohican, in which even he fails to believe, since his one ambition is to escape and return to Mother Russia and hide as quickly as possible (14:330). Katerina Ivanovna looks back to her love for Dmitry, now explicitly described as belonging to the past (14:331). The Snegirev family cling to the ritual aspects of religion to master their grief (14:335). The genre reverts to a kind of Dickensian pathos that seems to refer back to a much earlier phase of Dostoevsky's writing career. Even the treatment of the past is equivocal. Ivan is effectively written out of the script. We are left with a perfunctory reference to his health (14:324) and never find out whether he lives or dies. Zosima, for all that he may live on through Alyosha, is also ironically demoted by Ilyusha, whose corpse does not smell (14:334).

There seems to be a real sense in which the narrative is fighting with itself. Alyosha may acquire a new fluency in his speech at the stone, but the reader may remember that his previous attempts at extended communication have all ended in the failure of the medium, as in Zosima's hagiography, or in loss of control, as in the Cana of Galilee episode. His speech in the epilogue dwells on the value of memory and the need to perpetuate the memory of Ilyusha and of the camaraderie of the twelve boys into their future lives. Emotional intensity is conveyed through pathos and sentimentality which teeters on the edge of cliché, the point at which an excess of iteration attacks credibility. All previous narratives of children, whether from the Ilyusha / Kolya thread or from the iterating anecdotes of the suffering of children, have been characterised by excess either of shock or of sentimentality.

All have drawn attention, in the same way as the image of Saint John the Merciful / Saint Julien l'Hospitalier, to their status as narratives and have prompted the reader to assess their credibility. I think that this final image is profoundly ambiguous. We experience it in two dimensions, simultaneously aware of the attraction of its spiritual scope and of a rejection of its emotional overload. We are aware of the narrative skill and commercial power that have kept us reading for some seven hundred pages or almost two years of serialisation. But there is something unresolved in this resolution, a sense that the desired equilibrium is not to be had, that narrative has, indeed, become speculative. The fact that this dialogue continues right up to the closing pages of *The Brothers Karamazov* is an indication that, for Dostoevsky, no definitive answer exists. Like roulette, completion delivers only random outcomes. The fact that Dostoevsky does not resolve the balance between fictional credibility and the capacity of fiction to sustain a serious moral message may be an indication that, for him, there is no sustainable point of balance. The real moral challenge, for author and reader alike, is how to negotiate the continuous, fibrillating switchback from one to the other.

Dostoevsky calls the fictional town in which he sets *The Gambler* Roulettenburg. He returns again and again to the theme of speculation. The roulette table is both an object of addiction in his life, an iterated theme in his works and correspondence, and a symbol of the Russian character. By the time he started *The Brothers Karamazov,* though, his addiction had long since been overcome. The need to gamble had been replaced by a far more conservative attitude to risk as Anna Grigor'evna took over more and more of Dostoevsky's business dealings. Roulette is not mentioned a single time in the novel. Dostoevsky's writing habits, and particularly the planning of the novel, reveal a way of working that is fundamentally different from the impetuous approach to *The Idiot* of a decade earlier, which had led him to write the entire first book before working out the remainder of the plot. I think we should see *The Brothers Karamazov* as an exploration of ways of moderating the risk of failure in a changing publishing market. Perversely, this risk-management strategy is itself so novel that it creates an entirely new set of risks.

In the face of a publishing market that, to repeat, aped French mass-market publishing strategies without a comparable readership, Dostoevsky's strategy makes perfect sense. The choice of a courtroom drama clearly responded to a proven commercial driver in the growing boulevard newspaper industry: readers, and especially the newer readers from an emerging bourgeoisie, were interested in criminal psychology, detection, and legal process, particularly in their more sensational aspects. The genre of the courtroom drama plays to this readership and places a bet that future readerships will retain this fascination. But the actual readership of Katkov's thick journals was used to a quite different diet, much of which responds to the various strains of prospectus narrative with which Dostoevsky experiments, and with which he was directly familiar from his own experience of commercialising *Diary of a Writer*. With its emphasis on the competitive retelling of stories, the courtroom drama also provides a platform for experimentation from which an author can explore which variants attract which readers, particularly in a serialised format. Passages that may fail with one segment, or one generation, of the readership may still find favour with others. The genre itself also provides the subject of the novel, as the author imagines how the iterative revoicings of the narrative are received by his own in-story characters. The success of this risk-mitigation strategy is evidenced by the fact that the novel has travelled so well through time, has effectively penetrated the mass market, and has accumulated such a wide variety of competing explications.

The strategy also affords the modern critic an opportunity to observe how these commercial strategies influence the text itself. I have argued in this chapter that commercial drivers are evident within the text and are frequently referred to and discussed by Dostoevsky within the narrative itself. We can, for example, identify the patterns of iteration in the text and demonstrate that these serve both commercial and novelistic purposes. We can show how different genres of narration correspond to different modes of transaction and ways of constituting narrative value. We can suggest how these estimates of narrative value lead to further textual experimentation to explore how value can be modified. To ignore the commercial aspects of narrative leads to an incomplete understanding of the text.

Finally, we can perhaps suggest that Dostoevsky's famous "unfinalisability" is itself a successful commercial strategy. In attempting to write for an undeveloped but predicted mass audience as well as for a more limited contemporary audience, in trying to combine intellectual weight with compulsive narrative, in seeking ways to assert dearly held beliefs without alienating readers or inadvertently traducing his own case, a strategy of avoiding definition is perfectly logical. The value of his own memory, the perpetuity value of his own texts, depends in part on this ability to touch multiple audiences through multiple media whilst trying to maximise the likelihood of a good reception. "Dostoevsky and fiasco," writes John Jones, "are never far apart."[220] Playing the odds reduces the damage of any single fiasco and recognises that the constraints of writing within a fictional genre make it impossible to fix values even for a single reader. From the all-in strategy of the hero of *The Gambler*, playing his last coin on the tables in Roulettenburg, Dostoevsky has shifted to a more cautious tactic of multiple bets. His narrative plays are more deliberate, accepting fiasco as one losing bet amongst other winning ones. If Roulettenburg is where Dostoevsky learned to gamble, then *The Brothers Karamazov* is where he finally masters the art of placing the bet. Roulettenbook, perhaps?

3

Zola: The Business of Narrative

IF FEDOR DOSTOEVSKY WROTE for a mass readership that remained illusory in his lifetime, Emile Zola emerged into a French publishing industry ripe for change. A more literate, more urbanised and, albeit slowly, richer public could afford to buy not just newspapers and periodicals but books as well. Zola became the leading large-scale entrepreneur of this new market, borrowing freely from journalistic and commercial techniques to develop his business, as much businessman as novelist. His rise is that of big business, not just in the publishing industry but across the French industrial landscape as new forms of corporate ownership were introduced. His subject is big business, from the department store to the railways to the stock exchange. His novels are themselves products of the processes he describes. Even his naturalism is as much an economic as a literary phenomenon.

To illustrate the evolution of this process over the central span of Zola's writing career when he was publishing *Les Rougon-Macquart* (1871–1893), I have selected one work from each end of the cycle.[1] *La Curée* (1872) and *L'Argent* (1891), respectively the second and eighteenth works in the series, describe the business career of a single central character, Aristide Saccard. Their publication dates are separated by nineteen years. The first predates Zola's commercial breakthrough as a writer with *L'Assommoir* (1876) and allows us to understand some of the strategies Zola used to enhance narrative value. The second comes from a period when Zola's success had been firmly established for fifteen years and when he was about to introduce a new product range in the shape of *Les Trois Villes*. The comparison allows us to understand just how these narratives of business also become part of the business of narrative.

The Commercialisation of the Book

By the early 1880s in France, the book had reacquired a substantial degree of economic independence from the newspaper and periodical press. We have seen in the chapter on Honoré de Balzac how, in the 1830s, prose fiction was forced to migrate to the press, as the most effective platform on which to reach the contemporary reader, by a combination of the undeveloped reader market, inadequate technology, and lack of capital. By the 1880s many of the conditions that had forced this migration had radically altered. A mass-market readership for books independent from romans-feuilletons had begun to emerge. True, the overall size of the potential market had barely increased, with low birth rates and high infant mortality limiting population growth from 35.4 million in 1846 to just 38.3 million in 1891. But the urban population, where literacy was concentrated, had ballooned, rising over the same period from 8.6 million to 14.3 million.[2] Literacy, driven by state provision of primary education for males since the *loi Guizot* of 1833 and for females since the *loi Falloux* of 1850, was almost universal and would spread further with the *lois Ferry* of 1881 and 1882, which made primary education first free, then mandatory. François Furet and Jacques Ozouf's statistical evaluation of different methods of literacy assessment indicates levels of illiteracy of some 57 per cent in 1831–1835 but only around 6 per cent in 1891–1895.[3] Literacy among females, an important demographic for the novel, rose more slowly but had nonetheless reached 66 per cent by the early 1870s, rising to over 70 per cent in urban centres and over 92 per cent in the *département* of the Seine.[4]

Increasing leisure time, more disposable income available for spending on leisure pursuits such as reading, and reductions in the cover price of books all helped to increase the size of the readership. James Smith Allen suggests that, correcting for male / female and urban / provincial skew, the "real" readership for fiction had risen from just over 2 million readers in 1821, or some 6.7 per cent of the total population, to around 9.4 million in 1891, or around 24.5 per cent of the population. Within these overall estimates, he suggests that by far and away the fastest growth was recorded during the two decades of the 1870s and 1880s, each of which saw the addition of around 2 million new readers. Implicit in these estimates is the fact that the demographics of reading were changing, from the largely bourgeois, educated readership of the midcentury to the beginnings of a mass market that would eventually encompass a far broader social spectrum. Allen nonetheless cautions against the assumption that this was a swift process: the spread of literacy is scant evidence of the actual practice of reading fiction.[5]

The broader economic context suggests that there were many other reasons for the slow pace of change. Poor economic growth, and in particular the three decades of relative underperformance that began towards the end of the 1860s, impeded both the spread of literacy and the exploitation of its benefits. Competition from lower-cost imports, a series of natural and manmade disasters ranging from the loss of Alsace-Lorraine to phylloxera, and a failure to adapt to new technologies led to labour productivity growing by less than 1 per cent per annum over the thirty years to the late 1880s and early 1890s. By 1890 France's per capita income was under 60 per cent of that of Great Britain.[6]

This was no broad consumer revolution. Rather, it was confined to the bourgeoisie and uppermost layers of manual workers. Roger Magraw argues that only after 1870 did rising wages, falling food prices, and shorter working hours allow spending on nonessential items to increase. Even then, working-class families spent most of their income on food and rent. Less than 10 per cent were able to spend a tenth of their income on books, amusements, or other consumer goods.[7] Anne-Marie Thiesse, analysing reading habits in the Belle Epoque, suggests that no significant increase in disposable income for leisure pursuits among the lower classes occurred until after 1900. She points out that most books, other than the cheapest imprints, were still luxuries that could be easily replaced by much cheaper daily newspapers, and that even the bargain popular editions at one franc were still out of reach for many. In 1882 the wages of a Parisian cabinetmaker, by no means amongst the poorest, would have amounted to no more than eight francs per day, and would not grow for the rest of the decade.[8] Even though median industrial salaries had risen by 48 per cent between 1875 and 1905 (equivalent to an annual rise of some 1.25 per cent), a one-sou paper in 1900 was still equal to 12.5 per cent of the price of a kilo of bread, or one-third the price of a metro ticket. Women were typically even worse paid.[9]

To be competitive, books needed to be cheap and, if they were to reach a mass readership, their content had to address a layer of consumers more used to the cheaper flysheets and boulevard newspapers. Technological developments and improvements in distribution, pioneered by the newspaper industry, were indeed enabling books to be sold more cheaply, in ever-increasing volumes, to a wider audience. Hippolyte Auguste Marinoni's rotary press massively increased printing capacity, while improvements in mechanical composition, inking, and techniques for illustration, from lithography at the beginning of the century to photogravure at its end, all increased printing capacity, reduced costs through longer print runs, and improved product quality across the publishing spectrum.[10] Paper costs dropped significantly, from one hundred francs per kilogramme in 1870 to forty-four francs per kilogramme by 1888, with the increasing use of woodpulp-based paper in the 1860s and 1870s and the removal of paper tariffs.[11] The development of the railway network from 6,520 kilometres in 1857 to 22,000 kilometres in 1880 not only speeded access to the provinces but also created a new readership among the travelling public, which Louis Hachette addressed through both kiosks and special editions.[12] The size of the potential provincial audience was convincingly demonstrated by Moïse Millaud and *Le Petit Journal* (established in 1863), which rolled out its own distribution system across almost the whole of provincial France and by 1911 sold 80 per cent of its 835,000 circulation in the provinces.[13]

Many of the marketing tools developed for newspapers also proved relevant to books.[14] Price promotions had already reduced the prices of the cheapest imprints to one franc per volume across both Charpentier's and Hachette's entire popular editions by 1856. Distribution improved dramatically. Bookstore growth outpaced the rise in population, doubling outside Paris in the period 1851–1878.[15] Railway kiosks, another key outlet, grew from 43 in 1853 to 1,151 in 1895. Poster campaigns were used to promote new themes and new titles, as witness Millaud's 1865 promotion of the faits divers columns of *Le Petit Journal* by placards proclaiming "Crimes et Châtiments" in enormous letters— Dostoevsky *avant la lettre*.[16] Zola's own experience in the publicity department of Hachette, where he worked from 1862 to 1866, bartering free copies of new books against (he hoped) positive reviews in other papers, brought him face to face with the expanding market for prose fiction. While many of these advances related more to the newspaper and periodical industry than to the book trade, they left behind a fertile trail of new routes to market and new readers that the book was able to exploit in the course of its own quest for independence.

But perhaps the most important spin-off from newspapers to the book-publishing area lay in the vastly increased availability of capital and credit. Thomas Piketty demonstrates, with overwhelming evidence, that the Belle Epoque was a period when financial inequality in France across the social spectrum reached levels never previously—or indeed subsequently—seen.[17] Returns on investments—from government *rentes* to Parisian property—had exceeded the growth rate of the economy as a whole for much of the century. As a consequence, the amount of wealth passed on by inheritance grew exponentially, compounding the problem. The rich became richer while the poor, with nothing to invest, stagnated. Capital accumulation became a force for funding the development of a mass market while simultaneously stunting its growth. By the 1890s the top 10 per cent of the population owned almost 90 per cent of total wealth and the top 1 per cent almost 60 per cent, while the majority had virtually no accumulated savings at all. As Piketty notes on more than one occasion, Vautrin's advice to Rastignac to marry wealth, rather than try to earn it, turned out to be prescient.

As a consequence, though, the supply of capital did improve, and new corporate protections, such as the limited liability company (in the form of the *société anonyme*, introduced in the precursor to its present form in 1867), evolved to help control investment risk. The capital requirements for the development of the railway system were so huge—over 1.2 billion francs in 1852–1855 alone—as to demand a wholesale restructuring of the French equity and debt capital markets, which thereafter became important sources of capital to fund industrialisation in other sectors, from mines to textiles. Roger Price uses the volume of bills discounted at the Bank of France as a proxy for the evolution of the capital market, on the basis that faster circulation of goods ties up more credit, and shows an almost threefold rise from an annual average of 5.5 billion francs in 1851–1860 to 14.5 billion francs in 1861–1875.[18]

Capital flowed in particular to the publishing industry because, in the right hands, it had become an attractive investment proposition. By 1884 *Le Petit Journal* had paid-in capital of 25 million francs, an enormous sum for the age, and produced an annual profit of over 4.5 million francs.[19] It had also become a *société anonyme* in 1881, benefitting from changes in corporate law that promoted the creation of larger groups with better access to capital markets and less reliance on the family- or single entrepreneur–based wealth that had characterised the early growth of the press in the 1840s and 1850s.[20] By 1881 there were seventy-three press stocks quoted on the Paris Bourse.[21]

Newspapers, in particular, had become adept at creating multiple revenue streams. A growing readership led to higher circulation revenues, notwithstanding the price discounting needed to attract new readers. Total newspaper print runs increased from 73 copies per thousand inhabitants in 1881 to 244 copies per thousand in 1914, placing France on a par with the United States in terms of press penetration.[22] Brand extensions allowed leading titles to spawn a shoal of spin-offs targeting distinct market segments: Millaud clustered *Le Journal de Paris, Le Magasin pittoresque, La Musée des familles,* and an illustrated weekly, *Le Journal illustré,* around *Le Petit Journal.* New readers in turn allowed the development of an accelerating income stream from both classified and display advertising. For example, Patrick Eveno's analysis of profitability at *Le Figaro* shows that in the period from 1879 to 1881, the paper was profitable on the basis of copy sales alone—advertising revenues added a further 15 per cent of total revenues in 1878, representing almost pure profit—and that by 1889–1891 the proportion of advertising revenues has risen to 33 per cent of revenues, or some 2 million francs per annum.[23] The first advertising agencies emerged as early as the 1840s. New categories of advertising were allowed: pharmacies, for example, from 1867, following approval at their annual industry confederation conference.[24]

Paid editorial, almost always undisclosed as such, also developed into a substantial income stream. Hippolyte de Villemessant, the proprietor of *Le Figaro,* boasted that his target was to get every line of the paper paid for in this way. Between 1875 and 1890, the Crédit Foncier is recorded as having spent 60 million francs on press "subsidies," while the Panama Canal Company invested 12 million francs in paid articles in an attempt to boost its share price before its eventual bankruptcy. Stock and debt issues became virtually impossible without these payoffs. The Russian government continued to buy favourable press coverage right up till the outbreak of the First World War in support of its issue of foreign bonds—France was the only external market in which it was able to issue debt.[25] "In today's world newspapers are no longer created by political parties but by bankers. They create them to promote a deal," writes Jules Simon in *Le Matin* on August 12, 1884.[26] *La presse financière* became not just an important influence in shaping a new incarnation of Charles Augustin Sainte-Beuve's *littérature industrielle* but a driving force in promoting the long-delayed Industrial Revolution in France.

After years of serial bankruptcies, peaking in the 1840s and 1850s, the book-publishing industry was also finally becoming a better investment proposition.[27] Rising incomes and falling book prices combined to create an almost fourfold increase in household disposable income available for book purchases between 1840 and 1910, even if from a low base and with a marked acceleration towards the end of the period with the advent of Fayard's *livre populaire* at sixty-five cents in 1905.[28] The same technologies that had allowed the newspaper press to reduce prices, boost sales, and increase margins—cheaper paper, faster presses, productivity improvements, better distribution networks—also worked for the book trade. The number of books published, which had stayed in a range of 6,000–7,000 per annum throughout the 1830 and 1840s, started to rise towards the end of the 1850s and reached an annual average of around 13,000 by the 1880s.[29] Using a different source, Frédéric Barbier estimates that the number of titles published increased from 6,220 in 1840 to 28,143 in 1900, while over the same time average print runs increased from just under 2,000 to 11,239, implying a combined twenty-six-fold increase in the volume of books produced.[30] Publishing dynasties began to appear, such as those of Hachette, Havas, and Charpentier. The mutual attractions of wealth, influence, and status seem to have drawn publishers and financiers together: Calmann Lévy married his daughter to the banker Siegfried Propper and his son Paul married into the Dutch Becker-Fuld banking family.[31] Backed by inherited wealth and an investment market that favoured the media sector, publishers began investing directly in the book industry for the first time, as illustrated by Calmann Lévy's significant expansion of his book-distribution network in the 1880s.[32]

But it is equally clear that until the 1880s the book trade, as a separate business from press publishing, continued to be a struggle. Jean-Yves Mollier's analysis, in his *L'Argent et les lettres: Histoire du capitalisme d'édition*, of Georges Charpentier's business suggests that it made revenues in the three financial years from 1880 to 1882 of, respectively, 831,174 francs, 635,474 francs, and 815,706 francs, and profits before interest and tax of 181,190 francs, 100,523 francs, and 117,158 francs. Nonetheless, once the costs of financing the debts of an estimated 600,000–700,000 francs Charpentier had incurred in building his business were taken into account, Mollier speculates that he would have made a loss—and this for the foremost literary publisher of his time with writers from Gustave Flaubert, Guy de Maupassant, Joris-Karl Huysmans, Alphonse Daudet, and Edmond de Goncourt to Zola in his stable.[33] His financial situation deteriorated to such an extent that he came close to selling the business to Calmann-Lévy in 1883.

By 1885, though, Charpentier was back on his feet financially. What had driven the turnaround? A good part of the answer can be summarised in one word: Zola. The French book-publishing trade had seen spectacular successes before. Charles Joseph Panckoucke had established his publishing dynasty in prerevolutionary days on the back of the distribution in France of the *Encyclopédie:* Mollier argues that he was the first publisher to recognise the power of volume distribution, and Martin Lyons suggests that he reached the limits of practical economic scale within the ancien régime.[34] Alexandre Dumas *fils*'s *La Dame aux camélias*, first published in 1848, eventually required twenty-four successive editions to satisfy demand on top of an initial print run of 6,000, large for its day.[35] Ernest Renan's *Vie de Jésus*, published in 1863, sold 168,000 copies and had been translated into five languages by the end of 1864, earning its author an estimated 107,000 francs, an early demonstration of the power of scandal (in this case reinforced by a formal ecclesiastical ban) to open new readerships.[36]

But these were isolated successes. By and large, print runs remained stuck in the low thousands. The publishing history of Zola's early works illustrates how difficult it was to achieve scale in book format. *Thérèse Raquin*, after appearing as a three-episode serial in *L'Artiste* in August 1867, was eventually published in book form in December of the same year by Zola's first publisher, Lacroix, in an edition of 1,500 copies with a further 200 for overage and publicity.[37] The first edition of the opening volume of *Les Rougon-Macquart, La Fortune des Rougon*, published in October 1871, failed to sell out and, in a standard industry tactic, was remarketed in 1872 as the "second" edition. The launch of the next, *La Curée*, was interrupted by the imminent failure of Lacroix and Zola's transfer to his new publisher, Charpentier, who was able to buy from Lacroix the rights to the entire *Rougon-Macquart* series, together with the plates and unsold copies of the two previous volumes, for 800 francs. By the publication of *L'Assommoir* in 1877, the first five volumes of *Les*

Rougon-Macquart had sold a cumulative total of some 40,000–50,000 copies.[38]

L'Assommoir, printed in a first book edition of 4,000 in January 1877, sold over 40,000 copies in that year alone. Not only that, but it also reignited interest in the preceding titles. By the middle of the year, every copy of *L'Assommoir* sold led to the sale of almost the same number of copies of the earlier volumes in the series.[39] Over the course of 1877 and 1888, Charpentier would put on sale 75,000 copies of *L'Assommoir,* of which 15,000 in an expensive illustrated edition, 25,000 copies of *Une Page d'Amour,* and a further 10,000 copies of the earlier volumes. Henri Mitterand calculates that Zola made a total income of 65,000–80,000 francs from his publications over the course of 1877–1878, tax-free. Emboldened, Charpentier printed 55,000 copies of the first edition of *Nana* on February 15, 1880, and even so was forced to order a further 10,000 by the evening of the first day of sale.[40] The best seller had come of age. First print runs of subsequent works in the series averaged some 50,000 copies, rising to 66,000 for the final two. All three volumes of *Les Trois Villes* were printed in first editions of 88,000. By Zola's death in 1902, over 1.8 million copies in book format of *Les Rougon-Macquart* had rolled off the press.

The New Economics of Fiction

Why was Zola able to become the catalyst for the book's reacquisition of its economic independence in France? Was he simply in the right place at the right time to take advantage of a transition that would have happened anyway? Or was he able to impart additional "value" to his narratives that started or accelerated the process? And if the latter, are there specific qualities in his texts that can be identified with this economic function?

As we have seen, the conditions for the development of a mass readership for prose fiction both during and in the decade following the Second Empire were hardly propitious. The vast majority of the population lived on income levels too low to permit discretionary spending on anything but the popular press. Any attempt to expand this market had to contend with the fact that its tastes and expectations had already been conditioned by the boulevard newspapers. So to understand Zola's contribution to the way in which literary value was created, we need to consider the cultural context in which his fiction began to appear.

The steep growth in press circulation from the 1860s was fuelled not just by the economics of the volume and price but also by the techniques of popular journalism. Millaud's innovation with *Le Petit Journal* in 1863 was essentially one of degree rather than nature. There was little evidence of any fundamental shift in popular taste, more or less irrespective of social class. The key cultural drivers of voyeurism, fashion, the exotic, and the taxonomic had remained virtually unchanged since Emile de Girardin's earlier press revolution of 1836 despite the expansion in the readership over the intervening period.[41] Voyeurism, or the fascination of every social class with the mores of those they considered above and, especially, beneath them, as well as with the hidden *mœurs* of their own classes, had proved resiliently popular—notably demonstrated by Eugène Sue in *Les Mystères de Paris*. Fashion, or the thrill of the evanescent, had been identified as the focus of a key target reader demographic as early as Girardin's introduction of *La Mode* in 1829 and was able to adapt to expanding markets with ease, as Zola illustrates in *Au Bonheur des dames*.

The exotic, or the draw of all things foreign, was just as evident from the crowds flocking to each of the roughly decennial *expositions universelles* across the second half of the century as it had been to earlier readers of *Mille et une nuits*. And taxonomy, or the urge to understand through description and classification, could be traced back variously to the *Encyclopédie*, to Léon Curmer's *Les Français peints par eux-mêmes*, to the sociological and criminological investigations of an Alexandre Parent-Duchâtelet or a Eugène François Vidocq, or to the emergence of the detective novel. Dominique Kalifa's investigation in *Les Bas-fonds* of the links between this prurient interest in the underclasses, the mania for classification (which he calls "taximanie"), and the evolution of tastes in fiction shows clearly how popular tastes are able to travel through time.[42] Chapter 2 on Dostoevsky has also demonstrated that similar concerns were shared by Russian readers despite the remoteness and earlier stage of development of the Russian market. The relevance of these issues to today's press also suggests that to an extent they can be seen as cultural constants.

What was different, though, was the degree to which Millaud and, swiftly thereafter, his competitors were prepared to push the sensationalism of their coverage of these topics to attract the attention of readers. "Take 25 duels, 12 poisonings, 1 lost child, 1 policeman, 2 convicts, 4 spies, 1 mysterious good-looking male, 3 assassinations and 2 suicides. Place in a beaker and heat till white hot, then spread on paper with a goose quill, cut into strips and serve sequentially, referring each time to the 'next instalment,' and open your cash register with confidence."[43] The unnamed journalist from *Satan* in 1868 is satirising the roman-feuilleton but could just as easily have been writing about contemporary journalistic practice.

The link between sensationalism, excess, and profitability established itself rapidly. The Jean-Baptiste Troppmann murders of 1869 are frequently cited to demonstrate how a sensational crime was able to boost sales at *Le Petit Journal*, which jumped from 357,000 when Troppmann's first six bodies were found on September 23 to 594,000 by the time of his execution on January 16, 1870.[44] Kalifa's investigation of the links between crime and the press in *L'Encre et le sang* shows clearly how the volume and manner of crime reportage were linked to circulation. He cites Paul Féval, writing in 1866: "Crime is on the up, it sells, it fetches a premium price: to listen to the marketmakers, France has one or two million consumers who refuse to buy anything except crime, pure and simple."[45] By 1902 the journalist Henri de Noussanne, asking, "How much is the French daily press worth?" estimated that crime reporting had within a few decades become the sixth-largest category in the main daily newspapers.[46]

Nor did the quest for the sensational stop at crime stories. Alain Vaillant makes the point that the cycle of revolutions and wars that characterised the long nineteenth century created a backdrop against which the sensational was perhaps the only normal.[47] Periodicals used different aspects of sensation as a form of branding. *Gil Blas* became the place for louche anecdote, as Jules Bertaut notes in relation to the strategy adopted by its editor, Auguste Drumont: "The frenzy of the literary battle surrounding naturalism, together with consumer preferences for extremely risqué, even overtly explicit, material on the pretext of unadorned verismo, gave him the idea of creating a paper which would feature literature and a stunningly bold attitude to everything."[48] *Le Figaro*'s "Echo de Paris" column became the go-to source of society scandal: "Indiscretion has become an art form there. You read it to keep up with the scandals of the moment."[49] David Baguley suggests that Louis Napoleon's "rewriting" of himself as emperor after the 1851 coup d'état sets a tone of excess, political hyperbole, that characterises the whole of the Second Empire.[50]

The drive to sensationalism and excess affected not just content but the format and genre of journalistic narration as well. Compression, allied with sensation, became a hallmark of this new journalism. Paul Alexis, writing in 1888, records the process as follows: "For a few years now, alongside the grand style of political journalism, pushing literature down to the foot of the front page or locking it up on the third under the heading of 'Miscellany,' sandwiched between the faits divers and the advertisements, a new style has been tunnelling its way out under the name of 'Petit Journalisme'—livelier, more contemporary, fit for the purpose of interrogating the current age, propelled by immediacy, news, facts, relegating political theories to second level, giving greater space to literature."[51] Kalifa and others argue in *La Civilisation du journal* that Millaud brought the then experimental techniques of the department store, which Zola records in *Au Bonheur des dames*—"pile 'em high, sell 'em cheap"—to the newspaper through a combination of a pared-down presentation and a focus on trivia, delivered partly via the faits divers column and partly through the clipped style of Anglo-Saxon journalism.[52] Zola explicitly acknowledged the stylistic influence: "I love the news; it is the stuff of life, where you find passing epiphanies, fleeting impressions, all sorts of things that seem to me good because brief."[53]

The growth of the popular faits divers columns enabled more crimes, accidents, and scandals to be covered through compression of the material reported. Most newspapers stuck to the traditional four-page format until well into the 1880s, partly to reduce paper and composition costs but mainly because press speeds simply did not permit any more. Space was therefore at a premium, particularly with a significant and growing part of the back page taken up by advertising. Editorial compression, especially outside the main articles, was essential and became a significant influence on journalistic style. The "need to squeeze" favoured sensationalism through shock headlines and a concentration on gory detail.

Compression also eroded the distinction between fact and fiction. Real life could be stranger than fiction. Journalists reported the extraordinary in hyperbolic language. If the facts were not readily available, they invented them.[54] Some even became the heroes of their own stories as they tracked criminals or dug up scandal. Later French detective fiction represents the hero as a reporter—as witness Gaston Leroux's Rouletabille or Maurice Leblanc's Isadore Beautrelet.[55] The extravagant claims made in advertisements, a trend already established at the time Balzac was writing *César Birotteau,* revealed the commercial effectiveness of reality mediated by fiction. By the 1870s the practice had infected even classified advertisements, as illustrated by a series of libertine personal advertisements of a more or less fictitious character that appeared in certain papers from 1875.[56] Readers participated too: Marie-Eve Thérenty suggests that they became attuned by the compression of the faits divers to supplying their own fictionalised expansion of the headline, with the need to start the process often signalled by the use of a cliché such as "Vengeance au vitriol" or "Le Dégoût de vivre."[57]

Compression gave rise to "prefabrication," or the importation of quasi-industrial techniques into journalism. Producing a newspaper was a collective commercial and industrial exercise. Daily publication imposed daily work schedules, both on the profession of writing and on reader expectations.[58] Increasing demand for up-to-the-minute news gave rise to recognisable techniques of iteration, of shorthand rubrics and headlines, to allow readers to categorise articles instantly: *stereotype* and *cliché* are both words that derive from nineteenth-century press processes. Even the serialisation of literature led to a process of disassembling and reassembling akin to a production line. Popular works of literature became replicated as formats, sometimes parodied, sometimes seeking to capitalise on a popular success. Sue's *Les Mystères de Paris,* itself an undertaking on a commercial scale, is copied by Zola's *Les Mystères de Marseilles* and by Féval's *Les Mystères de Londres,* to name but two passengers on this particular bandwagon. And scale itself becomes an objective with clear market benefits. Balzac had led the way with *La Comédie humaine;* Zola would follow with *Les Rougon-Macquart.* As Zola remarked to Louis Desprez in 1882, "One book is a stone: twenty books are a wall."[59]

The drivers behind these stylistic shifts can be seen as predominantly (though of course not exclusively) economic. Increasing circulation meant, primarily, attracting new readers from the growing fringes of the market, from the new urban literate classes created by industrialisation and education and from the increased penetration of the provincial *départements* that better distribution and sales networks allowed. In the popular press, the tendency towards compression aligned with the need to establish a camaraderie with new readers unused to lengthy polemics. The pithy one-liners and backslapping familiarity of Timothée Trimm's Premiers-Paris in *Le Petit Journal* attest to this shift. "The *Petit Journal* pandered to the people, personified by concierges, manual workers, the little people," writes Zola, and Millaud confirms the strategy in a letter to Villemessant: "You have to have the courage to act dumb."[60]

These developments are intimately connected with the emergence of naturalism. Thérenty argues that the participation of naturalist writers in journalism evidences the closeness of naturalist fiction to contemporary reportage, but the influence flows in both directions.[61] Naturalism exploits the porosity of the boundary between fact and fiction by proposing a genre of fiction based apparently on a representation of everyday reality that overlaps substantially with the point of view and the stylistic modes of the popular press. Zola himself makes the comparison in an 1889 article in *Le Peuple:* "We make use, in our artistic creations, in the world of imagination, of the investigatory approach which today's journalist brings to bear on the real facts and actual events of everyday life."[62]

Compression, excess, and sensation, through an unalleviated focus on the worst of human nature, create texts in which fiction enhances realism. Roger Ripoll argues that the naturalist vision must incorporate a mythopoeic dimension, itself a product of sensation and hyperbole, as a means of uniting familiar and traditional modes of storytelling with current cultural perceptions and a documentary approach to description.[63] Thérenty suggests that a mixture of fiction and reality is seen by readers as a necessary mode of representing the real—that it does its job well, that reality itself needs to take account of the fictional in order to be properly credible.[64] In this context, Maupassant's claim, in the preface to *Pierre et Jean,* that reality can only be adequately represented by fiction seems more a confirmation of contemporary journalistic practice than a provocative new idea: "Rendering reality thus consists in creating a complete illusion of reality, following the logical order of events, not in transcribing servilely the pell-mell order they actually come in."[65] The proposal that fiction can be based on a process of experimentation through fact, scientific analysis, and rational deduction, which Zola will advance in his 1881 *Le Roman expérimental,* had already been tested much earlier by the new genre of the *roman policier* initiated in 1868 by

Emile Gaboriau and his detective hero, Monsieur Lecocq. And just as Gaboriau's serialised novels had helped drive the circulation of *Le Petit Journal,* so naturalism acquired an economic value as a genre capable of attracting readers.

But in emerging from the popularisation of journalism, naturalism was also forced to confront the separation of the book from the newspaper. Initially the roman-feuilleton remained a core part of the newspaper strategy, as it delivered an emotional punch that journalistic reporting could not match. Millaud again: "And more, you have to be on top of all the new discoveries, every invention, to bring out in plain speech all the stuff which gets buried in the heavyweight journals. It's the feuilleton which gave me life in the raw which the masses lap up: so, all of you, play me back what mister average is thinking, and talk about everything so as to appear to know more than the rest."[66] But as journalism invaded the territory of fiction, so the need to rely on serialised novels reduced. *Le Matin,* founded by an American in 1884 and published by the entrepreneur Philippe-Jean Bunau-Varilla from 1885, rejected the roman-feuilleton entirely in favour of what Zola describes as "the untrammelled flood of mass information" *(le flot déchaîné de l'information à outrance),* a journalistic style based on clipped, Americanised news reporting.[67] Although it was unusually radical in this, the fact that the newspaper no longer needed the feuilleton to make its economics work enabled a gradual divergence in content from the book. Zola goes on to describe it as what we would now call dumbing down: "News reporting . . . has transformed journalism, killed full-length articles, killed literary criticism, has given more space as every day passes to dispatches, to news great and small, to reporter and interviewer investigations."[68]

By the mid-1880s it seemed clear that the newspaper and the novel had become distinct products that could still coexist aesthetically within the same format if it suited but that no longer relied on each other economically. Zola concurs, but also points out the consequences: "The situation is the exact opposite of what happened before: now, you sell the newspaper on the strength of the newspaper, and you give away a feuilleton as an extra," and his section on the roman-feuilleton in "Les Romanciers contemporains" makes the point that naturalist novels do not operate as economic drivers for the daily press as effectively as the tearjerking sentimentality of an Emile Richebourg.[69] The would-be serious novelist needed to create a product that would satisfy both reader and publisher in a stand-alone format.

This had a series of implications for authors. Newspapers needed to rely less on star novelists or journalists to drive sales. *Le Matin,* under Bunau-Varilla, denied bylines to journalists as a matter of policy, as well as eschewing the roman-feuilleton.[70] Authorial identities were concocted by publishers: Timothée Trimm became nationally famous as the nom de plume of the leader writer for *Le Petit Journal*—but the real Napoléon Lespès, the man behind the *plume,* utterly failed when he moved, *cognito,* to a rival paper.[71] The world of the press is one where authorial identity can easily become confounded with the brand of the product. The Goncourt brothers, typically, fret about this: "This age is the beginning of the demolition of the book by the newspaper, of the man of letters by the journalist."[72] On the other hand, the author who chose to promote him- or herself had an array of promotional tools developed for the press but readily adaptable to the stand-alone book market, publishers willing and able to spend money on promotions or on longer print runs to satisfy growing demand, and a readership demonstrably prepared to devote more leisure spending to books.

Moreover, there could be little doubt that the power of the story, in both aesthetic and commercial terms, remained undiminished. The successes of Pierre Alexis Ponson du Terrail and Féval were rooted in the traditions of the *bibliothèque bleue,* in popular superstition, fairy stories, and heroic epics that demonstrate the enduring ability of these genres to withstand modernisation, and even mass production with all its defects, without losing their capacity to carry an audience. Stéphane Mallarmé, in "Etalages," celebrates the emergence of narrative fiction, for so long the unsung bedrock of the press, to its place as a product in its own right: "Rather, and only here in the French market, the Press sought status as writing. For a long time the traditional feuilleton at the foot of the front page supported the weight of the entire format, just as certainly as a fragile shopfront on the avenues, mirrors shimmering with flashing jewels or the subtle hues of drapery, supports a massive multistorey apartment block. More than that, true fiction, the narrative of imagination itself, fights its way through crowded 'dailies,' emerges victorious from main street to summit, and knocks feature articles and news stories off their pedestals."[73]

That this gift was not lost on the publishers as well is demonstrated by the increasing role of *la presse financière*. I have already referred to its role in improving newspaper profitability, but it also helped to display the raw power of narrative through its role in a series of share scams.[74] In the early 1850s Jules-Isaac Mirès, banker, press baron, and one of the prototypes for Saccard in *L'Argent,* turned the innocuously named *Journal des chemins de fer* into a financial paper that he then used to promote other companies in his portfolio, eventually owning a stable of six newspapers used for this purpose before the eventual failure of his main vehicle, the Caisse générale des chemins de fer, in 1860. The scandal of the Panama Canal Company, shown by a subsequent enquiry to have dispensed a total of 104.9 million francs over a nine-year period to support the price of its shares and bonds, 12 million francs of which went to the press, illustrated not just the scale of the financial operation but also the ability of press, readers, and holders of securities to sustain a good narrative, based on a genuine French success on the international scene at a point when France felt itself beleaguered. Payment for promotion, or for the suppression of negative publicity, became the norm, and in the 1880s specialised advertising agencies grew up to exploit this market. The power of the story had been recognised and captured by the financial community, which realised that if the illusion were created with enough skill and chutzpah, its dissociation from underlying reality would pass unnoticed. Prospectus fraud achieved its effect precisely by cutting through traditional expectations of genre and literary hierarchy to tap into underlying cultural constants.

Other essentially naturalist concerns blend easily with fiction. The marriage of contemporary scientific enquiry with the mystery story produced the detective story, first popularised by Gaboriau with Monsieur Lecoq and developed by the translations of Sherlock Holmes in the 1890s and by Maurice Leblanc's Arsène Lupin from 1905. Popular interest in the ability to convert scientific progress into industrial reality, symbolised by the Eiffel Tower and the *expositions universelles* of 1889 and 1900, combined with a long-established and essentially romantic thirst for exotic adventure to create a platform for Jules Verne, translations of H. G. Wells, and later extraterrestrial adventures. Frequently poor workmanship created texts that appeared approachable, down-to-earth, and *lisible* for an expanding audience. This is a literature that believed in itself and, as long as the power to create illusion rooted in the reader's own expectations, conventions, and prejudices remained intact, was relatively untroubled by the reflexivity and self-doubt that had always character-ised a section of the literary community.

Naturalism emerged as a genre that had both the cultural and com-mercial attributes to which readers and publishers of books could re-spond. Its radical aesthetic gave it novelty value as a new literary school. Its realism helped it to penetrate class barriers. Its espousal of the read-er's voyeuristic point of view and mania for classification mirrored stable popular tastes. Its stylistic tendency towards sensationalism and excess derived from the demonstrable success of just the same techniques in the context of journalism. And the equally demonstrable power of the right narrative to drive sales, combined with increasing pressure in some parts of the newspaper world to push the brand of the paper over the fame of the writer, created an environment that favoured the emergence of a powerful champion of the book.

Zola as Promoter of Story and Book

Zola shows an instinctive understanding of literature as an economic commodity. His clearest statements on the subject are to be found in an article entitled "Money in Literature" ("L'Argent dans la littérature") published first in the Russian thick periodical *Le Messager de l'Europe* in March 1880 and subsequently serialised in *Le Voltaire* from July 23 to July 30 of the same year. The mere fact that it was first published in, of all places, a Russian journal, tells its own story: when Zola's relation-ship with its publisher, Mikhail Stasyulevich, had started in 1874, Zola was a relative unknown and Stasyulevich's terms, both economic and editorial, were far more accommodating than anything he had been of-fered in the French market.[75] The article has long been recognised as an important statement of Zola's commercial awareness, but the key points bear restating here since they form an important part of my argument.[76] Zola emphatically rejects Sainte-Beuve's arguments that the commer-cialisation of literature has impaired its quality. On the contrary, he ar-gues that the ability to earn a living from writing allows new talent to emerge: "In earlier times it used to cost a fortune; today, even those of the most modest means can own a small library. These are key deter-minants: as soon as people learn to read, and to read cheaply, the publishing business grows tenfold, and a writer can live comfortably on the proceeds of his pen."[77] The increasing volume of production and the expansion of the readership, he claims, replace patronage by whim with a more democratic system of rewarding success: "It is the entire readership which sits in judgement and which makes successes happen. . . . The work is born of the many and for the many."[78] He even includes some thoughts on the trickle-down effect of greater investment in the entire publishing industry—"an entire race of little people who live from our works, who earn millions from our labour."[79]

But he is careful to distinguish between literature and the feuilleton, which in his mind have become two separate marketplaces characterised by different readerships and, consequently, different writers: "They [the *feuilletonistes*] have created their own special readership which reads only feuilletons; they target these new, illiterate readers who cannot recognise a properly made piece of writing. That said, perhaps we should rather thank them, because they are clearing uncultivated ground, like the penny flysheets which reach into the furthest depths of the provinces."[80]

The article was written at a time when Zola was himself about to suspend his own journalistic activities for an extended period, having finally reached a position where his income from publishing in book format was sufficient to permit this. Nonetheless, he still depended on the serialisation of his novels before their publication in book format, as a type of highly effective advertising (as well as a profitable activity in its own right). His dismissal of the *feuilletonistes* as a lesser species of *littérateur* comes across as slightly patronising and indicates that increasing wealth was, perhaps, accompanied by growing hubris. I will return to this issue later.

In reality, Zola had been introduced to the commercial aspect of literature before he even published his first work. His early career as a publicity clerk, later advertising manager, at Hachette from 1862 to 1866 would have given him a fine understanding of the economic value of literature, how public taste could be influenced, and, in turn, what the ingredients of literary success were. His job involved promoting new titles published by Hachette by distributing free copies together with favourable reviews, which he often wrote himself, for publication under the byline of a regular reviewer in the columns of other periodicals. Writing these *tract-annonces*, or miniprospectuses—a development

inaugurated during his time at Hachette, possibly by Zola himself—
required an understanding of what would resonate with both popular
and critical taste. His contemporary letters to his friend Antony Valabrègue show how thoroughly Zola took the commercial lesson on board:
"If you only knew how little talent counts for in a success, you would
put down your paper and pen and start studying literary life, the thousand sleazy little tricks which open doors, how to piggyback off other
people's credit, the brutality necessary to get ahead over the bodies of
your dear colleagues."[81]

The focus of Hachette's publishing roster on works of public reference and education, such as the collection *Bibliothèque des connaissances
utiles,* Emile Littré's *Dictionnaire de la langue française,* and Jules Miche-
let's *Histoire universelle,* would have revealed the commercial potential of
the scientific, the classificatory, and the comprehensive. The effectiveness of the volumes themselves as "gifts" in exchange for favourable reviews would have been tangible proof of literary value. And finally, the
experience of transformational financial success was there for all to see.
Louis Hachette was a self-made man who had created a publishing dynasty with three family branches involved in the business by the time
of Zola's arrival. It would eventually absorb close to half of the French
publishing industry. In Zola's time, its headquarters had grown to occupy a ten-thousand-square-metre city block with a new *galerie de ventes,*
opened in 1863, built on a cast-iron skeleton in the manner of the new
railway stations.[82]

"I'm going to make as much money as possible. In any case, I have
faith in myself and I'm marching on with good cheer."[83] The cocky self-
assurance of a slightly later letter to Valabrègue does indicate the seriousness with which Zola dedicated himself to learning the business of
being a writer. The terms of the 1864 contract with his publisher Albert
Lacroix for the publication of *Contes à Ninon* suggest strongly that Zola
was prepared to trade cash for distribution, since he agreed to take no
royalty payments on the entire first edition and self-financed the launch
publicity.[84] Despite the aversion to popular newspapers—and indeed, to
newspapers of any sort—that Alexis records,[85] in 1865 he started writing
for *Le Petit Journal* not, as he explained to Valabrègue, for money but to
reach a broader audience: "But I also consider journalism such a powerful
lever that I'm not at all averse to the chance to put myself regularly in
front of a considerable number of readers. That's the explanation for my

starting at *Le Petit Journal*.[86] On leaving Hachette, one of his first acts on joining Villemessant's newly minted team at *L'Evénement* was to announce his arrival by an exchange of polemical letters published in the columns of the paper with the editor of a rival paper, *Le Nain Jaune*, which had castigated Zola's own recently published *La Confession de Claude*.[87] His early training in authorial promotion seems to have borne fruit quickly.

Zola demonstrably remained conscious of the novel as an object of exchange throughout his career. I think this should be seen as a material influence on his output. *Thérèse Raquin* (1867) provides an immediate demonstration of how Zola uses devices that have both literary and commercial impact. We hardly need Louis Ulbach's outraged condemnation of it as "putrid literature" *(la littérature putride)* to understand that Zola is using the same technique of sensationalism and excess that had proved such a successful commercial tactic in Millaud's populist journalism.[88] Indeed, a much earlier article in the Lyon-based *Le Salut Public* had aligned Zola with what he clearly sees as a popular trend: "My taste, if you want, is depraved; I like strongly spiced literary dishes and decadent works where a sickly sensibility replaces the robust health of classical times. I'm a child of my time."[89] Murder, psychosis, and a double suicide are the staples of the faits divers.[90] The motif of the voyeur is everywhere. Thérèse and Laurent are spied on by the cat François, in their imaginations by Camille's corpse, and finally by the paralysed Mme Raquin.[91]

This is narrative targeted at a readership prepared to pay to be scandalised. Baguley identifies the violation of the "contractual relationship of shared conventional expectations" as a defining characteristic of naturalism.[92] *Thérèse Raquin* challenges conventional expectations of the limits of contemporary fiction in a manner likely, based on the precedent of *Le Petit Journal*, to expand its readership and commercial viability by seeking a *succès de scandale*. Zola had already admitted that this was a legitimate promotional gambit: "The trick is not to wait for readers once a work is done but to march straight towards them and force them to love you or abuse you."[93] He is therefore supplying a market need that, conveniently, happens to suit his personality and can be legitimised on the grounds of both morality and solvency. If the pursuit of scientific experimentation that Zola asserts in the preface to the novel leads involuntarily to more scandal, then the gratification of tabloid tastes cannot be laid at the door of the author: "The love affairs of my two heroes are the satisfaction of a need; the murder they commit a consequence of their adultery."[94] After all, making money is good for writers, as he will claim in "L'Argent dans la littérature": "Money has emancipated the writer. Money has created modern literature."[95]

In this Zola is evidently different from most of his contemporaries. The Goncourt brothers may have incurred their share of Ulbach's wrath for *Germinie Lacerteux*—"What a great idea to put all this mutilated flesh on show!" he spits.[96] But when they write, in the preface to the novel, "Living in the nineteenth century, in an age of universal suffrage, of democracy, of liberalism, we asked ourselves if what we call the 'lower classes' did not have a right to the Novel,"[97] it is quite clear that the right is to have a novel written *about* the lower classes for the benefit of an elite, middle-class audience peering over the brothers' shoulders, and that the assertion of democratic rights may be more that of the implied reader against the censor for his or her right to read about "les basses classes" than any promotion of an egalitarian morality.

The privileged financial position from which the Goncourts were able to write translates into a point of view significantly different from that of Zola. Most evidently, Zola's prose is simply more emphatic, more prone to excess, than that of the Goncourts. Compare the opening scene setting from *Thérèse Raquin* with that of *Germinie Lacerteux*. Zola's linguistic register is far from neutral and conveys a clear social commentary through repetitive emphasis: "Ce passage à trente pas de long et deux de large, *au plus;* il est pavé de dalles *jaunâtres, usées, descellées, suant* toujours une *humidité âcre;* le vitrage qui le couvre, coupé à l'angle droit, est *noir de crasse.*"[98] (This passageway is twenty paces in length and two wide, *at the most;* it is paved with *yellowing, worn, loose* flagstones, always *sweating an acrid humidity;* the glazed roof which covers it, cut short at its apex, is *black with filth.*) The Goncourts' text, by contrast, contains just three adjectives and is otherwise far more neutrally descriptive: "Ceci se passait dans une petite chambre dont la fenêtre montrait un étroit morceau de ciel coupé de trois noirs tuyaux de tôle, des lignes de toits, et au loin, entre deux maisons qui se touchaient presque, la branche d'un arbre qu'on ne voyait pas."[99] (This happened in a small room, through the window of which a narrow band of sky could be seen, intersected by three black metal chimneys, the outlines of some roofs and, between two houses which almost touched, a branch from a tree which could not be seen.)

Both passages convey a similar social context of poverty and constraint, but Zola's entire linguistic register here is more sensationalist, more visceral than that of the Goncourts. It is difficult not to see an element of commercialism in this comparison: the stronger colours of Zola's palette, combined with the proposition that this is a scientific investigation of human psychosis, are techniques designed to attract a broader spectrum of readers just as much as to articulate plot. Where others intellectualise, Zola talks, memorably, of being a bit of a mountebank, of what he calls "banquisme": "You, you've had a bit of private money which has given you a lot of freedom. Me, I've had to earn my living with nothing but my pen, I've been forced to make my way via all sorts of literature I'm ashamed of, like journalism, I've kept, how to put it, a bit of the mountebank about me. . . . Yes, just like you I really don't give a toss about this word *Naturalism*, but still I'm going to bang on about it because these things need a baptism for people to believe they are new."[100] Naturalism is at once a carnivalesque tool for attracting attention, just as mountebanks, *saltimbanques*, do, and for banking the profits from the resulting audience.

From Promoter to Managing Director

Over the course of Zola's career as a writer, there occurs a significant change in the way he uses commercial devices. The shift can be readily demonstrated, in headline terms at least, by a comparison of similar passages taken from works at different points in Zola's career. Zola returns time and again to descriptions of Paris. One of the first occurs in *La Curée*. We have previously met Aristide Saccard as a politically naive but ambitious Provençal journalist in *La Fortune des Rougon*. *La Curée* chronicles his arrival in Paris and the making of his first fortune. In an early flashback, Saccard recollects a panorama of Paris from the heights of the Butte Montmartre in the company of his first wife at the start of his rise to riches. The passage predates by several years Zola's emergence as a successful writer with *L'Assommoir* and dates from a period when he was still very much trying to establish himself both financially and in the literary canon.

On était à l'automne; la ville, sous le grand ciel pâle, s'alanguissait, d'un
gris doux et tendre, piqué çà et là de verdures sombres, qui ressemblaient
à de larges feuilles de nénuphars nageant sur un lac; le soleil se couchait
dans un nuage rouge, et, tandis que les fonds s'emplissaient d'une brume
légère, une poussière d'or, une rosée d'or tombait sur la rive droite de la
ville, du côté de la Madeleine et des Tuileries. C'était comme le coin enchanté d'une cité des *Mille et une Nuits,* aux arbres d'émeraude, aux toits
de saphir, aux girouettes de rubis. Il vint un moment où le rayon qui
glissait entre deux nuages fut si resplendissant, que les maisons semblèrent
flamber et se fondre comme un lingot d'or dans un creuset.

   "Oh!, vois, dit Saccard, avec un rire d'enfant, il pleut des pièces de
vingt francs dans Paris!" (1:388)

   [It was autumn; and under the great pale sky the town was growing
languid, a muted and tender grey punctured here and there by dark
green patches resembling the broad leaves of waterlilies floating on a
lake; the sun was setting in a cloud of red and, while a light mist was
filling the valley bottom, a dusting of gold, a golden dew was falling on
the right bank of the city, on the side of the Madeleine and the Tuileries. It was like some enchanted corner of a city from *A Thousand and
One Nights,* with trees of emerald, roofs of sapphire, weathervanes of
ruby. At one point a shaft of sunlight, sliding between two clouds, flared
out so brightly that the houses seemed to catch fire and melt like an ingot
of gold in a crucible.

   "Oh, look," said Saccard with a childlike laugh, "it's raining twenty-
franc pieces over Paris."]

This rather painterly passage is not just a description of Paris. It di-
rects the reader towards a representation of the process of wealth creation. It uses a sustained metaphor of wealth (the triple repetition of *or,*
the three precious stones) to foreshadow Saccard's rise, which the reader
will already anticipate. At the same time, the text proposes and promotes
its own worth as narrative. The direct allusion to *Mille et une nuits,* as
well as the indirect intertext to Balzac's representation of Rastignac challenging Paris at the conclusion of *Le Père Goriot,* links the text to an established literary success. It uses journalistic techniques of sensation and
compression to attract and retain the reader's attention. The image is
hardly naturalistic: it uses an exaggerated colour saturation ("rosée d'or,"
"girouette de rubis," "lingot d'or") picked out against a misty, defocal-
ised background ("gris doux et tendre," "verdure sombre," "brume légère") to create a memorable impression. The passage is compressed and
I quote it in its entirety: three sentences and a quotation to create the
picture and to move on to the next. It even refers twice to the process of

compression—the essence of *Mille et une nuits* in a "coin enchanté," the melting of streets into "un lingot d'or dans un creuset." It draws on established cultural stereotypes to accelerate the reader's ability to pigeonhole the effect the author is seeking to create. The reference to *Mille et une nuits* links not just to literary success but to the stock image of the Oriental pleasure dome and thence to a series of connections to the exotic that the vocabulary of dew, jewels, and gold reinforces. The viewpoint is doubly voyeuristic, with the reader permitted to peer over Saccard's shoulder to share what we assume is his view of a secret transformation.

And finally the painterly nature of the image is itself important. The reliance on a critical vocabulary based on visual perception and interpretation creates a link to modernity—to new ways of seeing reality, as the impressionists had proposed, and to new technologies such as the contemporary advances in chromolithography, the first appearance of colour in newspapers and magazines, and hand-coloured photographs. It could also be taken to refer to the uncertainties of artistic reception, which Zola had seen firsthand and had discussed extensively in his journalism during the 1860s, in relation to the reception of artists like Edouard Manet and Paul Cézanne who dared to contest established hierarchies, just as Saccard will do in his search for wealth.[101]

By journalistic intertext, by reference to modernity, and by claims of literary lineage, this narrative seeks to promote itself as sharing the same commercial inevitability of success as Saccard. But it can only do so much: ultimately the response is left up to reader reception. Zola is using narrative device as a tool for suggestion, to strengthen the psychological credibility of Saccard's desire for wealth and, in so doing, to convince readers of the value of the narrative they are reading.

Fourteen years later Zola returns to a series of descriptions of Paris, and particularly of the Seine, in *L'Œuvre* (1886):

> Et là, dans la Seine, éclatait la splendeur nocturne de l'eau vivante des villes, chaque bec de gaz reflétait sa flamme, un noyau qui s'allongeait en une queue de comète. Les plus proches, se confondant, incendiaient le courant de larges éventails de braise, réguliers et symétriques; les plus reculés, sous les ponts, n'étaient que des petites touches de feu immobiles. Mais les grandes queues embrasées vivaient, remuantes à mesure qu'elles s'étalaient, noir et or, d'un continuel frissonnement d'écailles, où l'on sentait la coulée infinie de l'eau. Toute la Seine en était allumée comme d'une fête intérieure, d'une féerie mystérieuse et profonde, faisant passer des valses derrière les vitres rougeoyantes du fleuve. En haut,

au-dessus de cet incendie, au-dessus des quais étoilés, il y avait dans le ciel sans astres une rouge nuée, l'exhalaison chaude et phosphorescente qui, chaque nuit, met au sommeil de la ville une crête de volcan.

Le vent soufflait, et Christine grelottante, les yeux emplis de larmes, sentait le pont tourner sous elle, comme s'il l'avait emportée dans une débâcle de tout l'horizon. (4:339–340)

[And there, in the Seine, blazed the splendour of an urban night-scape over flowing water. Each gas jet reflected its flame, a nugget of light stretching out into a comet tail. The closest, merging, set the current alight with fans of embers, regular and symmetrical, while the furthest, under the bridges, were fixed splashes of fire. But the huge glowing tails were alive, shifting as they pulsed, black and gold, in a continual shimmer of scales as the water flowed to infinity. The entirety of the Seine seemed to radiate with the light of an internal carnival, from some deep and mysterious fairy kingdom, waltzing behind the red-shifted windows of the river. Up above, over the conflagration, above the star-speckled quays, a red mist hung in the starless sky, the hot and phosphorescent breath which forms a volcanic cone over the city's sleep each night.

The wind blew and Christine, shivering, her eyes filled with tears, felt the bridge turn under her as though caught in the meltwaters of the entire skyline.]

By this time Zola had been established as a successful writer for almost a decade, was able to command the longest print runs in France for his novels, and was becoming wealthy from the proceeds of his writing. On first analysis, it seems that this text uses many of the same techniques we have identified in the passage from *La Curée*. The overall impression, though, is more self-consciously artistic than in the passage from *La Curée*. This sense of self-awareness is both central to the principal themes of this novel about an artist and the artistic temperament, and indicative of Zola's evolving approach to his readership.

The description of the Seine is not merely suggestive of the Impressionist viewpoint in its treatment of reflections on water but also betrays an increasing tendency to condition the reader's response. We are told how to view the scene: the entire composition of the image is carefully articulated, with a foreground and a background ("les plus proches, "les plus reculés," "en haut"), a colour palette ("noir et or," "une rouge nuée"), and perspective ("un noyeau qui s'allongeait," "des valses derrière les vitres rougeoyante"). We are given hints about how to interpret the scene.

The extract comes shortly before Claude's suicide, so an atmosphere of impending doom is in the air, picked up in this passage by the images of the volcano looming over Paris and by the forthcoming *débâcle*. We are, I think, left unsure whether this is the, by now, familiar Zolian practice of foreshadowing plot through metaphor, or whether it is some more fundamental view of Paris, one perhaps held by Zola himself.

This is not yet fully developed prospectus narrative, seeking to assert an authorial or narratorial point of view. But it does provide evidence of Zola developing further tools for manipulating reader response by channelling it into a preconstructed narrative frame that may, ultimately, lead to a different relationship with the reader. In *L'Œuvre* the effect is one of degree rather than of substance. By 1891, Zola's techniques had shifted once again, as we can see in this extract from *L'Argent*:

> Mme Caroline leva les yeux. Elle était arrivée sur la place, et elle vit, devant elle, la Bourse. Le crépuscule tombait, le ciel d'hiver, chargé de brume, mettait derrière le monument comme une fumée d'incendie, une nuée d'un rouge sombre, qu'on aurait crue faite des flammes et des poussières d'une ville prise d'assaut. Et la Bourse, grise et morne, se détachait, dans la mélancolie de la catastrophe, qui, depuis un mois, la laissait déserte, ouverte aux quatre vents du ciel, pareille à une halle qu'une disette a vidée. C'était l'épidémie fatale, périodique, dont les ravages balaient le marché tous les dix à quinze ans, les vendredis noirs, ainsi qu'on les nomme, semant le sol de décombres. (5:360–361)
>
> [Mme Caroline lifted her eyes. She had reached the square and saw before her the Bourse. Dusk was falling, and the mist-laden winter sky gave the monument a backdrop of smoke as if from a fire, a cloud of a dull red as if from the flames and dust of a town taken by storm. And from it the Bourse emerged, grey and bleak, in the melancholy aftermath of the catastrophe which, for a month now, had left it deserted, open to the four winds of heaven, like a market emptied by famine. This was the fatal epidemic which periodically swept through the market every ten to fifteen years, Black Fridays as they were known, strewing rubble in its wake.]

Saccard's ruin has happened: his fall has destroyed the lives and dreams of his less culpable followers. Mme Caroline reflects on the consequences. The description builds towards the final sentence, using the momentum of Saccard's defeat to extend the metaphor of war and plague across market, city, and sky. The final sentence, in a trick that, since

Germinal, had become a Zolian trademark, pans out cinematically to a global perspective. The ambiguity that, in *L'Œuvre,* had still allowed us to attribute the vision of the Seine as much to Claude's artistic sensibility as to Zola is here attenuated to the edge of credibility. Just possibly, and only on reflection, the "épidémie fatale" could still be Mme Caroline's point of view. More plausibly, and I think the way most readers would approach this sentence, this has become the assertion of Zola's own viewpoint, which we are expected to accept as the logical conclusion of an utterly compelling narrative.

A few years later, this trend has become dominant. In *Paris,* published in 1898 in the middle of the Dreyfus affair, Zola again describes a view from Montmartre:

> Pierre s'approcha du vitrage. C'était le même effet qu'il avait vu déjà, lors de sa première visite. Le soleil oblique, qui descendait derrière de minces nuages de pourpre, criblait la ville d'une grêle de rayons, rebondissant de toutes parts sur l'immensité sans fin des toitures. Et l'on aurait dit quelque semeur géant, caché dans la gloire de l'astre, qui, à colossales poignées, lançait ces grains d'or, d'un bout de l'horizon à l'autre. . . .
>
> En effet, à mesure que le soleil s'abaissait derrière le lacis des nuages, il semblait que le semeur de l'éternelle vie lançait sa flamme d'un geste volontaire, à cette place, puis à cette autre, dans un balancement rythmique qui choisissait les quartiers de labeur et d'effort. Là-bas, une brûlante poignée de semence tomba sur le quartier des Ecoles. Puis, là-bas, une autre poignée éclatante alla fertiliser le quartier des ateliers et des usines. . . .
>
> Et, devant eux, à longs gestes, de la vivante poussière d'or de ses rayons, le soleil ensemençait Paris, pour la grande moisson future de justice et de vérité.[102]
>
> [Pierre moved closer to the window. He had seen the same effect before, on his first visit. The low sun, going down behind thin purple clouds, bombarded the town with a hail of rays which bounced in all directions from the endless immensity of the roofscape. It seemed as if some giant sower, concealed in the glory of the heavens, was casting these golden grains in colossal fistfuls from one edge of the horizon to the other. . . .
>
> In fact, as the sun dropped behind the fretwork of clouds, it seemed as if the sower of eternal life was picking and choosing where to hurl his flame, now here, now there, in a rhythmic swing which favoured workful and productive districts. Over here a burning handful of seed fell on the university quarter. Then, over there, another bursting handful went to fertilise the zone of trades and industry. . . .

And in front of them, in broad sweeps of the life-bringing golden dust of its rays, the sun planted its seed in Paris for the future harvest of justice and truth.]

It is difficult to read this passage as anything except a direct ex cathedra pronouncement of an authorial viewpoint. Selling the narrative to the reader has become subordinate to the delivery of a message. If we accept Baguley's contention that the essence of naturalism is to shock the reader's preconceived critical hierarchies, then the attempt to manipulate rather than challenge seems like a faultline, a *fêlure*, in the concept of naturalism itself.[103] The commercial device of "saturation," so often effective before, is still in evidence but seems oddly overblown, attached not to the city but to a detached metaphysical construct of productivity ("semeur," "semence," "moisson"). It is as though Zola has become so convinced of his ability to carry his readership that he believes it will now follow him wherever he leads. The self-awareness that led him to write, in *Le Roman expérimental* of 1880, "In our age of science, setting yourself up as a prophet is a delicate task," has clearly deserted him by this point in his career.[104]

This progression towards prospectus narrative is familiar to all readers and critics of Zola. Zola himself had announced it shortly after publishing *L'Argent*, if we are to believe his contemporary biographer, Robert Sherard, who in his 1893 study records him being quite open about his intention to proselytise his views: "Later on, when my circumstances improved, when I felt I was becoming a power, the money question became only a secondary issue and I used my feuilleton as a tribune."[105] This process of gradual politicisation is, I think, intimately linked to Zola's rise as a commercial writer and to parallel changes in his perception of narrative value. Understanding how this shift occurs, and particularly how it affects the middle part of Zola's writing career as the *Rougon-Macquart* series comes to an end, is the subject of the remainder of this chapter.

Before developing this argument, it may be useful to situate it in the broader landscape of critical approaches to Zola. Most acknowledge the fact that he wrote for money, but few, if any, focus more than incidentally on how this might have affected his literary output, irrespective of their critical point of departure. Mitterand, in many ways the father of modern Zola criticism and author of a broad range of studies from the biographical to the narratological and the textual, consistently (if not consciously) seems to skirt the issue. His masterly biography tracks the parallel course of Zola's business life and his literary output but never quite investigates how the former influences the latter.[106]

Colette Becker, a disciple of Mitterand, does the same: her study of Zola's apprenticeship at Hachette again records the commercial experience Zola acquired from his time in the publishing world and juxtaposes the stories he wrote during this period, but seems to draw back from seeing them as experiments in selling, as much as in writing, narrative.[107] She and Mollier have, however, between them done more than any others to track down publication statistics for Zola's works during his lifetime, crucial for understanding the contemporary year-by-year evolution of Zola's business as a novelist.[108] My own efforts to follow this trail through direct enquiry of Hachette, now the owner of the Grasset-Fasquelle archives in which the Charpentier records are kept, has led me to believe that publication records before 1900 have been discarded, probably destroyed, so it may well be that their work remains the most detailed analysis of this process we are likely to obtain.

Those who approach Zola from a more narratological or sociological perspective tend to do the same. Ripoll's vast exploration of the role of myth in Zola barely acknowledges literature as a commercial product.[109] Jacques Noiray, similarly, investigates the role of the machine and automation as image, metaphor, and political symbol, the machine as midwife of the future *(accoucheuse de l'avenir),* but barely considers how the machine of Zola's own commercial enterprise fits into this schema.[110] Nor does Baguley, in many ways the bedrock of modern critical approaches to Zola in his analysis of the naturalist perspective, and despite his recognition of Zola's stylistic innovations, particularly in genre, as an ingredient in the recipe for commercial success.[111] Philippe Hamon comes closer, in recognising how many of Zola's characters are proxies for participants in the process of creating fiction, from author to critic to reader, but he sees this as Zola taking care to situate his characters in a historical landscape reinforced by links to literary as well as historical reality, rather than as an invitation to consider the novel itself as the subject of that process.[112] Adeline Wrona, in an all too brief article, starts to develop an argument about the role of the press in transforming economic transaction into narrative—a definition of prospectus, though she does not use the word—but lacks the space to develop the proposition fully.[113]

Those who take a sociological approach tend to recognise the innovations Zola brought to the representation of commerce and the changing demographics of its participants, often including the publishing industry, but by and large do not investigate the link between Zola's representation of business and his own agency as a businessman selling narrative. So Christophe Reffait, writing about the role of the Bourse in contemporary literature, sees Zola's representation essentially as a commentary on capitalism. In particular he recognises the importance of the stock exchange as a contemporary symbol of a growing gap between experience and the ability to interpret that experience, an aspect that I will develop as an important step in understanding Zola's evolving authorial position as someone who can bridge that gap for his readers.[114] Brian Nelson and William Gallois take similar standpoints: Nelson sees Zola as a commentator on the growth of the bourgeoisie, while Gallois treats Zola as a highly politicised author—"the aesthetic cannot be politically impartial"—and *Les Rougon-Macquart* as an encyclopaedia of the political economy of capitalism, with each novel describing a different aspect.[115] He does see the novel as an element of the economic cycle and, in particular, as an illustration of how capitalism appropriates and internalises narrative for its own purposes, but essentially this remains a political reading that does not follow up the questions about the way in which this process of internalisation has affected the product itself. David Bell, marrying political and economic analysis, comes closer to this question when he examines Saccard's sales techniques in both *La Curée* and *L'Argent,* which he sees as Zola's "economic" novels along with *Au Bonheur des dames.*[116] He recognises that Saccard is essentially selling forms of narrative, but never quite focusses on this aspect and does not make the connection that Zola is doing the same thing.

Three critics come closest to addressing this issue. Chantal Pierre-Gnassounou's 1999 *Zola: Les Fortunes de la fiction* not only recognises that many of Zola's novels are allegories of the process of creating fiction but also links this to Zola's own role in creating narrative for his public and the techniques he uses to ensure his readers follow what she sees as his purposes. She tends, however, to downplay economic motivation as a driver, as this quotation illustrates: "Losing the reader's attention is a threat which Zola certainly keeps testing, particularly in the laboratory of the *Ebauches* where the expectations of the reader, who wants to be 'riveted,' regularly run at cross purposes to the imperatives of the naturalist aesthetic which categorically insist that the novelist should not play for the reader's interest."[117] My argument here diverges from her position as regards the relative importance of the economic driver.

Hélène Gomart's comparison of financial dealings in Balzac's *César Birotteau* and Zola's *L'Argent* provides a compelling analysis of how Zola links narrative device with the representation of transaction.[118] Her notion of *Les Rougon-Macquart* as an extended financial transaction, the record of Félicité Rougon's investment in her offspring, is a good example of how Gomart has been successful in broadening the scope of Zola criticism.

Finally, Jean-Joseph Goux's work on the role of money in literature cannot be ignored, particularly in dealing with *L'Argent,* on which he has written specifically. More than anybody, he has drawn critical attention back to Zola's largely forgotten essay "L'Argent dans la littérature," discussed earlier in this chapter. He starts from the proposition, which he sees as self-evident, that writing is a commercial activity producing money, and that writing about the process of producing money is an entirely natural position for Zola, as the narrator of his age, to occupy.[119] That, too, is my starting point, and the remainder of this chapter takes us through the way the relationship between the fiction of business and the business of fiction evolves over the course of Zola's literary career, pausing to look in more detail first at *La Curée,* Zola's first novel about business and the second work of the cycle, and *L'Argent,* the last about business and eighteenth novel of *Les Rougon-Macquart.*

La Curée: *The Narrative of Business*

La Curée evidently occupied a significant place in Zola's plans for *Les Rougon-Macquart.* It figures twice in Zola's first recorded list, entitled "Notes générales" and dating from the end of 1868, of the ten works that were to make up the cycle, first as a novel about Georges-Eugène Haussmann's remodelling of Paris, "un roman sur les grandes démolitions de Paris," then as the story of a self-made man and his entourage, "un roman sur la famille d'un parvenu" (5:1735). It still occupies two of the ten slots in the plan that Zola submitted to Lacroix in 1869 as the basis of his contract, this time as novels about "the stupid, spoilt and sordid lives of our gilded youth" and "the corrupt speculative frenzy of the

Second Empire."[120] Ultimately, through *La Curée, Au Bonheur des dames,* and *L'Argent,* the theme of business would occupy a larger share of *Les Rougon-Macquart* than any other topic. Once the outlines of family genealogy had been established in *La Fortune des Rougon,* the very title of which signals a preoccupation with a commercial as well as familial heredity, it was the first subject to which Zola turned his attention.

But as only the second work in the series, and only the seventh work of prose fiction that Zola had published, *La Curée* should also be recognized as an experimental text in terms of what would work with readers and publishers. At the time when Zola was constructing his first outline of the cycle, he was also studying how to write, as illustrated by three notes all written around the turn of 1868–1869. His note titled "Différences entre Balzac et moi" not only shows his ambition as a writer but also identifies narratorial position—the Balzacian interpreter of society versus the Zolian reporter of fact—as a key point of differentiation (5:1736–1737). "Notes générales sur la marche de l'œuvre" (1868–1869) discusses how to integrate this narratorial point of view into a series of novels that deal with the representation of excess: "Orgy of appetites and ambition. Addiction to risk-taking . . . compulsive deal-making, craze for making a turn, for speculation."[121] "Notes générales sur la nature de l'œuvre" continues this theme but also, importantly, deals with matters of style. In these documents, Zola shows how closely the representation of excess is linked to the use of excess as a narrative device. The reader, he says, responds to strong sensation: "Keep the book going on a single strong blast which carries the reader along from first page to last."[122] Even this may not be enough: at times the reader must be pushed resolutely out of his or her comfort zone: "Don't forget that a drama grips the reader by the throat. He may get angry, but he won't forget. Always give him *over-the-top books* which at least stick in his memory, if they haven't give him nightmares first."[123] Zola clearly struggles to reconcile the theoretical hiatus between his insistence on a neutral, scientific narratorial stance and a mode of representation that seems to imply the opposite. Eventually, the need for a saleable product seems to win out: "You shouldn't assume," he reassures Lacroix in the first plan for the cycle (1869), "that this outline means that the work will be inflexible and dogmatic like a treatise on physiology or social science. I see it as being alive, really full of life."[124]

So *La Curée* is both a novel about business and an early exploration by Zola of the business of writing a novel. By comparing the way in which Zola represents business with the literary devices he uses to sell his novel to its readers, we can understand more about how the need to be commercially successful influences the text itself.

The Commercial Value of Sensation

La Curée is a novel of scandal and commercial intrigue. Haussmann is transforming the face of Paris. Fortunes can be made by those who know which buildings will be compulsorily purchased for demolition. Aristide Saccard, a sharp and driven Provençal from the Rougon family, has figured the game out and is at the apex of his wealth. Political patronage, from his minister brother Eugène, protects him as long as he stays away from Eugène's world. The pervasive corruption of the property market affords spiralling opportunities for an upwardly mobile entrepreneur to make money. But deal junkies make poor husbands and Renée, his trophy second wife, whom Saccard has also acquired on the cheap as sexually tarnished goods, is bored. She finds solace in the arms of Maxime, Saccard's son from his first marriage. Incest, even if not in the direct bloodline, is transgressive, titillating, and apparently tolerated if not too overt. But, inevitably, boundaries are overstepped. Renée forfeits Maxime, her inheritance, and eventually her life. Saccard, unperturbed, gets richer, strengthens his insider connections, and rebuilds his own relationship with Maxime.

The novel's very birth is also a story of scandal and commercial intrigue. Zola opened his dossier in preparation for *La Curée* in February 1869, started writing the novel itself in May 1870, was forced to pause after the first chapter for more than a year by war and revolution, and in all probability did not complete the text until the final months of 1871.[125] Serialisation began in Louis Ulbach's *La Cloche* on September 29, 1871 (before the novel had been completed) but was suspended thirty-eight days and twenty-seven episodes later, on November 5, as a result of reader protests and threats of a prosecution for obscenity. Publication of the entire text in book format followed later in the same month, but the impending bankruptcy of Zola's publisher, Lacroix, meant that the usual launch promotions could not be afforded, and the first edition of two thousand copies failed to sell out.[126] Despite the threat of an obscenity trial, which was normally good for business, its appearance remained critically unnoticed until Lacroix's successor, Charpentier, brought out a second edition a year later (5:1577–1578).

Zola's own financial position was barely better than that of his publisher. His contract with Lacroix provided for a monthly stipend of 500 francs for two novels a year. To pressure him to perform, Zola's commitment was evidenced by bills of exchange redeemable against delivery of manuscripts, a clause that would eventually cost Zola some 30,000 francs when it proved impossible to fulfil.[127] His basic annual income was thus 6,000 francs. His income from journalism had suffered from a peripatetic existence over the previous two years, as he moved from Paris to Marseille to escape the Prussian invasion of 1870, from Marseille to Bordeaux and thence to Versailles to report on the government in exile in 1871, and finally back to Paris in March 1871, a stay interrupted by the Commune, which caused a further temporary displacement. The cancellation of the serialisation of *La Curée* deprived him of a further source of income, and his tendency to sail close to the wind in his journalism came close to costing him his position at *La Cloche* again in 1872 and succeeded in sinking his new vehicle, *Le Corsaire*, at the end of that year.[128]

From the very beginning of Zola's writing career, there is a tension between sensation and commercial success. On the one hand, scandal was a key tool of journalism, as well as an effective method of self-promotion: it got a writer noticed and, as Balzac, Flaubert, and a host of other writers had demonstrated, could be a foundation stone of a successful literary career. On the other, the volatility of political sensitivities and the continued existence of censorship laws made for an unpredictable environment in which publications could be closed virtually overnight, as Zola had discovered with *Le Corsaire*. It was still difficult for a new novelist to achieve success without the direct help of the daily press, as Zola's experience with *La Curée* had shown. The few examples of success through publication only in book format, such as Victor Hugo's *Les Misérables*, tended to confirm that this avenue could only be used by established authors.

Increasingly, however, journalism and serialisation seem to have been perceived as promotional tools to be used alongside, rather than in substitution for, publication in book format. Zola exploits Ulbach's cancellation of the serialisation of *La Curée* by writing him a letter that he asks Ulbach to publish in *La Cloche* three days after the serial was pulled.[129] He uses it explicitly to promote his wider novelistic enterprise, in phraseology that might have been drawn straight from the advertising copy he was used to writing at Hachette: "*La Curée* is no isolated work: it is part of a great ensemble, it is one musical phrase from the vast symphony of which I dream. I want to write 'The Natural and Social History of One Family under the Second Empire.' The first episode, *La Fortune des Rougon,* which has just appeared in book format . . ." Scandal and sensation become at once justification and lure: "*La Curée* is the poisonous plant which grows on the imperial dungheap, it is incest grown tall in millionaire compost." But the idea that the book format serves a different purpose from the promotional tool of the newspaper is already present: "*La Curée* will only be understood when it appears in book format." Zola would later formulate his perception of journalism as a form of promotion more explicitly. Journalism, he maintains, is an essential tool for representing reality—"A writer who has not been a journalist is incapable of understanding and representing modern life"—as well as a platform for publicity: "My gavel is the journalism I do myself around my works."[130]

Sensation evidently had commercial value, as the preceding section has shown. Other writers apart from Zola formulated explicit commercial strategies based on it. The publisher P.-V. Stock, writing in 1933, recollects a letter received from a young and unknown Georges Darien (1862–1921), outlining a marketing plan in terms that could be applied almost word for word to *Les Rougon-Macquart:* "You need to let off a few fireworks, . . . some cracking bangers but spaced out. . . . I'd like to publish a pair each year, one inoffensive novel, sandwiched with a real firecracker. So for 7 years I need 14 novels."[131] It helped that the material of sensation required no invention but could be drawn directly from the pages of newspapers and from the lives of those around. Darien himself had been both a prison camp guard and an inmate in a notorious French penitentiary in Tunisia, and would later be suspected of being the author of daring robberies that he then wrote about in *Le Voleur.*

Despite its ostensible setting in 1862, *La Curée* dealt with issues that were still current and causing sensation at the time of its composition. Its plot derives in part from a polemical article by Jules Richard in *Le Figaro* on February 25, 1869, excoriating the excesses of Haussmann's modernisation of Paris.[132] Other sources, particularly Jules Ferry's 1868 *Les Comptes fantastiques d'Haussmann,* a collected series of articles chronicling Haussmann-related scandal, reveal how incestuously real-life events, sensation, and journalistic practice were conjoined. The power of journalism had been deployed by Mirès and the Péreire brothers to sell shares in the Caisse générale des chemins de fer and the Crédit Mobilier up to the very brink of bankruptcy, and the lesson had not been lost on Zola. In 1884 Desprez even recorded Zola's views on the relationship between real life and the press in terms that expressly link it to the process of literary creation: "The press provides information about everything. The courts produce documents precious to novelists. As M. Zola has written, *'a trial is an experimental novel played out in public.'*"[133] Ripoll argues that Zola transforms his sources, by the process of writing, into a description of animal appetites let loose. He uses the transformation as evidence of Zola's ability to link his material to the constants of myth. Another, simpler explanation is that Zola is merely selecting from his source material what will sell the narrative.

La Curée exploits the commercial power of excess in both subject and style. Its key plot threads of incest, property fraud, and the extravagance of the nouveaux riches are all variants on this single common theme. The suspension of its serialisation one episode ahead of the incest scene—which had already been typeset but which never appeared in print—is proof enough that sexual scandal attracted notice, even if unwelcome. Zola's protestations to his readers—that he was merely reproducing the "cesspit of deeds, the unbelievable stories of shame and folly, the money stolen and the women sold" that his three years of research had uncovered—conveniently omit mention of the commercial advantages of this strategy.[134] Even his choice of type of incest—between stepmother and stepson, rather than mother and son—implies a fine distinction between what would work commercially and what remained taboo.

Prurient material is mirrored in stylistic excess. Zola creates a kind of "high-definition" reality in which techniques of focus, colour saturation, and compression combine to produce an impression of a medium perfused by the very excess that it depicts. The long list of carriages in the Bois de Boulogne that opens the first chapter (1:320–321) is a technique borrowed literally from journalism, since the description is taken almost verbatim from an article in *Le Figaro* on April 10, 1870.[135] The length of the list mirrors the scale of the wealth it represents. Maxime and Renée, stuck in the traffic jam, take the place of faits divers columnists reporting titbits of scandal about those who pass within their focus. The sexually charged nature of their commentary serves to confirm the reader's expectations of the genre offered and offers a tantalising glimpse of even stronger revelations to come. Sexual and financial transgression is reflected in the intensity of the colour palette Zola chooses: "Ce pétillement des harnais et des roues, ce flamboiement des panneaux vernis dans lesquels brûlait la braise rouge du soleil couchant, ces notes vives que jetaient les livrées éclatantes perchées en plein ciel et les toilettes riches débordant des portières, se trouvèrent ainsi emportés dans un grondement sourd, continu, rythmé par le trot des attelages" (1:321). (This sparkle of harness and wheels, this blaze of varnished panels glowing with the embers of the setting sun, these splashes of colour thrown off by rainbow liveries perched high in the sky, these sumptuous dresses overflowing around the carriage doors, all found themselves swept along in a muted, ceaseless rumble to the rhythmic beat of the trot of the teams of horses.)

The intense spikes of vibrancy ("pétillement," "flamboiement," "braise," "éclatantes"), highlighted against a muted but possibly menacing background ("grondement sourd"), foreshadow the plot, with its contrast of excess and underlying threat.

Linguistic and stylistic excess is used to represent moral excess. Zola builds his climax carefully. From the Bois de Boulogne the reader is taken to the Hôtel Saccard, where architectural excess is used to the same effect (1:330–133). Thence to fashion, in the form of the tantalising layers of Renée's dress (1:336). Then the story itself acquires unexpected baggage in the shape of an immense flashback to fill in Saccard's history. The flashback covers two chapters out of seven, 80 pages out of 280. This is a story of excess, described by excess, told using excess as narrative device. "[The Saccard fortune] blazed in the middle of Paris like a giant bonfire. It was the killing hour, when the end of a hot chase filled a corner of the forest with baying hounds, cracking whips and flickering torches."[136] I shall have occasion to come back to this point in a different context later.

The technique culminates in Zola's description of the hothouse, the *serre*, at the Hôtel Saccard. Here the representation of an excess that will shortly translate into incest uses the medium of linguistic excess itself. "It was the gigantic rut of the hothouse itself, this corner of virgin forest ablaze with tropical greenery and blossom."[137] The list of plants that join the sexual frenzy, which stretches over three pages and twenty-six enumerated and capitalised Plant Species, comes to symbolise a sexual transgression so extreme that it can only be represented by a parallel narrative disruption.

It is, perhaps, questionable that this was Zola's intention. The list has a long history as a narrative device in French literature, from François Rabelais to Balzac and Flaubert, so Zola's use of it is perhaps no more than a form of experimentation with an established technique that seems to respond well to his own totalising apprehension, in addition to offering the convenience of a modern, factory-style manufacturing technique. Certainly, the narrative disruption echoes the sexual disruption of incest and the gender disruption of Renée's assumption of the male sexual role (1:485). But just as the cancellation of the novel's serialisation seems to take Zola by surprise, as the previously quoted letter to Ulbach indicates, so the bathetic effect of this lapse into narrative prolixity is at such odds with the intensity it seems intended to create that the question seems legitimate. He uses the technique again, more effectively, in *Le Ventre de Paris,* where lists seem an appropriate way to describe the functioning of a central market (for example, 1:626–628, 636–637), and then at even greater length and with multiple reprises in *La Faute de L'Abbé Mouret* (1:1345–1353, 1361–1364, 1377–1379, 1385–1390), then seems to recognise its pitfalls and avoids it thereafter. But it is, perhaps, a useful reminder that this is still only the second novel of *Les Rougon-Macquart* and that Zola is still learning his trade as a writer.

Both the *serre* and the list are also motifs of another import from journalism: compression. Again, *La Curée* represents compression by assimilating it as a stylistic device. It starts with an image of compression in the traffic jam in the Bois de Boulogne (1:320). Saccard's mansion compresses both architectural ornamentation (1:331) and social classes (1:335). Renée's corsets compress her body in a kind of sexual shorthand (1:336). Despite its length, the flashback history of Saccard's past is still a compression of his story and contains episodes of symbolic brevity, as for example the one-paragraph description, described as "a novel" *(un roman),* of Renée's fling with an employee known only by his first name, Georges (1:423). Her photograph album contains, in a single volume, a "gazette scandaleuse" of the sexual proclivities of the *monde* and the *demi-monde* (1:427). And the construction of the novel itself reflects Zola's sensitivity to the effects of compression as a novelistic device for managing suspense. The very first chapter gains narrative impulsion just as the traffic jam unblocks and gains pace from that point. The extended flashback is coitus interruptus in the progression of Renée and Maxime's affair after the foreplay of the first chapter. Even the ultimately bathetic list of flowers is intended, the reader suspects, as an orgasmic climax to sex in the *serre* (1:486–489).

La Curée is a novel that stays close to proven contemporary journalistic techniques for creating narrative value in the shape of text that, based on the evidence of the reception of contemporary newspapers, readers would both read and be prepared to pay for. Nonetheless, Zola's actual track record at converting theory into sales was still largely unproven. In choosing the subject of *La Curée* as a narrative of business, Zola also seems to be asking how his own business of writing works, what criteria readers use to assign value to a narrative, and how to reproduce those characteristics in his own works. That is the subject of my next section.

The Representation of Commerce

What business is Zola actually describing in *La Curée?* Ostensibly Saccard's property dealings, and by extension the reified social world of Paris in the Second Empire, where not only is everything and everyone ultimately for sale but values for properties in the *demi-monde* are almost tradeable commodities: "these creatures whose every expense was paid for by their lovers, and whose prices were quoted in high society just like securities on the Bourse."[138] *La Curée* has the potential to be a highly politicised, polemical narrative, and many critics read it that way. The rapidly jettisoned preface to the Lacroix edition, dated November 15, 1871, states a clear polemical objective: "I wanted to show the premature burnout of a race which lived too fast, in the shape of the she-male which degenerate societies produce; the overheated speculation of an age incarnated in an unscrupulous, thrill-seeking temperament; the nervous derangement of a woman living in a state of luxury which intensifies her natural desires tenfold. And, alongside these three social monstrosities, I have tried simultaneously to write a work of artistic and scientific merit and to record one of the strangest pages in our moral makeup."[139]

Becker agrees: "*La Curée* can only be a polemical work which denounces a regime and prefigures its speedy end. Expiation will, inevitably, follow."[140] Ripoll is less sure and argues that its polemical qualities are rapidly overtaken by the process of creating fiction.[141] Mitterand thinks that Zola is "above all a storyteller ["un conteur"]," and *La Curée* demonstrates his ability to spot a good story.[142] The carefully engineered contrast between the moral, sexual, and architectural excesses of the Hôtel Saccard and the puritanical abstemiousness of the Hôtel Béraud, home of Renée's parents, lends itself to a wide variety of different interpretations, mostly along political, moral, or social lines.[143] But it can also be seen, more simply, as an example of Zola's sensitivity to what will attract readers. The Hôtel Saccard, home of scandal, dominates the novel in part because, literally and literarily, it contains all the juicy bits, like a column from the *Echos de Paris*. The Hôtel Béraud provides contrast but not content and does not support the same weight of narrative. Of Christine Béraud, Renée's sister, Becker writes that she is the "antithesis of her sister, whose role is to represent what Renée could have become if she had been brought up differently and had lived in a different milieu." Perhaps, but she also serves to remind the reader that, if this had happened, there would have been no story at all.[144] Baguley's reading of the novel, which points out the proximity of *La Curée* to the world of fairy tale, with Renée as, successively, the heroines of "Sleeping Beauty," "Cinderella," "Snow White," and finally "Beauty and the Beast," rather supports the importance of simple "good stories" in the text.[145]

At this stage in his career, Zola seems to be at least as much interested in a saleable story as in polemic. Through his characters, he asks the direct question, What makes something saleable? "I'm not for sale," says Renée to Sidonie—but of course she is, and her saleability depends on a combination of desirable physical characteristics, sex appeal, availability, opportunity, and money.[146] And the same is true of the novel itself. Its appeal can be sexed up by precisely the combination of titillation, intrigue, and money Zola uses for its content; its availability can be enhanced through better distribution and longer print runs; opportunity comes from Zola's ability to spot a gap in the market that naturalism fills; and money comes from both the capital markets and the expanding readership.

In fact, narrative turns out to be a vital component of value in every dimension. In the fictional world of *La Curée*, objects acquire value not because of their intrinsic worth but because of the stories attached to them, and the implication is that narrative is equally essential in the world outside the novel. Saccard gives a fabulously expensive diamond necklace to Renée that, according to gossip, his mistress Laure d'Aurigny had been forced to sell (1:321, 337). In wearing the necklace, Renée displays the story as much as the stones, and the fiction duly distracts from Saccard's lack of real assets. But we later discover that this is only one level of the story. Saccard has himself conspired with Laure to invent another layer of the "histoire." In this version, she sells him her jewels, and he helps her use the money to buy back some of her debts at a huge discount (and takes a commission on the way through); the market believes this display of wealth proves he is solvent and she desirable, so his credit goes up, and she trades on the story of her attractiveness to lure other, richer lovers to replace her diamonds (1:465). Unlike real assets, stories are versatile, cheap, and effective. Saccard becomes a machine for converting reality into fiction: "The truth was that Renée's dowry had ceased to exist long ago; in Saccard's accounts it had been reclassified as an intangible asset [*valeur fictive*]."[147] His fortune is based on this device: inventing fictitious businesses producing fictitious profits for which real compensation is payable from Haussmann's valuation committees (1:392–393). His business philosophy is based on delivering the story rather than the goods: "He often said to himself: 'If I were a woman I might just sell my body, but I'd never deliver the goods—it's just too stupid.'"[148]

The notion of Saccard as a form of author is one to which I will return in more detail in the next section, since its role in *L'Argent* is even more significant. But even at this stage of Zola's own development as an author, it seems to be used as a tool to explore narrative value. There are overt similarities between Zola and Saccard. They share similar origins: both come from Provence, both started as journalists, both carry changed names (Zola from his father, Francesco Zolla), both build their fortune by peddling fictions of different types. Both share a similar method of work based on detail and meticulous preparation, Saccard in inventing the documentation for his claims to the expropriations committee, Zola in the 469 pages of the dossier for *La Curée*, a technique he had tried only once before but that was to serve him for the remainder of *Les Rougon-Macquart*. Zola automates his production line, while Saccard conceives of his family as a corporate enterprise: "The notion of family had been replaced in their setup by that of a sort of partnership in which everybody received an equal share of the profits."[149] The process of fiction is itself undergoing a commercialisation that Zola reflects in his narrative. Bell follows this theme in his analysis of *La Curée* as an economic novel and shows how, at the precise point when Saccard discovers Renée and Maxime's relationship and starts to think of himself for the first time as a husband and a father, his immediate reaction is to search for economic, not emotional, revenge in the shape of the contract for the sale of Renée's property (1:570–571).[150]

According to Saccard's formula, narrative value depends on preparation and pitch: "The events of the story don't much matter; it's the details, the gestures, the accent which are everything."[151] Zola shows Saccard doing exactly what he, Zola, is doing in real life as a writer, a would-be modern Balzac with his very own Rastignac. Both author and character are arch-manipulators of words. Saccard creates credibility through research, planning, on-the-ground detail, and "power narrative"—the projection and assertion of his story with a strength and intensity that brook no resistance. Time and time again, Zola shows us how he, Zola, and he, Saccard, achieve this. To illustrate the process, we can simply return to Saccard's vision from Montmartre of Paris overflowing with gold (1:388).[152] The intensity of the image is naturally associated with Saccard's own excitement, to the point where the reader tends to forget that the author is actually Zola. But Zola is in fact demonstrating just how commercially he, Zola, can manipulate words, just as his creature Saccard will mint money out of them.

Saccard's complex scheming with Larsonneau to defraud the compensation committee is credible partly because of the detail of his meticulous planning, which Zola describes at length (1:392–393). But Saccard's planning is also Zola's, and the very trick that Saccard uses to convince the compensation committee to accept his claim is precisely that which Zola is using to persuade the reader to accept the text. Later, Zola even has him describe the process in terms of authorship: "He had lost track of the number of strands he added to the most ordinary business deal. He tasted a real joy in the interminable tale he had just told to Renée, and what pleased him more than anything was the sheer audacity of the lie, the accumulation of impossibilities, the astonishing complexity of the intrigue. . . . In any case, he openly tried his hardest to turn the Charonne speculation into a real *financial melodrama*."[153]

In this context, excess and the naturalist perspective, which seem at first to be unlikely bedfellows, blend into a complementary sales strategy for Zola's fiction. The strategy is drawn from contemporary journalism and has the effect of increasing the credibility of the story and, at the same time, partially depoliticising it. Thérenty, writing about the sensational tone of the reporting of the 1869 Troppmann case, comments, "The roman-feuilleton of this period often takes the form of an extended and exaggerated fait divers, just at the moment when the fait divers was taking over the newspaper."[154] Zola's authorial viewpoint, based on copious research and preparation, resembles that of the journalist, as Zola himself confirmed in the 1888 preface to Parisis's *La Vie parisienne:* "We novelists who work from documents, who go out and observe life before writing about it, who collect card files of notes on the things and the people around us, we are working in just the same way as the news reporter."[155] Up to a point, the sensationalisation of the evidence serves to enhance its verisimilitude, just as high definition and vibrant colours can make a television picture seem more real. Here the novel has a clear advantage over journalism as sensationalism can be passed off as the viewpoint of an in-story character. Zola even provides an illustration of what happens when sensation is not perceived to be accompanied by adequate factual underpinning, in the shape of the Société générale des ports du Maroc, which fails because it never progresses beyond the stage of being a fiction: "A judicial enquiry had demonstrated that the Moroccan ports existed only in the shape of engineering drawings, admittedly very fine ones."[156]

The combination of an apparently factual representation with a linguistic and stylistic register that depends crucially on techniques of excess, high definition, colour saturation, and intensity is, if we are to believe Zola's representation of Saccard, the key to narrative value. The very subject of the novel itself, Saccard and his ability to construct the false prospectus, reinforces the probability of commercial success by allowing Zola to represent in his character's mouth exactly the narrative devices he is simultaneously using to convince his own readers. Polemicism, it turns out, is an effective sales strategy: the novel appears to condemn the excess it depicts, while simultaneously exploiting the representation of excess, via a text that itself relies on excess as a diegetic device, as an effective way to sell a book in the business environment of the early 1870s. *La Curée* is as much a commentary on the conditions of doing business as a professional writer in the newly minted Troisième République as it is a critique of *mœurs* in the Second Empire.

L'Argent: *The Business of Narrative*

By the time Zola came to write *L'Argent* in 1890, eighteen years after the publication of *La Curée*, his career as a novelist had become a big business. His choice of big business as a theme reflects not only his personal experience but also a perception that ways of doing business were themselves changing. *L'Argent*, whether deliberately or not, is both the story of that process and a demonstration of the process in action. The story has become big business, and big business has become the story.

Growing the Business

Making money was evidently important to Zola, as Alexis records: "At the end of the day, when all is said and done, apart from an innate penchant for scientific studies, apart from the original dream of an all-encompassing work, . . . it was money itself, and the question of making money, which drove him to undertake *Les Rougon-Macquart*."[157] Judging by the results, he was a capable businessman. Shortly after Zola published *La Débâcle* in 1892, a contemporary journalist in *Le Figaro* made an attempt to estimate Zola's total earnings for *Les Rougon-Macquart* to that date.[158] He arrived at a total of approximately 1,600,000 francs: 300,000 francs from serialisation rights in feuilletons (at prices rising from twenty-five cents to two francs per line over the period), 800,000 francs from book sales (by then a total of 1,338,000 copies had sold at royalties rising from forty to sixty cents per copy), 200,000 francs from foreign translation rights, and a further 300,000 francs from Zola's share of theatrical receipts. Only Hugo, who in 1862 had turned down an offer for *Les Misérables* of 150,000 francs from Hachette in favour of 240,000 francs from Lacroix, could match Zola. Others were far behind—Flaubert received 16,000 francs for *L'Education sentimentale*, 10,000 francs for *Salammbô*.[159]

The journalist comments that, for twenty years of work, this was actually less than might have been supposed. It indicated that Zola's business required continual attention to each strand of his commercial strategy to maximise its financial potential. The Zola "brand" first had to be established. The relatively muted reception of the first six volumes in the series, in terms of both copies sold and critical responses, suggests that this process was taking time and considerable effort. Only with the publication of *L'Assommoir* in 1876 did the brand gain real market acceptance and, with it, a definitive change in Zola's financial and commercial fortunes. It is difficult to pinpoint just what caused the change, and the real explanation may lie in an accumulation of small differences in both text and market. It received particularly heavy promotion from its feuilleton publisher, Yves Guyot, who saw it as a way to boost the circulation of his new journal, *Le Bien Public,* and a further boost when it was repromoted by Catulle Mendès, who had picked it up for his weekly, *La République des lettres,* in July 1876 after *Le Bien Public* had dropped it in the wake of subscriber complaints. The furore that surrounded the second half of the work, with accusations of "malpropreté" and pornography levelled at Zola, certainly seems to have played a part in its success, but the extent to which this debate amongst critics reached the wider public should not be overestimated.[160] Mitterand thinks that its combination of rigorous attention to detail, superior novelistic construction, and fortuitous timing at a moment of societal change enabled *L'Assommoir* to reach out to a far broader readership than before.[161]

Viewed as a commercial proposition, though, it seems evident that this was a much more successful attempt to establish the brand than before. *L'Assommoir* is more assertive in its themes, more graphic in its descriptions, and above all closer to a predominantly urban readership than its recent predecessors. Anatole France, writing contemporaneously in *Le Temps* on June 27, 1877, certainly thought so: "The characters, and there are many, speak the language of the streets. When the author, without putting words in their mouths, finishes their thoughts or describes their state of mind, he uses the same register himself. . . . *L'Assommoir* may not be a particularly likeable book, but it is certainly a powerful one. Life comes across with immediacy and directness."[162] It established a clear Zolian voice, incapable of being mistaken for the work of any other contemporary novelist. It must have been an indication to Zola that the commercial strategies he had begun to develop in *La Curée* of naturalism and sensation were capable of paying off now that the brand had become visible.

It also demonstrated that what we would now call a multimedia approach to distribution could also be a successful way of diversifying Zola's sources of income. For the first time, the volume of copies sold in book format showed that this was a profitable activity on a stand-alone basis for publisher and writer. *L'Assommoir* was published in book form on January 24, 1877, sold thirty-eight thousand copies in its first year, and reached its ninety-first edition on December 31, 1881.[163] At an approximate average royalty of fifty cents per copy, this represented income of some 45,500 francs over five years, and a stream of income that would continue to accrue until its copyright expired. By comparison, Zola's one-time earnings from the feuilleton publication rights were 9,000 francs. It was clear that if enough copies could be sold, then the future value of the income stream from selling titles in book format was substantially greater than the one-off feuilleton rights.

With *L'Assommoir*, Zola had demonstrated not just that it was possible to attract a book-buying readership of this size but that it was possible to achieve this by a novelistic formula that appeared to be repeatable in a way that previous successes, such as Renan's *Vie de Jésus*, were evidently not. It meant that the role of the feuilleton in the publishing process could change to that of a promotional platform, as *L'Assommoir* had, perhaps fortuitously, demonstrated. It gave publishers the confidence to plan longer initial print runs. From *L'Assommoir* onwards, every Zola novel had sold more than fifty thousand copies in the Charpentier edition by the time the series came to an end in 1893; of the earlier works, only *La Faute de l'abbé Mouret* had broken this barrier. Six had exceeded one hundred thousand copies. First-year print runs of over fifty thousand for the most popular titles were the norm. Charpentier's willingness to increase Zola's royalties in regular steps from forty cents per copy to an eventual seventy-five cents per copy in 1892 is a good indication of the increasing profitability that scale production brought. Finally, others had also proved that this was a replicable phenomenon: the popular romantic melodramas of Georges Ohnet, published by Paul Ohllendorff, had achieved volumes similar to that of Zola, with *Serge Panine* (1880) and *Le Maître des forges* (1883) reaching cumulative sales of three hundred thousand copies over four years.[164]

Zola's approach to improving his earnings potential seems to have become more and more businesslike. Diversity remained important. Out of Zola's total earnings in 1876 of 34,200 francs, less than a third came from the sale of serialisation rights for *L'Assommoir*, while 6,000 francs came from his monthly salary from Charpentier, and a further 19,200 francs from journalism. Royalties from book sales of *L'Assommoir* began to flow in 1877, and, as I have shown, its success had a knock-on effect on sales of prior titles, which also picked up significantly, allowing Zola to negotiate the first of a series of increases in his royalty rate with Charpentier.[165] Even though this distribution would change with the increasing importance of *Les Rougon-Macquart,* the continuing diversity of income sources indicates that Zola was intent on developing the business of being a writer across multiple fronts. Journalism was dropped for an extended period from 1880, by which time it had become more a means of publicity for "brand Zola," his name was well enough known and he could make more by writing books. He experimented with brand extensions, particularly into theatre where, despite a consistent lack of critical acclaim for his theatrical adaptations jointly with the impresario William Busnach, he still seems to have made good money. The 1879 stage version of *L'Assommoir,* for example, ran for over 350 performances and earned box office takings of over 600,000 francs, while *Nana* had a run at *L'Ambigu* in 1881 of some 135 shows and box office receipts of some 400,000 francs.[166] His business skills improved. From 1881, on the back of the worldwide success of *Nana* in translation, he took personal charge of selling the foreign rights to his novels separately from the domestic rights, which Charpentier had retained under the 1877 contract: *Pot-Bouille,* for example, fetched 10,000 francs from the *Neue Freie Presse* of Vienna.[167] He took to selling domestic serialisation rights by auction and managed to raise the price from the 8,000 francs paid by *Le Bien Public* for the initial rights to *L'Assommoir* to, ultimately, 50,000 francs for the rights to each of the *Trois Villes* trilogy.[168] Zola even tried his hand at writing erotica.[169]

Success brought wealth, critical acclaim, at least in some quarters, and a belief in his own abilities as a storyteller. Naturalism became formulated in *Le Roman expérimental* and was elevated to the status of literary school. Followers, in the shape of various literary circles, Les Cinq, the devotees of "Bœuf nature," and the invitees of the Soirées de Médan, were recruited. Zola used the prominence of his journalism to promote his status as the nation's novelist in chief. An article in *Le Messager de l'Europe* incautiously exhibited his disdain for most of his contemporary competitors.[170] Along with this, Zola's own work began to show a greater concern with artistic control and with the ability of the writer to replicate predictable effects on the reader. We have already seen how Claude Lantier's framing of his painting of the Seine in *L'Œuvre* betrays a technique that steers the viewer's eye to a preselected perspective. But Claude struggles again and again with the impossibility of condensing fragmentary experience into an artistic whole (4:46–47, 203). Claude may fail to complete the task, but Zola succeeded. He alone could narrate the world. Claude leaves nothing behind: even his sketches have been destroyed. Zola left not only *L'Œuvre* but also the entire body of his creative output.

Completion is permanence, the creation of posterity value. Zola was conscious of being the man of the hour, "l'homme nécessaire," in Sandoz's words (4:359), just as Eugène Delacroix and Gustave Courbet rose at their appointed times (4:45). Judgement is in the hands of the reader, but, if the contemporary audience fails to understand, posterity will provide a second chance. The positioning is almost Napoleonic (and, as with the Goncourts, with an ironic overtone of the romantic), with the artist uniquely able to apprehend reality in its full state of fragmentation and to reassemble the jumbled pieces into a relevant political and social order.

Zola's increasing self-confidence as a novelist is perhaps most forcefully displayed in *Le Rêve* (1888). Its self-conscious differentiation from its immediate precursor, *La Terre* (1887), marks it as an experiment. Zola chose a genre partway between fairy tale and hagiography, a *conte bleu* told in a register of simple pathos that had been a staple of popular literature and oral tradition. His selection of the only real mass medium that predated the popular press both exploited a genre with proven commercial credentials and announced a confidence in his ability to reinterpret this classical genre for a modern readership. It also, I think, betrayed a degree of hubris in his ability to pick whatever narrative modality he wished, secure in his ability to turn any genre into a blockbuster. He even uses his own reputation as a novelist of sex and violence to maintain narrative tension: part of the suspense is derived from an expectation of the irruption of typical Zolian excess into the self-aware demureness of the text. Anatole France notes sarcastically, "For my part, I would prefer a less flashy kind of chastity."[171] The very fact that the sex never really happens is an indication of the sheer strength of "brand Zola" by this stage: he has, in effect, kept readers reading to the end precisely by *not* behaving as usual.

Le Rêve is, in equal measure, an example of Zola's narrative virtuosity, an assertion of his own belief in his storytelling powers, and a demonstration of the commercial power of this combination. A first edition of forty-four thousand sold out immediately, and at Zola's death it was his fourth most frequently bought novel after *Nana, La Débâcle,* and *L'Assommoir. L'Argent,* which followed three years later in 1891, turns this combination into the very subject matter of the novel itself and, in doing so, reveals an important aspect of the relationship between a narrative of business and the business of narrative.

Manufacturing the Story

While the story was assuming the form of a business, the form of business in France was itself changing. A new law in 1867 had introduced the *société anonyme* and permitted capital to flow into businesses with the protection of limited liability, provoking a wave of corporate consolidation and the foundation or expansion of many modern corporate groups, including France's largest book publisher, Hachette Livre, now part of the Lagardère group. The notion of limited liability had long been associated with speculation and fraud. England had forbidden all forms of companies limited by shares without specific permission by government charter from 1720 in consequence of the speculative bubbles caused by John Law in France and by the South Sea Bubble in England. A form of limited liability had been proposed under the French Revolution but had not come into effect until 1808, and even then it could only be used with specific government approval on a case-by-case basis, a situation that obtained until the change of law in 1867. Despite interim legislation in 1856 in response to liberalisation of the laws on joint-stock companies in England, the system remained cumbersome, difficult to access, and open to abuse through back doors such as limited partnerships, which were widely preferred until the 1856 legislation cut off this avenue.

The "baggage" that the concept of limited liability brought with it consisted of two rather contradictory strands. On the one hand, it had historically been associated with fraud and underhand dealings, either through direct abuse of the concept or through indirect avoidance of the controls it was meant to impose. On the other, it stood for a kind of remote and ponderous respectability as a form of governance adopted by some of the largest corporations, principally in the financial, transport, mining, and public works sectors, licensed under government authority with a history of capricious inconsistency in the way in which control was exercised. From 1867 the requirement for government approval was removed and limited liability became accessible to all forms of corporate activity. The *société anonyme* became effectively normalised and, although it took time to become established, the number of S.A.s established more than doubled in the second half of the 1870s to over 400, compared to a cumulative total of 651 during the entire prior period from 1808 to 1867.[172]

In writing about the growth of the corporate entity, Zola was tackling a topical and modern issue. Its chief characteristic was, as the name suggests, anonymity. The *société anonyme* could not be identified with a single owner. Responsibility for its actions lay with the nebulous concept of the company itself, separated from its owners by an insulating barrier of limited liability. The very etymology of one of its signifiers in both French and English, *corporation* / corporation, suggests an image of a body bound by a set of rules rather than controlled by a head.[173] The corporation was indeed represented by a board of directors who in theory could not delegate their responsibilities but in practice could temporise and obfuscate for extended periods. And yet corporate power over the growing workforce working within the larger corporations, from railways to banks, as industrialisation and urbanisation progressed was evidently considerable. Even the concept of being an employee, in Balzac's day used almost exclusively to designate a civil servant, had been privatised. By 1881, French banks employed over 50,000. The number of employees in Paris would rise from 126,000 in 1866 to 352,000 in 1911. Le Bon Marché employed 1,788 in 1877; by 1887 the number had almost doubled.[174] The press itself had followed suit, as evidenced by the seventy-three quoted media companies on the Paris Bourse in 1881. As Mollier writes, "A page has been turned, that of the publisher as feudal lord. Another, more anonymous, is opening: that of the corporate entity, comparable to any other limited liability company of the time."[175] This was the world Zola was writing about.

Where Zola clearly differentiates himself from his contemporaries, I think, is in his apperception and critique of the rise of "big business," represented by its avatar, the corporate entity, as the political and sociological phenomenon of the age.[176] At one level, Zola's intuition leads to an aesthetic that denies subjectivity, individuality, and rationality in favour of automated responses, mindless consumption, and complete subjugation to the corporation—the railway workers of *La Bête humaine*, the department store customers of *Au Bonheur des dames*, the miners of *Germinal*. At another, it allows him to recognise a "comprehension gap" in the shape of the inability of a society contemporaneously to understand the basic principles of its own functioning. At a third level, it allows him, I believe, to present *Les Rougon-Macquart,* and particularly *L'Argent,* as the story of the rise of the business of narration.

As *Les Rougon-Macquart* progresses, so Zola opposes two quite separate models of corporate behaviour. On the one hand we have a model in which the corporation is still capable of being controlled by a superior individual; on the other a situation in which any possibility of control has passed into the hands of the corporate entity itself. The fissile Rougon-Macquart family itself becomes a metaphor for this process, with its tendency towards entropic autonomy pitted against Félicité Rougon's quest for total control of the dynasty, which frames the entire narrative, from her attempt to direct its history in *La Fortune des Rougon* to her struggle to rewrite it in *Le Docteur Pascal.* Both the Saccard of *La Curée* and Octave Mouret of *Au Bonheur des dames* belong to this model of the *homme nécessaire,* in the right place at the right time, and represented as able to control both their businesses and their destinies just as Zola is himself able to control his narrative. The closeness with which Mouret's ability to control stock units is matched by Zola's narrative prowess in marshalling the detail of his descriptions of the department store sends an apparently unequivocal message to the reader that the business of narrative can be managed as efficiently as that of women's fashion. Yet we are, I think, still left with a sense of lurking *fêlure.* Just as the market itself in *Le Ventre de Paris* assumes a brooding presence that seems capable, at this stage in an unformulated way, of influencing the lives of those who live within it, so the business of the department store—not its physical incarnation, nor even its complexity, but the idea that this is a form of corporate machine with its own momentum and direction—seems poised to overwhelm Mouret's fragile control at any moment.

In the *ébauche* for *Germinal,* Zola is quite explicit about the need to choose between these two models of commercial behaviour. "There are two alternative scenarios. Should I take an individual boss who would himself personify the role of capital, which would make the battle more immediate and perhaps more dramatic? Or should I take a limited liability company, shareholders, in other words the world of big business, with the mine run by an appointed director and a team of employees and, behind them, capital itself as a passive shareholder? That would certainly be more topical, more relevant, and would pitch the debate in a way big business is used to. I think it would be better to adopt the latter scenario."[177] In his contemporary notes on Paul Leroy-Beaulieu's *La Question ouvrière au XIXe siècle*, Zola goes further in considering how to represent big business in a novelistic context: "So on one side I'd have the workers, on the other management, and behind would be the share-holders, the boards etc. (a whole apparatus to be studied). But once the whole structure had been discreetly introduced, I think I would leave the shareholders, the committees, etc., to one side in favour of a sort of tabernacle in the background, a kind of living god eating workers in the shadows. That would be more effective and I wouldn't have to burden the book with boring details of corporate administration."[178] Taken to-gether, these two statements form a powerful case for considering Zo-la's "mythologising" prism as, at least in part, a method of describing the rise of "la grande industrie."

The Compagnie des mines de Montsou, referred to throughout as "La Compagnie" in a typical Zolian device that transforms a single pit into a generic representative of its entire species, is a clear manifestation of the faceless power of the corporate in *Germinal*. In *L'Œuvre*, even art it-self can be corporatized. Naudet, "a speculator and stock trader who fun-damentally cared nothing for real art,"[179] reinvents art, in a reflection of Zola's own past career at Hachette, as a product of marketing: con-sumer desire is created through the perception of monetary value, not artistic worth (4:185–186). He owns artists: Fagerolles, a rising name, is "one of his painters, . . . a hired hand."[180] And the final scene of Lanti-er's funeral is saturated with images of corporate invasion—the indus-trialisation of death in the neat, factory-like lines of the new cemetery at Clignancourt (4:358), the shunting train that drowns out the funeral service (4:361), and finally, in a typical Zolian expansion, the represen-tation of the entire century as a failed corporation.[181] In *La Bête humaine* it is the railway company, the Compagnie de l'Ouest, that owns the workers and controls not just their waking hours, through the railway timetable, but also who they sleep with or marry, through supervised accommodation (4:1224–1225, 1242). The corporation is the emblem of an apparently inexorable evolutionary process towards a more efficient society, yet it disrupts causality through its inability to explain its ap-parently irrational actions—and how, indeed, could a headless body re-spond? The Compagnie de l'Ouest, not the organs of government, de-cides whether the truth of Grandmorin's murder is revealed or suppressed

(4:1124–1125, 1315–1317). The railway becomes its ambiguous, slippery symbol, on the one hand, of ownership, possession, and order and, on the other, of exploitation, abuse of power, and dispersal.

The shift of agency to a formless corporate machine evidently makes life harder to interpret: the "comprehension gap," the hiatus between the occurrence of an event and the point at which its origins or motivation becomes generally understood, expands. Zola devises many symbols to illustrate this, from the shrouded decision-making processes of the mining company in *Germinal* and *La Bête humaine* to the opaque procedures and transaction structures of the Bourse in *L'Argent*. Reffait specifically links the latter to the growth in importance of the quoted *société anonyme*.[182] Since, under this structure, shareholders are free to transact their shares independently, with no reference to any form of central control or, in the case of bearer shares, knowledge of the transaction, understanding what is happening *en temps utile* is a virtual impossibility. His argument implies that the failure of the Banque Universelle is somehow implicit in the structure of modernity, which obliges it to take a form that will ultimately destroy it, an argument that echoes Baguley's presumption of entropy as a condition of the naturalist perspective.[183] We may question how Zola's own ability to understand this comprehension gap is consistent with its essential unknowability, and in due course my argument will return to the point. For the moment, though, let us continue to follow the trail of the corporate entity.

Zola represents the corporate as infinitely replicable once critical mass is achieved, and definable only by narrative—just like his own business. The Compagnie des mines de Montsou will simply reallocate capital to buy or dig new mines to replace those lost—unlike the individual pits under private ownership, which, like Deneulin in *Germinal*, are forced to sell to big business (3:1523). Its business is effectively invisible as it exists underground: what gives it reality are the stories of its operations rather than the pits themselves. The corporation exists fully only through its narrative: its scope is verifiable only by its books of accounts. The railway conglomerate simply rewrites its own story if threatened. Reality is manipulated or suppressed to ensure narrative continuity. Senior employees spend their time grooming the narrative to make it as attractive as possible for the shadowy boards of directors, and behind them shareholders, who take the place of corporate readers. M. Camy-Lamotte, agent of the company, feeds evidence to the judge and destroys compromising documentation (4:1314–1323). Narrative is the true creator of lasting value: even the runaway train that closes *La Bête humaine* is perhaps less a political symbol than a metaphor of the posterity value of the story in the hands of the reader. The driverless coaches, glimpsed from town to town as they rush through the night on endless rails, represent the survival of the tale of the end of empire just as much as the end of empire itself (4:1330–1331).

L'Argent is the novel in which narrative itself becomes big business. The plot is based on three real-life corporate dramas: the rise and fall of the Union Générale from its incorporation in May 1878 to its bankruptcy in January 1882; the fate of the Caisse générale des chemins de fer and its promoter, the banker and press baron Mirès, in the 1850s; and the story of the epic battle between the Péreire brothers and the Rothschilds that led ultimately to the bankruptcy of the Péreire's corporate vehicle, the Crédit Mobilier, in 1867. The Union Générale scandal had happened less than a decade before the publication of *L'Argent* itself, within the personal experience of many of Zola's readers. Mitterand has demonstrated how closely the plot of *L'Argent* mirrors that of the Union Générale, down to the level of the exact scale and timing of individual share price movements (5:1238–1242). Halina Suwala has also shown how the sensational demise of the Union Générale had itself spawned a shoal of other literary works, creating, as it were, its own literary subsidiary.[184]

In adopting such a high-profile corporate history as the basis for his novel, Zola is, I think, suggesting several important propositions to his readers. The simple choice of a plot revolving around a corporate debacle implies that the world of the corporate entity, distinct from that of a specific commerce or an industry, is itself a compelling and contemporary object of literary focus. He implies that the corporate vehicles from which big business operates are themselves projections in narrative of an underlying structure too complex to grasp. Further, these narratives may be an independent source of durable value, just as the story of the Union Générale has survived its bankrupted business. And as a virtuoso creator of narrative, he proposes himself to the reader as the scribe of business, capable of rendering legible its baffling complexity. It is worth examining each of these propositions in more detail.

Zola's focus is now firmly on the corporate vehicle. *L'Argent* tells the story of the rise and fall of the Banque Universelle, S.A. Saccard, down on his luck after the (omitted) failure of his property empire from *La*

Curée, chances on an engineer, Georges Hamelin, and his sister, Mme Caroline, recently returned from the Middle East with tales of fabulous wealth and riches to be won if the capital to exploit them could only be raised. Saccard scrapes the barrel of his reputation, his contacts, and his wallet to raise the money to establish a bank, the Banque Universelle, for this purpose. He buys up and bribes entire swathes of the press to promote the projects. He seduces shareholders, speculators, and Mme Caroline alike. The bank grows like topsy in a Ponzi scheme that rewards shareholders from their own contributions. The bank is quoted on the stock exchange and its share price rises inexorably. But success breeds enemies, including Gundermann, king of the Bourse, and the Busch clan, a family of sinister fraudsters who discover Victor, a forgotten illegitimate child of Saccard's, and try to blackmail Saccard. Eventually, inexorably, the bankruptcy and stock market crash, which forms the climax of the novel, arrive. Saccard's brother Eugène abruptly removes his political protection. Saccard and many of his investors are ruined. But he survives, possibly to rise again to another fortune, and his vicious, mentally deranged son disappears into the Parisian netherworld.

The novel is the history of a company, not of the underlying business, since much of that business is a fraud and never exists. The corporation itself, however, is very much in focus. Zola spares no detail: readers are subject to the arcana of subscription rules for new shares in a *société anonyme* (5:113), to the rules for the selection of board directors (5:132), and to a two-thousand-word description of an annual general meeting (5:164–168). The role and importance of the corporation have clearly changed since the time of *La Curée*, when a single superior individual had no need of corporate structures to create a business, and, indeed, since that of *Au Bonheur des dames*, when such a man could dominate the company he has founded. In *L'Argent*, Saccard cannot realise the scale of his plans without the help of collective capital mobilised through the structures of the *société anonyme*. The whole of the first three chapters, almost a third of the novel, is devoted to showing Saccard's attempts to raise this capital. His rise is also that of the corporate, as the dominant form of big business.

The corporate entity is visibly more the *narrative* of a business than it is the business itself. The Banque Universelle is essentially a story told, or a prospectus sold, by Saccard. His credibility is its creditworthiness and vice versa: narrative terminology becomes irredeemably confused with that of business. Credo leads to credit, *croyance* to *créance*, when he mixes religion with business and persuades the Beauvilliers family to subscribe based on faith (5:126). Shareholders are described as a crowd of believers (*la foule croyante;* 5:129). Like the earlier Société des ports du Maroc of *La Curée*, the Banque Universelle has a far more convincing existence in narrative than it does in reality. Its very name projects scale but gives no indication of whether anything lies behind the story. It exists through its stock, trading as inscriptions in a register until paid up and then as bearer certificates (5:241). Its growth is recorded in narrative rather than in constructions: the literary device of its profit-and-loss account allows the narrative of profits to be written and published long ahead of the reality: "Then, you're not taking into account the colossal impact of this profit forecast appearing in all the papers. . . . The Bourse will ignite."[185]

The business project itself is more a compendium of literary genres than a business plan: from the *Mille et une nuits,* thrice cited in the text (5:82, 233, 252), comes the exotic Middle Eastern setting; from mediaeval Grail epics the quest for the Trésor du Saint-Sépulcre (5:80); from Verne-esque travel literature the concept of voyaging through terra incognita on railways and steamers (5:61–63); from fairy tale the image of the pot of gold at the end of the rainbow, or, in this case, in Saccard's vaults: "In the basement, where the securities department lived, strongboxes were sealed in, immense, opening maws deep as ovens, behind clear glass screens so the public could see them, lined up like the fabled casks in which the incalculable treasures of the fairies sleep."[186]

Saccard's rise is therefore the story of how he constructs the story of the Banque Universelle. He has regularly been compared to an author in critical analyses, and he is indeed referred to in terms as a virtuoso *littérateur,* the *poète* of the financial world (5:101, 219, 243).[187] But his position is as much that of the chief executive of a publishing business as that of an author. He acts as publisher and editor. He receives contributions from others, like articles in a newspaper—from Hamelin the main lines of the story (5:61–63, 75), from Mme Caroline the infill detail (5:75)—edits them into a coherent prospectus, then puts the product into circulation (5:125). He also performs the functions of a corporate executive: he develops its business plan (5:74–75); he names the company (5:82); he raises capital for the business (5:107); he worries about its corporate profile (5:115); he promotes the business in the press (5:119). He imitates the press barons of the age by buying not just advertising space but also titles, journalists, and critics, and the story of his press subsidiary forms a distinct subplot to the main story of the novel. *L'Argent* is, in a very real sense, a narrative of the business of fiction.

It explores how narrative value is created and destroyed. In the very first chapter, Zola, through the medium of Saccard, compares and contrasts a complete range of transaction types. They fall into three distinct categories: those where value can be controlled, those where it is constantly challenged but can be manipulated, and those where it cannot be controlled at all. The first category comprises prospectus and theft; the second, auction and speculation; the final, gift, charity, and political redistribution. Prospectus is represented by the plans that Saccard begins to construct for his as yet unformulated new project, a narrative that projects a view of value and seeks to control the reception of that message to the last degree (5:22). Theft, represented by Busch and his attempt to blackmail Saccard, which this chapter initiates, turns out to be remarkably similar to prospectus. It is simply another form of narrative that acquires value through preparation, detailed research, and careful presentation: the parallels with Saccard's narrative and with Zola's are heavily ironic (5:33–38). Busch, trading shares by weight, even has his own variant form of scale.

Just as prospectus and theft are opposite sides of the same coin, so auction and speculation are also subdivisions of a continuum. The Bourse, introduced to the reader on the first page, operates an auction mechanism in which the value of shares and the narratives they represent is determined by the operation of the market (5:11–22). It can be manipulated to an extent via its propensity to convert credulity into credit, but its greatest threat is its scale, the opacity that its size brings, and the apparent dislocation between risk and reward, which converts auction into speculation. Speculation itself is a form of auction where excess, another kind of scale, obscures motivation and thus renders the process ungovernable. The cameo of Baronne Sandorff, who sells sex for investment tips, in the first chapter shows precisely this: her mixture of predictable financial motivation and sexual excess leads to capricious investment behaviour (5:29–30). Finally, gift is represented by three forms of exchange that are all dismissed as impractical because they lack scale or the ability to be scaled: by a demonetised exchange in the shape of the sexual favours of the local stationer, Mme Conin, who sleeps around for free, but only with men she likes, much to Saccard's frustration (5:32–33); by charity, which Busch's ailing Marxist son Sigismond rejects as insulting (5:42) and which the religious philanthropist Princesse Orviedo will later show to be ineffectual; and by political redistribution, rejected even by Sigismond as utopian (5:46). Marcel Mauss also notes this conflict between industrial scale and the relevance of gift: "It appears that the whole field of industrial and commercial law is in conflict with morality. The economic prejudices of the people and producers derive from their strong desire to pursue the thing they have produced once they realise that they have given their labour without sharing in the profits."[188]

The value of Saccard's story is precisely measured and converted, through the mechanism of the Bourse and the share price of the Banque Universelle, into monetary equivalents. From an initial issue price of 500 francs, it rises to a high of 3,060 francs before crashing to its final suspension price of 430 francs, and that, in a nutshell, is the plot of the book (5:131, 252, 333). The stock price itself becomes a lever to create narrative value by regulating dramatic tension and pace. The rise from the initial issue value to 2,000 francs takes 121 pages (5:131–252); from there to the peak valuation takes 58 pages (5:252–310); the crash itself, just 23 pages (5:310–33). The share price of the Banque Universelle tracks, and eventually becomes, its narrative. The Bourse becomes a metaphor for a collective readership, of such a scale that its methods of valuation become utterly opaque and immune to challenge. Like the mine in *Germinal* and the railway in *La Bête humaine*, it is characterised by images of consumption and circulation, another body with no head. It is another variant of the Zolian corporate, a collective entity that is both an unavoidable platform for modern business and an ultimate surrender of individual agency.

Scale must be met with scale in the modern world. The conclusion that Saccard's investors, as the collective readers of his prospectus, must reach is that scale, in terms both of the reach of the story and of the narrative force with which it is created and projected, is the defining characteristic of success. In order to survive, the story must become big business. "We need a gigantic project, of a scale to match the occasion," says Saccard, in the same breath as he describes the *société anonyme* as the only vehicle for the size of his ambitions.[189] Even he is mistaken, Zola suggests, in believing in his own importance: ultimately narrative outlives both individuals and corporates. Saccard is not required for the posterity of the Banque Universelle, just as Bontoux is no longer required to tell the story of the Union Générale. Its continuation depends not on creditworthiness, which is fallible, but on the credibility of its story. The techniques that Saccard uses to present this story are themselves derived from the business of merchandising narrative. In the hands of Jantrou, the editor of his tame newspaper, business and narrative become one: "At first he thought of writing a brochure, twenty pages or so on the main enterprises the Universelle was undertaking, but brought to life in the manner of a mini novel, dramatized in colloquial style, and he wanted to flood the provinces with this brochure, which would be distributed for free to the furthest depths of the countryside."[190] Even fictional scale works: the rumour of the size of Sabatani's penis is enough to guarantee his success with the Parisian ladies, just as that of the Banque Universelle's success is enough to fill the fraudulent accounts that he is fronting for Saccard (5:118, 215). And when Saccard fails, his excuse is that even he failed to act on a large enough scale: "As for me, if I had had the few hundred millions I needed to chuck into the pit, I'd be the master of the universe."[191]

The Story of a Crash, or the Crash of the Story?

Saccard's narrative is not Zola's. Zola, in contrast to Saccard, is manifestly capable of managing scale. *L'Argent* is the eighteenth novel of a series that had sold over 1,200,000 copies at the time of its publication. No other French writer came close to the size of his publishing empire. Following its publication, Zola's next novel, *La Débâcle*, appeared simultaneously in French and in translations into German, English, Spanish, Portuguese, Italian, Czech, Danish, Norwegian, Swedish, and Russian.[192] The feuilleton was serialised in London one day after its appearance in France. Saccard, implicitly, has failed to control the corporate monster, while Zola has succeeded, and the fact that subsequent generations continue to read the story demonstrates how Zola has successfully laid the foundations for the posterity value that has eluded Saccard.

Zola implies that he is able to remain unaffected by the hubris that Saccard displays. Gundermann, "the master of the Bourse and the universe" *(le maître de la Bourse et du monde)* (5:21), part portrait of James de Rothschild, the epitome of big business in the financial world, Saccard's nemesis, shows some characteristics strangely reminiscent of Zola (or perhaps of how Zola would like to see himself).[193] Like Zola as businessman, Gundermann represents scale. Like Zola as naturalist, he operates without emotion on the basis of observation, preparation, and deduction, a fine workman (5:96). Like Zola as writer, he is a simple, unaffected virtuoso: "He was no speculator, no adventure captain manipulating the fortunes of others, dreaming, as Saccard did, of heroic battles in which he would triumph, would win a colossal payback on the back of the mercenary gold at his command; he was, as he said frankly, just a moneybroker, the most skilled and the most assiduous that ever existed."[194]

Gundermann is also a reader and critic of Saccard's prospectus, and a hint that Zola, too, is a fine judge of narrative value. Overt manipulation of investors or readers, Zola implies, is the hallmark of an unskilled operator, the sort of behaviour to which Saccard and Jantrou, plotting to deceive the subscribers to their newspapers, may resort but to which neither he, Gundermann, nor he, Zola, needs to stoop: "And out of their [Saccard's and Jantrou's] prodigality, out of all this money they noisily threw around to the four corners of the heavens, emerged only their immense disdain for the public, the contempt of the entrepreneurial mind for the unenlightened ignorance of the herd, ready to believe any old story, so far removed from the complex operations of the Bourse that the most barefaced scams set the neighbourhood alight and made it rain millions."[195]

But Zola may be closer to Saccard than he cares to admit. Gomart memorably describes Zola's own drive for scale as an operation on the *marché à terme* in which Zola is a perpetual short seller of his novelistic output to Charpentier, trying to cover his position by risk-mitigation strategies to ensure each novel will realise full value when delivered.[196] All his risk-mitigation strategies involve exactly what he condemns: reader manipulation. Her analysis shows how manipulative Zola's narrative style in *L'Argent* has become, using prolepsis, iteration, and concatenation as ways to modify the reader's perception of value, just as the in-story characters use the same techniques to manipulate the outcomes of their own deals.[197] Goux argues that Zola's search for scale is another aspect of manipulative risk mitigation: he sees it as Zola's way of discounting the uncertain future value of his novels into immediate present value by maximising the size of the immediate readership without the need to wait for the judgement of posterity, just as Saccard tries to

anticipate the profits of the Banque Universelle.[198] The need to maximise the readership requires predictable narrative values and, hence, a
series of ultimately fruitless strategies to impose a kind of narrative gold
standard with absolute values against which success or failure can be
measured.

Both show how Zola's narratives become more manipulative of the
reader as *Les Rougon-Macquart* progresses. In part this can be attributed,
as Goux implies, to the establishment of "brand Zola" as a known narrative commodity. Before the Zola-aware reader has even opened to the
first page of *L'Argent,* he or she will be expecting a plot that ends in the
death or ruin of the main characters. From the outset, Zola quietly hints
that Saccard's rise will end in failure: the construction of the very first
chapter, which shifts from Saccard's ambition, up through the apex of
the stock exchange in the shape of Gundermann, then back down to
the threat from the underworld of Busch and La Méchain, mirrors the
shape of the work as a whole (5:11–49). By the end of the novel, as the
price of Banque Universelle stock tumbles, even the weather joins in presaging Saccard's defeat (5:323). The entropic essence of the naturalist
perspective is a trademark that conditions readers as much as it pretends
to be a dispassionate record of observed reality.

Zola's confidence in his narrative virtuosity leads to a degree of slop-
piness in the construction of the narrative. As many critics have noted,
the story of Saccard's private life, and in particular of his illegitimate
son Victor, is poorly integrated into the central plot about the Banque
Universelle. Mitterand traces this fault line back to the *ébauche:* "There
are *two* novels in *L'Argent:* . . . that of the private man and that of the financier."[199] Successful narrative devices are overworked: the construction of the first chapter as a mirror of the entire plot of the novel, tracking
a process of rise and fall, is copied in the fifth and ninth chapters, all
three of which end with a salutary reminder of the alternative world of
Busch and La Méchain (5:32–49, 137–138, 281–294). Minor characters
seem to be treated as disposable stage props. Mère Eulalie, mistress of
the precocious Victor in the cité de Naples, is used as a rather transparent
device for intensifying the picture of degradation Zola is seeking to
convey (5:150). Once the effect has been created, she is conveniently dis-
posed of a mere six pages later in order to allow Victor's rescue by Mme
Caroline (5:156). Characters become caricatures: the trio of monothe-
matic brokers, Pillerault the optimist, Moser the pessimist, Salmon the

silent (5:14–18, 297); later Jacoby of the heavy stomach and the thundering bass voice (5:88, 301). Even Saccard, the pirate with charisma, described five times as "corsaire" (5:56, 130, 275, 331, 336) and twice as "bandit" (5:228, 278), comes close to caricature at times. Perhaps most seriously, Mme Caroline's vacillations, whether in her relations with Saccard, in her investment in the Banque Universelle, or in her view of money as productive or destructive, seem at odds with her portrayal as a strong, independently minded woman.

Through these cracks in the narrative emerges a more politicised perspective. Even in *La Curée* it is noticeable that passages where the story falters allow a much more direct authorial voice to emerge. From the bathos of the enumeration of the plants in the *serre* slides a sudden polemical edge: "This pretty youngster . . . found himself, in Renée's hands, in one of those decadent orgies which, on occasion in a decaying nation, drain the flesh and unhinge the mind."[200] As time goes on and Zola's belief in his own role as national storyteller in chief strengthens, so the adoption of a political or moral position becomes more and more difficult to avoid. He is clearly aware of this and tries a number of tactics to mitigate it. In *L'Argent* he confronts squarely, from the *ébauche* onwards, the evident danger that writing about money implies taking a position on the impact of capitalism in society. His solution is to adopt a deliberately neutral stance, hiding behind the justification he expresses in *Le Roman expérimental* of the role of novelists as "moralistes expérimentateurs" and for the novel as a powerful tool of political and social analysis.[201] He explicitly recognises money as a force for both good and evil: "Don't do money down. The best and the worst of things. All the great things you can do with it."[202] In the text of the novel itself, he transplants these arguments into the reported thoughts of the already impaired character of Mme Caroline, contrasting "this horrible money, which defiles and devours!" with money as "the manure in which grew the humankind of the future."[203]

But what he fails to recognise is that this decision not to take a stance is a stance in itself. The *ébauche* also reveals how close he felt personally to the portrayal of Mme Caroline—"Put myself completely into her"—and perhaps some of her contradictions have also crept in.[204] Her inner voice of reason suspects that the mere process of achieving scale involves a loss of agency: "A company with a capital of five hundred million, with three hundred thousand shares, quoted at three thousand francs each, representing a value of nine hundred million: could that be justified; wasn't there a terrible risk in paying out the colossal dividend required for such an amount of paid-up capital, even at just five per cent?"[205] Perhaps, too, these are evidence of Zola's own doubts that have leached into the character of Mme Caroline. He, however, has a vested interest in the viability of the process of scaling up, at least insofar as the publishing industry is concerned, since that is the very basis of his own success. Saccard discovers that, as scale increases, so the process requires more and more intervention by its manager to avoid a loss of control. Zola's fiction undergoes a similar evolution.

Politicisation sneaks in by the back door, much as it had in *Germinal* through the record of the politicised reality of the mining communities he was describing. Charle sees this as characteristic of the contemporary press as well, which moved, under the influence of advertising and paid advertorial, from passively reflecting public tastes to actively trying to shape them, and it is perhaps not surprising to see Zola in the vanguard of this movement.[206] In *L'Argent* the opposition of two alternative political realities does not make either less political. The many, often diametrically opposed, political readings of *L'Argent* attest to its continuing polemical resonances; and it remains clearly possible to impose a political reading on the work, from Nelson's view of it as evidence of how far Zola had shifted towards a stance supportive of an enlightened form of bourgeois capitalism, to Reffait's perception of it more as a dialectical discussion of the incompatibilities of market-based capitalism and democracy, to Gallois's reading of it as a commentary on French cultural imperialism.[207] Pierre-Gnassounou sensibly sees this increasing level of authorial intrusion as less a political statement per se and more what she calls the fear of narrative "incomplétude," a lacuna in which an interpretation other than that of Zola can emerge.[208] She sees the golden fly in *Nana,* the representation of *Phèdre* in *La Curée,* and the battle of the Maigres and the Gras in *Le Ventre de Paris* as examples of this tendency to make sure the reader "gets it."

Perhaps, though, this is simply another successful commercial strategy? After all, texts that follow the politicisation of their readership, and that can be interpreted to appeal to many constituencies in an increasingly splintered society, represent a credible way of maximising market share. The technique, however, comes at a price. Married with scale and financial resources, politicisation has the potential to turn narrative into a powerful *tribune,* as Sherard records Zola's contemporary intentions in 1893.[209] Politicised narrative requires a greater level and visibility of authorial control, just as Saccard is forced to intervene more and more actively as his need for the narrative of the Banque Universelle to prevail becomes more acute. Serious contradictions start to appear at this juncture. Zola describes a world in which the acquisition of scale irresistibly disempowers the individual and assumes autonomous agency, yet when it comes to his own business, he appears to be confident that this process can somehow be averted. Goux wonders whether Zola has run out of road as a novelist: "Is it not legitimate to ask whether, in the unbridled whirl of this demented game which upends any notion of stable values and of reality, Zola has not reached the limits of his own realist or naturalist representation of society?"[210] The entire naturalist perspective points to a universal principle of entropy, yet *Les Rougon-Macquart* describes an imploding society that has manifestly survived to the point of its description twenty years later. And even if aspects of that society have disappeared, like the Banque Universelle, Zola's narrative has successfully re-created them. Durable narrative value is attainable only at the price of contradicting the very tenets of naturalism itself.

Le Docteur Pascal can perhaps be seen as an attempt by Zola to resolve some of these contradictions. Pascal has spent his career in an individual search for a new chemical compound to cure diseases. His withdrawal from society, from big business, from the compromises of scale, is symbolised both by his physical isolation in a remote house and by his enforced abstention from money as bankruptcy looms. He eventually realises that the placebo effect of plain water, injected under the right circumstances, can produce just as powerful a therapeutic response as the elusive drug itself. It is an apparent affirmation of the power of the individual as author, who alone can render the narrative of a drug as effective as the drug itself. The job of the doctor, or the writer, is to create not the drug but the conditions under which the story of the drug acquires credibility.

Like Pascal, part portrait of Zola himself as the autobiographical detail in the text indicates, Zola believes he, as an individual, has that gift.[211] But Pascal's voice eventually fails because, as an individual, he is too weak to promote it sufficiently and cannot compete with the scale of Félicité Rougon, corporate representative of the Rougon empire and its reputation. The very fact that Zola's novel about Dr. Pascal was printed in three editions totalling 88,000 copies in the first year of its publication (1893) suggests that Zola had made his own choice in favour of scale. The same would remain true of all his further output despite its increasingly politicised and tendentious tones. All three volumes of the *Trois Villes* cycle had initial editions of 88,000. By Zola's death in 1902, *Lourdes* had been through seven editions totalling 143,000, while *Rome* and *Paris* had two editions each with totals of 100,000 and 93,500 copies, respectively. Even though sales were slowing, and would slow more with *Les Quatre Evangiles*, these were still enormous print runs for the time. Zola, as Goux implies in relation to *L'Argent*, seems to have been trying to anticipate posterity value by generating as much current value from the titles as possible.[212] By this stage, rather than the power of the story, it was the reach of Zola's brand, the muscle of the production machine behind him, and the willingness of capital providers to invest that sustained the business of Zola, Inc.

In a sense, Zola was indeed *l'homme nécessaire*. He arrived on the literary scene at a time when technological advances enabled a mass readership to be reached with affordable products. He used the techniques of popular journalism, which had already opened up this market, as a springboard to establish his brand. He brought some of the methods of the production line to the manufacture of novels. He acquired the commercial skills of promoting literature early in his career. Even naturalism became in his hands as much a sales tool as a literary philosophy. He showed how literature could become big business. And, inevitably, the business of literature becomes his subject. More than any other French writer of his time, he captures the emergence of the corporate entity, the faceless *société anonyme*, as the vehicle and emblem of big business, and the loss of individual agency that this brings. And, with magnificent irony, he eventually falls victim to the phenomenon he has done so much to document, as his later novels succumb to a self-defeating demand for authorial control. But the very fact that we still read Zola today attests to his ultimate success in creating a narrative with true posterity value, even if history has adjusted the relative valuations. Saccard, I feel, would have understood.

Conclusion: Accounts

THIS BOOK HAS REVEALED a curious lacuna in critical analysis of nineteenth-century prose fiction. Scholars discuss the novel's representations of economic realities, or how an author uses the novel to critique aspects of political economics. They admit the importance of economic influences in the author's own life. They investigate at length the commercialisation of the press and the means of production of printed works. But when it comes to seeing novelistic narrative as an economic commodity in its own right and, as such, a revealing commentary on the conditions of its own production, all but a few back off. This book has tried to show how that omission can be remedied and the potential benefits of doing so.

With hindsight, it is not difficult to understand how this lacuna has developed. In France, successive waves of criticism first created it and then, over time, have begun a slow and, so far, incomplete process of filling it in. The initial rejection of the industrialisation of literature by Charles Augustin Sainte-Beuve and his followers reinforced a prejudice against judging aesthetic production by commercial standards that has never been entirely eradicated. Over the last fifty years, the importance of historical, cultural, and economic context has become far more widely recognised. Critics such as Jean-Hervé Donnard, Henri Mitterand, and Jean-Yves Mollier have shown how research into economic, publishing, and biographical detail can generate a richer background from which new critical interpretations can spring. The current wave, led by Dominique Kalifa, Marie-Eve Thérenty, Judith Lyon-Caen, and Alain Vaillant, not only has linked developments in the popular press and popular culture with the development of prose fiction but has also shown how economic analysis, especially of press and book production, can be relevant to literary criticism. In Russia this process has barely started, while in English literary criticism it is rather more fully developed, as my introductory chapter has demonstrated. But for all this growing awareness of the relevance of economics as a tool in the critic's armoury, there still seems to be a reluctance to recognise that prose fiction does function as a commodity and that it is legitimate to discuss it as such. Even attempts to promote "economic criticism" as a discrete field of study in its own right have largely foundered because of this hesitation to see the text itself as an economic agent and to develop the tools to examine it as such.

So this book is a logical extension of the direction of travel of current critical trends. It uses the growing evidential base relating to the economics of the publishing industry and the development of readership demographics to support a view of how an author might have perceived and responded to the demands of both readership and publisher. It builds on analysis of the poetics of transfers of style and content between the press and the extensively serialised prose fiction of the nineteenth century. It incorporates current work on cultural history to achieve a better understanding of economic drivers. Finally, it applies the economic concepts that have been so widely recognised in studies of publishing as an industry to the study of individual narratives, not in the sense of seeking a statistical approach but rather in terms of thinking of literary devices as having economic as well as aesthetic agency.

In each of these areas, the book has shown that the economic perspective plays a more important role than critics have so far allowed. As a means of interpreting texts, it can generate a quite different critical point of view by focussing attention on the nature of the exchange between author and reader. As a method of analysing authorial behaviour, it throws light on commercial motivations, or on reactions to external economic developments, both as evidenced by the text itself, which were previously ignored or underplayed. As a way of understanding social and cultural drivers, it supplies a framework for linking changes in patterns of commerce, particularly within the publishing industry, with changes in the production of novels. As a branch of economic investigation, it allows us to import tools and techniques from a related discipline that have seldom been used in literary analysis and that enable us to uncover the economic agency of the text itself.

This is hardly a radical departure in critical approaches; rather, it simply imports into the critical viewpoint the commercial changes that have been such an important part of the novel's development over the last two centuries, particularly in Europe. It does not attempt to deny or diminish the reality and role of the many other forms of literary value, from aesthetic to ethical to pedagogic, on which critics have traditionally focussed. But it does require us to recognise that any given literary device may have a dual role as both aesthetic and economic agent. Unravelling the functions of each requires detailed textual analysis, since the text itself is the best evidence we have of the author's "point of sale" perspective. The text contains valuable clues, often overlooked, about how authors perceived the reception of their works, about whom they thought they were writing for, and about how they shaped the text to try to manipulate reader reception.

The methodological framework developed here specifically addresses economic context, modes of transaction between author and reader, and pragmatic definitions of literary value, but the framework is neither mandatory nor exclusive. It is, however, broad enough to be widely applicable: there is no reason why it should not be as valid for a modern internet author as for an eighteenth-century writer financed by patronage. At either extreme, the publishing context defines a contemporary notion of "reach," or the extent of penetration of the possible readership, and a direction of travel as the readership evolves. Considering literature as transaction differentiates succinctly and successfully between writing under patronage, writing for payment by the column inch, and writing for free (whether enabled by technology or enforced through piracy), and forces the critic to consider how the differing nature of the transaction with the reader changes authorial strategy and, consequently, the economic as well as the aesthetic implications of that strategy. And defining literary value as that synchronically accessible at the point of sale to the author, as demonstrable by contemporary evidence, helps to establish a basis of comparison between, say, an eighteenth-century author of independent means writing for a small readership of literate and aristocratic friends and a modern internet author writing for a potentially huge but anonymous audience and trying to develop techniques to get noticed amidst the clutter.

The methodology has been able to demonstrate that it can produce new critical insights. Chapter 2 on Fedor Dostoevsky's *Brothers Karamazov,* for example, takes the literary device of iteration, a central pillar of the genre of the courtroom drama, and shows the role that this device plays in an economic context as a means of testing audience reception to different modes of retelling. Analysis of the publishing context provides an explanation for why this experimental technique might be required, in the shape of the demonstrable disconnect between contemporary publishing strategies and the stage of development of the contemporary readership. An examination of the many representations within the text of characters offering narrative for consumption to other in-story characters not only alerts a modern reader to his or her own role as the recipient of Dostoevsky's narrative but also provides a framework by which he or she can evaluate its credibility. When these are taken together, a text more often treated as a novelistic discussion of philosophical and ethical issues acquires a new dimension as an enquiry into what constitutes a successful novel.

"Economic criticism" can also suggest new angles on authorial motivation. Rereading *Splendeurs* in its economic context, as a rolling commentary on the evolution of the press during a period of momentous change in the industry, prompted a quite new approach to the novel as a kind of experimental test-bed for new modes of prose fiction. The approach highlighted the correlations between external economic trends in the industry—for example, the changing competitive dynamics between Honoré de Balzac and Eugène Sue, or the growing importance of the periodical press as the leading vehicle for prose fiction—and stylistic or diegetic changes in the product that Balzac offered to his readers. Combining this with parallel changes in the way in which Balzac represents transaction in *Splendeurs* produced a body of evidence pointing to significant differences in the way in which Balzac produces, and relates to, his own output over time. From this, a change in authorial motivation could be demonstrated based on textual and economic analysis rather than on surmise about authorial intention.

An economic perspective on the text can also indicate new aspects of social and cultural development. Chapter 3 on Emile Zola shows how his own commercial strategies for engaging with the growing mass readership for his novels are intimately linked to changing modes of corporate structure and commerce in contemporary France, as well as to the growing importance of narrative as a phenomenon in French cultural life. Zola's own writings are themselves a form of big business. The novels simultaneously perform what they describe. Telling the story has become an enterprise of industrial scale in its own right, with its own distinctive brand, style, and promotion. Representations of his in-story characters telling stories or concocting fictions, surprisingly frequent once the reader is sensitised to notice them, become test-beds for Zola's own commercialisation of the novel. The literary devices that Zola uses become an integral part of the sales strategy of the novel. Naturalism is reinterpreted as an economic driver for the development of a mass readership. Zola's evolving representation of the power of the story over the course of the cycle of *Les Rougon-Macquart,* and from there to what we now see as the collapse of his narrative power in later works, both chronicles and critiques the role of the story in society, as well as providing new perspectives on Zola's own authorial motivation.

Economic criticism is just as much a branch of economics as it is an avenue of literary scholarship. This book has demonstrated how tracing the history of the book format across the French publishing industry of the 1830s to the 1880s, with cross-references to its parallel evolution in some other markets, particularly that of Russia, has identified changes in the terms of trade between authors, publishers, and readers and has been able to link these to changes in authorial production. It has also illustrated how categorising transactions—both those represented in the text and those implicit between author and reader—into known economic categories (prospectus, auction, speculation, gift) can provide an analytical framework that emphasises a particular mode of economic agency. Once we start to notice how the author represents transaction between the in-story characters, we becomes sensitised to our own transaction with the author, even at a distance of over a century. In turn, this leads to reflections on why the narrative has survived over time, and how it has acquired posterity value. It can also highlight the importance of narrative as a commodity in nonliterary spheres as a tool of communication used by all of society, from politics to business to human relations. No doubt an economist would have framed the analysis differently, and perhaps conducted it in different terms. But this approach has relevance as a method of analysing economic and cultural history, just as it has to literary criticism.

"Que 'vaut' le récit?" There may be no definitive answer to Roland Barthes's question, but perhaps his point was not to answer but simply to ask it. His quotation marks around *vaut* imply an awareness that this economic term may not be fully transferable to the world of aesthetics, but that the question still needs to be asked. I began this book with a quotation from *The Way We Live Now* in which Anthony Trollope pokes fun at Lady Carbury's view of the novel as an exclusively economic commodity, and literary value as equivalent to sales potential. He, too, is reminding us that it is possible to think of the novel in terms other than those of artistic appreciation. Our modern world provides us with countless everyday examples of the importance of narrative, the power of the story, to everything from advertising to business, to politics, and to literature. Over the past two centuries, selling the story has evolved from a cottage industry into, arguably, the biggest business in the world. Understanding and manipulating narrative is fundamental to countless professions and is overwhelmingly the most powerful argument for the importance of the humanities as a university discipline. This book is not an attempt to impose economics on literature. It is, simply, a demonstration of how narrative is inseparable from the creation of economic value.

Appendix A

Serialisation of *The Brothers Karamazov*[1]

		Book
1879	Jan.	Preface, 1, 2
	Feb.	3
	Mar.	
	Apr.	4
	May	5, chaps. 1–4
	June	5, chaps. 5–7
	July	
	Aug.	6
	Sept.	7
	Oct.	8, chaps. 1–4
	Nov.	8, chaps. 5–8
	Dec.	(apology for delay)
1880	Jan.	9
	Feb.	
	Mar.	
	Apr.	10
	May	
	June	
	July	11, chaps. 1–5
	Aug.	11, chaps. 6–10
	Sept.	12, chaps. 1–5
	Oct.	12, chaps. 6–14
	Nov.	Epilogue

[1] William Mills Todd III, "*The Brothers Karamazov* and the Poetics of Serial Publication," *Dostoevsky Studies* 7 (1986): 87–97, 97.

Appendix B

The Thirty-Eight Retellings of the Murder of Fedor Karamazov

Iteration	Full or partial	Summary	Page reference
1	F	The murder as related by the narrator (bk. 8, chap. 4, "In the Darkness").	14:29–32
2	P	Dmitry to Fenya, reported direct dialogue about his blood-covered clothes.	14:34
3	P	Dmitry to Perkhotin, same type of dialogue. Dmitry alleges a fight.	14:36–37
4	P	Perkhotin's speculations in the inn. Reported indirect speech and direct dialogue.	14:43–44
5	P	Dmitry's reflections on the murder at Mokroye. Reported internal monologue in the form of a prayer.	14:66–67
6	P	Dmitry's arrest at Mokroye. He is accused of parricide. Reported direct dialogue.	14:72
7	P	Perkhotin interrogates Fenya. Reported direct dialogue, indirect speech, narratorial description.	14:73
8	P	Perkhotin interrogates Mme Khokhlakova. Speculation about a possible murder. Reported direct dialogue.	14:75–77

(*continued*)

Iteration	Full or partial	Summary	Page reference
9	F	The narrator's report of what the police have learned of the murder from the inhabitants of the Karamazov house. Reported direct dialogue, indirect speech, narratorial description.	14:79–81
10	F	Dmitry's interrogation, as reported by the narrator. Reported direct dialogue, indirect speech, narratorial description.	14:82–116
11	P	The evidence of the innkeeper, Trifon Borisovich, and his staff, Stepan and Semyon, and of the driver Andrey. Reported direct dialogue, indirect speech, narratorial description.	14:118
12	P	The evidence of Kalganov. Reported direct dialogue.	14:118
13	P	The evidence of the two Poles and Dmitry's offer of 3,000 roubles for them to leave Grushenka. Reported indirect speech, narratorial description.	14:118–120
14	P	The evidence of Maksimov. Reported direct dialogue, indirect speech, narratorial description.	14:120
15	P	The evidence of Grushenka. Reported direct dialogue, indirect speech, narratorial description.	14:120–122
16	F	The newspaper report of the crime written by Rakitin in the Petersburg newspaper *Rumours,* as told to Alyosha by Mme Khokhlakova, followed by Mme Khokhlakova's speculations about Dmitry's guilt. Indirect speech, paraphrased article by narrator, dialogue.	14:175–179
17	P	Alyosha tells Ivan that he (Ivan) is not the murderer. Reported direct dialogue.	14:198
18	F	Dmitry's version of the murder as told to Ivan. Reported direct dialogue, indirect speech, narratorial description.	14:200–201

19	F	Smerdyakov's confession, in three parts. Reported direct dialogue, indirect speech, narratorial description.	14:201–206, 208–211, 215–224
20	P	Discussion between Ivan and Alyosha about Ivan's motivation for the murder. Reported direct dialogue.	14:206
21	P	Revelation of Dmitry's incriminating letter to Katya Ivanovna. Narrated description, verbatim reproduction of letter.	14:211–213
22	P	Ivan's intention to confess, as told to Alyosha after the devil scene. Reported direct dialogue.	14:240–241
23	P	The evidence of the witnesses for the prosecution: 1. Grigory. Reported direct dialogue, indirect speech, narratorial description.	14:249–252
24	P	The evidence of the witnesses for the prosecution: 2. Rakitin. Reported direct dialogue, indirect speech, narratorial description.	14:252–253
25	P	The evidence of the witnesses for the prosecution: 3. Snegirev. Reported direct dialogue, indirect speech, narratorial description.	14:253–254
26	P	The evidence of the witnesses for the prosecution: 4. Trifon Borisovich and staff. Reported direct dialogue, indirect speech, narratorial description.	14:254
27	P	The evidence of the witnesses for the prosecution: 5. the Poles. Reported direct dialogue, indirect speech, narratorial description.	14:254
28	P	The evidence of the expert witnesses at the trial: 1. Dr. Herzenstube (as both expert witness and witness for the defence). Reported direct dialogue, indirect speech, narratorial description.	14:255–256, 258
29	P	The evidence of the expert witnesses at the trial: 2. the Moscow doctor. Reported indirect speech, narratorial description.	14:256–257

(*continued*)

Iteration	Full or partial	Summary	Page reference
30	P	The evidence of the expert witnesses at the trial: 3. Dr. Varvinsky. Reported indirect speech, narratorial description.	14:257
31	P	The evidence of the witnesses for the defence: 1. Alyosha. Reported direct dialogue, indirect speech, narratorial description.	14:259–262
32	P	The evidence of the witnesses for the defence: 2. Katerina Ivanovna (twice). Reported direct dialogue, indirect speech, narratorial description.	14:262–264, 269–272
33	P	The evidence of the witnesses for the defence: 3. Grushenka. Reported direct dialogue, indirect speech, narratorial description.	14:264–266
34	P	The evidence of the witnesses for the defence: 4. Ivan. Reported direct dialogue, indirect speech, narratorial description.	14:267–269
35	F	The speech of the prosecutor. Reported direct speech.	14:273–299
36	F	The speech of the defence counsel. Reported direct speech.	14:300–320
37	P	Dmitry's final plea. Reported direct speech.	14:320–321
38	P	The jury's verdict. Reported direct dialogue, indirect speech, narratorial description.	14:321–323

Notes

Introduction

1. "Que 'vaut' le récit? . . . Le récit est, par une astuce vertigineuse, la représentation du contrat qui le fonde: dans ces récits exemplaires, la narration est théorie (économique) de la narration: . . . on raconte pour obtenir en échangeant, et c'est cet échange qui est figuré dans le récit lui-même: le récit est à la fois produit et production, marchandise et commerce." Roland Barthes, *S/Z* (Paris: Editions du Seuil, 1970), 81.
2. I should make it clear from the outset that I use the term *narrative* and its derivatives in a loose sense, to denote all the forms of discourse that combine to create the novels under consideration here, rather than to differentiate narrative from alternative forms of literary discourse such as argument, exposition, description, and so on. As we will see, the conditions of serial publication invite sliding between different types of discourse: both newspapers and periodicals published a wide variety of text types, from the polemic to the poetic, and the novels that appeared in their pages engaged all of them. I make the case that the novels with which this book deals, from Balzac to Dostoevsky and Zola, cross generic and discursive boundaries and make use of this slippery fluidity to create new forms of literary value—a term I shall also consider at some length in this introduction—for their readers.
3. I am grateful to Helen Small, professor of English literature at Oxford University, for her guidance on recent developments in economic criticism in English literature. I have not extended my exploration to American literature, for reasons of space and time, but since a number of the major contributors to the current debate are scholars from US universities, there may be reason to suppose an equally active investigation of the field.
4. Richard Altick, *The English Common Reader: A Social History of the Mass Reading Public, 1800–1900*, 2nd ed. (Columbus: Ohio State University Press, 1998). Among the many histories of modes of publication and reception in England in the nineteenth century, Paul Delany's *Literature, Money and the Market:*

From Trollope to Amis (Basingstoke, UK: Palgrave, 2002) is a useful and more recent extension of Altick with a particular emphasis on the changing modes of commercialisation of the novel in the latter part of the nineteenth and the first part of the twentieth centuries. Kate Flint, ed., *The Cambridge History of Victorian Literature* (Cambridge: Cambridge University Press, 2012), gives a good general overview of the publishing environment.

5. John Vernon, *Money and Fiction: Literary Realism in the Nineteenth and Early Twentieth Centuries* (Ithaca, NY: Cornell University Press, 1984).

6. Claude Bellanger et al., *Histoire générale de la presse française*, 5 vols. (Paris: Presses universitaires de France, 1969).

7. Roger Chartier and Henri-Jean Martin, eds., *Histoire de l'édition française*, 4 vols. (Paris: Fayard / Promodis, 1990).

8. René Guise, "Le Roman-feuilleton, 1830–1848: La Naissance d'un genre," 36 microfiches (doctorat d'état diss., Nancy II University, 1975).

9. Jean-Yves Mollier, *Michel et Calmann Lévy, ou, la naissance de l'édition moderne* (Paris: Calmann-Lévy, 1984); Jean-Yves Mollier, *L'Argent et les lettres: Histoire du capitalisme d'édition, 1880–1920* (Paris: Fayard, 1988); Jean-Yves Mollier, *Le Commerce de la librairie en France au XIXe siècle, 1789–1914* (Paris: IMEC Editions, 1997); Jean-Yves Mollier, *Louis Hachette, 1800–64: Le Fondateur d'un empire* (Paris: Fayard, 1999).

10. Françoise Parent-Lardeur, *Lire à Paris au temps de Balzac: Les Cabinets de lecture à Paris, 1815–1830* (Paris: Ecole des hautes études en sciences sociales, 1999).

11. Dominique Kalifa et al., eds., *La Civilisation du journal* (Paris: Nouveau monde éditions, 2011).

12. Guillaume Pinson, *L'Imaginaire médiatique: Histoire et fiction du journal au XIXe siecle* (Paris: Garnier, 2012).

13. Judith Lyon-Caen, *La Lecture et la vie: Les Usages du roman au temps de Balzac* (Paris: Tallandier, 2006).

14. Christophe Charle, *Histoire sociale de la France au XIXe siècle* (Paris: Editions du Seuil, 1991); Christophe Charle, *Le Siècle de la presse, 1830–1939* (Paris: Editions du Seuil, 2004).

15. Martin Lyons, *Reading Culture and Writing Practices in Nineteenth-Century France* (Toronto: University of Toronto Press, 2008).

16. Alain Vaillant, *La Crise de la littérature: Romantisme et modernité* (Grenoble: ELLUG, 2005), in particular the third section, "Mesure de la littérature," 75–102.

17. Edmund Birch, *Fictions of the Press in Nineteenth-Century France* (Cham, Switzerland: Palgrave, 2018).

18. György Lukács, *The Theory of the Novel: A Historico-philosophical Essay on the Forms of Great Epic Literature*, trans. Anna Bostock (London: Merlin, 1978); György Lukács, *Balzac et le réalisme français*, trans. Paul Laveau (1951; repr., Paris: François Maspero, 1967).

19. Charles Augustin Sainte-Beuve, "De la littérature industrielle," *Revue des deux mondes* 4, no. 19 (1839): 675–691.

20. Pierre Bourdieu, *La Distinction: Critique sociale du jugement* (Paris: Editions de Minuit, 1979); Pierre Bourdieu, *Les Règles de l'art: Genèse et structure du champ littéraire* (Paris: Editions du Seuil, 1992).

21. Pierre Barbéris, *Le Prince et le marchand: Idéologiques: La Littérature, l'histoire* (Paris: Fayard, 1980).

22. Jean-Joseph Goux, *Frivolité de la valeur: Essai sur l'imaginaire du capitalisme* (Paris: Blusson, 2000), 249–271. Also see his long analysis of Gide's *Les Faux-Monnayeurs* in *Les Monnayeurs du langage* (Paris: Editions Galilée, 1984), 27–124.

23. Alexandre Péraud, *Le Crédit dans la poétique balzacienne* (Paris: Garnier, 2012), 25, 42–44.

24. Mikhail Kufaev, *Istoriya russkoi knigi v XIX veke* (1927; repr., Moscow: Pashkov Dom, 2003).

25. Mikhail Muratov, *Knizhnoe delo v Rossii v XIX i XX vekakh: Ocherk istorii knigoizdatel'stva i knigotorgovli, 1800–1917 gody* (Moscow: Gosudarstvennoe sotsialno-ekonomicheskoe izdatel'stvo, 1931).

26. William Mills Todd III, ed., *Literature and Society in Imperial Russia, 1800–1914* (Stanford, CA: Stanford University Press, 1978).

27. Abram Reitblat, *Ot Bovy k Bal'montu: Ocherki po istorii chteniya v Rossii vo vtoroi polovine XIX veka* (Moscow: MPI, 1991); Abram Reitblat, *Kak Pushkin vyshel v genii: Istoriko-sotsiologicheskie ocherki o knizhnoi kul'ture Pushkinskoi epokhi* (Moscow: Novoe literaturnoe obozrenie, 2001).

28. Jeffrey Brooks, *When Russia Learned to Read: Literacy and Popular Literature, 1861–1917* (Princeton, NJ: Princeton University Press, 1985).

29. William Mills Todd III, "*The Brothers Karamazov* and the Poetics of Serial Publication," *Dostoevsky Studies* 7 (1986): 87–97; William Mills Todd III, "Dostoevsky and Tolstoy: The Professionalization of Literature and Serialized Fiction," *Dostoevsky Studies*, n.s., 15 (2011): 29–36; William Mills Todd III, "Serialization: Institutions of Literature as Patterns of Communication" (unpublished paper delivered at Oxford University, May 31, 2012); William Mills Todd III, "'To Be Continued': Dostoevsky's Evolving Poetics of Serialized Publication," *Dostoevsky Studies*, n.s., 18 (2014): 22–33; William Mills Todd III, "Dostoevsky and the Moral Hazards of Serial Publication" (unpublished paper delivered at the annual conference of the Association for Slavic, East European, and Eurasian Studies, Philadelphia, PA, November 2015).

30. Louise McReynolds, *The News under Russia's Old Regime: The Development of a Mass-Circulation Press* (Princeton, NJ: Princeton University Press, 1991).

31. Deborah Martinsen, ed., *Literary Journals in Imperial Russia* (Cambridge: Cambridge University Press, 1997).

32. Boris Mironov, *The Social History of Imperial Russia, 1700–1917*, with Ben Eklof (Boulder, CO: Westview, 1999–2000).

33. Susanne Fusso, *Editing Turgenev, Dostoevsky and Tolstoy: Mikhail Katkov and the Great Russian Novel* (DeKalb: Northern Illinois University Press, 2017).
34. Martha Woodmansee and Mark Osteen, eds., *The New Economic Criticism: Studies at the Intersection of Literature and Economics* (London: Routledge, 1999).
35. Mikhail Gronas, ed., "Novaya Ekonomicheskaya Kritika," *Novoe literaturnoe obozrenie* 58 (2002): 7–87.
36. For example, Kirill Postoutenko, "Die Geburt des Rubels aus dem Geist des Platonismus," *Wiener Slawistischer Almanach* 49 (2003): 75–91; and Kirill Postoutenko, "Mezhdu monetoi i ikonoi: Sakral'naia ekonomika Nikolaia Vtorogo," *Die Welt der Slaven* 45 (2000): 2, 315–338.
37. Mark Osteen and Martha Woodmansee, "Taking Account of the New Economic Criticism: An Historical Introduction," in Woodmansee and Osteen, *New Economic Criticism*, 2–43, 35–38.
38. Mary Poovey, *Genres of the Credit Economy: Mediating Value in Eighteenth- and Nineteenth-Century Britain* (Chicago: University of Chicago Press, 2008), 11.
39. Delany, *Literature, Money and the Market*, 1–4.
40. Rémy de Gourmont, *Le Problème du style* (Paris: Société du Mercure de France, 1907), 193–202.
41. Theodor Adorno, *Aesthetic Theory*, trans. R. Hullot-Kentor (Minneapolis: University of Minnesota Press, 1997), 8.
42. Jean-Hervé Donnard, *Balzac, les réalités économiques et sociales dans "La Comédie humaine"* (Paris: Armand Colin, 1961).
43. Bernard Guyon, *La Pensée politique et sociale de Balzac*, 2nd ed. (Paris: Armand Colin, 1969).
44. André Maurois, *Prométhée, ou, La Vie de Balzac* (Paris: Hachette, 1965).
45. Harry Levin, *The Gates of Horn* (New York: Oxford University Press, 1966).
46. Louis Chevalier, *Classes laborieuses et classes dangereuses à Paris pendant la première moitié du XIXᵉ siècle* (Paris: Plon, 1958).
47. Lukács, *Balzac et le réalisme*.
48. Walter Benjamin, *The Writer of Modern Life* (1935–1939), ed. Michael Jennings, trans. Howard Eiland et al. (Cambridge, MA: Harvard University Press, 2006).
49. Karl Marx, "The Power of Money," in *Economic and Philosophical Manuscripts of 1844*, trans. Martin Mulligan (Moscow: Progress, 1959), https://www.marxists.org/archive/marx/works/1844/manuscripts/preface.htm.
50. Regenia Gagnier, *The Insatiability of Human Wants: Economics and Aesthetics in Market Society* (Chicago: University of Chicago Press, 2000), esp. chap. 4, "Production, Reproduction and Pleasure in Victorian Aesthetics," 115–145. The quotation is from 2.
51. Christopher Prendergast, *The Order of Mimesis* (Cambridge: Cambridge University Press, 1986), 83–118. The comments on narrative as economic exchange are at 101–111.
52. Terry Eagleton, *Literary Theory: An Introduction*, rev. ed. (1983; Oxford: Blackwell, 1996).

53. Vernon, *Money and Fiction,* 18–19.
54. Wolfgang Iser, *The Act of Reading: A Theory of Aesthetic Response* (published in German 1976; London: Routledge and Kegan Paul, 1978).
55. Hans Robert Jauss, *Toward an Aesthetic of Reception,* trans. Timothy Bahti (Minneapolis: University of Minnesota Press, 1982).
56. Poovey, *Genres of the Credit Economy,* 1–2.
57. Delany, *Literature, Money and the Market,* 4.
58. Catherine Gallagher, *The Body Economic: Life, Death, and Sensation in Political Economy and the Victorian Novel* (Princeton, NJ: Princeton University Press, 2006), 63.
59. Franco Moretti, *The Bourgeois: Between History and Literature* (London: Verso, 2013), 125–131, 74–100. The quotations are, respectively, at 130 and 81.
60. Claire Tomalin, *Charles Dickens: A Life* (London: Viking, 2011), 249–251.
61. Osteen and Woodmansee, "Taking Account of the New Economic Criticism."
62. See Altick's analysis of the book trade in England in Altick, *English Common Reader,* 260–317.
63. Since this is a summary of propositions I will develop more fully in the chapters on Balzac and Zola, readers are referred to those chapters for details of the source materials underlying my arguments.
64. Readers are referred to Chapter 2 for source material on the Russian publishing market.
65. Wilkie Collins, "The Unknown Public," *Household Words* 18, no. 439 (August 21, 1858): 217–222, 218.
66. All three concepts are present in current definitions in the *Oxford English Dictionary*—for example, *Oxford Living Dictionaries Online,* s.v. "transaction," https://en.oxforddictionaries.com/definition/transaction, and in historical texts such as the 1835 *Dictionnaire de L'Académie française,* 6th ed., 2 vols. (Paris: Firmin-Didot, 1832–1835), 2:874, s.v. "transaction"; Larousse's *Grand Dictionnaire universel du XIXᵉ siècle,* 17 vols. (Paris: Administration du grand Dictionnaire universel, 1866–1877), 15:411, s.v. "transaction"; and the contemporary *Dictionnaire de la langue française* of Littré, 4 vols. (Paris: Hachette, 1873–1874), 4:2312, s.v. "transaction."
67. Georg Simmel, *The Philosophy of Money,* ed. David Frisby, trans. Tom Bottomore and David Frisby (London: Routledge, 2004), 82–83.
68. Robert Gildea, *Children of the Revolution: The French, 1799–1914* (London: Penguin, 2009), 91–117.
69. Lee Erickson, *The Economy of Literary Form: English Literature and the Industrialization of Publishing, 1800–1850* (Baltimore: Johns Hopkins University Press, 1996), 17–18.
70. William Wordsworth, "Essay Supplementary to the Preface," in *Lyrical Ballads* (1815), http://spenserians.cath.vt.edu/TextRecord.php?textsid=35963.
71. Mikhail Bakhtin, *The Dialogic Imagination,* ed. Michael Holquist, trans. Caryl Emerson and Michael Holquist (Austin: University of Texas Press, 1981), 342–344.

72. Poovey, *Genres of the Credit Economy*, 30–31.

73. "Toutes les activités, toutes les pensées, toutes les productions de l'intelligence ou de l'imagination, sont entrainées sur un marché, une bourse, où dans le modèle de Walras, la valeur qui n'a pas d'autre fondement que l'échange instantané, se décide par une 'vente à la criée.'" Goux, *Frivolité de la valeur*, 26–27.

74. E. C. Maddison, *The Paris Bourse and the London Stock Exchange* (London: Effingham Wilson, 1877), 16–18.

75. Thomas M. Kavanagh, *Dice, Cards, Wheels: A Different History of French Culture* (Philadelphia: University of Pennsylvania Press, 2005), 10.

76. And, as Marcel Mauss debates in his seminal work on gift, it raises the question of whether any gift is so truly altruistic as to expect no return of whatever nature to the giver. See Marcel Mauss, *The Gift: Forms and Functions of Exchange in Archaic Societies*, trans. Ian Cunnison (Glencoe, IL: Free Press, 1954; repr., Mansfield Center, CT: Martino, 2011), 63–81.

77. Jillian Cooper, *Economies of Feeling: Russian Literature under Nicholas I* (Evanston, IL: Northwestern University Press, 2017), 89–106.

78. For a more extensive discussion of the role of paper currency and bank bills as a literary genre, see Poovey, *Genres of the Credit Economy*, 42–51.

79. Thomas Bridges, *Adventures of a Bank-Note*, 4 vols. (1770–1771; repr., New York: Garland, 1975). See also Poovey's argument that this text represents a bridge between economic and imaginative narrative, in Poovey, *Genres of the Credit Economy*, 144–152.

80.
      Zu wissen sei es jedem ders begehrt:
      Der Zettel hier ist tausend Kronen wert.
      Ihm liegt gesichert als gewisses Pfand
      Unzahl vergrabnen Guts im Kaiserland.
      Nun ist gesorgt damit der reiche Schatz
      Sogleich gehoben, diene zum Ersatz.

Johann Wolfgang von Goethe, *Faust*, pt. 2, lines 6057–6062, http://guten berg.spiegel.de/buch/-3645/13.

81. Anthony Trollope, *The Way We Live Now*, ed. John Sutherland (1875; Oxford: Oxford University Press, 1982; reissued 2008), 1:423.

82. William Henry Wills, "Review of a Popular Publication: In the Searching Style," *Household Words* 1, no. 18 (July 27, 1850): 426–431, 426, http://www .djo.org.uk/household-words/volume-i/page-426.html.

83. En 15 jours de temps, j'ai vendu 50 colonnes à la *Chronique*, pour mille francs; cent vingt colonnes à *La Presse*, pour huit mille francs, 20 colonnes à une *Revue musicale* pour mille francs; un article au *Dictionnaire de la conversation* pour mille francs, cela a fait onze mille francs en 15 jours, j'ai travaillé 30 nuits sans me coucher, et j'ai fait *La Perle brisée* (pour la *Chronique* et qui a paru): *La Vieille Fille* (pour *La Presse* et qui paraît demain). J'ai fait *Le Secret des Ruggieri* pour Werdet. Dans 15 jours les deux derniers volumes des *Etudes de mœurs* paraissent: me voilà quitte. J'ai vendu *deux mille francs* mon 3me *dixain* (cela fait 13,000fr). Enfin, je vais faire *La Torpille* et *La Femme supérieure* pour *La Presse*,

et *les Souffrances de l'Inventeur* pour *La Chronique*. En même temps, je suis en train de vendre, pour *18,000 francs*, les réimpressions de *La Torpille* et de *La Femme supérieure*, accompagnés de *Un Grand Homme de province [à Paris]*, et des *Héritiers Boirouge*, tous deux commencés, ce qui me fera *trente et un mille francs*. Puis, n'ayant plus à m'appuyer sur cette planche pourrie de Werdet, je vais contracter avec une maison riche et solide pour les 14 derniers volumes des *Etudes de mœurs*, les tomes de 12 à 26, qui devront bien monter à 56 francs de droits d'auteur, sur lesquels j'en veux immédiatement 30,000. Si cela réussit, j'aurais trouvé par ces deux dernières affaires, que je vais poursuivre avec activité, 63 mille francs qui me sauveront de tout. Non seulement je ne devrai plus rien, mais j'aurai quelque argent. Mais il me faudra travailler nuit et jour pendant six mois et après, au moins 10 heures par jour pendant deux ans. (Honoré de Balzac, *Lettres à Madame Hanska,* ed. Robert Laffont, 2 vols. [Paris, Editions Robert Laffont, 1990], 1:341–342; Balzac's emphasis. Balzac's maths is somewhat shaky.)

84. Quoted in Tomalin, *Charles Dickens,* 230, from the *Economist* of April 3, 1852.

85. Victoria Glendinning, *Trollope* (London: Pimlico, 1993), 441–442.

86. See Mollier, *Michel et Calmann Lévy,* 400.

87. For a fuller discussion of the various forms of literary value, see Poovey, *Genres of the Credit Economy,* 285–335. Although this only deals with the literary scene in England, the forms she identifies are, in broad terms, equally valid in France and Russia. For a particular discussion of Ruskin's views on literary value, see Marc Shell, *The Economy of Literature* (Baltimore: Johns Hopkins University Press, 1978), 129–151. The paragraph that follows draws on both sources to identify a more comprehensive list of competing notions of literary value.

88. See Walter Besant, "The Art of Fiction," lecture given at the Royal Institution on April 25, 1884, in *The Art of Fiction,* by Walter Besant and Henry James (Boston: Cupples and Hurd, 1884), https://ia600205.us.archive.org /23/items/cu31924027192941/cu31924027192941.pdf; Henry James, *Theory of Fiction: Henry James,* ed. James Miller Jr. (Lincoln: University of Nebraska Press, 1972), 27–44, for James's September 1884 response to Besant's lecture; and Robert Louis Stevenson, "A Humble Remonstrance," December 1884, http://virgil.org/dswo/courses/novel/stevenson-remonstrance.pdf, for Stevenson's response to both.

89. Sainte-Beuve, "De la littérature industrielle."

90. For example, John Ruskin, *The Political Economy of Art* (London: Smith, Elder, 1857).

91. Stepan Shevyrev, "O Kritike voobshe i u nas v Rossii," *Moskovskii nablyudatel'* 1 (1835): 494–525.

92. See Shell, *Economy of Literature,* 134.

93. John Ruskin, *Sesame and Lilies* (New York: John Wiley and Sons, 1891), 14–15.

94. Pierre Bourdieu, *The Forms of Capital,* trans. Richard Nice (1986), https://www .marxists.org/reference/subject/philosophy/works/fr/bourdieu-forms -capital.htm.

95. "D'abord, l'instruction se répand, des milliers de lecteurs sont créés. Le journal pénètre partout, les campagnes elles-mêmes achètent des livres. En un demi-siècle, le livre, qui était un objet de luxe, devient un objet de consommation courante." Emile Zola, *Le Roman experimental*, ed. François-Marie Mourad (Paris: Flammarion, 2006), 167–202, 181. The article was first published in the Russian *Le Messager de l'Europe* of May 1880, then serialised in *Le Voltaire* from July 23 to July 30 of the same year.

96. "Peut-être faut-il que le vaste ensemble de romans auquel je me suis consacré soit terminé complètement, pour qu'on le comprenne et qu'on le juge. Et j'attendrai très bien dix ans encore." Zola to Louis Bosses de Fourcaud, September 23, 1876, in Emile Zola, *Correspondance*, ed. Bard Bakker et al., 10 vols. (Montreal: Presses de l'Université de Montréal; Paris: CNRS, 1978–1995), 2:495.

97. "J'écris ceci, sans mentir j'espère, sans me faire illusion, avec plaisir comme une lettre à un ami. Quelles seront les idées de cet ami en 1880?" Stendhal, *Vie de Henri Brulard*, ed. Béatrice Didier (Paris: Gallimard, 1973), 32.

98. Christopher Prendergast, *For the People by the People? Eugène Sue's "Les Mystères de Paris": A Hypothesis in the Sociology of Literature* (Oxford: Legenda, 2003), 13.

99. Peter Brooks, *Reading for the Plot* (Cambridge, MA: Harvard University Press, 1984), xiii–xiv.

100. Brooks, *Reading for the Plot*, 171. Zola, reviewing *L'Education sentimentale* in *La Tribune* of November 28, 1869, can hardly disguise his impatience with Flaubert's obsession with detail. "*L'Education sentimentale* (suite): Vu par Emile Zola et Henri James," http://www.alalettre.com/flaubert-oeuvres-education-sentimentale-suite.php.

101. Tzvetan Todorov, *Genres in Discourse*, trans. Catherine Porter (Cambridge: Cambridge University Press, 1990), 19.

102. See, for example, his schematic representation of the nature of genre in Jean-Marie Schaeffer, *Qu'est-ce qu'un genre littéraire?* (Paris: Editions du Seuil, 1989), 116.

103. Poovey, *Genres of the Credit Economy*, 25–55.

104. Robert Darnton, *The Business of Enlightenment: A Publishing History of the "Encyclopédie," 1775–1800* (Cambridge, MA: Belknap Press of Harvard University Press, 1979), 6.

105. Todd, "Dostoevsky and the Moral Hazards of Serial Publication."

106. Tim Farrant, "Fragmentation, *Feuilleton*, Form: Balzac, Baudelaire, Zola," *Dix-Neuf* 21, no. 4 (April 2018): 245–257.

1. Balzac

1. "*La Comédie humaine*. Œuvres complètes de M. H. de Balzac. Edition de luxe à bon marché. 1ère livraison, in-8° de 3 feuilles plus une vignette.... L'ouvrage sera publié en 12 volumes. Chaque volume, orné de huit gravures, se composera de 10 livraisons. On souscrit ici." The advertisement is shown

on the website of the Groupe international de recherches balzaciennes: Robert Tranchida, "Historique de l'édition Furne," Groupe international de recherches balzaciennes, 2001, http://www.v2asp.paris.fr/commun/v2asp /musees/balzac/furne/historique.htm.

2. References to works in *La Comédie humaine* are, unless otherwise indicated, to the twelve-volume Pléiade edition of *La Comédie humaine* of 1975, ed. Pierre-Georges Castex. See Notes on Citation for citation methodology. The text of *Splendeurs et misères des courtisanes*, additionally edited by Pierre Citron, René Guise, André Lorant, and Anne-Marie Meininger, is at 6:425–935. Both Castex and Antoine Adam, the editor of the 1964 Garnier edition of *Splendeurs* (hereafter *Splendeurs*, ed. Adam), include extensive notes on the history of the text (at 6:1309–1316 in the Pléiade edition and on i–ix of the introduction to the Garnier edition) on which I have relied without further detailed reference in the following section.

3. Publication details are taken from Stéphane Vachon's *Les Travaux et les jours d'Honoré de Balzac: Chronologie de la création balzacienne* (Paris: Presses du CNRS, 1992), usually without further specific reference beyond the dates in the text, which correspond to the relevant dated sections in Vachon's work. The more important references are, however, given.

4. Arthur de Gobineau in *Le Commerce*, October 29, 1844. The article is reprinted in full in *La Querelle du roman-feuilleton: Littérature, presse et politique: Un débat précurseur (1836–1848)*, ed. Lise Dumasy (Grenoble: ELLUG, Université Stendhal, 1999), 87–94, 93.

5. Jean Pommier, *L'Invention et l'écriture dans "La Torpille" d'Honoré de Balzac* (Geneva: Droz, 1957). Examples of the more generalist critical literature of the 1960s have been referenced in the Introduction.

6. Agathe Novak-Lechevalier, *Splendeurs et misères des courtisanes* (Paris: Gallimard, 2010). See in particular her chapter entitled "Lire le réel," 92–121.

7. Lucien Dällenbach, "Du fragment au cosmos (*La Comédie humaine* et l'opération de lecture I)," *Poétique* 40 (1979): 420–431; Lucien Dällenbach, "Le Tout en morceaux (*La Comédie humaine* et l'opération de lecture II)," *Poétique* 42 (1980): 159–169.

8. Christopher Prendergast, *Balzac: Fiction and Melodrama* (London: Edward Arnold, 1978), 89. More generally, see his chapter "Connection and Totality," in *Balzac: Fiction and Melodrama*, 61–89; and Christopher Prendergast, *The Order of Mimesis* (Cambridge: Cambridge University Press, 1986), 83–118.

9. Frederick Hemmings, *Culture and Society in France, 1789–1848* (Leicester: Leicester University Press, 1987), 125.

10. Maurice Crubelier, "L'Elargissement du public," in *Histoire de l'édition française*, ed. Roger Chartier and Henri-Jean Martin, 4 vols. (Paris: Fayard / Promodis, 1990), 3:14–41, 18.

11. Roger Price, *An Economic History of Modern France, 1730–1914* (London: Macmillan, 1981), 1–26.

12. Crubelier, "L'Elargissement du public," 3:24–25.

13. Martin Lyons, *Reading Culture and Writing Practices in Nineteenth-Century France* (Toronto: University of Toronto Press, 2008), 20–27.

14. Crubelier, "L'Elargissement du public," 3:39; Odile Martin and Henri-Jean Martin, "Le monde des éditeurs," in Chartier and Martin, *Histoire de l'édition française,* 3:176–244, 194–195.

15. Robert Gildea, *Children of the Revolution: The French, 1799–1914* (London: Penguin, 2009), 174.

16. Martin and Martin, "Le monde des éditeurs," 3:194–196.

17. For example, in his open letter to French writers, Honoré de Balzac, "Lettre adressée aux écrivains français du XIXe siècle," *Revue de Paris,* n.s., 9 (1834): 62–82, 68: "While the poor French bookseller struggles to sell one of your books to a thousand wretched *cabinets de lecture,* which are killing our literature, that Belgian over there is selling two thousand at a knock-down price to the wealthy aristocrats of Europe" (Quand le pauvre libraire français vend à grand'peine un de vos livres à un millier de misérables cabinets de lecture, qui tuent notre littérature, le Belge, lui, en vend deux milliers au rabais à la riche aristocratie européenne).

18. See Castex's note at 9:1635.

19. Françoise Parent-Lardeur, *Lire à Paris au temps de Balzac: Les Cabinets de lecture à Paris, 1815–1830* (Paris: Ecole des hautes études en sciences sociales, 1999), 10, 123.

20. Balzac, "Lettre aux écrivains français," 68.

21. Nicole Felkay, *Balzac et ses éditeurs, 1822–1837: Essai sur la librairie romantique* (Paris: Promodis, 1987), 81–99.

22. Guy Lemarchand, *L'Economie en France de 1770 à 1830* (Paris: Armand Colin, 2008), 260–268.

23. Jean Morienval [Henri Thévenin], *Les Créateurs de la grande presse en France: Emile de Girardin, H. de Villemessant, Moïse Millaud* (Paris: Editions Spes, 1934), 53–57.

24. René Guise, "Le Roman-feuilleton, 1830–1848: La Naissance d'un genre," 36 microfiches (doctorat d'état diss., Nancy II University, 1975), 3:210–331. I use the anachronistic phrase "short story" as a useful shorthand to refer to works typically printed as a complete unity in a single edition of the periodical in which they appear: as Tim Farrant points out, much of Balzac's writing in this period was shifting towards the longer formats of the *nouvelle* and eventually that of the multiepisode novel. Tim Farrant, *Balzac's Shorter Fictions: Genesis and Genre* (Oxford: Oxford University Press, 2002), 129–152.

25. "Le roman-livre a abdiqué; le roman-feuilleton règne et gouverne." Unsigned article entitled "Du Roman et du roman-feuilleton," quoted in Judith Lyon-Caen, *La Lecture et la vie: Les Usages du roman au temps de Balzac* (Paris: Tallandier, 2006), 67.

26. Guise makes the point that the reader saturation point with the short story had been reached by the end of 1833 and led naturally to experimentation with longer, more sustained forms of fiction that allowed experimentation

in genre and literary technique in a more extended frame. Guise, "Le Roman-feuilleton, 1830–1848," 3:318–331.

27. "Il faut enfin obtenir qu'un volume se fabrique exactement comme un pain, et se débite comme un pain." Honoré de Balzac, "De l'état actuel de la librairie," *Le Feuilleton des journaux politiques*, March 1830, reproduced in *Œuvres diverses*, ed. Pierre Georges Castex and Roland Chollet (Paris: Gallimard, 1990) 2:667.

28. "Où en serions-nous tous s'il fallait rechercher les origines des fortunes?" (11:119).

29. "Il faudra peut-être transiger, dit l'avoué" (3:333).

30. "Il semble hors de doute qu'en bien de cas, Balzac a été tour à tour poussé à écrire ou découragé d'écrire dans la mesure où il était plus ou moins harcelé par ses difficultés financières." René Bouvier and Edouard Maynial, *Les Comptes dramatiques de Balzac* (Paris: Fernand Sorlot, 1938), 271 for the quotation and 200–271 for their analysis of his accounts over the period from 1835 to 1838. Their account perhaps overemphasises economic necessity as a driver at the expense of psychological factors: the sheer volume of Balzac's creation, as well as his obsessive attitude to proof correction, seems to indicate a compulsive, even pathological, urge to write.

31. Vachon, *Les Travaux et les jours*, 212–216.

32. "Oh! qu'il est beau, le spéculateur, lorsque, mollement étendu sur un fauteuil à la Voltaire, il lit voluptueusement le prospectus d'une entreprise étourdissante, où il apportera toute sa capacité, et ses amis tout leur argent! Comme il en étudie les chances! Elle lui paraît d'autant plus magnifique, qu'elle a l'air à peu près impraticable." Vicomte d'Arlincourt, "Le Spéculateur," in *Les Français peints par eux-mêmes: Encyclopédie morale du dix-neuvième siècle*, ed. Léon Curmer, annotated by Pierre Bouttier, 2 vols. (Paris: Omnibus, 2003), 1:373–400, 387.

33. For a wider discussion of the significance and iconography of paper money, see Marc Shell, "The Issue of Representation," and Jean-Joseph Goux, "Cash, Check, or Charge?," in *The New Economic Criticism: Studies at the Intersection of Literature and Economics*, ed. Martha Woodmansee and Mark Osteen (London: Routledge, 1999), 53–74 and 114–128, respectively; and Jean-Joseph Goux, *Frivolité de la valeur: Essai sur l'imaginaire du capitalisme* (Paris: Blusson, 2000), 221–248.

34. Niall Ferguson, *The Ascent of Money* (London: Allen Lane, 2008), 138–155.

35. Jean-Hervé Donnard, *Balzac, les réalités économiques et sociales dans "La Comédie humaine"* (Paris: Armand Colin, 1961), 301–303; Gildea, *Children of the Revolution*, 111–113; Ferguson, *Ascent of Money*, 81–91.

36. For a useful discussion of the role of advertising in Balzac's time, see Sara Thornton, *Advertising, Subjectivity and the Nineteenth-Century Novel* (Basingstoke, UK: Palgrave, 2009), 119–171.

37. "On doit faire remarquer que, d'après les recherches statistiques les plus authentiques, les capitaux rapporteront un dividende net de 18fr. 71c pour

100"; "De NAFE D'ARABIE . . . SEULS pectoraux approuvés et reconnus SUPER-IEURS à tous les autres, par un RAPPORT Fait à la Faculté de médicine, un Brevet, et par 54 Certificats des plus célèbres médecins." *La Presse,* March 19, 1838, 4, https://gallica.bnf.fr/ark:/12148/bpt6k4273305/f4.item.

38. The fictional prospectus for Birotteau's *huile céphalique* (6:156–157), first published in *César Birotteau* at the end of 1837 after the novel had undergone many false starts, may seem an ironic commentary on the 1840 prospectus for *La Comédie humaine.*

39. Fifty-six, according to an online text search at http://artflx.uchicago.edu /cgi-bin/philologic31/showrest_?conc.6.1.41168.0.55.balzacTEST2, but since this site proved on a more recent attempt to be no longer accessible, I have reverted to the fifty-two examples in *La Comédie humaine* recorded in Kazuo Kiriu's dictionary of words found in Balzac's works, "Vocabulaire de Balzac," Maison de Balzac, http://www.v2asp.paris.fr/commun/v2asp /musees/balzac/kiriu/ch/tome76ch.pdf. His dictionary also records four instances in *Œuvres diverses,* four in Balzac's theatrical works, and six in his correspondence.

40. "Monsieur, dit Popinot, un prospectus est souvent toute une fortune"; "Et pour les roturiers comme moi, dit Andoche, la fortune n'est qu'un prospectus" (6:155).

41. Marie-Eve Thérenty, *Mosaïques: Etre écrivain entre presse et roman (1829–1836)* (Paris: Honoré Champion, 2003), 101–183.

42. For examples of discounted remaindering, see Christophe Charle, "Le Champ de la production littéraire," in Chartier and Martin, *Histoire de l'édition française,* 3:137–175; and Roland Chollet, *Balzac journaliste* (Paris: Klincksieck, 1983), 516–518.

43. "La pâte des sultanes et l'Eau carminative se produisirent dans l'univers galant et commercial par des affiches colorées, en tête desquelles étaient ces mots: *Approuvées par l'Institut!* Cette formule, employée pour la première fois, eut un effet magique" (6:65).

44. "[Il] rédigea lui-même un prospectus dont la ridicule phraséologie fut un élément de succès: en France, on ne rit que des choses et des hommes dont on s'occupe, et personne ne s'occupe de ce qui ne réussit point" (6:65).

45. Peter Brooks, *The Melodramatic Imagination: Balzac, Henry James, Melodrama and the Mode of Excess* (1976; repr., New Haven, CT: Yale University Press, 1995), 111–112.

46. Prendergast, *Balzac: Fiction and Melodrama,* 147–173.

47. Guise, "Le Roman-feuilleton, 1830–1848," 3:210–331.

48. Brooks, *Melodramatic Imagination,* 22.

49. Charles Maturin, *Melmoth the Wanderer,* ed. Douglas Grant and Chris Baldick (Oxford: Oxford University Press, 2008), 5.

50. Christopher Prendergast's chapter "Type and Transgression" in *Balzac: Fiction and Melodrama,* 147–173, analyses how Balzac departs from culturally accepted norms to defamiliarise the reader, implying an awareness in the

reader's mind of an alternative and culturally conforming text, although he does not focus on the consequences of this.

51. "A l'auteur de *La Vieille Fille*. Il nous vient de si nombreuses réclamations contre le choix du sujet et la liberté de certaines descriptions . . . que le g[érant] de *La Presse* demande à l'auteur de *La Vieille Fille* de choisir un autre sujet que celui de *La Torpille*." *Corr.*, 2:155, November 17, 1836.

52. Vachon, *Les travaux et les jours*, 172, 175.

53. Guise, "Le Roman-feuilleton, 1830–1848," 3:254–263.

54. "Qui n'a pas remarqué que là . . . il est une façon d'être qui révèle ce que vous êtes" (6:431).

55. "Quiconque a trempé dans le journalisme, ou y trempe encore, est dans la nécessité cruelle de saluer les hommes qu'il méprise, de sourire à son meilleur ennemi, de pactiser avec les plus fétides bassesses, de se salir les doigts en voulant payer ses agresseurs avec leur monnaie" (6:437).

56. "A nous tous, nous pouvions faire une reine. . . . Vernou lui aurait fait des réclames, Bixiou lui aurait fait ses mots!" (6:441).

57. "Où sont peintes les existences, dans toute leur vérité, des espions, des filles entretenues et des gens en guerre avec la société qui grouillent dans Paris" (6:423).

58. "Le monde fantastique d'Hoffmann le Berlinois est là" (6:447).

59. "De ces paroles que Rabelais prétend s'être gelées et qui fondent" (6:447).

60. "Les conditions atmosphériques y sont changées: on y a chaud en hiver et froid en été" (6:447).

61. *Splendeurs*, ed. Adam, xvi–xix, and a series of notes on sources throughout the text, in particular 32n1. The sources are also demonstrated in Pommier, *La Torpille*, 31–67. For a broader assessment of the urban underworld and its literary representation in the nineteenth century, see Dominique Kalifa, *Les Bas-fonds* (Paris: Seuil, 2013).

62. "Il faut bien accorder quelque chose au Dieu moderne, la *majorité*, ce colosse aux pieds d'argile" (6:428; Balzac's italics).

63. See Kyoko Murata, *Les Métamorphoses du pacte diabolique dans l'œuvre de Balzac* (Osaka: Osaka Municipal Universities Press, 2003), 126–179, for an analysis of the *pacte diabolique* and the *pacte angélique* and 229–255 for a discussion of its role in *Splendeurs*.

64. "Des billets qui ne représentent ni marchandises ni valeurs pécuniaires fournies" (10:360).

65. However, Balzac's contemporaries, unlike ours, might have recognized the pyramid as a buried reference to E. T. A. Hoffmann's *Salvator Rosa*, dealing precisely with a charlatan and evaporating value.

66. "Insensible aux jolies rondeurs d'un sein" (6:450).

67. "Ce n'était plus une courtisane, mais un ange qui se relevait d'une chute" (6:463).

68. "Aucun regard n'aurait pu lire ce qui se passait alors en cet homme; mais pour les plus hardis il y aurait eu plus à frémir qu'à espérer à l'aspect de ses

yeux, jadis clairs et jaunes comme ceux des tigres, et sur lesquels les austérités et les privations avaient mis un voile semblable à celui qui se trouve sur les horizons au milieu de la canicule: la terre est chaude et lumineuse, mais le brouillard la rend indistincte, vaporeuse, elle est presque invisible" (6:455).

69. See *Splendeurs,* ed. Adam, 62n1.

70. "Cet homme vit donc en ce moment la nature humaine à fond" (6:458).

71. "Blanches comme les mains d'une femme en couches de son second enfant"; "comme un œuf miraculeux dans un nid de brins de soie" (6:464).

72. "Personne ne pouvait répondre à ces questions ni mesurer l'ambition de cet Espagnol comme on ne pouvait prévoir quelle serait sa fin" (6:474).

73. "La passion d'un poète devient alors un grand poème où souvent les proportions humaines sont dépassées" (6:475).

74. "Il ne faut pas briser le balancier avec lequel nous battons monnaie" (6:477).

75. This was a need driven not only by commercial considerations but, as Farrant argues, also by aesthetic requirements, reflecting the rationale of the characters and situations Balzac had created thus far. Farrant, *Balzac's Shorter Fictions,* 211–216.

76. Bouvier and Maynial, *Les Comptes dramatiques de Balzac,* 305–309, 325–331, 346–351, 366–371.

77. Christopher Prendergast, *For the People by the People? Eugène Sue's "Les Mystères de Paris": A Hypothesis in the Sociology of Literature* (Oxford: Legenda, 2003), 1.

78. Emile de Girardin in *Musée des familles* 2 (November 1834): 45–47, cited in Thérenty, *Mosaïques,* 34–35.

79. Irene Collins, *The Government and the Newspaper Press in France, 1814–1881* (Oxford: Oxford University Press, 1959), 80.

80. Balzac to Mme Hanska, July 1, 1843, in *EH,* 1:701.

81. Vachon, *Les travaux et les jours,* 237, 250.

82. "Tout le monde a dévoré *Les Mystères de Paris,* même les gens qui ne savent pas lire: ceux-là se les sont fait réciter par quelque portier érudit et de bonne volonté." Théophile Gautier, review of *Les Mystères de Paris,* by Eugène Sue and Dinaux, performed at the Théâtre de la Porte-Saint-Martin, *La Presse,* February 19, 1844, 1, https://gallica.bnf.fr/ark:/12148/bpt6k4294950/f1 .image.langFR.

83. Balzac to Mme Hanska, May 31, 1843, in *EH,* 1:693.

84. Anne O'Neil-Henry, *Mastering the Marketplace: Popular Literature in Nineteenth-Century France* (Lincoln: University of Nebraska Press, 2017), 87–118.

85. Eugène Sue, *Les Mystères de Paris,* pt. 1, *Journal des débats,* June 19, 1842, 1, http://gallica.bnf.fr/ark:/12148/bpt6k4458735/f1.item.zoom. The full text reads as follows: "Un tapis-franc, en argot de vol de meurtre, signifie un estaminet ou un cabaret du plus bas étage. Un repris de justice, qui, dans cette langue immonde, s'appelle un ogre, ou une femme de même dégradation, qui s'appelle une ogresse, tiennent ordinairement ces tavernes, hantés par le

rebut de la population parisienne: forçats libérés, escrocs, voleurs, assassins y abondent. Un crime a-t-il été commis, la police jette, si cela peut se dire, son filet dans cette fange; presque toujours elle y prend les coupables. Ce début annonce au lecteur qu'il doit assister à de sinistres scènes: s'il y consent, il pénétrera dans des régions horribles, inconnues; des types hideux, effrayants, fourmilleront dans ces cloaques impurs comme les reptiles dans les marais."

86. "Nous conduirons le lecteur dans ce triste logis." Eugène Sue, *Les Mystères de Paris,* ed. Judith Lyon-Caen (Paris: Gallimard, 2009), 394–399, 198–229. The quoted passage is at 394.

87. "J'avais lu son livre, j'avais bu son philtre, je m'étais enivrée de sa magie." Fanny Denoix to Eugène Sue, in Sue, *Les Mystères de Paris,* ed. Lyon-Caen, 1264.

88. "En même temps, au-dessus même du rédacteur en chef, et pour mener son journal, pour le conduire chaque matin où il faut qu'il aille, vous avez la foule que ce journal représente, c'est la foule qui lui donne ces inspirations, qui lui impose ses colères et ses vengeances." Jules Janin, "Le Journaliste," in Curmer, *Les Français peints,* 2:9–63, 54.

89. Prendergast, *For the People?,* 64.

90. Lyon-Caen, *La Lecture et la vie,* particularly the chapter entitled "Au Miroir du roman: Lettre au romancier et expérience sociale," 190–243.

91. Christiane Mounod-Anglès, *Balzac et ses lectrices* (Paris: Indigo, 1994), 31–46.

92. Janin, introduction to Curmer, *Les Français peints,* 1:9–22, 11.

93. Honoré de Balzac, *Monographie de la presse parisienne,* in *Œuvres complètes,* ed. Maurice Bardèche, 28 vols. (Chambéry, France: Club de l'honnête homme, 1963), 27:360–421.

94. A selection of the letters to Sue is reproduced in the dossier to *Les Mystères de Paris,* ed. Lyon-Caen, 1259–1294, and others are cited throughout Prendergast, *For the People?* A selection of critical responses, including that of Nettement, which appears in his *Lettres à une jeune femme du monde sur "Les Mystères de Paris,"* is set out on 1219–1244 of Lyon-Caen's edition.

95. "L'homme aux trois francs vous a donc acheté, payé, emporté sous le coup de cette opération involontaire [the runaway success]. Il rentre chez lui, il rentre en lui-même. Vous êtes un nom tout neuf, il se défie de vous. Il se connait, il se défie de lui; il a grand-peur de son jugement, il n'a pas l'habitude de penser lui-même, une opinion lui a toujours paru une propriété nationale, quelque chose que tous prêtent à chacun. . . . Notez par là-dessus que cet homme est un public: il vous jalouse comme un lecteur jalouse un auteur. Il faut que vous passiez sur le corps à tous ces préjuges-là, et qu'à la dernière page de votre livre l'homme aux trois francs soit convaincu qu'il croit que vous avez du talent." Edmond de Goncourt and Jules de Goncourt, *Charles Demailly,* ed. Adeline Wrona (Paris: Flammarion, 2007), 132.

96. "Le commerce de *La Presse* se trouve bien de cette longue immolation de la vertu sur la caisse du journal." *La Mode,* September 15, 1842, reproduced in the dossier to Sue, *Les Mystères de Paris,* ed. Lyon-Caen, 1227.

97. Sainte-Beuve to Juste Olivier, July 28, 1843, in Sue, *Les Mystères de Paris,* ed. Lyon-Caen, 1224.

98. "Qui fit révolution dans le journalisme par la révélation d'une manière neuve et originale" (5:399).

99. "Parlons donc capital, parlons argent! Matérialisons, chiffrons la pensée dans un siècle qui s'enorgueillit d'être le siècle des idées positives! L'écrivain n'arrive à rien sans des études immenses qui représentent un capital de temps ou d'argent: le temps vaut l'argent, il l'engendre." Balzac, "Lettre aux écrivains français," 66.

100. "Le *Premier-Paris,* qui n'existe que par la divination perpétuelle des pensées de son abonné, le surprend le lendemain agréablement en lui panifiant sa pensée." Balzac, *Monographie de la presse parisienne,* in *Œuvres complètes,* ed. Bardèche, 27:365.

101. "Phénomène du roman feuilleton devenu politique et social," *Gazette de France,* November 29, 1844, quoted at 9:1243.

102. Lyon-Caen, *La Lecture et la vie,* 180–185.

103. Marie-Eve Thérenty, "Chapitres et feuilletons: Les Scansions-fantômes de *La Comédie humaine,*" in *Balzac et alii, génétiques croisées: Histoires d'éditions,* ed. Takayuki Kamada and Jacques Neefs, proceedings of the meeting organised by the Groupe international de recherches balzaciennes, June 3–5, 2010, 8–14, with the quotation from Sand at 13, http://balzac.cerilac.univ-paris-diderot.fr/balzacetalii.html.

104. René Guise, "Balzac et le roman feuilleton," *L'Année balzacienne,* 1964, 283–338, 298–299.

105. "Je ne peux pas, je ne dois pas, je ne veux pas subir la dépréciation qui pèse sur moi par les marchés de Sue et par le tapage que font ses deux ouvrages" (Balzac to Mme Hanska, September 17, 1844, in *EH,* 1:910).

106. Sue, *Les Mystères de Paris,* ed. Lyon-Caen, 63–70.

107. "L'un de ces pactes infernaux qui ne se voient que dans les romans" (6:502).

108. Louis Chevalier, *Classes laborieuses et classes dangereuses à Paris pendant la première moitié du XIXᵉ siècle* (Paris: Plon, 1958). See especially 469–496 for Chevalier's discussion of Balzac as a representative of bourgeois opinion on the lower and criminal classes.

109. "Une fille de bonne maison" and "La maison d'une bonne fille" (6:510, 514). The pun is somewhat clumsier in English.

110. "L'un de ces pactes infernaux qui ne se voient que dans les romans, *mais dont la possibilité terrible a souvent été démontrée aux Assises par de célèbres drames judiciaires*" (6:502; my emphasis).

111. "Je suis l'auteur, tu seras le drame" (6:504).

112. "Pour la première fois, les deux artistes en espionnage rencontraient donc *un texte indéchiffrable,* tout en soupçonnant une ténébreuse histoire" (6:629;

my emphasis). The final phrase in the 1844 Potter edition is even "un ténébreux roman."

113. "Cent mille francs placés en Asie" (6:571). Again, the pun works better in French as character and continent carry the same name.

114. Armine Kotin Mortimer, "*La Maison Nucingen,* ou le récit financier," *Romanic Review* 69, nos. 1–2 (January–March 1978): 60–71.

115. "Chapitre ennuyeux car il explique quatre ans de bonheur" (6:487).

116. Charles Bernheimer, *Figures of Ill Repute: Representing Prostitution in Nineteenth-Century France* (Cambridge, MA: Harvard University Press, 1989), 53–54.

117. "Le dandy, le faussaire et la courtisane" (6:505).

118. "Ce vieillard dodeliné de vices, calme comme un Vitellius dont le ventre impérial reparaissait, pour ainsi dire, palingénésiquement" (6:529).

119. Herrera is "Le Mal, dont la configuration poétique s'appelle le Diable" (6:504). Lucien is "cet homme à moitié femme" (6:505).

120. "Dans Esther, dont la fable est excessivement compliquée . . . l'action circule avec peine à travers les labyrinthes laborieusement construites; elle se brise mille fois en route et, à la fin, au lieu de se dénouer, elle se casse définitivement sans qu'on puisse deviner pourquoi ce livre s'arrête là"; "Les courtisanes devenues des modèles de chasteté, les forçats luttant de dévouement et de délicatesse avec les plus beaux modèles de l'antiquité et des temps modernes, nous sommes accoutumés à ces singularités qui n'ont rien d'extraordinaire pour nous"; "Ainsi, à les bien considérer, les *Splendeurs et misères des courtisanes* peuvent nous servir, tout comme un autre livre médiocre, à inaugurer un système d'indulgence envers le roman-feuilleton. Ici, il peut venir un doute: ce roman a-t-il réellement paru au bas d'un journal quelconque? Notre réponse sera catégorique; peu importe que le fait matériel ait eu lieu, il suffit qu'Esther porte les marques évidentes de l'intention." Arthur de Gobineau in *Le Commerce,* October 29, 1844, reproduced in Dumasy, *La Querelle du roman-feuilleton,* 87–94. The quotations are at 91, 92, 93.

121. Balzac to Mme Hanska, July 16, 1844, in *EH,* 1:803, 882.

122. Guise, "Balzac et le roman feuilleton," 307; Vachon, *Les travaux et les jours,* 217–219, 228–231.

123. Guise, "Balzac et le roman feuilleton," 305–324.

124. Bouvier and Maynial, *Les Comptes dramatiques de Balzac,* 410–445.

125. "Le moment exige que je fasse deux ou trois œuvres capitales qui renversent les faux dieux de cette littérature bâtarde . . . il faut pour la fin de juin, que j'aie fait 150 f[euille]ts, 10 par jour en moyenne" (Balzac to Mme Hanska, June 16, 1846, in *EH,* 2:213).

126. *Splendeurs,* ed. Adam, xxvi.

127. Prendergast, *Order of Mimesis,* 109.

128. Brooks, *Melodramatic Imagination,* 148.

129. Eric Bordas, "Pratiques balzaciennes de la digression," *L'Année balzacienne,* n.s., 2, no. 20 (1999): 293–316, 315–316.

Notes to Pages 82–87

130. "Mais avant d'entrer dans le drame terrible d'une instruction criminelle, il est indispensable, comme il vient d'être dit, d'expliquer le marché normal d'un procès de ce genre" (6:700).

131. "Ce petit détail peut indiquer aux gens les moins compréhensifs combien est vive, intéressante, curieuse, dramatique et terrible la lutte d'une instruction criminelle, lutte sans témoins, mais toujours écrite" (6:746).

132. "Ainsi, comme on le voit, les plus grands événements de la vie sont traduits par de petits faits-Paris plus ou moins vrais" (6:798).

133. "Néanmoins, Jacques Collin ou Carlos Herrera (il est nécessaire de lui donner l'un ou l'autre de ces noms selon les nécessités de la situation) connaissait de longue main les façons de la police, de la geôle et de la justice" (6:703).

134. "Il faut faire observer ici que Jacques Collin parlait le français comme une vache espagnole, en baragouinant de manière à rendre ses réponses presque inintelligibles et à s'en faire demander la répétition. Les germanismes de monsieur de Nucingen ont déjà trop émaillé cette Scène pour y mettre d'autres phrases soulignées difficiles à lire, et qui nuiraient à la rapidité d'un dénouement" (6:746).

135. This discarded chapter heading does not translate: an approximation might be "One end against another end—where will it all end?" but the French also contains a notion of a contest between "finely" matched opponents.

136. "La digression balzacienne, c'est l'aveu stylistique d'une disparate discursive qui prétend à la complétude et à la cohérence, mais dont l'énonciation ne cesse de faire entendre le rythme des brisures, des décalages et des contradictions." Bordas, "Pratiques balzaciennes," 316.

137. Sue, *Les Mystères de Paris,* ed. Lyon-Caen, 1157–1212.

138. See "The Old Curiosity Shop," Charles Dickens Page, accessed December 11, 2018, https://charlesdickenspage.com/curiosityshop.html.

139. "Onze heures sonnent. J'ai fait ma dernière prière, je vais me coucher pour mourir" (6:763).

140. "Une âme si jeune, si fraiche, une beauté si magnifique, un enfant, un poète" (6:764).

141. "Chez les gens dont le caractère ressemble à celui de Lucien, et que Jacques Collin avait si bien analysé, ces passages subits d'un état de démoralisation complète à un état quasiment métallique, tant les forces humaines se tendent, sont les plus éclatants phénomènes de la vie des idées" (6:776).

142. "En lui remettant en mémoire le dénouement de Roméo rejoignant Juliette" (6:787).

143. Marcel Proust notes perceptively that these allusions are more credible in Balzac's voice than Lucien's. Marcel Proust, *Contre Sainte-Beuve,* ed. Pierre Clarac (Paris: Gallimard, 1971), 293.

144. "C'est la plante vénéneuse aux riches couleurs qui fascine les enfants dans les bois. C'est la poésie du mal" (6:790). "C'est" refers to the use of power to pervert and corrupt.

145. "Amants de la vérité, les magistrats sont comme les femmes jalouses, ils se livrent à mille suppositions et les fouillent avec le poignard du soupçon comme le sacrificateur antique éventrait les victimes; puis ils s'arrêtent non pas au vrai, mais au probable, et ils finissent par entrevoir le vrai" (6:767).

146. "Ces cartons fournissent en quelque sorte l'envers de la tapisserie des crimes, leurs causes premières, et presque toujours inédites" (6:726).

147. "Les sept à huit publics qui forment le public" (6:719).

148. "Il n'y a qu'un cri sur sa publication. On trouve cela hideux et honteux, il est perdu" (Balzac to Mme Hanska, August 5, 1846, in *EH*, 2:291).

149. "L'immense succès de *La Cousine* a causé des réchauffements chez les journaux, ils voudraient de moi" (Balzac to Mme Hanska, October 24, 1846, *EH*, 2:389).

150. Guise, "Balzac et le roman feuilleton," 327–332; Vachon, *Les travaux et les jours,* 255–275.

151. "'On doit, avant d'admettre quelqu'un, bien connaitre sa fortune, ses parents, tous ses antécédents . . .' Cette phrase est la morale de cette histoire, au point de vue aristocratique" (6:883).

152. "Aussi la duchesse avait-elle conservé ces lettres émouvantes, comme certains vieillards ont des gravures obscènes, à cause des éloges hyperboliques donnés à ce qu'elle avait de moins duchesse en elle" (6:877).

153. "La hardiesse du vrai s'élève à des combinaisons interdites à l'art" (6:873).

154. "Le petit épagneul mort, on se demande si son terrible compagnon, si le lion vivra!" (6:813).

155. "Dans la vie réelle, dans la société, les faits s'enchaînent si fatalement à d'autres faits, qu'ils ne vont pas les uns sans les autres" (6:813).

156. "La solitude n'est habitable que pour l'homme de génie qui la remplit de ses idées, filles du monde spirituel" (6:849).

157. Walker Gibson, "Authors, Speakers, Readers and Mock Readers," *College English* 11, no. 5 (February 1950): 265–269.

158. *Splendeurs,* ed. Adam, 502n1.

159. "Jacques Collin, surnommé Trompe-la-Mort dans le monde des bagnes, et à qui maintenant il ne faut donner d'autre nom que le sien" (6:812).

160. Prendergast, for example, argues that this is an essential part of Balzac's totalising vision, in which vice, symbolised by motifs of debased sexuality common to all classes, erases social and moral distinctions. Prendergast, *Balzac: Fiction and Melodrama,* 61–89.

161. The murders in a sealed room are this time explained by Calvi's diminutive girlfriend, who climbs down the chimney to let him in, then locks the door and climbs back out once the crime has been committed.

162. First published in *Graham's Magazine,* April 1841, translated into French and published in *La Quotidienne,* June 11–13, 1846.

163. "Les états qu'on fait dans le monde ne sont que des apparences; la réalité, c'est l'idée!" (6:911).

164. André Gide, *Journal, 1889–1939* (Paris: Gallimard, 1992), 1225–1226.
165. Proust, *Contre Sainte-Beuve*, 292.
166. Bernheimer suggests that this is a cornerstone of Sue's moral viewpoint: "The model of enlightened behaviour Sue proposes for the rich thrives on plotting the elimination of characters whose erotically charged deviance provides the plot of *Les Mystères de Paris* with its most narratable story lines." Deviance is tolerable only as long as it provokes the appropriate counterdiscipline. Bernheimer, *Figures of Ill Repute*, 51.
167. "En mariant leurs richesses et leurs misères" (7:499).
168. Dällenbach, "Le Tout en morceaux."
169. For example, Donald Fanger in *Dostoevsky and Romantic Realism: A Study of Dostoevsky in relation to Balzac, Dickens, and Gogol* (Chicago: University of Chicago Press, 1967), 44–65. Balzac's own suggestion to this effect comes, tellingly, in the final part of *Splendeurs:* "Il est impossible de faire une longue digression au dénoûement d'une scène déjà si étendue et qui n'offre pas d'autre intérêt que celui dont est entouré Jacques Collin, espèce de colonne vertébrale qui, par son horrible influence, relie pour ainsi dire le *Père Goriot* à *Illusions perdues*, et *Illusions perdues* à cette Etude" (6:851). The fact that Balzac is about to make just the digression he denies so emphatically may be an indication that his tongue is firmly in his cheek.

2. Dostoevsky

1. "Уж не роман ли и это?" Fedor Dostoevsky, *Polnoe sobranie sochinenii F. M. Dostoevskogo v XVIII tomakh*, ed. G. N. Seleznev et al., 18 vols. (Moscow: Voskresen'e, 2003–2005; hereafter *PSS 2003–2005*), 14:307. See Notes on Citation for citation methodology.
2. "Нас упрекают что мы насоздавали романов. А что же у защитника как не роман на романе?" (14:319).
3. At the time of writing, we still await William Mills Todd III's promised work on serialisation, but he has nonetheless accumulated a body of work in a series of articles, edited volumes, and unpublished papers, of which the most important for the present study are the following: "*The Brothers Karamazov* and the Poetics of Serial Publication," *Dostoevsky Studies* 7 (1986): 87–97; "Dostoevsky and Tolstoy: The Professionalisation of Literature and Serialised Fiction," *Dostoevsky Studies*, n.s., 15 (2011): 29–36; "Serialisation: Institutions of Literature as Patterns of Communication" (unpublished paper delivered at Oxford University, May 31, 2012); "'To Be Continued': Dostoevsky's Evolving Poetics of Serialised Publication," *Dostoevsky Studies*, n.s., 18 (2014): 22–33; and "Dostoevsky and the Moral Hazards of Serial Publication" (unpublished paper delivered at the annual conference of the Association for Slavic, East European, and Eurasian Studies, Philadelphia, PA, November 2015).

Of Robin Feuer Miller's works, *Dostoevsky's Unfinished Journey* (New Haven, CT: Yale University Press, 2007); *Dostoevsky and "The Idiot"* (Cambridge, MA: Harvard University Press, 1981); and *The Brothers Karamazov* (New York: Twayne, 1992) are the most relevant. Robert Belknap's two major works on *The Brothers Karamazov* are *The Structure of "The Brothers Karamazov"* (The Hague: Mouton, 1967; repr., Evanston, IL: Northwestern University Press, 1989); and *The Genesis of "The Brothers Karamazov"* (Evanston, IL: Northwestern University Press, 1990).

4. Leonid Grossman, *Poetika Dostoevskogo* (Moscow: Gosudarstvennaya akademiya khudozhestvennykh nauk, 1925), in particular the first chapter, entitled "Kompositsiya v romane Dostoevskogo," 7–63.

5. John Jones, *Dostoevsky* (Oxford: Clarendon, 1983), pt. 3, "Parajournalist," 199–362, and in particular the final chapter, *"The Brothers Karamazov,"* 297–362; Jacques Catteau, *Dostoevsky and the Process of Literary Creation*, trans. Audrey Littlewood (Cambridge: Cambridge University Press, 1989), 180–191.

6. See in particular Gary Saul Morson, introduction to *A Writer's Diary*, by Fedor Dostoevsky, trans. Kenneth Lantz (Evanston, IL: Northwestern University Press, 2009), xix–lxxiii, as well as broader studies such as Harriet Murav, *Russia's Legal Fictions* (Ann Arbor: University of Michigan Press, 1998); and Irina Paperno, *Suicide as a Cultural Institution in Dostoevsky's Russia* (Ithaca, NY: Cornell University Press, 1997).

7. Igor' Volgin, *Dostoevsky-zhurnalist: "Dnevnik pisatelya" i russkaia obshchestvennost'* (Moscow: Izdatel'stvo Moskovskogo universiteta, 1982). In his introduction to Peter Sekirin's *Dostoevsky Archive* (Jefferson, NC: McFarland, 1992), 28, Volgin summarises his conclusions on the *Diary* thus: "The ordinary readers of this periodical . . . felt the richness and diversity of different points of view united by some hidden denominator which defined the unity of publication and brought it out of the traditional limitations of the journalistic genre."

8. "Моя идея, это—стать Ротшильдом" (10:61).

9. Bruce W. Lincoln, *The Great Reforms: Autocracy, Bureaucracy and the Politics of Change in Imperial Russia* (DeKalb: Northern Illinois University Press, 1990), particularly chap. 5, "Testing the Great Reforms," 159–191; Olga Maiorova, *From the Shadow of Empire: Defining the Russian Nation through Cultural Mythology, 1855–1870* (Madison: University of Wisconsin Press, 2010), particularly chap. 1, "A Shifting Vision of the Nation," 26–52.

10. Ekaterina Pravilova, *A Public Empire* (Princeton, NJ: Princeton University Press, 2014).

11. Sarah Young, *Dostoevsky's "The Idiot" and the Ethical Foundations of Narrative* (London: Anthem, 2004), 168–182.

12. John Jones, *Dostoevsky*, 308.

13. Victor Terras, *A Karamazov Companion* (Madison: University of Wisconsin Press, 1981), 108–109. The theme is slightly further developed in a later

essay, Victor Terras, "The Art of Fiction as a Theme in *The Brothers Karamazov*," in *Dostoevsky: New Perspectives*, ed. Robert Louis Jackson (Englewood Cliffs, NJ: Prentice-Hall, 1983), 193–205.

14. Malcolm Jones, *Dostoevsky after Bakhtin* (Cambridge: Cambridge University Press, 1990), 187.

15. Susan McReynolds provides a good survey of the critical school that regards Dostoevsky as a Christian prophet and imputes messages to his works accordingly: see *Redemption and the Merchant God* (Evanston, IL: Northwestern University Press, 2008), 3–19, and particularly 5–6.

16. Mikhail Konotopov and Stanislav Smetanin, *Istoriya ekonomiki Rossii* (Moscow: KnoRus, 2008), 158.

17. A series of exhibitions called the All-Russia Industrial Exhibitions (Vserossiskie promyshlennye vystavki) were sponsored by the Ministry of Finance every four years from 1829, alternating between Saint Petersburg, Moscow, and Warsaw. "Industrial Exhibitions," Saint Petersburg Encyclopaedia, http://www.encspb.ru/object/2804001685?lc=en.

18. Aleksandr Polunov, *Russia in the Nineteenth Century: Autocracy, Reform and Social Change, 1814–1914*, ed. Thomas Owen and Larissa Zakharova (Armonk, NY: Sharpe, 2005), 73. See also Jillian Porter, *Economies of Feeling: Russian Literature under Nicholas I* (Evanston, IL: Northwestern University Press, 2017), for a discussion of the impact of the volatility of the Russian currency on literature in general, 7–8, and on Dostoevsky in particular, 89–106.

19. Polunov, *Russia in the Nineteenth Century*, 129.

20. For a more extended discussion of the development and financing of the railway network, see Frit'of Shenk, *Poesd v sovremmenost'* (Moscow: Novoe literaturnoe obozrenie, 2016), 61–78.

21. Polunov, *Russia in the Nineteenth Century*, 130–135. The relative value calculation is taken from https://www.measuringworth.com/calculators/uscompare /relativevalue.php.

22. Polunov, *Russia in the Nineteenth Century*, 135–136.

23. For a general discussion of the rise of the merchant classes during the Great Reforms, see Thomas Owen, *Capitalism and Politics in Russia: A Social History of the Moscow Merchants 1855–1905* (Cambridge: Cambridge University Press, 1981), esp. 53–71.

24. Polunov, *Russia in the Nineteenth Century*, 135.

25. For a more extended discussion of the impact of the Great Reforms on agriculture and industry, see Arcadius Kahan, *Russian Economic History: The Nineteenth Century*, ed. Roger Weiss (Chicago: University of Chicago Press, 1989), 6–19.

26. Pravilova, *Public Empire*, 89–92.

27. For more extended discussions of the impact of the terms of emancipation on the economy, see Konotopov and Smetanin, *Istoriya ekonomiki Rossii*, 166–170; and Polunov, *Russia in the Nineteenth Century*, 106–109.

28. Leo Tolstoy, *Anna Karenina*, bk. 8, chap. 11.

29. Polunov, *Russia in the Nineteenth Century*, 13.

30. Sergei Antonov, *Bankrupts and Usurers of Imperial Russia: Debt, Property and the Law in the Age of Dostoevsky and Tolstoy* (Cambridge, MA: Harvard University Press, 2016).

31. Konotopov and Smetanin, *Istoriya ekonomiki Rossii*, 172–184; Polunov, *Russia in the Nineteenth Century*, 135–138.

32. Konotopov and Smetanin, *Istoriya ekonomiki Rossii*, 179.

33. Polunov, *Russia in the Nineteenth Century*, 135.

34. Shenk, *Poesd v sovremmenost'*, 62.

35. "Мы . . . при всаднике имеющем меру в руке своей, так как все в нынешний век на мере и на договоре" (8:153).

36. Mikhail Kufaev, *Istoriya russkoi knigi v XIX veke* (1927; repr., Moscow: Pashkov Dom, 2003), 129.

37. Miranda Beaven, "Aleksandr Smirdin and Publishing in St. Petersburg, 1830–1840," *Canadian Slavonic Papers* 27, no.1 (March 1985): 15–30, 22–29.

38. Jean Morienval [Henri Thévenin], *Les Créateurs de la grande presse en France: Emile de Girardin, H. de Villemessant, Moïse Millaud* (Paris: Editions Spes, 1934), 73–75.

39. Abram Reitblat, *Ot Bovy k Bal'montu: Ocherki po istorii chteniya v Rossii vo vtoroi polovine XIX veka* (Moscow: MPI, 1991), 32–47, 78–97.

40. Robert Gildea, *Children of the Revolution: The French, 1799–1914* (London: Penguin, 2009), 174.

41. Abram Reitblat, *Kak Pushkin vyshel v genii: Istoriko-sotsiologicheskie ocherki o knizhnoi kul'ture Pushkinskoi epokhi* (Moscow: Novoe literaturnoe obozrenie, 2001), 14–15; Reitblat, *Ot Bovy k Bal'montu*, 10.

42. James Smith Allen, *In the Public Eye: A History of Reading in Modern France, 1800–1914* (Princeton, NJ: Princeton University Press, 1991), 27, 38 (table A).

43. Jeffrey Brooks, *When Russia Learned to Read: Literacy and Popular Literature, 1861–1917* (Princeton, NJ: Princeton University Press, 1985), 61.

44. Louise McReynolds, *The News under Russia's Old Regime: The Development of a Mass-Circulation Press* (Princeton, NJ: Princeton University Press, 1991), appendix A, table 4.

45. Reitblat, *Ot Bovy k Bal'montu*, 109–129; Louise McReynolds, *News under Russia's Old Regime*, 52–63.

46. For a fuller discussion of the rise of the Russian thick journals, see Reitblat, *Ot Bovy k Bal'montu*, chap. 2, "The Thick Journal and Its Readers" [Tolstyi zhurnal i ego publika], 32–47; and Deborah Martinsen, ed., *Literary Journals in Imperial Russia* (Cambridge: Cambridge University Press, 1997), particularly William Mills Todd III, "Periodicals in Literary Life of the Early Nineteenth Century," 37–63, and Robert Belknap, "Survey of Russian Journals, 1840–1880," 91–116.

47. Todd, "'To Be Continued,'" 26.

48. Isabelle Luquet, "Les Lecteurs de Zola," in *Histoire de l'édition française*, ed. Roger Chartier and Henri-Jean Martin, 4 vols. (Paris: Fayard / Promodis,

1990), 566–567. Although editions were usually of one thousand copies, this was not always the case, especially for first impressions, so the number of editions is more reliable as a minimum than as an accurate indicator of published copies.

49. Alexis Pogorelskin, "The Messenger of Europe," in Martinsen, *Literary Journals in Imperial Russia*, 129–149, 142–143.

50. Nikolai Strakhov, "Iz vospominanii," *Semeinye vechera*, February 1881, 235–248, quoted in an unattributed translation in Sekirin, *Dostoevsky Archive*, 148.

51. Katia Dianina, "The *Feuilleton*, an Everyday Guide to Public Culture in the Age of the Great Reforms," *Slavic and East European Journal* 47, no. 2 (Summer 2003): 187–210, 191.

52. "Фельетон в наш век—это . . . это почти главное дело. . . . Я думаю так: если б я был не случайным фельетонистом, а присяжным, всегдашним, мне кажется я бы пожелал обратиться в Эженя Сю, чтоб описывать петербургские тайны." From Fedor Dostoevsky, *Petersburg Dreams in Verse and Prose* [*Peterburgskie snovideniya v stikhakh i proze*] (4:8).

53. Vladimir Zakharov, "A Genius *Feuilletonist*" [Genial'ny fel'etonist], in *PSS 2003–2005*, 4:501–513.

54. Catteau, *Dostoevsky and the Process*, 190.

55. Reitblat, *Ot Bovy k Bal'montu*, 11–12, and more generally 8–32. Reitblat's categories are stated as being derived ultimately from definitions proposed in 1862 by the censor F. F. Veselago, so they may reflect a contemporary view of the readership.

56. S. Shashkov, "Literaturny trud v Rossii," *Delo* 8 (1876): 1–48, 36–37 (table).

57. Thomas Piketty, *Le Capital au XXIᵉ siècle* (Paris: Editions du Seuil, 2013); Thomas Piketty, *Capital in the Twenty-First Century*, trans. Arthur Goldhammer (Cambridge, MA: Belknap Press of Harvard University Press, 2014), 103–104. If Shashkov's estimates are right (his evidence is anecdotal rather than scientific), the comparison provides a dramatic illustration of the short-term economic impact of the Great Reforms.

58. Shashkov, "Literaturny trud v Rossii," 37–40.

59. Strakhov, "Iz vospominanii," cited in Sekirin, *Dostoevsky Archive*, 152.

60. Reitblat, *Ot Bovy k Bal'montu*, 12.

61. Jeffrey Brooks, *When Russia Learned to Read*, 114–125.

62. Konotopov and Smetanin, *Istoriya ekonomiki Rossii*, 158; Polunov, *Russia in the Nineteenth Century*, 135.

63. Jeffrey Brooks, *When Russia Learned to Read*, 112.

64. Thais Lindstrom, "From Chapbooks to Classics: The Story of the *Intermediary*," *American Slavic and East European Review* 16, no. 2 (April 1957): 190–201, 194.

65. Jeffrey Brooks, "Readers and Reading at the End of the Tsarist Era," in *Literature and Society in Imperial Russia, 1800–1914*, ed. William Mills Todd III (Stanford, CA: Stanford University Press, 1978), 119–120; Reitblat, *Ot Bovy k*

Bal'montu, 17. Brooks makes the point that literacy rates in many subgroups of the general population were considerably higher, particularly amongst younger urban males. French and English literacy rates are derived from, respectively, Jean Hébrard, "Les Nouveaux lecteurs," in Chartier and Martin, *Histoire de l'édition française,* 526–567, and Richard Altick, *The English Common Reader: A Social History of the Mass Reading Public, 1800–1900,* 2nd ed. (Columbus: Ohio State University Press, 1998), 171.

66. Dostoevsky's correspondence contains too many references to his parlous financial condition to list individually. A letter to his publisher, Mikhail Nikiforovich Katkov, in September 1865, sent from Wiesbaden, asks for a minimum payment of 125 roubles per printer's sheet (*pechatnyi list,* a standard measure of printed text equivalent to about sixteen printed pages; vol. 15, bk. 2, p. 118); another, to Apollon Maikov in August 1867, details his gambling losses, as well as the increasing frequency of his epileptic fits (vol. 15, bk. 2, pp. 173–182). Over a dozen years later, in May 1878, after his gambling has long stopped and he has put his financial affairs in far better order, he is still writing to Nikolai Alekseevich Lyubimov, his editor, to complain of his immediate need for money (vol. 16, bk. 2, p. 100). Joseph Frank's biography, *Dostoevsky,* 5 vols. (Princeton, NJ: Princeton University Press, 1976–2002), traces his financial fortunes throughout his life in passages far too numerous to list separately, while Catteau provides a useful summary of his financial affairs in *Dostoevsky and the Process,* 135–168.

67. Frank, *Dostoevsky,* 3:32, 162–163.

68. Frank, *Dostoevsky,* 1:137–139, in relation to *Poor People;* 1:308–309, in relation to *The Double;* 2:213–216, in relation to *Notes from the House of the Dead;* 2:311–314, in relation to *Notes from the Underground.*

69. "Вот хоть бы и Ратазяев,—как берет! Что ему лист написать? Да он в иной день и по пяти листов писывал, а по триста рублей, говорит, за лист берет. Там анекдотец какой-нибудь, или из любопытного что-нибудь—пятьсот, дай не дай, хоть тресни, да дай!" (1:40).

70. Gary Saul Morson, *The Boundaries of Genre* (Austin: University of Texas Press, 1981), 20.

71. "Но неужели, неужели вы и в самом деле до того легковерны, что воображаете, будто я это все напечатаю, да еще вам дам читать? И вот еще для меня задача—для чего, в самом деле, называю я вас господами, для чего обращаюсь как будто и вправду к читателям?" (6:28).

72. Frank, *Dostoevsky,* 2:74–75. Dostoevsky's editorial introducing the Poe stories is to be found at 5:63–65 of *PSS 2003–2005.*

73. Oliver Ready, introduction to *Crime and Punishment,* by Fedor Dostoyevsky, trans. Oliver Ready (London: Penguin, 2014), xxv.

74. "У меня свой особенный взгляд на действительность (в искусстве) и то что большинство называет почти фантастическим и исключительным, то для меня иногда составляет самую сущность действительного" (vol. 15, bk. 2, p. 300).

75. "В каждом номере газет Вы встречаете отчет о самых действительных фактах и о самых мудрёных. Для писателей наших они фантастичны, да они не занимаются ими, а между тем они действительность, потому что они *факты.*" Dostoevsky to Strakhov, February 26, 1869 (vol. 15, bk. 2, p. 300; Dostoevsky's italics).

76. "Главная мысль романа—изобразить положительно прекрасного человека." Dostoevsky to Sofya Ivanova, January 1, 1868 (vol. 15, bk. 2, pp. 216–217).

77. Marcel Mauss proposes just such a description of a "gift" economy in which such fixed values, typical of a society based on commercial exchange, give way to ethical or emotional exchanges. See Marcel Mauss, *The Gift: Forms and Functions of Exchange in Archaic Societies,* trans. Ian Cunnison (Glencoe, IL: Free Press, 1954; repr., Mansfield Center, CT: Martino, 2011): 69–76.

78. "Рискнул как на рулетке: 'Может-быть под пером разовьётся!'" Dostoevsky to Maikov, December 31, 1867 (vol. 15, bk. 2, p. 209).

79. For a fascinating analysis of the Gothic markers that allow the reader to recognise the genre, see Miller, *Dostoevsky and "The Idiot,"* 108–126.

80. Morson, introduction to *Writer's Diary,* ed. Morson, xxv, xliv–xlv, xlix–l.

81. *Diary of a Writer,* 10/76, 1.1 (11:520–524); 11/76, 1 (11:548–574). The numbering of articles in *Diary of a Writer* uses the following sequence: [volume]/[year], [section].[subsection], together with page references to *PSS 2003–2005* in parentheses.

82. For example, as the guardian of Orthodoxy (e.g., *Diary of a Writer,* 6/76, 2.4 [11:437–441]), on the Eastern question (e.g., 7–8/76, 4.5 [11:485–487]), or through his anti-Semitism (e.g., 3/77, 2.1–4 or 3.1–2 [12:69–85]).

83. For example, in defence of war as a socially useful phenomenon (*Diary of a Writer,* 4/76, 2.2 [11:387–390]).

84. *Diary of a Writer,* 5/76, 1.3 (11:402–410).

85. "Два рассказа 'при существенном единстве целого'" (13:8).

86. "Конечно никто ничем не связан, можно бросить книгу и с двух страниц первого рассказа, с тем чтоб и не раскрывать более" (13:7–8).

87. See Appendix A for a full schedule of the serialisation of *The Brothers Karamazov.*

88. Fedor Dostoevsky, *The Notebooks for "The Brothers Karamazov,"* ed. and trans. Edward Wasiolek (Chicago: University of Chicago Press, 1971), 12–18.

89. Todd, "Poetics of Serial Publication," 90.

90. Belknap, *Genesis of "The Brothers Karamazov,"* 45–56.

91. *Russkii Vestnik* 139 (January 1879). The essays cited are at 5–35, 36–64, and 264–291; the poem and fictional works at 262–263, 291–308, and 309–396. The first part of *The Brothers Karamazov* is at 104–207.

92. For example, in the story of Alyosha's childhood, bk. 1, chap. 4, where the narrator shifts from omniscient penetration of the four-year-old Alyosha's deepest feelings for his mother to gossipy disapproval of the sort of expressions children learned in the modern world, and all within the space of a couple of pages (13:19–20).

93. "Да, Дмитрия Федоровича еще не существует" (13:33).

94. An example of a direct approach to the reader on the basis of an assumption of shared common experience occurs in the final sentences of the very first chapter: "In most cases people, even the bad ones, are far more naïve and straightforward than we think. And we are just the same." (В большинстве случаев люди, даже злодеи, гораздо наивнее и простодушнее чем мы вообще заключаем. Да и мы сами тоже.) (13:11)

95. Mikhail Bakhtin, *The Dialogic Imagination,* ed. Michael Holquist, trans. Caryl Emerson and Michael Holquist (Austin: University of Texas Press, 1981), 342–349, 342.

96. "Уверовал он лишь единственно потому, что желал уверовать" (13:25, compared to the same image in similar terms in Ivan's dream at 14:227).

97. Belknap, *Genesis of "The Brothers Karamazov,"* chap. 5, "The Theme of Memory," 73–87.

98. Nina Perlina, *Varieties of Poetic Utterance: Quotation in "The Brothers Karamazov"* (New York: University Press of America, 1985), esp. 11–52 for a discussion of Perlina's proposed hierarchy.

99. Bakhtin's arguments on the relationship of the carnival to the notion of testing are set out in Mikhail Bakhtin, *Problems of Dostoevsky's Poetics,* ed. and trans. Caryl Emerson (Minneapolis: University of Minnesota Press, 1984), 134–136.

100. "Для пикантности присочинил" (13:37).

101. "А когда заколачивали, то блудные плясавицы пели песни и играли на гуслях, то есть на фортоплясах" (13:75).

102. "И непременно в либеральном и атеистическом направлении, с социалистическим оттенком, с маленьким даже лоском социализма, но держа ухо востро, то есть в сущности держа нашим и вашим и отводя глаза дуракам" (13:71).

103. "Я читал вот как-то и где-то про 'Иоанна Милостивого' (одного святого): что он, когда к нему пришел голодный и обмерзший прохожий и попросил согреть его, лег с ним вместе в постель, обнял его и начал дышать ему в гноящийся и зловонный от какой-то ужасной болезни рот его" (13:196).

104. Terras, *Karamazov Companion,* 221n120.

105. A full discussion of this approach to *Trois contes* is beyond the scope of this book. Its premise, that the mismatch between what is represented and the genre of its representation is a way of testing the boundaries of reader acceptance, would perhaps not be seen as a conventional interpretation of these stories, but the way in which Dostoevsky seems to have responded to this probable source suggests that even then such an interpretation was actively considered.

106. Julien ôta ses vêtements; puis, nu comme au jour de sa naissance, se replaça dans le lit; et il sentait contre sa cuisse la peau du lépreux, plus froide qu'un serpent et rude comme une lime. . . .
   [Il] s'étala dessus complètement, bouche contre bouche, poitrine sur poitrine.

> Alors le lépreux l'étreignit; et ses yeux tout à coup prirent une clarté d'étoiles; ses cheveux s'allongèrent comme les rais du soleil; le souffle de ses narines avait la douceur des roses; un nuage d'encens s'éleva du foyer, les flots chantaient. . . . Le toit s'envola, le firmament se déployait;—et Julien monta vers les espaces bleus, face à face avec Notre-Seigneur Jésus, qui l'emportait dans le ciel. (Gustave Flaubert, *Œuvres complètes,* 16 vols. [Paris: Club de l'honnête homme, 1971–1975], 4:249)

107. Alex de Jonge, *Dostoevsky and the Age of Intensity* (London: Secker and Warburg, 1975), 88.

108. *Diary of a Writer,* 10 / 76, 1.3 (11:529); 11 / 76 (11:548–574).

109. "Вот это предположение о записавшем все стенографе (после которого я обделал бы записанное) и есть то, что я называю в этом рассказе фантастическим." *Diary of a Writer,* 11 / 76, ch. 1 (11:548), and in Dostoevsky, *Writer's Diary,* ed. Morson, 236.

110. Richard Terdiman, "The Mnemonics of Musset's *Confession,*" *Representations* 26 (Spring 1989): 26–48, 26–27.

111. Robin Feuer Miller, "Transformations, Exposures and Intimations of Rousseau in *The Possessed,*" in *Dostoevsky's Unfinished Journey,* 86–104, 94.

112. "Ну, вот сам видишь, как может выйти вдруг сумбур природы. Я здесь на секрете и стерегу секрет. Объяснение впредь, но понимая, что секрет, я вдруг и говорить стал секретно, и шепчу как дурак, тогда как не надо" (13:88).

113. See Terras, *Karamazov Companion,* 170–171, for the identification and origins of the various quotations and allusions used by Dmitry.

114. "И вот в самом-то этом позоре я вдруг начинаю гимн. Пусть я проклят, пусть я низок и подл, но пусть и я целую край той ризы, в которую облекается бог мой; пусть я иду в то же самое время вслед за чортом, но я все-таки и твой сын, господи, и люблю тебя, и ощущаю радость, без которой нельзя миру стоять и быть" (13:91).

115. In Balzac's *Ursule Mirouët,* for example, Docteur Minoret conceals Ursule's inheritance of 36,000 francs in bearer bonds in the third volume of Justinian's *Pandectes.* Honoré de Balzac, *La Comédie humaine,* ed. Pierre-Georges Castex, 12 vols. (Paris: Pléiade, 1976–1981), 3:831, 916.

116. "Алеша слушал чрезвычайно внимательно" (13:93).

117. "Let me explain it to you now in a couple of words. In Moscow their affairs took a new turn with lightning speed and all the unexpectedness of an Arabian fairy tale." (Поясняю тебе теперь в двух словах. В Москве у них дела обернулись с быстротою молнии и с неожиданностью арабских сказок.) (13:98)

118. "Братья Карамазовы производят здесь фурор—и во дворце и в публике, и в публичных чтениях, что в прочем увидите из газет (Голос, Молва и проч)" (vol. 16, bk. 2, p. 92).

119. Dostoevsky to K. K. Romanov, March 21, 1879 (vol. 16, bk. 2, p. 93); Frank, *Dostoevsky,* 5:413, 424–425.

120. William Mills Todd III, "Contexts of Criticism: Reviewing *The Brothers Karamazov* in 1879," in "Literature, Culture, and Society in the Modern

Age: In Honor of Joseph Frank," ed. Edward J. Brown et al., special issue, *Stanford Slavic Studies* 4, no. 1 (1991): 293–310; Terras, *Karamazov Companion,* 33–38, 36.

121. Respectively, Fedor Dostoevsky, *The Brothers Karamazov,* trans. Constance Garnett, ed. Susan McReynolds Oddo (New York: W. W. Norton, 2011); Fedor Dostoevsky, *The Brothers Karamazov,* 2 vols., trans. David Magarshack (London: Penguin, 1958); Fedor Dostoevsky, *The Brothers Karamazov,* trans. David McDuff (London: Penguin, 1993, reissued 2003); and Fedor Dostoevsky, *The Brothers Karamazov,* trans. Richard Pevear and Larissa Volokhonsky (London: Vintage, 2004).

122. Belknap, *Structure of "The Brothers Karamazov,"* 37–45.

123. Christopher Prendergast, *Balzac: Fiction and Melodrama* (London: Edward Arnold, 1978), 7–8.

124. Peter Brooks, *The Melodramatic Imagination: Balzac, Henry James, Melodrama and the Mode of Excess* (1976; repr., New Haven, CT: Yale University Press, 1995), 55.

125. "Любить пассивно он не мог, возлюбив, он тотчас же принимался и помогать. . . . Но вместо твердой цели во всем была лишь неясность и путаница. 'Надрыв' произнесено теперь! Но что он мог понять хотя бы даже в этом надрыве? Первого даже слова во всей этой путанице он не понимает!" (13:155). I have included alternative translations of *nadryv* to give a sense of the genre differences between the two.

126. "Мысль ее, как Вы уже увидите из посланного текста, есть изображение крайнего богохульства и зерна идеи разрушения нашего времени в России, в среде оторвавшейся от действительности молодежи, и рядом с богохульством и анархизмом." Dostoevsky to Lyubimov, May 10, 1879 (vol. 16, bk. 2, p. 98).

127. Dostoevsky to Lyubimov, June 11, 1879 (vol. 16, bk. 2, p. 104).

128. Dostoevsky to Lyubimov, July 8, 1879 (vol. 16, bk. 2, p. 111).

129. Terras, *Karamazov Companion,* 224n158, in relation to the source of the anecdote about the hunted boy.

130. Myshkin establishes his credibility with the Epanchin family by means of three stories, of the prisoner reprieved from execution, of the final moments of a man sentenced to execution, and of his own relationship with the handicapped Marie in Switzerland (8:49–50, 52–53, 54–61). Like Ivan, his skills as a narrator and the sensational or sentimental aspects of his stories are shown as being key attributes enabling him to attract and hold an audience.

131. "Все что говорится моим героем в посланном Вам тексте, основано на действительности. Все анекдоты о детях случились, были напечатаны в газетах и я могу указать где, ничего не выдумано мною." Dostoevsky to Lyubimov, May 10, 1879 (vol. 16, bk. 2, p. 98).

132. John Jones, *Dostoevsky,* 314.

133. "Скотское сладострастие, со всеми последствиями, до жестокости, до преступления, до Маркиза де Сада" (*PSS 2003–2005,* suppl. 3:114).

134. "Бестолковая поэма бестолкового студента" (13:217).

135. "Чуть лишь человек отвергнет чудо, то тотчас отвергнет и бога, ибо человек ищет не столько бога, сколько чудес" (13:212).

136. "Темная, горячая и 'бездыханная' ночь" (13:207).

137. "Да, мы заставим их работать, но в свободные от труда часы мы устроим им жизнь как детскую игру, с детскими песнями, хором, с невинными плясками" (13:214).

138. "Тихо умрут они, тихо угаснут во имя твое и за гробом обрящут лишь смерть" (13:215).

139. Charles Maturin, *Melmoth the Wanderer,* ed. Douglas Grant and Chris Baldick (Oxford: Oxford University Press, 2008), 73–261.

140. Samuel Taylor Coleridge, review of *The Monk,* by Matthew G. Lewis, *Critical Review* 2, no. 19 (February 1797): 194–200, 195.

141. Dostoevsky to Lyubimov, June 11, 1879 (vol. 16, bk. 2, p. 104).

142. "Вместо твердого древнего закона,—свободным сердцем должен был человек решать впредь сам, что добро и что зло, имея лишь в руководстве твой образ пред собою,—но неужели ты не подумал, что он отвергнет же наконец и оспорит даже и твой образ и твою правду, если его угнетут таким страшным бременем, как свобода выбора?" (13:215).

143. "Да и совсем не может быть такого фантастического лица, как твой инквизитор. Какие это грехи людей, взятые на себя? Какие это носители тайны, взявшие на себя какое-то проклятие для счастия людей? Когда они виданы?" (13:215).

144. William Leatherbarrow, *Fyodor Dostoyevsky: "The Brothers Karamazov"* (Cambridge: Cambridge University Press, 1992), 38–41.

145. Diane Oenning Thompson, *"The Brothers Karamazov" and the Poetics of Memory* (Cambridge: Cambridge University Press, 1991), 136–140. The three episodes referred to are at 13:105 and 13:110.

146. "Иван Федорович попробовал было 'не думать,' но и тем не мог пособить. Главное, тем она была досадна, эта тоска, и тем раздражала, что имела какой-то случайный, совершенно внешний вид; это чувствовалось" (13:220).

147. "Ибо ответом на всю эту *отрицательную сторону,* я и предложил быть вот этой 6ꙗ книге, *Русский Инок,* которая появится 31 Августа. А потому и трепещу за нее в том смысле; будет ли она достаточным ответом. Тем более что ответ-то ведь не прямой, не на положения прежде выраженные (в *Великом Инквизиторе* и прежде) по пунктам, а лишь косвенный. . . . А тут вдобавок еще обязанности художественной потребовалось представить фигуру скромную и величественную, между тем жизнь полна комизма . . . так что поневоле, из-за художественных требований, принужден был, в биографии моего инока коснутся и самых пошловатых сторон, чтобы не повредить художественному реализму." Dostoevsky to Pobedonostsev, August 24, 1879 (vol. 16, bk. 2, p. 152; Dostoevsky's italics).

148. "Дух спекулятивного реализма." Dostoevsky to Pobedonostsev, August 9, 1879 (vol. 16, bk. 2, p. 136; Dostoevsky's italics). The words "speculative

realism" appear at least in part to be a euphemism for "Jewish greed" in this context.

149. "Мало того: мне в романе предстояло провести несколько идей и положений, которые, как я боялся, им будут очень не по нутру, ибо до окончания романа, действительно, можно эти идеи и положения понять превратно." Dostoevsky to Putsykovich, June 11, 1879 (vol. 16, bk. 2, p. 106).

150. Mauss, *Gift*, 6–16.

151. Reviewing the considerable body of criticism on both sides of this debate is beyond the scope of this chapter. As noted already, the introductory chapter to Susan McReynolds's *Redemption and the Merchant God*, 3–19, provides a good overview of the "Dostoevsky as a prophet" school of thought, while those who voice doubts over the effectiveness of "A Russian Monk" as a repudiation of Ivan's position include Grossman, Jackson, Leatherbarrow, Morson, and Wasiolek.

152. "А главное эти фразы и словечки, самые неожиданные эти словечки, так что никак не ожидаешь, а вдруг оно и выскочит" (13:176).

153. "И много еще было чего и не припомнить, и не вписать" (13:238).

154. Caryl Emerson, "Zosima's 'Mysterious Visitor': Again Bakhtin on Dostoevsky, and Dostoevsky on Heaven and Hell," in *A New Word on "The Brothers Karamazov,"* ed. Robert Louis Jackson (Evanston, IL: Northwestern University Press, 2004), 155–179, 163.

155. William Mills Todd III, "Dostoevsky's Russian Monk in Extra-literary Dialogue: Implicit Polemics in *Russkii Vestnik*, 1879–1881," *California Slavic Studies* 17 (1994): 124–133.

156. For a summary of critical attitudes to the role and status of religion in Dostoevsky's work, see Malcolm Jones, *Dostoevsky and the Dynamics of Religious Experience* (London: Anthem, 2005), particularly the section entitled "An Introduction to Current Debate," 25–43.

157. For example, Todd sees Leont'ev's representation of Father Kliment as Christian by force of intellectual conviction as opposed to Dostoevsky's portrait of Zosima as Christian by emotional disposition. Todd, "Dostoevsky's Russian Monk," 127–128.

158. Dostoevsky, *Notebooks*, ed. Wasiolek, 91.

159. Morson, *Boundaries of Genre*, 83.

160. Dostoevsky to Pobedonostsev, August 24, 1879 (vol. 16, bk. 2, p. 151).

161. "Тверд[ое], небоящ[ее]ся слов[о]." Dostoevsky to Pobedonostsev, August 24, 1879 (vol. 16, bk. 2, p. 151).

162. Dostoevsky to Lyubimov, September 16, 1879 (vol. 16, bk. 2, p. 155).

163. Joseph Brodsky, *Less than One: Selected Essays* (1986; repr., London: Penguin, 2011), 161.

164. Dostoevsky to Lyubimov, September 8, 1879 (vol. 16, bk. 2, p. 155).

165. Kate Holland, *The Novel in the Age of Disintegration* (Evanston, IL: Northwestern University Press, 2013), 176.

166. Yuri Corrigan, *Dostoevsky and the Riddle of Self* (Evanston, IL: Northwestern University Press, 2017), 120–141, 140.

167. "Это только басня, но она хорошая басня, я ее, еще дитей была, от моей Матрены, что теперь у меня в кухарках служит, слышала" (13:288).

168. "Самая существенная во всей книге, а может быть и в романе." Dostoevsky to Lyubimov, September 16, 1879 (vol. 16, bk. 2, p. 155). Dostoevsky uses similar language to describe "A Russian Monk" in letters to Lyubimov and Putsykovich from August 8 and 9, 1879, respectively (vol. 16, bk. 2, pp. 135, 137).

169. "Какая-то как бы идея воцарялась в уме его. . . . 'Кто-то посетил мою душу в тот час'" (13:296).

170. Petr Mikhailovich Bitsilli, "O vnutrennei forme romana Dostoevskogo," in *O Dostoevskom: Stat'i*, ed. Donald Fanger (Providence, RI: Brown University Press, 1966), 4–56, 41–43.

171. Based on the frequency of occurrence of derivatives of the Russian for *thousand* (тысяч), the overwhelming majority of which refer to money: part 1—62; part 2—33; part 3—146; part 4—126.

172. Boris Christa, "Dostoevskii and Money," in *The Cambridge Companion to Dostoevsky*, ed. William Leatherbarrow (Cambridge: Cambridge University Press, 2002), 91–110, 108–109.

173. Brodsky, *Less than One*, 157–158.

174. Sophie Ollivier, "L'Argent chez Dostoïevski," *Europe* 510 (October 1971): 70–84.

175. "Тут дело в том, что—один оборот колеса и все изменяется. . . . Что я теперь? Zero. Чем могу быть завтра? Я завтра могу из мертвых воскреснуть и вновь начать жить!" (6:313).

176. For example, Dostoevsky's letter to Maikov from August 16, 1867, which talks of the impact on his wife of his latest gambling losses (vol. 15, bk. 2, pp. 176–177).

177. Belknap, *Structure of "The Brothers Karamazov,"* 59–61.

178. John Jones, *Dostoevsky*, 341.

179. "Этот анализ подводит нас к осознанию противоречий писателя, который умозрительно ясно различал—как ему казалось—идеально-положительное и отрицательное, но который, переходя к художественному воплощению этих умозрительных представлений, мучительно убеждался в том, что его положительное—вовсе не так положительно, а отрицательное имеет оттенки и оттеночки, не позволяющие взять все отрицательное за скобки." Iakov Zundelovich, "Romany Dostoevskogo," in *Stat'i* (Tashkent: Gosudarstvennoe izdatel'stvo, srednyaya i vysshaya shkola UzSSR, 1962; repr., Moscow: Ardis, 1984), 70.

180. *PSS 2003–2005*, suppl. 3:129. The difference is also picked up by Wasiolek in his edition of the notebooks to *The Brothers Karamazov*. Dostoevsky, *Notebooks*, ed. Wasiolek, 63.

181. In their analysis of serialisation in the Victorian novel, Linda Hughes and Michael Lund also note how the format of serial publication is especially well suited to the courtroom drama, with sequential episodes from different narratorial positions as witnesses and counsel present alternative versions of the plot. Linda Hughes and Michael Lund, *The Victorian Serial* (Charlottesville: University Press of Virginia, 1991), 91–92.

182. See Appendix B for a full list with textual references. Some iterations are evidently more comprehensive than others, but I consider it relevant to include even partial iterations of the story to demonstrate how many different points of view Dostoevsky represents. The appendix also describes briefly the manner of representation, which varies from simple narratorial description (albeit from a narrator whose point of view can vary unpredictably from limited to omniscient) to indirect speech, to reported direct dialogue.

183. Colette Becker, *Dictionnaire d'Emile Zola,* with Gina Gourdin-Servenière and Véronique Lavielle (Paris: Laffont, 1993), 425.

184. "В газетах уже сам читал раза три обвинения и инсинуации на Редакцию Русского Вестника в том что она нарочно (для каких-то причин непонятных) растягивает романы (Льва Толстого и мой) на два года." Dostoevsky to Lyubimov, December 8, 1879 (vol. 16, bk. 2, p. 162).

185. "Роман читают всюду, пишут мне письма, читает молодежь, читают в высшем обществе, в литературе ругают или хвалят и никогда еще, по произведенному кругом впечатлению, я не имел такого успеха." Dostoevsky to Lyubimov, December 8, 1879 (vol. 16, bk. 2, p. 161).

186. "Вот здесь в газете *Слухи,* в Петербургской. Эти *Слухи* стали издаваться с нынешнего года, я ужасно люблю слухи, и подписалась, и вот себе на голову: вот они какие оказались слухи" (14:175).

187. Terras, *Karamazov Companion,* 316n40.

188. André Gide, *Dostoïevsky* (Paris: Plon, 1923), 170.

189. "Не один только сюжет романа важен для читателя, но и некоторое знание души человеческой, (психологии): чего каждый автор вправе ждать от читателя." Dostoevsky to E. N. Lebedeva, November 8, 1879 (vol. 16, bk. 2, p. 158).

190. Jean Genet, "A Reading of *The Brothers Karamazov,*" trans. Arthur Goldhammer, *Grand Street* 47 (Autumn 1993): 172–176, 176.

191. "Право, мне все кажется, что у нас наступила какая-то эпоха всеобщего 'обособления.' Все обособляются, уединяются, всякому хочется выдумать что-нибудь свое собственное, новое и неслыханное. . . . Между тем, ни в чем почти нет нравственного соглашения—все разбилось и разбивается и даже не на кучки, а уж на единицы." *Diary of a Writer,* 3/76, 3 (11:346). The translation is taken from Dostoevsky, *Writer's Diary,* ed. Morson, 145.

192. See, for example, John Jones, *Dostoevsky,* 325. Jones argues that the dream is the turning point in a series of details that have so far marked Dmitry's descent and from this point on will mark his spiritual rebirth.

193. "Кстати, я очень доволен что книга 'Мальчики' . . . столь отдельна и эпизодна: читатель будет не столь претендовать, как если бы на самом оконченном месте вдруг прервать и поставить: продолжение будет." Dostoevsky to Lyubimov, April 29, 1880 (vol. 16, bk. 2, p. 181).

194. "Знаю, я только для красоты слога сказал" (14:134).

195. "Будьте же не такой как все; хотя бы только вы оставались не такой, а все-таки будьте не такой" (14:163).

196. Susanne Fusso, *Discovering Sexuality in Dostoevsky* (Evanston, IL: Northwestern University Press, 2006), 45.

197. Miller, *Brothers Karamazov*, 108.

198. Belknap, *Structure of "The Brothers Karamazov,"* 89.

199. "[Вот у меня] одна книга, я читала про какой-то где-то суд" (14:184).

200. Алеша, зачем вы меня совсем, совсем не любите!—закончила [Лиза] в исступлении.—

    Нет, люблю!—горячо ответил Алеша. (14:185; translation from Magarshack, 2:686)

    Both Magarshack and Garnett, translating this scene, can only muster "warmly" for *goryacho,* while McDuff and Pevear and Volokhonsky choose, respectively, "ardently" and "hotly" (Garnett, ed. Oddo, 493; McDuff, 748; Pevear and Volokhonsky, 585).

201. As, for example, Dostoevsky states in relation to Myshkin in a letter to his niece Sofya Ivanova from January 1, 1868 (vol. 15, bk. 2, p. 216).

202. "Отрицая реальность призрака, он [мой герой], когда исчез призрак, стоит за его реальность." Dostoevsky to Lyubimov, August 10, 1880 (vol. 16, bk. 2, p. 227).

203. "Фома поверил не потому, что увидел воскресшего Христа, а потому, что еще прежде желал поверить" (14:227, vs. the use of a very similar phrase to describe Alyosha's belief at 13:25).

204. "Ваш земной реализм. Тут у вас все очерчено, тут формула, тут геометрия" (14:229).

205. "Видят такие сны иной раз вовсе не сочинители, совсем самые заурядные люди, чиновники, фельетонисты, попы" (14:229).

206. "Я икс в неопределенном уравнении" (14:232).

207. "Je pense donc je suis, это я знаю наверно, остальное же все, что кругом меня, все эти миры, бог и даже сам сатана,—все это для меня не доказано, существует ли оно само по себе, или есть только одна моя эманация" (14:232).

208. "За что купил за то и продал" (14:234).

209. The references are to the following articles in *Diary of a Writer:* "The Sentence" ("Prigovor," 10/76, 1.4 [11:529–531]); "The Meek One" ("Krotkaya," 11/76 [11:548–574]); and "On Suicide and Arrogance" ("O samoubiistve i o vysokomerii," 12/76, 1.5 [11:593–595]).

210. "Несчастный молодой человек, возвратясь домой, в ту же ночь застрелился; я был при нем неотлучно до последнего момента" (14:235).

211. See the note to 14:235 at 14:379, which explains the origins of the anecdote in an epigram about a French actress of the eighteenth century.

212. For example, in his "Treatise on Smerdyakov," which the prosecutor spins to prove that Smerdyakov could not have been the murderer, while the reader knows the opposite (14:285–292).

213. "Тут, главное, можно осадить и в прах разбить торжествующего романиста подробностями, теми самыми подробностями, которыми всегда так богата действительность и которые всегда, как совершенно будто бы незначащая и ненужная мелочь, пренебрегаются этими несчастными и невольными сочинителями и даже никогда не приходят им в голову" (14:297).

214. "Вот именно это соображение и было причиною предложения обвинителя, что деньги где-то спрятаны в расщелине в селе Мокром. Да уж не в подвалах ли Удольфского замка, господа? Ну не фантастическое ли, не романическое ли это предложение?" (14:305).

215. "Затем поднялся страшный хаос" (14:323).

216. "Похороны Илюши и надгробная речь Алексея Карамазова мальчикам, в которой отчасти отразится смысл всего романа." Dostoevsky to Lyubimov, April 29, 1880 (vol. 16, bk. 2, p. 181).

217. "Но возрождается и идет новая интеллигенция. Та хочет быть с народом. А первый признак неразрывного общения с народом есть уважение и любовь к тому, что народ, всею целостью своей, любит и уважает более и выше всего, что есть в мире,—т.е. своего Бога и свою веру." Dostoevsky to Blagonravov, December 19, 1880 (vol. 16, bk. 2, p. 254).

218. Miller, *Brothers Karamazov,* 131–133.

219. "Я говорю лишь о братстве людей и о том что ко всемирному, ко всечеловечески-братскому единению сердце русское может быть изо всех народов предназначено, вижу следы сего в нашей истории, в наших даровитых людях, в художественном гении Пушкина" (12:330).

220. John Jones, *Dostoevsky,* 314.

3. Zola

1. Emile Zola, *Les Rougon-Macquart: Histoire naturelle et sociale d'une famille sous le Second Empire,* ed. Henri Mitterand, 5 vols. (Paris: Gallimard-Pléiade, 1960–1967). See Notes on Citation for citation methodology. For a fuller description of the origins, preparation, and evolution of *Les Rougon-Macquart,* see Colette Becker, *La Fabrique des Rougon-Macquart: Edition de dossiers préparatoires,* 7 vols., with Véronique Lavielle (Paris: Honoré Champion, 2003).

2. Roger Price, *An Economic History of Modern France, 1730–1914* (London: Macmillan, 1981), 215; Michael Palmer, *Des petits journaux aux grandes agences: Naissance du journalisme moderne, 1863–1914* (Paris: Aubier, 1983), 11n2.

3. François Furet and Jacques Ozouf, *L'Alphabétisation des Français de Calvin à Jules Ferry,* 2 vols. (Paris: Editions de Minuit, 1977), 1:30, 292.

4. Anne Sauvy, "Une littérature pour les femmes," in *Histoire de l'édition française,* ed. Roger Chartier and Henri-Jean Martin, 4 vols. (Paris: Fayard / Promodis, 1990), 3:496–508, 496–497.

5. James Smith Allen, *In the Public Eye: A History of Reading in Modern France, 1800–1914* (Princeton, NJ: Princeton University Press, 1991), 56–70, table A.7, "Estimate of Active Readers in France 1801–1936."

6. Robert Tombs, *France, 1814–1914* (Harlow, UK: Longman, 1996), 154.

7. Roger Magraw, "Producing, Retailing, Consuming: France 1830–70," in *French Literature, Thought and Culture in the Nineteenth Century: A Material World*, ed. Brian Rigby (Basingstoke, UK: Macmillan, 1993), 59–85, 63–66.

8. Christophe Charle, *Histoire sociale de la France au XIXe siècle* (Paris: Editions du Seuil, 1991), 292.

9. Anne-Marie Thiesse, *Le Roman du quotidien: Lecteurs et lectures populaires à la Belle Epoque* (Paris: Le Chemin Vert, 1984), 11–24.

10. For fuller descriptions of technological improvements over the period, see particularly Frédéric Barbier, "L'industrialisation des techniques," in Chartier and Martin, *Histoire de l'édition française*, 3:51–67, 57–67; Claude Bellanger et al., *Histoire générale de la presse française*, 5 vols. (Paris: Presses universitaires de France, 1969), 3:63–99; Gilles Feyel, "Les transformations techniques de la presse au XIXe siècle," Gilles Feyel, "L'économie de la presse au XIXe siècle," and Gilles Feyel and Benoît Lenoble, "Commercialisation et diffusion des journaux au XIXe siècle," all in *La Civilisation du journal*, ed. Dominique Kalifa et al. (Paris: Nouveau monde éditions, 2011), respectively at 97–139, 141–180, and 181–212.

11. Bellanger et al., *Histoire générale de la presse française*, 3:284; Barbier, "L'industrialisation des techniques," 3:53–56, 61–63; Feyel, "Les transformations techniques de la presse," 122.

12. Price, *Economic History of Modern France*, 22–25.

13. Palmer, *Des petits journaux aux grandes agences*, 341.

14. For a good general survey of the evolution of the commercialisation strategies of the press in the nineteenth century, see Feyel and Lenoble, "Commercialisation et diffusion."

15. Allen, *In the Public Eye*, 44. For statistics on bookstore and railway kiosk growth, see Jean-Yves Mollier, "Zola, le Champ littéraire et l'argent," *Cahiers naturalistes* 78 (2004): 91–102, 93–94. He records 2,428 bookstores outside Paris in 1851, 5,086 in 1878.

16. Jean Morienval [Henri Thévenin], *Les Créateurs de la grande presse en France: Emile de Girardin, H. de Villemessant, Moïse Millaud* (Paris: Editions Spes, 1934), 219.

17. Thomas Piketty, *Le Capital au XXIe siècle* (Paris: Editions du Seuil, 2013); Thomas Piketty, *Capital in the Twenty-First Century*, trans. Arthur Goldhammer (Cambridge, MA: Belknap Press of Harvard University Press, 2014). Page numbers refer to the translation. What follows is a very abbreviated summary of the complex argument that Piketty makes in relation to inequality. He also underlines the fact that French tax and inheritance records are amongst the most complete and extensive in the world, such that the reliability of the data and conclusions relating to France is correspondingly

higher. The available data series for France begin in the early 1800s. Key passages on Belle Epoque France are at 260–264, 337–343, and 393–396. His references to Vautrin's lesson occur at 238–242, 279, 404–407, 410, and 412.

18. Price, *Economic History of Modern France*, 22, 153–155.
19. Feyel, "L'économie de la presse au XIXᵉ siècle," 175.
20. Tombs, *France, 1814–1914*, 147–148.
21. Patrick Eveno, *L'Argent de la presse française des années 1820 à nos jours* (Paris: Editions du CTHS, 2003), 29.
22. Eveno, *L'Argent de la presse française*, 29.
23. Eveno, *L'Argent de la presse française*, 32.
24. Theodore Zeldin, *France, 1848–1945: Taste and Corruption* (Oxford: Oxford University Press, 1980), 169.
25. Zeldin, *France*, 165–176. For more general surveys of the economics of the French press in the latter half of the nineteenth century, see Feyel, "L'économie de la presse au XIXᵉ siècle"; Bellanger et al., *Histoire générale de la presse française*, 3:100–293; and Eveno, *L'Argent de la presse française*, 19–75.
26. "Aujourd'hui ce ne sont plus les partis qui créent les journaux, ce sont les banquiers. Ils les créent pour lancer une affaire." Jules Simon, *Le Matin*, August 12, 1884, https://gallica.bnf.fr/ark:/12148/bpt6k551991r.
27. Frédéric Barbier, "Une production multipliée," in Chartier and Martin, *Histoire de l'édition française*, 3:105–130, 125 (table 8).
28. Barbier, "L'industrialisation des techniques," 3:108.
29. Allen, *In the Public Eye*, 38, table 1.1, sourced from the returns to the *Bibliographie de la France*.
30. Barbier, "Une production multipliée," 3:122, 129n48; the statistics are based on official returns from printers in the years 1840, 1860, and 1880. Despite the difference between the sources, there is clear evidence of a substantial increase.
31. Jean-Yves Mollier, *Michel et Calmann Lévy, ou, la naissance de l'édition moderne* (Paris: Calmann-Lévy, 1984), 446.
32. Mollier, *Michel et Calmann Lévy*, 441.
33. Jean-Yves Mollier, *L'Argent et les lettres: Histoire du capitalisme d'édition, 1880–1920* (Paris: Fayard, 1988), 220–223; Mollier, *Michel et Calmann Lévy*, 453–454.
34. Mollier, *L'Argent et les lettres*, 20–30; Martin Lyons, *Reading Culture and Writing Practices in Nineteenth-Century France* (Toronto: University of Toronto Press, 2008), 45.
35. Mollier, *Michel et Calmann Lévy*, 265.
36. Mollier, *Michel et Calmann Lévy*, 322; Elizabeth Parinet, "Un succes de librarie: 'La Vie de Jésus' de Renan," in Chartier and Martin, *Histoire de l'édition française*, 3:441–443.
37. Henri Mitterand, *Zola*, 3 vols. (Paris: Fayard, 1999–2002), 1:571.

38. For the sources of all the data on the print runs of Zola works, see Collette Becker, *Dictionnaire d'Emile Zola,* with Gina Gourdin-Servenière and Véronique Lavielle (Paris: Laffont, 1993), 421–427; and Mollier, "Zola, le Champ littéraire."

39. Precise evidence for this statement is not available. However, comparison between figures for the initial print runs given by Paul Alexis in his memoirs of Zola, *Emile Zola: Notes d'un ami* (Paris: Charpentier, 1888; repr., Paris: Maisonneuve et Larose, 2001), 105 (also at http://solo.bodleian.ox.ac.uk /OXVU1:oxfaleph012282998), and later publication totals for 1877 and 1880 cited in Becker, *Dictionnaire d'Emile Zola,* 421, along with private correspondence with Jean-Yves Mollier, all indicate that the acceleration that the success of *L'Assommoir* would lead one to expect did in fact happen.

40. Mitterand, *Zola,* 2:510, although Alexis records slightly different figures. Alexis, *Emile Zola,* 119.

41. Establishing and defending the parameters of what constitutes a "key cultural driver" is beyond the scope of this book. I rely here on distinctions drawn by others, in particular Dominique Kalifa in *L'Encre et le sang* (Paris: Fayard, 1995) and *Les Bas-fonds* (Paris: Seuil, 2013), together with Louis Chevalier in *Classes laborieuses et classes dangereuses à Paris pendant la première moitié du XIXᵉ siècle* (Paris: Plon, 1958), for the notions of voyeurism and "taximanie," the urge to know through classification; Anne Green, in *Changing France: Literature and Material Culture in the Second Empire* (New York: Anthem, 2011), for the importance of fashion; and René Guise, in his extensive investigation of the 1832–1834 "folie du conte" in "Le Roman-feuilleton, 1830–1848: La naissance d'un genre," 36 microfiches (doctorat d'état diss., Nancy II University, 1975), for the emphasis he places on the role of the exotic in the early development of the press.

42. Kalifa, *Les Bas-fonds,* chap. 4, "L'Empire des listes," 145–170.

43. "Mettez dans votre cornue 25 duels, 12 empoisonnements, 1 enfant perdu, 1 agent de police, 2 forçats, 4 mouchards, 1 beau jeune homme mystérieux, 3 assassinats et 2 suicides: faites chauffer à blanc et étendez sur le papier avec une plume d'oie, coupez par tranches que vous servirez une à une, en renvoyant chaque fois 'au prochain numéro,' et ouvrez avec confiance votre coffre-fort." *Satan,* January 29, 1868, quoted in Roger Bellet, *Presse et journalisme sous le Second Empire* (Paris: Armand Colin, 1967), 200.

44. Palmer, *Des petits journaux aux grandes agences,* 332–333; Morienval [Thévenin], *Les Créateurs de la grande presse,* 229–230.

45. "Le crime est en hausse, il se vend, il fait prime: au dire des marchands, la France compte un ou deux millions de consommateurs qui ne veulent plus rien manger, sinon du crime, tout cru." Paul Féval, "La Fabrique des crimes," *Le Grand Journal,* December 2, 9, and 16, 1866, quoted in Kalifa, *L'Encre et le sang,* 29.

46. "Que vaut la presse quotidienne française?" Quoted in Kalifa, *L'Encre et le sang,* 19. Noussanne records it as occupying some 4.9 per cent of overall edi-

torial copy, but Kalifa thinks the true figure was nearer 8 per cent and still rising. For a broader analysis of the importance of crime and court reporting to the press, see the whole of the chapter that this quotation introduces, entitled "L'irrésistible essor du récit de crime," in *L'Encre et le sang*, 19–52.

47. Alain Vaillant, "Ecrire pour raconter," in Kalifa et al., *La Civilisation du journal*, 773–792, 777–778.

48. "La frénésie de la bataille littéraire autour du naturalisme, le goût du public pour les choses très osées et même tout à fait crues, sous prétexte de vérisme intégral, lui ont donné l'idée de créer une feuille ou la littérature aura une large place et où l'on manifestera une belle audace en toute matière." Jules Bertaut, *L'Opinion et les mœurs* (Paris: Editions de France, 1931), 139.

49. "L'indiscrétion y est érigée en art. On le lit pour être au courant de la chronique scandaleuse." Quoted in Dominique Kalifa, Marie-Eve Thérenty, and Alain Vaillant, "Le quotidien," in Kalifa et al., *La Civilisation du journal*, 269–294, 286, from an August 1877 article in *Le Messager de L'Europe*.

50. David Baguley, *Napoleon III and His Regime: An Extravaganza* (Baton Rouge: Louisiana State University Press, 2000), 90–95.

51. "Depuis quelques années, à côté du grand journalisme politique, reléguant la littérature au rez-de-chaussée, ou l'enclavant à la troisième page, sous la rubrique 'Variétés,' entre les faits divers et les annonces, il en sortait de terre un nouveau, dit 'Petit Journalisme' mais plus vivant, plus moderne, approprié au besoin d'enquête de l'époque, nourri surtout d'actualité, d'informations, de faits, reléguant les théories politiques au second plan, accordant plus de place à la littérature." "Petit Journalisme" references what we would now call a more tabloid style of journalism as well as its origins in Millaud's *Le Petit Journal*. Alexis, *Emile Zola*, 65–66.

52. See Dominique Kalifa et al., "Les Scansions internes à l'histoire de la presse," in Kalifa et al., *La Civilisation du journal*, 249–268; and Anne-Claude Ambroise-Rendu, "Les Faits divers," in Kalifa et al., *La Civilisation du journal*, 979–997.

53. "J'aime la presse d'informations; elle est la coupe de la vie; on y puise les extases passagères, les impressions fugitives, toutes choses qui me paraissent bonnes, parce qu'elles sont courtes." Mario Fenouil, "M. Zola et le journalisme," *Le Gaulois*, August 22, 1888, 1–2, directly quoting Zola, https://gallica.bnf.fr/ark:/12148/bpt6k526602r.

54. See, for example, Sarah Mombert, "La Fiction," in Kalifa et al., *La Civilisation du journal*, 811–832.

55. Kalifa, *L'Encre et le sang*, 102, and more generally the chapter "Portrait du reporter en héros," 82–104.

56. Kalifa, Thérenty, and Vaillant, "Le quotidien," 286.

57. Thérenty, *La Littérature au quotidien*, 135–144.

58. For a more extended discussion of the impact of the professionalisation (and perhaps also the industrialisation) of journalism on style, layout, and content, see chap. 1 of Thérenty, *La Littérature au quotidian*, 47–120.

59. "Un livre, c'est une pierre, vingt livres, c'est un mur." Louis Desprez, *L'Evolution naturaliste* (Paris: Tresse, 1884), 215.

60. "Au *Petit Journal,* on flattait le peuple, personnifié par les concierges, les ouvriers, les petites gens"; "Il faut avoir le courage d'être bête," both quoted in Bellet, *Presse et journalisme,* 59, 60.

61. Thérenty, *La Littérature au quotidien,* 149.

62. "Nous nous servons, dans nos créations d'artistes, dans l'imaginaire, de l'investigation que le journaliste actuel porte sur les faits réels et sur les actions vivantes du drame quotidien." "Le Reporteur," *Le Peuple,* March 11, 1889, quoted in Palmer, *Des petits journaux aux grandes agences,* 87n102.

63. Roger Ripoll, "Réalité et mythe chez Zola," 2 vols. (PhD diss., Université de Paris IV, 1977; reproduced by Champion, 1981), 1:1–28.

64. Thérenty, *La Littérature au quotidien,* 150–151.

65. "Faire vrai consiste donc à donner l'illusion complète du vrai, suivant la logique ordinaire des faits, et non à les transcrire servilement dans le pêlemêle de leur succession." Guy de Maupassant, preface to *Pierre et Jean,* ed. Daniel Leuwers and Pierre Cogny (Paris: Flammarion, 1999), xv.

66. "Et avec ça, soyez au courant de toutes les découvertes, de toutes les inventions, vulgarisez toutes les choses qui s'enfouissent dans les lourdes revues. C'est le feuilleton qui me procura le palpitant qui plaît aux masses: vous autres, donnez l'écho de l'opinion moyenne, et parlez de tout pour avoir l'air d'en savoir plus long que tout le monde." Quoted in Palmer, *Des petits journaux aux grandes agences,* 29n26, from a report by "Jean-Jacques" in "A Thomas Grimm," *La Petite République Française,* November 23, 1887.

67. Emile Zola, "Le Journal," *Les Annales politiques et littéraires,* July 22, 1894, 51.

68. "L'information . . . a transformé le journalisme, tué les grands articles, tué la critique littéraire, donné chaque jour plus de place aux dépêches, aux nouvelles grandes et petites, aux procès-verbaux des reporters et des interviewers." Zola, "Le Journal," 51.

69. "La situation est exactement contraire à celle de jadis: on vend aujourd'hui le journal pour le journal, et l'on donne un feuilleton par-dessus le marché." From a long article entitled "Les Romanciers contemporains," in *Le Messager de L'Europe,* September 1878, reprinted in *Le Figaro,* December 22, 1878, supplément littéraire, https://gallica.bnf.fr/ark:/12148/bpt6k273817c.r=.langFR .textePage.

70. Bellanger et al., *Histoire générale de la presse française,* 3:312.

71. Morienval [Thévenin], *Les Créateurs de la grande presse,* 205–208.

72. "Ce temps est le commencement de l'écrasement du livre par le journal, de l'homme de lettres par le journaliste de lettres." Quoted in Bellet, *Presse et journalisme,* 142, from the *Journal* of the Goncourt brothers without reference.

73. "Plutôt la Presse, chez nous seuls, a voulu une place aux écrits—son traditionnel feuilleton en rez-de-chaussée longtemps soutint la masse du format

entier: ainsi qu'aux avenues, sur le fragile magasin éblouissant, glaces à scintillation de bijoux ou par la nuance de tissus baignées, sûrement pose un immeuble lourd d'étages nombreux. Mieux, la fiction proprement dite ou le récit, imaginatif, s'ébat au travers de 'quotidiens' achalandés, triomphant à des lieux principaux, jusqu'au sommet; en déloge l'article de fonds, ou d'actualité, apparu secondaire." Stéphane Mallarmé, "Etalages," 3, http:// short-edition.com/fr/classique/stephane-mallarme/etalages.

74. For a wider discussion of the venality of the French press in the latter part of the nineteenth century, from which the details in this paragraph are drawn, see Zeldin, *France, 1848–1945,* 144–266; and Eveno, *L'Argent de la presse française,* 57–75.

75. Mitterand, *Zola,* 2:230–239.

76. Colette Becker refers to it as a very important article (Colette Becker, *Les Apprentissages de Zola* [Paris: Presses universitaires de France, 1993], 97), and Christophe Charle uses it in support of his illustration of the contemporary economic power of the theatre (Christophe Charle, *La Crise littéraire à l'époque du naturalisme* [Paris: Presses de l'Ecole Normale Supérieure, 1979], 79), but it has in fact more often been ignored in critical appraisals, perhaps as overshadowed by *Le Roman expérimental* published later in the same year. It merits a one-line note in Mitterand's three-volume biography (Mitterand, *Zola,* 2:475n3) and is not mentioned at all in, for example, Frederick Brown's *Zola: A Life* (London: Macmillan, 1995) or Frederick Hemmings's *Emile Zola* (Oxford: Clarendon, 1966).

77. "Autrefois, il coûtait très cher; aujourd'hui, les bourses des plus humbles peuvent se faire une petite bibliothèque. Ce sont là des faits décisifs; dès que le peuple sait lire, et dès qu'il peut lire à bon marché, le commerce de la librairie décuple ses affaires, l'écrivain trouve largement le moyen de vivre de sa plume." Emile Zola, "L'Argent dans la littérature," in *Le Roman expérimental,* ed. François-Marie Mourad (Paris: Flammarion, 2006), 182.

78. "C'est la foule des lecteurs elle-même qui juge et qui fait les succès. . . . L'œuvre naît de la foule et pour la foule." Zola, "L'Argent dans la littérature," 190, 191.

79. "Tout un petit people qui vit de nos œuvres, qui gagne des millions avec notre travail." Zola, "L'Argent dans la littérature," 193.

80. "Ils [les feuilletonistes] se sont créé un public spécial qui lit uniquement les feuilletons, ils s'adressent à ces lecteurs nouveaux, illettrés, incapables de sentir une belle œuvre. Dès lors, il faudrait plutôt les remercier, car ils défrichent les terrains incultes, comme les journaux à un sou qui pénétrent jusqu'au fond des campagnes." Zola, "L'Argent dans la littérature," 195.

81. "Si vous saviez combien peu le talent est dans la réussite, vous laisseriez là plume et papier, et vous vous mettriez à étudier la vie littéraire, les milles petites canailleries qui ouvrent les portes, l'art d'user du crédit des autres, la

cruauté nécessaire pour passer sur le ventre des chers confrères." Zola to Valabrègue, September 24, 1865, in *Emile Zola: Correspondance*, ed. Bard Bakker et al., 10 vols. (Montreal: Presses de l'université de Montréal; Paris: CNRS, 1978–1995), 1:413.

82. For more details on Zola's career at Hachette, see Mitterand, *Zola*, 2:321–348; Becker, *Dictionnaire d'Emile Zola*, 95–111; and Brown, *Zola*, 101–125, from which the details given here are variously sourced.

83. "Je battrai monnaie autant que possible. D'ailleurs, j'ai foi en moi et je marche gaillardement." Zola to Valabrègue, January 8, 1866, in Bakker et al., *Correspondance*, 1:434–435.

84. Mollier, "Zola, le Champ littéraire," 91.

85. Alexis, *Emile Zola*, 58.

86. "Mais je considère aussi le journalisme comme un levier si puissant que je ne suis pas fâché du tout de pouvoir me produire à jour fixe devant un nombre considérable de lecteurs. C'est cette pensée qui vous expliquera mon entrée au *Petit Journal*." Zola to Valabrègue, February 6, 1865, in Bakker et al., *Correspondance*, 1:405.

87. Henri Mitterand, *Zola journaliste* (Paris: Armand Colin, 1962), 51.

88. Louis Ulbach, *Le Figaro*, January 23, 1868, 1, https://gallica.bnf.fr/ark:/12148/bpt6k2710070.

89. "Mon goût, si l'on veut, est dépravé; j'aime les ragoûts littéraires fortement épicés, les œuvres de décadence où une sorte de sensibilité maladive remplace la santé plantureuse des époques classiques. Je suis de mon âge." Émile Zola, "Mes Haines," *Le Salut Public*, February 24, 1865, in *Œuvres complètes*, ed. Henri Mitterand et al., 21 vols. (Paris: Nouveau monde, 2002–2010), 1:754.

90. See, for example, Kalifa, *L'Encre et le sang*, 19–53, and Ambroise-Rendu, "Les Faits divers," for more extended analyses of the typical content of the *faits divers* columns.

91. Emile Zola, *Thérèse Raquin*, ed. Robert Abirached (Paris: Gallimard, 2001), 196, 212, 240.

92. David Baguley, *Naturalist Fiction: The Entropic Vision* (1990; repr., Cambridge: Cambridge University Press, 2005), 167.

93. "L'habileté consiste une fois l'œuvre faite, à ne pas attendre le public mais à aller vers lui et à le forcer à vous caresser ou vous injurier." Zola to Valabrègue, January 8, 1866, in Bakker et al., *Correspondance*, 1:434–435.

94. "Les amours de mes deux héros sont le contentement d'un besoin; le meurtre qu'ils commettent est une conséquence de leur adultère." Zola, preface to *Thérèse Raquin*, ed. Abirached, 24.

95. "L'argent a émancipé l'écrivain. L'argent a créé les lettres modernes." Zola, "L'Argent dans la littérature," 192.

96. "Le beau procédé que celui d'étaler des chairs meurtries!" Louis Ulbach, *Le Figaro*, January 23, 1868, 1.

97. "Vivant au XIXe siècle, dans un temps de suffrage universel, de démocratie, de libéralisme, nous nous sommes demandés si ce qu'on appelle 'les basses classes' n'avait pas droit au Roman." Edmond de Goncourt and Jules de Goncourt, *Germinie Lacerteux*, ed. Nadine Satiat (Paris: Flammarion, 1990), 55.

98. Zola, *Thérèse Raquin*, ed. Abirached, 15; my emphasis.

99. Goncourt and Goncourt, *Germinie Lacerteux*, ed. Satiat, 59.

100. "Vous, vous avez eu une petite fortune, qui vous a permis de vous affranchir de beaucoup de choses. Moi qui ai gagné ma vie absolument avec ma plume, qui ai été obligé de passer par toutes sortes d'écritures honteuses, par le journalisme, j'en ai conservé, comment vous dirai-je cela? un peu de *banquisme*. . . . Oui, c'est vrai que je me moque comme vous de ce mot *Naturalisme*, et cependant, je le répéterai sans cesse parce qu'il faut un baptême aux choses, pour que le public les croie neuves." As recorded by the Goncourts in their journal: Edmond de Goncourt and Jules de Goncourt, *Journal: Mémoires de la vie littéraire*, ed. Robert Ricatte et al., 3 vols. (Paris: Robert Laffont, 1956), 2:728–729; their italics.

101. For example, "A mon ami Paul Cézanne" and "M. Manet" in "Mon Salon" (1866); his 1867 study of Manet, "Edouard Manet, étude biographique et critique"; and a further article on Manet in the 1868 "Mon Salon," entitled "Edouard Manet," all reprinted in *Emile Zola: Ecrits sur l'art*, ed. Jean-Pierre Leduc-Adine (Paris: Gallimard, 1991), 90–93, 112–119, 137–170, 196–200.

102. Emile Zola, *Paris*, ed. Jacques Noiray (Paris: Gallimard, 2002), 415–416.

103. Baguley, *Naturalist Fiction*, 164–183.

104. "Dans notre temps de science, c'est une délicate mission que de prophétiser." Zola, "Le Roman expérimental," 88.

105. Robert H. Sherard, *Emile Zola: A Biographical and Critical Study* (London: Chatto and Windus, 1893, reprinted 2019 from the University of California Libraries), 142.

106. Henri Mitterand, *Zola: L'Histoire et la fiction* (Paris: Presses universitaires de France, 1990).

107. Becker, *Les Apprentissages de Zola*, 8.

108. Becker, *Dictionnaire d'Emile Zola*, 421–427; Mollier, "Zola, le Champ littéraire."

109. Ripoll, "Réalité et mythe chez Zola."

110. Jacques Noiray, *Le Romancier et la machine*, 2 vols. (Paris: Corti, 1981), 2:284.

111. Baguley, *Naturalist Fiction*; David Baguley, *Zola et les genres* (Glasgow: University of Glasgow French and German Publications, 1993).

112. Philippe Hamon, *Le personnel du roman: Le système des personnages dans les Rougon-Macquart d'Emile Zola* (Geneva: Droz, 1983), 39–55.

113. Adeline Wrona, "Mots à crédit: *L'Argent* de Zola, ou la presse au cœur du marché de la confiance," *Romantisme* 1, no. 151 (2011): 67–79.

114. Christophe Reffait, *La Bourse dans le roman du second XIXe siècle* (Paris: Champion, 2007).

115. Brian Nelson, *Zola and the Bourgeoisie* (London: Macmillan, 1983); William Gallois, *Zola: The History of Capitalism* (Bern: Peter Lang, 2000), 31.

116. David Bell, *Models of Power: Politics and Economics in Zola's "Rougon-Macquart"* (Lincoln: University of Nebraska Press, 1988).

117. "Assurément, la perte du lecteur est un péril que Zola n'a cessé d'expérimenter, en particulier sur le chantier des Ebauches, où régulièrement se croisent les attentes du lecteur, qui veut qu'on 'l'intéresse beaucoup' et les impératifs d'une poétique naturaliste qui exige en définitive du romancier qu'il ne fasse pas son intéressant." Chantal Pierre-Gnassounou, *Zola: Les Fortunes de la fiction* (Paris: Nathan, 1999), 206.

118. Hélène Gomart, *Les Opérations financières dans le roman réaliste* (Paris: Honoré Champion, 2004). The example of *Les Rougon-Macquart* as a financial investment is at 183.

119. Jean-Joseph Goux, "Emile Zola: De l'Argent de l'écriture à l'écriture de *L'Argent*," in *Les Frontières littéraires de l'économie*, ed. Martial Poirson, Yves Citton, and Christian Biet (Paris: Editions Desjonquères, 2008), 145–160.

120. "La vie sotte et élégamment crapuleuse de notre jeunesse dorée"; "les spéculations véreuses et effrénées du Second Empire" (5:1772).

121. "Orgie d'appétits et d'ambition. Soif de jouir . . . poussée du commerce, folie de l'agio et de la spéculation" (5:1738–1741).

122. "Garder dans mes livres un souffle un [*sic*] et fort qui, s'élevant de la première page, emporte le lecteur jusqu'à la dernière" (5:1742).

123. "Ne pas oublier qu'un drame prend le public à la gorge. Il se fâche, mais n'oublie plus. Lui donner toujours, sinon des cauchemars, du moins *des livres excessifs* qui restent dans la mémoire" (5:1744; my emphasis). The translation of *excessifs* as "over-the-top" may be mildly anachronistic but accurately conveys what I think Zola meant.

124. "Il ne faudrait pas croire, d'après ce plan, que l'œuvre sera dure et rigide comme un traité de physiologie ou d'économie sociale. Je la vois vivante, et très vivante" (5:1758).

125. For a detailed discussion of the probable composition dates of *La Curée*, see Robert Lethbridge, "La Préparation de *La Curée:* Mise au point d'une chronologie," *Cahiers naturalistes* 51 (1977): 37–48.

126. Alexis, *Emile Zola*, 105.

127. Mollier, *L'Argent et les lettres*, 218.

128. Mitterand, *Zola journaliste*, 168–170.

129. Zola to Ulbach, November 6, 1871, published in *La Cloche*, November 8, 1871, in Bakker et al., *Correspondance*, 3:303–305, from which the three quotations in this paragraph are drawn: "*La Curée* n'est pas une œuvre isolée, elle tient à un grand ensemble, elle n'est qu'une phrase musicale de

la vaste symphonie que je rêve. Je veux écrire l''Histoire naturelle et sociale d'une famille sous le second Empire.' Le premier épisode, *La Fortune des Rougon*, qui vient de paraître en volume . . .'; "*La Curée*, c'est la plante malsaine poussée sur le fumier impérial, c'est l'inceste grandi dans le terreau des millions"; "Quand *La Curée* paraîtra en volume, elle sera comprise."

130. "Un écrivain qui n'a pas été journaliste est incapable de prendre et de peindre la vie contemporaine"; "Mon marteau c'est le journalisme que je fais moi-même autour de mes œuvres." The first quotation is from an 1878 article in *Le Messager de L'Europe*, in Emile Zola, *Œuvres complètes*, ed. Henri Mitterand, 15 vols. (Paris: Cercle du livre précieux, 1962–1969), 14:329–330. The second is a quote from Zola recorded by the Goncourt brothers in their journal: Goncourt and Goncourt, entry for February 19, 1877, *Journal*, 2:728–729.

131. "Il s'agit de faire du pétard . . . du pétard à haute dose mais du pétard intermittent. . . . De ces romans inoffensifs entrelardés de romans à pétard je voudrais faire paraître une paire tous les ans. . . . Pour une période de 7 ans il me faut donc 14 romans." P.-V. Stock, *Mémorandum d'un éditeur*, 3 vols. (Paris: Stock, 1935–1938), 1:74–75.

132. See Robert Lethbridge, "Du nouveau sur la genèse de *La Curée*," *Cahiers naturalistes* 45 (1973): 28. For a fuller review of the many journalistic and other sources of *La Curée*, see particularly Colette Becker, *Genèse, structure et style de "La Curée,"* with Henri Mitterand and Jean-Pierre Leduc-Adine (Paris: SEDES, 1987); and the notes to the Pléiade edition (1:1570–1580).

133. "La presse nous renseigne sur tout. Les tribunaux livrent aux romanciers des documents précieux. Comme l'écrit M. Zola: *un procès est un roman expérimental qui se déroule devant le public.*" Desprez, *L'Evolution naturaliste*, 231; his italics.

134. "Faits orduriers, les aventures incroyables de honte et de folie, l'argent volé et les femmes vendues." Zola to Ulbach, November 6, 1871, published in *La Cloche*, November 8, 1871, in Bakker et al., *Correspondance*, 2:303–305, 304.

135. See Becker, *Genèse, structure et style*, 60–61, for a side-by-side comparison of the two texts.

136. "Elle [la fortune des Saccard] brûlait en plein Paris comme un feu de joie colossal. C'était l'heure où la curée ardente emplit un coin de forêt de l'aboiement des chiens, du claquement des fouets, du flamboiement des torches" (1:435).

137. "C'était le rut immense de la serre, de ce coin de forêt vierge où flambaient les verdures et les floraisons des tropiques" (1:487).

138. "Ces créatures dont les amants payaient le luxe, et qui étaient cotées dans le beau monde comme des valeurs à la Bourse" (1:510).

139. "J'ai voulu montrer l'épuisement prématuré d'une race qui a vécu trop vite et qui aboutit à l'homme-femme des sociétés pourries; la spéculation furieuse d'une époque s'incarnant dans un tempérament sans scrupule,

enclin aux aventures; le détraquement nerveux d'une femme dont le milieu de luxe décuple les appétits natifs. Et, avec ces trois monstruosités sociales, j'ai essayé d'écrire une œuvre d'art et de science qui fût en même temps une des pages les plus étranges de nos mœurs" (1:1583). See also Zola to Ulbach, November 6, 1871, in Bakker et al., *Correspondence*, 2:304.

140. "*La Curée* ne peut être qu'une œuvre polémique qui dénonce un régime et prédit sa fin prochaine. L'expiation viendra fatalement." Becker, *Genèse, structure et style*, 62.

141. Ripoll, "Réalité et mythe chez Zola," 2:487–514.

142. Mitterand, *Zola: L'Histoire et la fiction*, 8.

143. For example, Janice Best sees it as a moral commentary in "Espace de la perversion et perversion de l'espace: La génération du récit dans *La Curée*," *Cahiers naturalistes* 63 (1989): 109–116; while Bernard Joly sees it as part of an extended metaphor that contrasts old and new France in "Le Chaud et le froid dans *La Curée*," *Cahiers naturalistes* 51 (1977): 56–79, 73; and Clayton Alcorn sees it as a study of sociological types in "*La Curée*: Les deux Renée Saccard," *Cahiers naturalistes* 51 (1977): 49–55.

144. "Antithèse de sa sœur, dont le rôle est de représenter ce que Renée aurait pu devenir si elle avait été élevée autrement et si elle avait vécu dans un autre milieu." Becker, *Genèse, structure et style*, 95.

145. Baguley, *Zola et les genres*, 33–41.

146. "Je ne suis pas à vendre" (1:506).

147. "La vérité était que la dot de Renée n'existait plus depuis longtemps; elle avait passé, dans la caisse de Saccard, à l'état de valeur fictive" (1:463).

148. "Il se disait souvent: 'Si j'étais femme, je me vendrais peut-être, mais je ne livrerais jamais la marchandise; c'est trop bête'" (1:421).

149. "L'idée de famille était remplacée chez eux par celle d'une sorte de commandite où les bénéfices sont partagés à parts égales" (1:426).

150. Bell, *Models of Power*, 78. His reading of *La Curée* as an economic novel, rather different from mine, is in chap. 3, "Deeds and Incest: *La Curée*," 57–97.

151. "Le fond de l'histoire importe peu; ce sont les détails, le geste et l'accent qui sont tout" (1:525).

152. See the section earlier in this chapter entitled "From Promoter to Managing Director."

153. "Il n'avait pas conscience du nombre incroyable de ficelles qu'il ajoutait à l'affaire la plus ordinaire. Il goûtait une vraie joie dans ce conte à dormir debout qu'il venait de faire à Renée; et ce qui le ravissait, c'était l'impudence du mensonge, l'entassement des impossibilités, la complication étonnante de l'intrigue. . . . D'ailleurs, il mettait la plus grande naïveté à faire de la spéculation de Charonne tout un *mélodrame financier*" (1:526; my emphasis).

154. "Le roman-feuilleton de cette époque se présente souvent comme un fait divers continu et exacerbé au moment où le fait divers triomphe à la tête

des journaux." Marie-Eve Thérenty, "Le réel," in Kalifa et al., *La Civilisation du journal*, 1533–1542, 1536.

155. "Nous autres romanciers qui faisons nos livres de documents, qui allons regarder la vie avant d'en parler, qui ne coordonnons que des notes prises sur les choses et les gens de notre entourage, nous procédons identique-ment comme le journalisme étudiant l'actualité." Emile Zola, preface to *La Vie parisienne*, by Parisis [Emile Blavet] (Paris: Ollendorff, 1889), vi, http://gallica.bnf.fr/ark:/12148/bpt6k215491q.

156. "Une enquête judiciaire avait démontré que les ports du Maroc n'existaient que sur les plans des ingénieurs, de fort beaux plans" (1:540).

157. "Enfin, pour tout dire, outre ce penchant inné vers les études scientifiques, outre le rêve ancien d'une œuvre générale, . . . l'argent lui-même, la ques-tion d'argent, le poussa à entreprendre *Les Rougon-Macquart*." Alexis, *Emile Zola*, 85.

158. Gaston Davenany, "Les Bénéfices de Zola," *Le Figaro*, September 9, 1892, 1, http://gallica.bnf.fr/ark:/12148/bpt6k282284r.

159. Mollier, "Zola, le Champ littéraire," 97.

160. As, for example, in Albert Millaud's article of September 1, 1876, in *Le Fi-garo*, 1–2, http://gallica.bnf.fr/ark:/12148/bpt6k276077s.

161. Mitterand, *Zola*, 2:313–314.

162. "Les personnages, fort nombreux, y parlent le langage des faubourgs. Quand l'auteur, sans les faire parler, achève leur pensée ou décrit leur état, d'esprit, il emploie lui-même leur langage. . . . *L'Assommoir* n'est certes pas un livre aimable, mais c'est un livre puissant. La vie est rendue d'une façon immédiate et directe." Anatole France, "Les Romanciers contemporains: M. Emile Zola," *Le Temps*, June 27, 1877, 3–4, http://gallica.bnf.fr/ark:/12148/bpt6k226951d.

163. See Mitterand, *Zola*, 2:308–309 and more generally 301–315, for a fuller account of the publication of *L'Assommoir*.

164. Mollier, *Michel et Calmann Lévy*, 435.

165. Mitterand, *Zola*, 2:304n1.

166. Mitterand, *Zola*, 2:470–472, 655.

167. Mitterand, *Zola*, 2:615, 614, 431.

168. Alain Pagès and Owen Morgan, *Guide Emile Zola* (Paris: Ellipses, 2002), 145–146.

169. Mitterand, *Zola*, 2:607.

170. *Le Messager de L'Europe*, September 1879, cited in Mitterand, *Zola journaliste*, 212.

171. "Je préférerais pour mon goût une chasteté moins tapageuse." Anatole France, "Le Rêve, par Emile Zola," *Le Temps*, October 21, 1888, 2, http://gallica.bnf.fr/ark:/12148/bpt6k231936g.

172. For a more detailed discussion of the introduction of the *société anonyme*, see Anne Lefebvre-Teillard, *La société anonyme au XIXe siècle: Du Code de*

commerce à la loi de 1867, histoire d'un instrument juridique du développement capitaliste (Paris: Presses universitaires de France, 1992), 1–35, 419–449.

173. Pierre Larousse, *Grand Dictionnaire universel du XIXe siècle* (Paris: Larousse, 1869), 5:167–169, http://gallica.bnf.fr/ark:/12148/bpt6k2053572/f171.

174. Christophe Charle, *Histoire sociale de la France au XIXe siècle* (Paris: Editions du Seuil, 1991), 187–193.

175. "Une page est tournée, celle de la féodalité des éditeurs, un autre plus anonyme lui succède, celle de la société, comparable en cela à n'importe quelle SA ou SARL du temps." Mollier, *L'Argent et les lettres,* 318.

176. He is, of course, not entirely alone, but the trend seems to have been more widespread in English literature, as might be expected given the earlier development of the joint-stock company in England. Balzac's theatrical drama *Mercadet, ou Le Faiseur* (written 1840, first published 1848), which deals with a conman who is himself duped by another conman, was pirated by Georges Lewes for his comedy *A Game of Speculation* (1851), which turns the hero into a fraudulent promoter of the Great Indian Emerald Company. Anthony Trollope's *Way We Live Now* (1875), with its central plot of Melmotte's Great South Central Pacific and Mexican Railway company, is perhaps the closest parallel to Zola's *L'Argent* and, indeed, the plots bear some resemblance. Even Gilbert and Sullivan joined in with their 1893 *Utopia Limited,* a satire on limited liability companies and the legislation that created them, in which the king of Utopia transforms his entire country into a limited liability corporation. See Jane Moody, "The Drama of Capital: Risk, Belief, and Liability on the Victorian Stage," in *Victorian Literature and Finance,* ed. Francis O'Gorman (Oxford: Oxford University Press, 2007), 91–109.

177. "Mais deux cas se présentent: prendrai-je un patron qui personnifie en lui-même le capital, ce qui rendrait la lutte plus directe et peut-être plus dramatique? Ou prendrai-je une société anonyme, des actionnaires, enfin le monde de la grande industrie, la mine dirigée par un directeur appointé avec tout un personnel, et ayant derrière lui l'actionnaire oisif, le vrai capital? Cela serait certainement plus actuel, plus large, et poserait le débat comme il se présente toujours dans la grande industrie. Je crois qu'il vaudra mieux prendre ce dernier cas" (quoted at 3:1827).

178. "Alors, j'aurai d'une part les ouvriers et de l'autre la direction, puis derrière les actionnaires, avec les conseils d'administration, etc. (tout un mécanisme à étudier). Mais, après avoir posé ce mécanisme discrètement, je pense que je laisserai de côté les actionnaires, les comités, etc., pour en faire une sorte de tabernacle reculé, de dieu vivant et mangeant les ouvriers dans l'ombre; l'effet à tirer sera plus grand, et je n'aurai pas à compliquer mon livre par les détails d'administration peu intéressants." Quoted in Ripoll, "Réalité et mythe chez Zola," 2:703.

179. "Un spéculateur, un boursier, qui se moquait radicalement de la bonne peinture" (4:186).

180. "Un peintre à lui, . . . un ouvrier à ses gages" (4:290).

181. "C'était une faillite du siècle" (4:360).

182. Reffait, *La Bourse dans le roman*, 440–443.

183. Baguley, *Naturalist Fiction*, 204–223.

184. Halina Suwala, *Autour de Zola et du naturalisme* (Paris: Champion, 1993), which incorporates and revises an earlier article, "Le Krach de l'Union Générale dans le roman français avant *L'Argent* de Zola," *Cahiers naturalistes* 27 (1964): 80–90. The relevant chapter from the 1993 work is to be found at 155–192.

185. "Et puis, vous ne voyez pas l'effet colossal de ce bilan anticipé paraissant dans tous les journaux. . . . La Bourse va prendre feu" (5:243).

186. "Dans le sous-sol, où se trouvait le service des titres, des coffres-forts étaient scellés, immenses, ouvrant des gueules profondes de four, derrière les glaces sans tain des cloisons, qui permettaient au public de les voir, rangés comme les tonneaux des contes, où dorment les trésors incalculables des fées" (5:229).

187. The point is a critical commonplace too frequent to reference exhaustively. Corinne Saminadayar-Perrin, in "Fictions de la Bourse," *Cahiers naturalistes* 78 (2004): 41–62, analyses *L'Argent* as a mirror of the process of fiction, as does Philippe Hamon in his preface to the 1988 Livre de poche edition of *L'Argent*. Pierre-Gnassounou's already-cited *Zola*, 25–88, contains perhaps the most complete survey of how Zola places his characters in roles that resemble positions in the publishing process, from author to critic and reader.

188. Marcel Mauss, *The Gift: Forms and Functions of Exchange in Archaic Societies*, trans. Ian Cunnison (Glencoe, IL: Free Press, 1954; repr., Mansfield Center, CT: Martino, 2011), 64.

189. "Il faut un projet vaste, dont l'ampleur saisisse l'occasion" (5:115).

190. "Il songeait d'abord à écrire une brochure, une vingtaine de pages sur les grandes entreprises que lançait l'Universelle, mais en leur donnant l'intérêt d'un petit roman, dramatisé en un style familier; et il voulait inonder la province de cette brochure, qu'on distribuerait pour rien, au fond des campagnes les plus reculées" (5:175).

191. "Moi, si j'avais eu à jeter au gouffre les quelques centaines de millions nécessaires, je serais le maître du monde" (5:383).

192. Mitterand, *Zola*, 2:1067.

193. Mitterand notes that Zola's preparatory notes for *L'Argent* include several pages on James de Rothschild, drawn principally from his reading of Ernest Feydeau's *Mémoires d'un coulissier*, which were incorporated almost in their entirety into his portrait of Gundermann (5:1255).

194. "Il n'était point un spéculateur, un capitaine d'aventures, manœuvrant les millions des autres, rêvant, à l'exemple de Saccard, des combats héroïques où il vaincrait, où il gagnerait pour lui un colossal butin, grâce à l'aide de l'or mercenaire, engagé sous ses ordres; il était, comme il le disait avec

bonhomie, un simple marchand d'argent, le plus habile, le plus zélé qui pût être" (5:95).

195. "Et, de leur prodigalité, de tout cet argent qu'ils jetaient de la sorte en vacarme, aux quatre coins du ciel, se dégageait surtout leur dédain immense du public, le mépris de leur intelligence d'hommes d'affaires pour la noire ignorance du troupeau, prêt à croire tous les contes, tellement fermé aux opérations compliquées de la Bourse, que les raccrochages les plus éhontés allumaient les passants et faisaient pleuvoir les millions" (5:176).

196. Gomart, *Les Opérations financières,* 269.

197. Gomart, *Les Opérations financières,* 121–164.

198. Goux, "Emile Zola," 153.

199. "Il reste *deux* romans dans *L'Argent:* . . . celui de l'homme privé et celui de l'homme de Bourse" (5:1252; Mitterand's italics).

200. "Ce joli jeune homme, . . . se trouva être, aux mains de Renée, une de ces débauches de décadence qui, à certaines heures, dans une nation pourrie, épuisent une chair et détraquent une intelligence" (1:486).

201. Zola, "Le Roman expérimental," 71.

202. "Ne pas frapper sur l'argent. La pire et la meilleure des choses. Les grandes choses qu'on fait avec" (5:1246).

203. "L'horrible argent, qui salit et dévore!" (5:221); "le fumier dans lequel poussait cette humanité de demain" (5:224).

204. "Me mettre tout entier là-dedans" (5:1248).

205. "Une société au capital de cent cinquante millions, et dont les trois cent mille titres, cotés trois mille francs, représentent neuf cents millions: cela pouvait-il se justifier; n'y avait-il pas un danger effroyable dans la distribution du colossal dividende qu'une pareille somme engagée exigeait, au simple taux de cinq pour cent?" (5:382–383).

206. Christophe Charle, *Le Siècle de la presse, 1830–1939* (Paris: Editions du Seuil, 2004), 141.

207. Nelson, *Zola and the Bourgeoisie,* 158–188; Reffait, *La Bourse dans le roman,* 331–455; Gallois, *Zola,* 119–148.

208. Pierre-Gnassounou, *Zola,* 91–122.

209. Sherard, *Emile Zola,* 142.

210. "N'est-il pas légitime de se demander alors si Zola n'atteint pas là, dans le jeu déchainé de ce tourbillon qui devient démentiel et qui déroute toute notion de valeur stable et de réel, les limites de sa propre représentation réaliste ou naturaliste de la société?" Jean-Joseph Goux, "Monnaie, échanges, spéculations: La mise en représentation de l'économie dans le roman français au XIXᵉ siècle," in *La Littérature au prisme de l'économie,* ed. Francesco Spandri (Paris: Garnier, 2014), 51–70, 67.

211. For a summary of the similarities, both autobiographical and philosophical, between Zola and Pascal, see 5:1570–1575.

212. Goux, "Emile Zola," 153.

Acknowledgements

Returning to academia after a forty-year career as an investment banker is an odd experience. "You'll have to learn to concentrate," said one banking colleague to me—and he was right: scholarly study requires a quite different intellectual approach.

So my first acknowledgement must go to Hermione Lee who, as president of Wolfson College, took me in and made me feel less like the duck out of water I certainly was. Julie Curtis, professor of Russian literature at Oxford University, also from Wolfson, and Tim Farrant, professor of French literature at Pembroke College, Oxford, my supervisors on, respectively, the Russian and French aspects of my doctoral work, have provided encouragement, inspiration, and, above all, real engagement with the subject of this book as it began to emerge.

Through them I have developed a network of contacts and friends who have helped me to explore many different aspects of the French and Russian literary, publishing, and economic scene in the nineteenth century. Philip Ross Bullock, professor of Russian literature and music at Oxford, and Diana Greenwald, a fellow graduate student, coorganised with me our first conference, entitled "Genius for Sale! Artistic Production and Economic Context in the Long Nineteenth Century," and we have since continued to develop a new approach to the use of an economic perspective in aesthetic appreciation. Robin Feuer Miller, Edytha Macy Gross Professor of Humanities at Brandeis University, and William Mills Todd III, Harry Tuchman Levin Professor of Literature at Harvard University, both Dostoevsky scholars of world renown, not only participated in the first conference but have since joined me on other conference podiums to develop the economic perspective. Robin, in addition, has followed the development of my Dostoevsky chapter from the start; her enthusiasm is contagious, and her openness to positions far away from her own areas of focus is utterly refreshing. Bill, too, has been a staunch supporter of this project, and has been invaluable in persuading Harvard University Press to take this first-time author seriously.

Deborah Martinsen, associate dean of alumni education and adjunct associate professor of Slavic at Columbia University, and Carol Apollonio, professor of the practice of Slavic and Eurasian studies at Duke University, have welcomed me into the International Dostoevsky Society, for which I now act as treasurer, and Deborah, together with Olga Maiorova, associate professor at the University of Michigan, has also invited me to contribute my first academic publication, a chapter on economics and the press, to their 2016 edited volume *Dostoevsky in Context*. The text of this chapter is reprinted in Chapter 3 by permission of Cambridge University Press.

Ann Jefferson, professor of French literature at Oxford, provided me with the best formulation of the topic of the present book: "the novel as a self-reflexive commentary on the conditions of its own production." Helen Small, professor of English literature at Oxford, has provided invaluable guidance on recent developments in economic criticism in English literature. Jean-Yves Mollier, Alain Vaillant, and Marie-Eve Thérenty, professors at, respectively, the Université de Versailles Saint Quentin, the Université Paris Ouest, and the Université de Montpellier, have been generous with their time and their interest in my work. André Derval, *directeur des collections* at the Institut pour la Mémoire de l'Edition Contemporaine, the repository of the Grasset and Fasquelle publishing archives, and Ronald Blunden, senior vice president of corporate communications at Hachette, have helped me track down the extant records of the publication details of *Les Rougon-Macquart*.

My employer, Rothschild, has demonstrated an extraordinary tolerance of this curious employee who combined investment banking and academic scholarship, much to the despair of my long-suffering assistant, Kathryn Ohle, without whose assistance most of the finer points of word processing would have escaped me. To all of these I owe my gratitude and appreciation.

Finally, my family has borne my part-time approach to family life over the past several years, as this project has taken an ever-deeper hold, with a level of support and encouragement that has kept me going. To them this book is dedicated, to my wife, Julie, to my children, Claire, Alex, and Olivia, in gratitude and love.

Index

Levin, Harry, 7
Lévy, Calmann, 189–190
Lévy, Michel, 26
Lewis, Matthew, *The Monk*, 142
Library for Reading (*Biblioteka dlya chteniya*),
  107
Lincoln, Bruce, 101
Literary device: Balzac, use of literary
  device, 62, 71–79, 81–88; Dostoevsky,
  use of literary device, 114–119,
  121–126, 127–153, 161–165, 175–182;
  Zola, use of literary device, 200–205,
  206–211, 216–226, 231–232, 239–242.
  See also Auction; Cliché; Compression;
  Excess and sensation; Genre; Iteration;
  Literary value; Prospectus; Publishing
  context; Reader reception; Speculation;
  Transaction; *and under specific works*
Literary value, 12, 23–35, 49–56,
  113–119, 191–200. *See also* Auction;
  Genre; Literary device; Point of sale;
  Prospectus; Publishing context; Reader
  reception; Speculation; Transaction;
  and under specific works
Littré, Emile, 16n66, 67, 202
Lukács, György, 4, 8
Lyon-Caen, Judith, 3, 48n25, 66–67, 71,
  249; *Les Mystères de Paris* (ed.) dossier,
  66n87, 68n94, 69nn96–97
Lyons, Martin, 3, 46, 190
Lyubimov, Nikolai Alekseevich, 113n66,
  139, 140n131, 143n41, 153, 154n164,
  155n168, 164nn184–185, 168, 173,
  178n216

Madame Firmiani, 49
Magasin pittoresque, Le, 188
Magraw, Roger, 185
Maikov, Apollon, 113n66, 117n78, 122,
  159n176
Maiorova, Olga, 101
Maison Nucingen, La, 57, 75–76
Maître des forges, Le, 229
Mallarmé, Stéphane, 26, 198
Malthus, Thomas Robert, 8
Martin, Henri-Jean, *Histoire de l'édition
  française*. *See* Chartier, Roger
Martinsen, Deborah, 5, 109n46
Marxist thought, 4, 6–8, 16, 241
Matin, Le, 188, 197–198
Maturin, Charles, 73; *Melmoth the
  Wanderer*, 55, 142

Maupassant, Guy de, 190; *Bel-Ami*, 15;
  Pierre et Jean, 196
Mauss, Marcel, 22n76, 117n77, 147, 241
Maynial, Edouard, 50, 64n76, 81n124
McReynolds, Louise, 5, 108nn44–45
McReynolds, Susan, 102n15, 147n151
Melmoth réconcilié, 60–61
Melodrama. *See* Genre
Menger, Carl, 8
Messager de l'Europe, Le (*Vestnik Evropy*),
  28n95, 109, 193n49, 197n69, 200,
  218n130, 230
Mill, John Stuart, 8
Millaud, Moïse, 68, 108, 186, 188, 192,
  194, 196–197, 203
Mille et une nuits. See *Arabian Nights*;
  Genre
Miller, Robin Feuer, 100, 117n79, 131,
  169, 178
Milyukov, Alexandr Petrovich, 109
Mirès, Jules-Isaac, 199, 219, 237
Mironov, Boris, 5
Mitterand, Henri, 197n69, 203n87,
  211–212, 217n128, 218n132, 223,
  230n170, 237, 243n193, 244, 249; *Zola*,
  190n37, 191, 200nn75–76, 202n82,
  228, 229n163, 230nn165–167, 230n169,
  242n192
Mode, La, 58, 69, 192
Mollier, Jean-Yves, 3, 26n86, 186n15,
  189–190, 191nn38–39, 202n84, 212,
  217n127, 227n159, 229n164, 233, 249
Monographie de la presse parisienne, 67, 70
Moretti, Franco, 9–10
Morienval, Jean, 48n23, 107n38, 186n16,
  193n44, 198n71
Morson, Gary Saul, 100, 114, 118,
  147n151, 151–152
Mortimer, Armine Kotin, 76
Mounod-Anglès, Christiane, 67
Murata, Kyoko, 60
Muratov, Mikhail, 4
Murav, Harriet, 100
Muse du département, La, 70
Musée des familles, La, 47, 64, 188
Musset, Alfred de, 131
Mystères de Paris, Les, 31, 33, 54, 64–69,
  72n106, 80, 83, 85, 135, 161, 192, 195

Nain Jaune, Le, 203
Nana, 191, 230, 232
Naturalism. *See* Genre